Quakers Living in the Lion's Mouth

Southern Dissent

UNIVERSITY PRESS OF FLORIDA

Florida A&M University, Tallahassee
Florida Atlantic University, Boca Raton
Florida Gulf Coast University, Ft. Myers
Florida International University, Miami
Florida State University, Tallahassee
New College of Florida, Sarasota
University of Central Florida, Orlando
University of Florida, Gainesville
University of North Florida, Jacksonville
University of South Florida, Tampa
University of West Florida, Pensacola

Quakers Living in the Lion's Mouth

The Society of Friends in Northern Virginia,
1730–1865

A. GLENN CROTHERS

Foreword by Stanley Harrold and Randall M. Miller

University Press of Florida

Gainesville · Tallahassee · Tampa · Boca Raton
Pensacola · Orlando · Miami · Jacksonville · Ft. Myers · Sarasota

Portions of this book draw on A. Glenn Crothers's previously published work: "Quaker Merchants and Slavery in Early National Alexandria, Virginia: The Ordeal of William Hartshorne," *Journal of the Early Republic* 25 (Spring 2005): 47–77; "'I Felt Much Interest in Their Welfare': Quaker Philanthropy and African Americans in Antebellum Northern Virginia," *Southern Friend* 29 (2007): 3–36; and "Northern Virginia's Quakers and the War for Independence: Negotiating a Path of Virtue in a Revolutionary World," in Joseph S. Tiedemann and Eugene R. Fingerhut, eds., *The Other Loyalists: The Common Sort, Royalism, and the Revolution in the Middle Colonies, 1763–1787* (New York: State University of New York Press, 2009), 105–30.

First cloth printing, 2012
First paperback printing, 2013

Library of Congress Cataloging-in-Publication Data
Crothers, A. Glenn.
Quakers living in the lion's mouth : the Society of Friends in Northern Virginia, 1730–1865 / A. Glenn Crothers ; foreword by Stanley Harrold and Randall M. Miller.
p. cm. — (Southern dissent)
Includes bibliographical references and index.
ISBN 978-0-8130-3973-2 (acid-free paper)
ISBN 978-0-8130-4954-0 (pbk.)
    1. Quakers—Virginia, Northern—History—18th century. 2. Quakers—Virginia, Northern—History—19th century. 3. Society of Friends—Virginia, Northern—History. 4. Dissenters—Virginia, Northern—History. 5. Pacifism—Virginia, Northern—History. 6. Antislavery movements—Virginia, Northern—History. 7. Quaker women—Virginia, Northern—History. 8. Religious pluralism—Virginia, Northern—History. 9. Whites—Virginia, Northern—Attitudes—History. 10. Virginia, Northern—Social conditions. I. Title.
F232.N867C76 2012
289.6755—dc23   2012001005

The University Press of Florida is the scholarly publishing agency for the State University System of Florida, comprising Florida A&M University, Florida Atlantic University, Florida Gulf Coast University, Florida International University, Florida State University, New College of Florida, University of Central Florida, University of Florida, University of North Florida, University of South Florida, and University of West Florida.

University Press of Florida
15 Northwest 15th Street
Gainesville, FL 32611-2079
http://www.upf.com

This book is dedicated to the memory of my father, Albert Crothers.

Contents

Illustrations

Foreword

Dissent in America is an old and perpetually relevant topic. Dissenters simultaneously reflect and refute the nation's values. And since the beginning of America they have often acted on religious conviction. Based on their interpretation of the Bible, Anne Hutchinson and Roger Williams, during the 1630s, challenged authority in the Puritan Massachusetts Bay colony. A century later, Mormons faced persecution for practicing a revised version of Christianity. At the same time, Roman Catholics provoked a Protestant and nativist reaction through their loyalty to the Pope and insistence on their right to educate their children in their faith. During the twentieth century, Jehovah's Witnesses affected American perceptions of civil liberties through their refusal to allow government to stand between them and their religious commitment. Other examples of religious dissent abound.

Probably no American religious group, however, is better known for dissent from prevailing social and cultural practices than the Society of Friends, or Quakers. The Society organized in England during the seventeenth century. It stressed the existence of a divine spark in all human souls and a determination not to engage in or resist violence. Starting during the 1670s, large numbers of Quakers moved to England's North American colonies to practice their faith more openly. By 1750 Quaker meeting houses were the third most common places of worship in the thirteen colonies. Their numbers trailed only those of Congregationalists and Anglicans. Yet by 1775 Quakers had declined to the fifth largest American denomination. They were ninth by 1820 and sixty-sixth by 1981. In 2009 there were only 107,000 Quakers in North America.

Many factors produced this decline over two and one half centuries. But, during the eighteenth and nineteenth centuries, Quakers' diminishing numbers owed a great deal to their engagement with the world around them and the demands in self-discipline that standing against that world made on them. Unlike such pietist groups as the Amish and Mennonites that shunned aspects of materialism, Quakers became merchants, manufacturers, commercial farmers, and politicians. Even as Quakers adopted forms of worship, dress, and speech that set them apart, they sought to prosper materially and to spread their social views in ways that forced them to interact with larger regional societies. By the late eighteenth century, in such states as Pennsylvania, New Jersey, Maryland, and Virginia, they organized antislavery societies and lobbied governments in efforts to express their opposition to violence and their commitment to the spiritual equality of all human beings. These economic, social, and moral initiatives led Quakers simultaneously to challenge the dominant society and to compromise with it.

The stress, anguish, and contradiction that accompanied this awkward engagement with the world form the central theme of A. Glenn Crothers's thoughtful study of the Quaker community in northern Virginia between 1730 and 1865. Crothers's approach is multifaceted as he analyzes the development of a dissenting religious community located on the Old South's northern periphery. In his detailed narrative, Crothers explores several interrelated themes. One of them is Quaker pacifism versus the larger society's demands for military service during the War for Independence, the War of 1812, and the Civil War. Another is the Quakers' intensifying opposition to slavery in a slaveholding society, where pressure to conform to a pervasive, oppressive, race-based system affected them much more directly than it did their antislavery coreligionists in the North. Throughout his book, Crothers also portrays the evolving role of Quaker women in a community that (sometimes grudgingly) accorded them wider prerogatives than existed in the larger American culture.

Most important, Crothers shows how Quakers helped shape life in northern Virginia from the early eighteenth century through the Civil War period. While attempting to uphold their beliefs, Quakers changed over time in regard to religious obligations, community, and civic duty. In some cases, individual Quakers compromised the denomination's most central principles; some left the Society altogether. And often Quaker dissent encouraged other Virginians to strengthen their contrary views. In short, throughout his book, Crothers addresses the issue of means-and-ends in dissent by relocating the question to a place and a people too little studied. He does so in ways that suggest dissent was, and is, not easy. Although dissent is essential to democracy, it is often costly for individuals and groups that engage in it. That was all the more true in the Old South. Crothers's book is a welcome addition to the Southern Dissent series.

Stanley Harrold and Randall M. Miller
Series editors

Acknowledgments

Sixteen years ago, in what seems like a different life, I came across a marine insurance policy issued by the Alexandria Marine Insurance Company—no. 2157—archived in the Virginia Historical Society. The policy insured thirty slaves valued at nine thousand dollars transported from Alexandria to New Orleans on the vessel *Dorchester*. The policy was signed by the president of the insurance company, William Hartshorne. At the time, I found the policy an intriguing example of economic modernization within a slave society. But it was so much more. Hartshorne was a prominent Alexandria Quaker, a member of the Society of Friends, and the policy provided my first glimpse of the world and dilemmas of Quakers in northern Virginia and the South. Sometime in the late 1990s, I realized that I must write an article about William Hartshorne. But as I investigated the Quaker community of northern Virginia more fully, it dawned on me that I had material for a book-length study. The work that follows sprang from that single marine insurance policy discovered years ago.

The intellectual and personal journey that I have taken to finish this study would not have been possible without the assistance, support, intellectual engagement, friendship, and love of many people. Financial support was provided by a variety of institutions and organizations: the Virginia Historical Society, Friends Historical Library at Swarthmore College, Quaker and Special Collections at Haverford College, the University of Louisville, and—for summer fellowships and the purchase of microfilm—Marcia Segal at Indiana University Southeast. The support of these institutions was, and is, greatly appreciated. Above all, the staff at the Friends Historical Library at Swarthmore College proved invaluable at all stages of the research. The knowledge, assistance, and advice of the library's inestimable director, Christopher Densmore, along with the aid of the library staff, Patricia O'Donnell, Charlotte Blandford, and Susanna Morikawa, made working at Swarthmore a pleasure. My thanks, too, to the Friends at Pendle Hill, who offered a welcoming and warm environment for an interloper into Quaker history and culture.

I had equally enjoyable and productive visits to Magill Library at Haverford College, where Emma Lapsansky generously shared her rich knowledge of all things Quaker with me (and demonstrated great understanding when I discovered that the records of my Hicksite Friends were housed primarily at Swarthmore). At the Virginia Historical Society, Frances Pollard and Nelson Lankford (among others) have been extremely helpful and generous with their time through many visits, beginning in the early 1990s. At the Indiana Historical Society, Wilma Gibbs provided assistance as I worked in the Clarence H. and Robert B. Smith collections. At Earlham College, Thomas Hamm, Quaker historian extraordinaire, helped identify research collections, answered a variety of uninformed questions with good grace, and provided a generous manuscript review. The significance of his scholarship can be gleaned from my endnotes. Many staff members at the Library of Virginia have provided important assistance over the years, including Minor Weisiger, Gregg Kimball, Brent Tarter, and John Deal.

I can't forget the many local historians whose research has guided my own over the years. Bronwen and John Souders of Waterford, Virginia, have shared key documents and insights with me (though I have never had the pleasure of meeting John), as has Deborah Lee. Rebecca Ebert, a librarian at the Handley Regional Library in Winchester and a Quaker, gave me a tour of the Hopewell Meeting House and introduced me to the richness of silence during that visit. Taylor Chamberlin's careful research has been extremely helpful to me, as has the work of Jay Worrall, whose history of Virginia Quakers guided me as I began this project in earnest. A variety of professional historians have provided friendship and insights over the years, beginning with my graduate school companions and long-time friends: Granddad (Andy Chancey), Dutch (Stan Deaton), Ignatius (Mark Greenberg), Snuggles (Dan Kilbride), and Gomez (Chris Olsen). Bertram Wyatt-Brown continues to inspire as a historian, and Darrett Rutman's rigor first taught me what good history could be. The rotating members of the Kentucky Early American History group, begun by Wayne Lee over a decade ago, have been a constant source of insight and (friendly) criticism, especially Bradford Wood, Wayne Lee, Kelly Ryan, Tom Baker, Daniel Krebs, and Darrell Meadows. Kelly Ryan's close reading of chapter 6 was particularly helpful, as was Rhonda Lee's reading of chapter 5. Likewise, Christopher Phillips's review of chapter 8 saved me from many errors (while his good humor as coeditor of *Ohio Valley History* never ceases to amaze). My gratitude to all the other readers who took the time to read and comment on my work in its various iterations.

So many people have been helpful at various stages, some in conversation, some as friends, and others through their scholarship. They include

Dee Andrews, Diane Barnes, John Brooke, Peter Carmichael, Andrew Cayton, Peter Coclanis, Stephanie Cole, John Findling, Paul Finkelman, Andrew Frank, William Freehling, Craig Hammond, Warren Hofstra, Jim Holmberg, Charles Irons, Nancy Isenberg, Helena Kaler, Jacob Lee, William Link, Cathy Matson, Michael McDonnell, Jack McKivigan, T. Michael Miller, Monica Najar, John Quist, Stacey Robertson, Randolph Scully, Jewel Spangler, Lisa Tenderich, Frank Thackeray, Joe Torre, Frank Towers, Mark Wetherington, and Robert Wright. My apologies to those I have overlooked, though my notes reveal my intellectual debts. Student researchers have also provided important assistance, both in collecting materials and acting as sounding boards. My thanks to Kris Allen-Hanks, Rebekah Dement, Kelley Greene, and Mary Southard. My greatest scholarly debt, however, is owed to Randall Miller and Stanley Harrold, whose patience during the long completion of this manuscript and whose critical insights have saved me from many errors and made the book inestimably better. Stan's blue pen, reflecting his critical eye, became something of a crutch. The prose is much stronger and the arguments more pointed because of his time and expertise. The errors that remain are there despite Stan and Randall's best efforts. One could not ask for better editors. And Meredith Babb's good humor, enthusiasm, and patience have been greatly appreciated.

My family has supported me throughout my scholarly journey, from graduate school to the present. My father did not live to see this book in print, but I suspect he would conclude wryly, as he did of my dissertation, that it's a "little dry." His humor and encouragement is missed every day, and this study is affectionately and gratefully dedicated to him. My mother remains my biggest cheerleader, even if her opinion of me is a little—but only a little—overinflated. My sister and brother remain friends and supporters, with lots of good advice about Red Bull, white wine, and such. My beautiful, brilliant, brash, loud, and amazing children, Norah and Colin, have filled my life with joy and affection (and noise) for the last nine years. I can't imagine life without them. But my greatest thanks go to my best friend, my love, my intellectual partner and critic, my greatest supporter and wife, Tracy K'Meyer. She makes me and every day I spend with her better, richer, and fuller. As a wise man from Petty Harbor once said, "Remember our life is nothing but a song."

Prologue

Quakers Living in the Lion's Mouth

In 1849, Samuel M. Janney, a respected Loudoun County, Virginia, educator and minister in the Society of Friends (or Quakers), discovered the limits of the white South's tolerance of religiously based opposition to slavery. Janney embraced Quakers' antislavery testimony, but before the 1840s he had, like most Friends, called in restrained tones for gradual emancipation. An 1842 visit to the region by the northern abolitionist and Quaker Lucretia Mott inspired Janney to renewed vigor in his antislavery campaign. Employing deferential language, he published a series of articles in Chesapeake newspapers between 1843 and 1850 to convince white southerners that self-interest should convince them to end slavery. Janney argued that slavery had decimated the Virginia economy and that black emancipation—immediate, if possible, gradual and compensated, if necessary—would improve the lives of the "oppressed and oppressor," the slave and the slaveholder. He also opposed the forced colonization of former slaves back to Africa, and advocated black education to prepare the South's enslaved population for freedom. Ultimately, he envisioned freedpeople living peacefully alongside white southerners. Although he recognized that "a vast amount of prejudice" had "to be removed before" the free labor future he envisioned could occur, he believed that he could "promote the anti-slavery sentiment."[1]

Janney's optimism soon confronted antebellum southern realities. In April 1849, William A. Smith, a Methodist minister and the president of Randolph-Macon College in Ashland, Virginia, gave a proslavery lecture at the county courthouse in Leesburg, arguing that the Bible sanctioned slavery. Janney's response, published in a local Whig paper in August, refuted Smith's argument in a "moderate and temperate" tone, in part by quoting Methodist founder John Wesley's opposition to slavery. But in rebutting the scriptural defense of slavery, Janney discovered that he had gone a step too far for slaveholders. Days after Janney published a second essay, a Loudoun County grand jury indicted him on charges of publishing an article "calculated to incite persons of color to make insurrection or rebellion." The editor of the local paper, C. C. McIntyre, declined to print a third Janney essay. After the court refused to bring the case to trial because the charge was "expressed in illegal form," the grand jury indicted Janney again at its November session. This time, it charged him with writing that slaveholders "had no right of property in their slaves." When the court met in June 1850, Janney refuted the facts of the charge. Never, he argued, did he deny that masters owned their slaves. In fact, his "strongest objection" to slavery was that "it degrades men by regarding them as property." Most striking, he argued that county residents had a right to defend themselves against interlopers like Smith. "A person from another county," Janney proclaimed, had "traversed" Loudoun "publicly maintaining that slavery was right" and ridiculing "the leading doctrine of the Declaration of Independence." How could the court deny the right of "a native citizen of the county" to answer a public address that "maintained doctrines at variance with the sentiments of Washington, Jefferson, Madison, Patrick Henry, and all the great statesmen of Virginia?" Janney claimed the right to defend the honor of Loudoun from a meddling outside agitator.[2]

As a Virginian, Janney constructed a defense that employed regional tropes to novel ends. Southerners had long denied the right of outsiders to question their "domestic institutions." Their insistence on this demand rose after the 1830s when northern abolitionists called for an immediate end to slavery and pursued the goal more aggressively. Janney's ironic use of southern arguments to attack proslavery speech illustrates the bifurcated identity of northern Virginia Quakers. Friends had first settled in the region—Virginia's Potomac watershed, from Alexandria in the east to the lower Shenandoah Valley in the west—in the 1730s. During their long residence, Friends developed an attachment to the land and identified themselves as Virginians and southerners. Janney used the sobriquet "A Virginian" for many of his antislavery newspaper essays, reflecting his regional identity and his belief that southerners would more likely listen to one of their own than to a northern intruder.

Nonetheless, Friends' spiritual beliefs and distinctive community made them outsiders in Virginia, where an honor culture grounded in violence and a commitment to African American slavery defined white society. Speech, dress, marriage, and settlement patterns set Friends apart from

Map 1. Antebellum northern Virginia, Society of Friends Meetings.

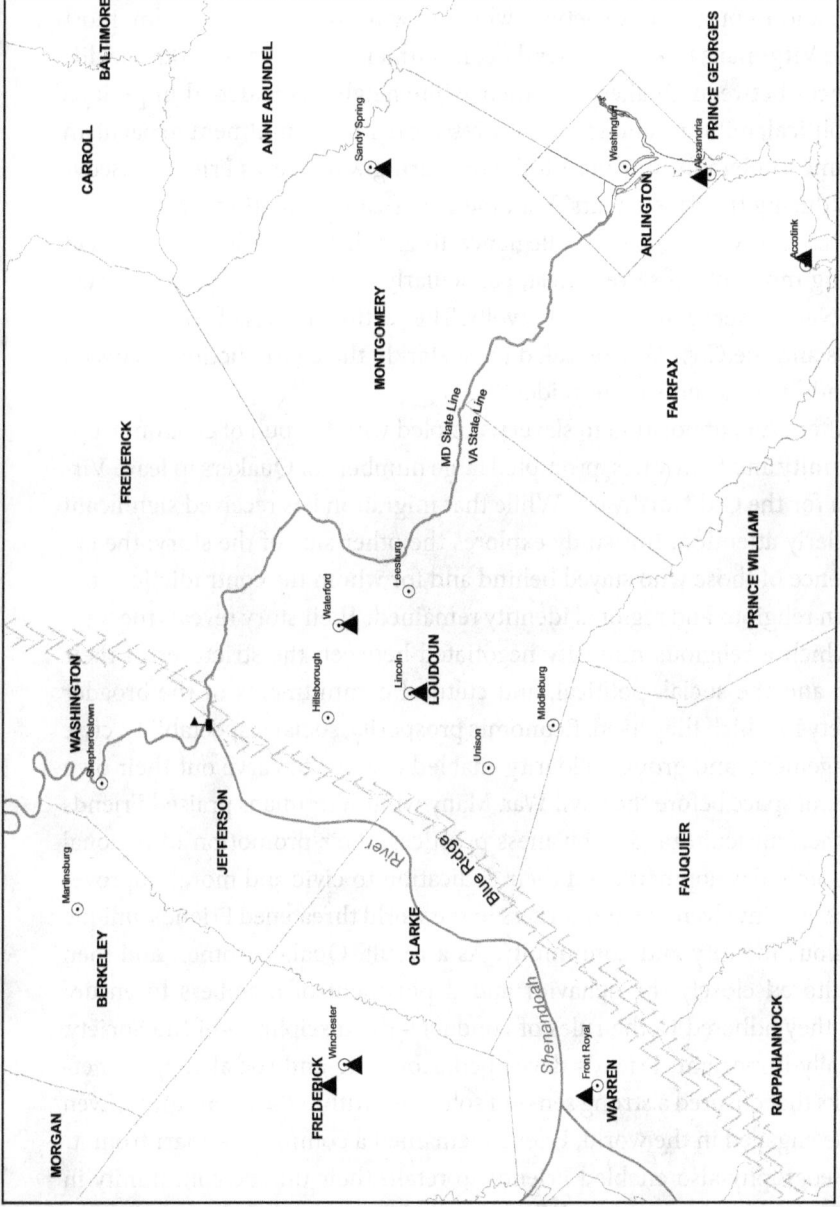

Prepared by Stacy Lamar Brooks

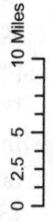

Source Data: Minnesota Population Center. National Historical Geographic Information System: Pre-release Version 0.1. Minneapolis, MN: University of Minnesota 2004.

Legend

- ☉ Town
- ▲ Quaker Meeting
- ⚓ Harpers Ferry

- ⋀⋀⋀ Blue Ridge
- ⋙ Potomac River
- — Shenandoah River

0 2.5 5   10 Miles

their non-Quaker neighbors. More important, Friends' belief that all individuals possessed an inward light, a portion of divinity within, led them to embrace ethical concerns—most notably pacifism and, in the 1780s, antislavery—that contravened the values of white Virginians. From the Revolution through the Civil War, Friends believed they had a moral duty to transform and improve the society in which they lived. In times of calm, most white Virginians tolerated Friends' commitment "to do good."[3] But the differences between Quakers and their white neighbors widened in periods of political, military, and sectional stress. Friends' commitment to pacifism became intolerable to white Virginians during wartime, as Friends discovered during the Seven Years' War, the American Revolution, and the War of 1812. Likewise, Quakers' allegiance to antislavery made them suspect during moments of slave unrest, particularly in the aftermath of Gabriel's and Nat Turner's 1800 and 1831 revolts. The sectional crisis of the 1840s and 1850s and the Civil War revealed most starkly the contradictions between Friends' values and southern identity.

After 1790, opposition to slavery, coupled with the pull of economic opportunity and family ties, prompted large numbers of Quakers to leave Virginia for the Old Northwest. While that migration has received significant scholarly attention, this study explores the other side of the story: the experience of those who stayed behind and for whom the contradictions between religious and regional identity remained. Their story reveals the ways in which a religious minority negotiated between the strictures of their faith and the social, political, and cultural commitments of the broader society in which they lived. Economic prosperity, social respectability, civic engagement, and group solidarity enabled Friends to carve out their own cultural space before the Civil War. Many white Virginians praised Friends for their agricultural and business practices, their promotion of regional economic development, and their dedication to civic and moral improvement. But involvement and success in the world threatened Friends' unique religious identity and community. As a result, Quaker women and men monitored closely the behavior and deportment of members to ensure that they adhered to the rules of conduct—the discipline—of the Society. Equally important, Friends developed economic and social support networks that ensured a strong sense of solidarity within the community. Even while engaged in the world, Friends remained a community apart from it.

Geography also enabled Friends to retain their unique community in the midst of a slave society. When northern states ended slavery after the American Revolution, northern Virginia lay on the border between slavery and freedom. Whites in the region emulated northern models of economic development while retaining their commitment to slavery and southern cultural values. As a result, they often tolerated dissenting voices associated with the North during the early national and antebellum era. That openness evaporated, however, when the institutions and values of the white community came under attack from external and internal enemies. At those moments, Friends faced censure and repression as white northern Virginians closed ranks in defense of their cultural and social traditions. White Virginians' changing attitudes toward local Friends provides one measure of the process by which white northern Virginians became "southern," committed to sectional political and social institutions, economic ties, and cultural values. Over time, white Virginians came to see once tolerated and even respected Friends as pariahs who threatened their racial and cultural solidarity.

Despite these challenges, Friends maintained their distinctiveness and their commitment to pacifism and antislavery. But external threats sparked a variety of responses among Friends that transformed their community. Many Quakers decided to leave Virginia for the free states in the Old Northwest. Between 1780 and 1860, outmigration halved the number of Friends in northern Virginia, creating a gender imbalance and weakening the economic and social networks that bound the community. Doctrinal disputes in the late 1820s sparked by the rise of evangelicalism separated Friends into Hicksite and Orthodox factions. The schism weakened the community, preoccupied its spiritual leaders, and sparked disputes over property and identity. Friends also debated how to respond to radical abolitionism after 1831. Local Quaker leaders feared abolitionist tactics would engender violence, deepen the sectional crisis, and provoke a backlash against southern Friends. They cautioned members to eschew northern antislavery organizations and adopt circumspect tactics. In the face of these challenges, the status of Quaker women rose. Friends had always recognized the spiritual equality of women and had given them leadership roles in the Society. In the antebellum era, northern Virginia's Quaker women expanded their responsibilities within the meetings. More important, female networks of friendship and family helped ensure the solidarity of the shrinking Quaker community. When the Civil War erupted in 1861, women played a central role in articulating Friends' Unionism.

The Civil War accelerated the internal changes within northern Virginia's Quaker community, giving rise to a more individualist and tolerant faith. Living in a borderland contested by Union and Confederate forces through most of the war, Friends faced depredations from both sides. However, the vast majority of Friends never wavered in their allegiance to the Union. Indeed, their loyalty increased after Abraham Lincoln's Emancipation Proclamation transformed the war into a crusade against slavery. But in embracing the Union cause, Friends' commitment to the peace testimony faltered. A small number of Friends fought for the Union. Many more abandoned the neutrality that the Quaker adherence to peace demanded. By war's end, large numbers of northern Virginia Friends had violated the peace testimony, and the Society's leadership realized they could not enforce it strictly without doing serious damage to their community. In response, Friends forged a more tolerant policy and eased their disciplinary rules. Friends retained their central spiritual principle—the belief in the inward light within all people—but they recognized that individuals might pursue its guidance along different paths. In the Civil War, Friends forged a new kind of Quakerism.

From the moment Friends settled in northern Virginia, their spiritual beliefs set them apart from the white society. The depredations they suffered during the Seven Years' War and the American Revolution prompted them to refine and tighten their testimonies and discipline, and widened the divide between themselves and white Virginians. The experience of these two wars convinced Friends that they must reform themselves and set a moral example for the broader society. Their embrace of antislavery in the 1780s represented a major step in this process of moral reformation. But it ensured that the differences between themselves and white Virginians remained wide for the next eighty years. Paradoxically, Friends also identified themselves as Virginians—and southerners—and many white Virginians accepted them, at least during times of peace and political calm. But social acceptance presented different moral dangers to Friends. They worried it would weaken their spiritual values and the moral imperative to improve the world. The tension between Friends' spiritual commitments and their participation in the broader society lay at the heart of their experience in northern Virginia.

Always fragile and often threatened, Friends' dual identity faced its greatest threat after 1840. The deepening crisis over slavery made the white slaveholders of northern Virginia fearful and defensive. Living close to the free states, they demanded ideological conformity from the region's white inhabitants and rejected Friends' attempts to broaden southern identity. They insisted on protecting the intertwined racial, class, and gender hierarchies that ensured their dominance, and they lashed out at those, like

Samuel Janney, who refused to embrace their social and cultural values. Lydia Wierman, a Quaker minister who traveled to northern Virginia in 1845, recognized the moral and physical dangers Friends faced. "We of the north," she noted, "know not what it is like to live in the lion's mouth," in the midst of slavery and slaveholders. She urged northern Friends not to judge "how, or in what manner our southern brother or sister must labor" to end slavery. "Their peculiar circumstances," she concluded, "must modify their views." It had always been so for the Friends of northern Virginia. They believed they must set a moral example—or, in Wierman's words, "hold . . . up the light in the world around them."[4] However, living among slaveholders, Friends had to chart their path carefully. Push too far and they could alienate their white neighbors, snuff out their "light," and lose the opportunity "to do good" among black and white Virginians. Push too little and they faced the danger of compromising their spiritual values. Herein lay the dilemma of northern Virginia's Friends. Their experience reveals the nature and the parameters of southern identity in the nineteenth-century borderland South.

1

Friends Come to Northern Virginia

In December 1754, just as the Seven Years' War erupted in North America, Quaker minister Samuel Fothergill ventured across the Blue Ridge Mountains to visit Friends recently settled in the lower Shenandoah Valley. A "traveling Friend" from England who paid visits to Quaker religious meetings throughout Great Britain and North America, Fothergill was concerned that Quakers in the "remotest part of Virginia" might not continue to follow the ideological and moral precepts of the Society since they had moved some distance from the center of Quaker society in Pennsylvania. He worried that living in what Europeans considered a wilderness would corrupt Friends and turn them from the paths of spiritual "Truth." What he found shocked him. "My passage seems through briars and thorns," he wrote from the valley, "a too general languor having spread amongst the people." "The state of the Church in this province," he concluded a few days later, "is low and painful." Catherine Phillips, an English itinerant minister who traveled from North Carolina to Pennsylvania "up the Sherrando [Shenandoah] River, and by Opeekan [Opequon] Creek to Fairfax," was similarly disturbed by what she found among Friends in the region, concluding that "many of their souls" were "oppressed by a dark carnal spirit," and "the discipline"—the moral and ethical rules of the Society—was "in some places so perverted, that this designed wall of defence, is rather a stumbling-block."[1]

Traveling Friends such as Fothergill and Phillips worried that the southern frontier posed a threat to Quaker patterns of behavior, worship, and belief, and feared for the spiritual welfare of their coreligionists who resided there. Their successful settlement of the northern and western frontier after 1730 had won them a grudging toleration from colonial officials, and many Friends assimilated into the colony's economic and social life. As a result, the community revealed signs of laxity in its attachment to Friends' faith and traditions, providing grounds for Fothergill's fears. Yet Quaker spiritual values and practices—especially their pacifism and evolving egalitarianism—represented a continuing (if often unspoken) challenge to the hierarchical culture and society of white Virginians. Moreover, the experience of the Seven Years' War made Virginia Friends more determined to live according to their values, setting them on a divergent path from their white neighbors.

I

By the time of Fothergill's visit, Friends had lived in colonial Virginia for nearly one hundred years. The first Friends arrived in Virginia in the 1650s, a few years after their 1652 founding in England. Born in the unrest of the English Civil War and the Interregnum, a political climate that gave rise to a variety of religious sects committed to social and political equality or "leveling," Friends grew out of the religious seeking of the charismatic George Fox. For nine years, Fox wandered England in search of spiritual enlightenment, seeking divine revelation, disputing with ministers and disrupting church services, facing frequent imprisonment, and gaining a few disciples. In 1652, he traveled to the north of England, where he attracted a large following of Seekers, one of the era's small sects that had rejected the established church and sought a return to primitive Christianity. Margaret Fell, the wife of a wealthy and prominent judge, numbered among Fox's converts, and her home, Swarthmoor Hall, soon became the focal point of the movement. In the 1650s, despite the fierce repression they suffered at the hands of English authorities, Fox and his most ardent converts began taking their spiritual message throughout England and gained a substantial following.[2]

By 1656, Friends had reached Maryland and Virginia, where they received a similar reception, gaining a growing number of adherents but facing official repression. In the next few decades, Friends established religious meetings on Virginia's Eastern Shore and along the lower James River. George Fox's visit to Virginia in 1672 gained Friends more adherents, and they began creating a more formal organizational structure. But growth took place in the face of a colonial government committed to ensuring conformity to the established Anglican Church. Beginning in the late 1650s, the Virginia House of Burgesses passed a series of acts designed "for the suppressing of Quakers." The legislation banned all Friends' religious meetings and publications, required Anglican ministers to perform all marriages and baptize all children within the colony, fined ship captains who transported Quakers to the colony, and called for the removal of all Friends whom authorities arrested or who arrived after the passage of the legislation. Over the next forty years, Quaker missionaries to Virginia suffered detention, imprisonment, corporal punishment, and removal, while resident Friends faced arrest and banishment for meeting and had their property impressed for refusing to pay tithes to the established church. A 1666 militia law that imposed steep fines on all militia-age men who refused to muster also posed a challenge for Friends, who opposed the use of violence.[3]

In the first decades of the eighteenth century, Friends continued to face disabilities even as their status improved. Not until 1699, ten years after the British Parliament passed its first toleration act, did Virginia authorities grant Friends (and a small number of Presbyterians) official toleration. Thereafter, they no longer faced arrest for meeting but they continued to suffer fines and occasional arrest if they refused to pay tithes to the established church. Friends petitioned the Virginia assembly in 1692, 1696, and again in 1727, requesting exemption from militia service, and they gained the right to send a substitute to war in 1736 (although this measure did not relieve Quaker scruples). They had more success addressing the issue of oath taking, which they rejected because they believed people should always speak the truth. This conscientious concern, however, denied them access to the courts. Recognizing the legal disability, the British Parliament passed an affirmation act in 1695, enabling Friends to testify in court without taking an oath. The Virginia legislature recognized the act ten years later. Friends' slowly improving legal status reflected their growing acceptance in Virginia. Before 1740, their numbers remained small, and colonial leaders soon recognized that they posed little threat to the Anglican establishment. After gaining toleration, moreover, Friends proved themselves loyal, law-abiding (aside from their religious oddities), and productive citizens who developed a reputation for honesty and uprightness.[4]

This early history informed the reception Friends received when larger numbers of them began migrating from Pennsylvania and New Jersey southwest into northern and western Virginia in the 1730s. In the eighteenth century, almost two thousand Friends, more than half from southeastern Pennsylvania, traveled south on the Great Wagon Road, which extended from Philadelphia through Lancaster and western Maryland, into the Shenandoah Valley of Virginia. The vast majority of these migrants—over

80 percent—settled in northern Virginia, in the Potomac River watershed, extending from the lower Shenandoah Valley in the west, across the Blue Ridge Mountains to the east, into what in 1757 became Loudoun County, and then southeast along the Potomac River, past the Great Falls, the port of Belhaven (or Alexandria), and into Prince William County. Although Virginia's eighteenth-century colonial officials remained suspicious of non-Anglicans, they accepted the settlement of ethnic and religious minorities, including Quakers, on the western and northern frontiers of Virginia. Immersed in a three-way contest with the French and Native Americans for control of the continent, Virginia's leaders recognized that the newcomers would help establish English claims to the land while providing a buffer zone between western Indians and eastern settlements. Moreover, despite Friends' objection to the Church of England, Virginia's established church, and their avowed pacifism, they possessed attributes that made them admirable settlers. Friends came to Virginia in family groups, seeking middling-sized tracts of land on which each family could establish a "competency," or a "comfortable independence," to support itself and future generations. This type of settlement, colonial officials realized, would discourage Native American intrusion from the west and solidify Virginia's claim to the region. No less crucial, Friends had not yet embraced their antislavery testimony. A large population of white settlers on Virginia's frontier denied the colony's growing enslaved population an escape route to the west, something Virginia Governor Alexander Spotswood had recognized as early as 1721.[5]

The first Friends arrived in the Shenandoah Valley in the early 1730s. They were led by Alexander Ross, a Scots-Irish Quaker who came to Pennsylvania as an indentured servant in the early 1690s. In the years after he gained his freedom, Ross purchased five hundred acres on Conowingo Creek in Lancaster County, and by 1730 he was a member in good standing of the Nottingham Monthly Meeting. The same year, he and his business partner and fellow Quaker Morgan Bryan received from the Virginia council a grant of one hundred thousand acres of land "on the west and North Side of the River Opeckan [Opequon]," lying north of what would become the town of Winchester in future Frederick County. Seeking permanent settlers, the council agreed to issue full title to the grant if the pair remained two years and established one hundred families on the land. Within a few years Bryan moved on, eventually settling on the Yadkin River in North Carolina, but Ross remained, taking over two thousand acres for himself and settling some seventy Quaker families in the Opequon settlement. In return, the Virginia council issued permanent patents to Ross for the land in November 1735.[6]

Other Friends settled in what would become Loudoun County, east of the Blue Ridge Mountains during the same decade, though a proprietary claim to the land complicated their settlement. In 1649, Charles II granted five million acres between the Potomac and Rappahannock rivers to some of his loyal supporters. By the early eighteenth century, the grant had come into the hands of Lord Thomas Fairfax, and instead of treating with colonial officials, Quaker migrants purchased land from Fairfax's agents, Robert "King" Carter and William Fairfax. Amos Janney, the first Friend to settle in the area, had by the early 1740s purchased over three thousand acres, most of them along Catoctin Creek, in the vicinity of what would become the town of Waterford. He also worked as a surveyor and land agent for Lord Fairfax. Like Alexander Ross in the valley, Janney's knowledge of the local topography and official connections enabled him to attract more northern Friends to the region. Pennsylvania Quaker John Hough soon joined Janney and also worked as a surveyor and land agent for Fairfax. The two amassed significant personal landholdings, on which much of the region's growing Quaker population settled, including Amos's younger brother Jacob and his wife Hannah. They arrived in 1745, settling near Goose Creek, eight miles south of Amos's home, after purchasing nearly seven hundred acres of land. As at Waterford, a significant Quaker community grew up around their homestead.[7]

Economic and religious motives brought these settlers south to Virginia. In Pennsylvania and New Jersey, the place of origin for over fourteen hundred of the migrants, Friends' unique child-raising techniques led to landholding and inheritance patterns that placed a premium on significant land ownership. As historian Barry Levy argues, Friends used persuasion and instruction from parents, rather than coercion or harsh discipline, to bring their children into a state of "holy conversation" and enable them to avoid sin. Inculcating a devout path, however, required creating an environment free from the corruptions of the wider world. To encourage their sons and daughters to remain in the company of people who lived pious lives, Friends sought landed wealth. Quaker farmers in southeastern Pennsylvania acquired relatively large tracts of land—they believed around three hundred acres per son to be sufficient—to ensure that they could distribute land to their offspring and that their children could avoid the moral dangers of indenture to artisanal and commercial occupations among non-Friends. Such generous land practices soon pushed up the price of land and many second-generation parents could not provide for their children as their parents had for them. Commercial opportunities abounded in what was a prosperous region, but creating a protected environment in which parents could inculcate holiness among their children became more difficult. The alternative for some Pennsylvania Friends was "moving south." Pennsylvania Quakers moved to Virginia, Barry Levy notes, "when they began experiencing or fearing childrearing 'failures' due to the newly diversified, consumer-oriented economy" of the colony. The inexpensive land of backcountry Virginia, they hoped, would enable them to create an environment in which they could more effectively instill Quaker values.[8]

But settlement in Virginia also presented difficulties for Friends. Despite the colony's policy of toleration, they did not enjoy religious freedom as they had in Quaker-dominated Pennsylvania, nor did they always receive a warm welcome. In 1738, just as Friends had begun settling in western Virginia, they got a taste of some Anglicans' hostility to and suspicion of dissenters. That year, eastern Friends had unsuccessfully petitioned the Virginia assembly for relief from parish levies. They received instead a long diatribe in the *Virginia Gazette* by "W. W.," entitled "Composition for Making a Quaker." Friends, according to this critic, consisted of "the herb of Deceit," the "leaves of Folly," some "buds of Envy and a few blossoms of Malice," "the seeds of Pride" and "Hypocrisy," "an ounce of Ill-Manners," and a "mortar of Defiance." Mix these ingredients together "in a Stony-hearted jug," strain them "through a cloth of Vanity" and "a spout of Ignorance," and, concluded W. W., "in a little time . . . you will become a perfect Quaker." Colonial officials recognized that this antagonistic environment made many dissenters reluctant to settle in Virginia. To encourage western settlement, they sometimes exempted newcomers from parish taxes, but such measures were temporary. Indeed, colonial officials viewed Friends— and all dissenters—as parishioners of the established church and subject to its tithes. A 1748 act for the support of the clergy, passed during a period of rapid parish creation and church growth, stipulated that anyone who refused to pay the parish levy would have their property seized and sold at auction. The act reflected not only widespread support for the Anglican establishment but also concern about the colony's small but growing population of Quakers and Presbyterians, who had settled on Virginia's periphery where the church establishment remained undeveloped. These dissenters, many Anglicans feared, promised to bring "schism" to "a colony . . . famous for uniformity of religion."[9]

Living on the colony's frontier also presented dangers and difficulties. Quakers who arrived in the 1730s and 1740s settled in what contemporaries considered a "wilderness." Still, the land was neither uninhabited nor devoid of human manipulation. Warfare among American Indians had by the mid-seventeenth century emptied northern Virginia of a sedentary Native American population, but Indians still frequented the region. When Europeans started settling the Virginia piedmont after 1720, Native Americans moved their main trade and travel routes between northern and southern tribes into the Shenandoah Valley. As a result, early European settlers had frequent, if intermittent, contact—and occasional conflict—with various Indian groups. In addition to their movement through the region, nearby Native peoples hunted in the valley, periodically using fire to drive and trap game, a practice that thinned out northern Virginia's forests and led to the "spotty" appearance of grasslands. To avoid the arduous task of clearing the land, many of the region's early settlers sought out what the Shenandoah Valley's earliest historian, Samuel Kercheval, called "the Indian old fields." Nevertheless, the region remained largely forested in the early eighteenth century, and although it abounded in a variety of game, including bear, deer, and buffalo, it remained difficult terrain in which to establish a family farm.[10]

Despite the challenges, this was a region of great promise. Land-hungry settlers from Pennsylvania, Quakers among them, found in northern Virginia a bountiful supply of cheap and fertile land for cultivation. In part, such positive impressions were a product of the publicity efforts of early land speculators like Jost Hite, who worked assiduously to attract settlers to the one hundred and forty thousand acre tract he received from the Virginia government in 1730. But travelers to the region echoed Hite's positive appraisals. Arriving in the valley for the first time in 1755, Captain Charles Lewis, of the Virginia Regiment, pronounced the region "beautiful, and the best land I ever yet saw." Similarly, German traveler Johann Schoepf believed northern Virginia had "much and very good land." Nicholas Cresswell, an English visitor traveling west from Alexandria, found the lands around the port town poor but noted that "the Land begins to grow better" in Loudoun County. The land east of the Blue Ridge Mountains, he reported, was "a Gravelly soil," but it "produces good Wheat." Once Cresswell crossed the Blue Ridge, his appraisal of the land rose higher. "Here is some of the finest land I ever saw for the plough or pasture," he reported, "very rich . . . all Limestone, well watered and very level." "I am sorry," he lamented, "it is not in my power to settle here." As word of the fertility and promise of land in northern Virginia spread, Friends flocked to the region, experiencing their greatest population growth in the 1760s.[11]

II

In the first years after their arrival, local Friends set about creating religious meetings, modeled on and linked to the broader system of Quaker government, to regulate their spiritual lives. In the late seventeenth century, English Friends, following the advice of Quaker founder George Fox, established a hierarchical structure of business meetings, headed by the London Yearly Meeting. Friends met twice weekly in meetings for worship, but to help ensure doctrinal unity and police the behavior of members who might bring disrepute upon the sect, Fox believed a more elaborate church government was necessary. Over time, yearly, quarterly, monthly, and preparative meetings became the vehicles through which Quakers established, distributed, and enforced the sect's discipline (or rules of conduct) that all adherents were expected to follow upon pain of disownment (removal from membership). Beyond this punitive function, Friends depended on the system of meetings to help them resist persecution from government authorities and the established church. The meetings became a primary source of mutual aid and encouragement for Friends in times of spiritual need or material suffering.[12]

Most Friends had limited contact with the yearly meeting. For them, the preparative and monthly meetings provided the most visible sign of the broader Quaker community and government. Each preparative meeting (a small, local meeting not yet large enough to attain monthly meeting status) had several overseers who supervised the conduct of local Friends and prepared business for the monthly meeting, which was mostly concerned with violations of the discipline and problems that the smaller meeting could not solve. The monthly meetings, which stood next in the Quaker organizational hierarchy, represented the principal governing structure within the Society of Friends. Upon them devolved most of the tasks of defining membership and documenting and regulating the lives of Friends: supervising marriages, recording births and deaths, overseeing transfers to other meetings, identifying and recognizing Quaker ministers, dispensing aid to Friends in need, and communicating with other meetings. Elders and overseers, selected by the preparative meeting with the approval of the monthly, quarterly, and yearly meetings, assumed most of the responsibilities of the monthly meeting, working through a variety of ad hoc committees assigned to undertake specific tasks. In addition, each monthly meeting appointed a respected member as clerk, who recorded the group consensus—the sense of the meeting—at each session of the monthly meeting and as a result often possessed significant influence. Following Fox's suggestion, each monthly meeting also included a women's meeting, which oversaw the disciplinary infractions of female members and the care of the sick and poor. The creation of women's meetings gave female Friends a degree of authority within the Society and their households that was unknown in other churches and proved among the "most radical" innovations made by Friends.[13]

Two or more monthly meetings joined together to form a quarterly meeting, which worked to ensure doctrinal and behavioral uniformity among the monthly meetings, helped Friends reach decisions on disputed issues, and served as a court of appeal for members dissatisfied with the judgments of their monthly meetings. The quarterly meetings also selected representatives to attend the yearly meeting, which codified Quaker principles and doctrine through a series of "advices" and queries issued to the quarterly and monthly meetings. In the mid-eighteenth century, yearly meetings also created meetings for sufferings, which documented oppressive measures directed against Quakers by the colonial and state governments. In time, these meetings, which met as needed, came to exercise an executive function within the Society. In the American colonies, Friends established yearly meetings and their constituent structures in New England, New York, Baltimore, Virginia, and North Carolina. However, the most influential yearly meeting, established soon after William Penn founded the colony of Pennsylvania in 1682, was in Philadelphia. The elaborate hierarchy of meetings produced a sense of community and solidarity among members on matters of doctrine and discipline, ensuring a continuity of Quaker spiritual values and behavior across geographic space and sparsely settled regions. Moreover, from their earliest settlement, Friends in northern Virginia carried on an extensive correspondence with meetings throughout America, fielded annual queries from the Philadelphia Yearly Meeting, and welcomed frequent visitations by traveling or public Friends "called" to testify and witness in far-flung Quaker communities.[14]

The process of integrating the growing Quaker population of northern Virginia into the Society's governing structure began soon after first settlement, reflecting the importance Friends placed on internal government and achieving community stability. In 1733, Alexander Ross requested that

Figure 1.1. Hopewell Meeting House, Frederick County, Virginia, built in 1759 and enlarged in 1788. Courtesy of Swarthmore College Friends Historical Library.

the Nottingham Monthly Meeting of Pennsylvania establish "a meeting for worship . . . among'st" the "friends att Opeckon." After some consideration, the Nottingham meeting, along with the Concord Quarterly Meeting, granted Ross's request in December 1734, establishing a meeting for worship at Hopewell. The following year, the quarterly meeting granted Hopewell Friends "the liberty of having a Monthly Meeting set up among them," and early settlers soon took leadership roles within it. As the Quaker population in the Shenandoah Valley rose, the Hopewell meeting created a number of new meetings for worship to accommodate the growing settlements of Friends. At least initially, the homes of leading Friends, around which significant Quaker populations often formed, served as places of worship. The Providence or Tuscarora meeting, for example, was located north of Hopewell on Tuscarora Creek at the home of Richard Beeson, who in 1737 had purchased 1,650 acres of land in what would become Berkeley County. Likewise, Hopewell Friends agreed to the request of Friend Robert McKay—whose father had purchased forty thousand acres in the vicinity—to establish the Crooked Run meeting for worship, located in eastern Frederick County near Front Royal. And the Luptons, another early settler family, requested the creation of a meeting at their home on Apple Pie Ridge, just west of Hopewell.[15]

Figure 1.2. Fairfax Meeting House, Waterford, Virginia, built in 1761, enlarged in 1771, and restored in 1866. Meeting house and land sold in 1937. Courtesy of Swarthmore College Friends Historical Library.

Figure 1.3. Old Goose Creek Meeting House, Lincoln, Virginia. Stone meeting house built in 1765; new brick meeting house built in 1817; older stone buildings used as caretaker's residence after 1817. Courtesy of Swarthmore College Friends Historical Library.

Quakers east of the Blue Ridge Mountains also hastened to establish religious meetings, with the most prominent early settlers again taking leadership roles. By 1734, Friends at Waterford had obtained permission from Pennsylvania to establish a meeting for worship, which came under the care of Hopewell Monthly Meeting. Rapid growth of the Waterford settlement led Friends to seek the creation of their own monthly meeting, a request Pennsylvania Friends granted in 1744. A year later, the Fairfax meeting granted Goose Creek Quakers their own meeting. As the Quaker population of the region grew, so did the number of subsidiary meetings. In 1759, two years after the creation of Loudoun County, Jonas Potts requested a meeting at his home near Vestal's Gap, one of the passages through the Blue Ridge and close to the future site of the town of Hillsboro. Likewise, in 1768 Isaac Votaw requested a meeting at his home, located at South Fork, some six miles west of Goose Creek, which later became the small town of Unison. Friends in northern Virginia established regular contact with Virginia Quakers to the south and east, but they remained part of the Philadelphia Yearly Meeting and were subsequently influenced by developments within America's most significant meeting.[16]

The system of meetings played an important role for geographically dispersed Friends. Despite their distance from the centers of Quaker settlement in Pennsylvania, local Friends shared with the broader Quaker community a set of constantly renewed religious principles and practices that set them apart from their neighbors and reflected their belief in the spiritual equality of all people. Since the late seventeenth century when George Fox issued a series of apostolic letters designed to codify Quakers' spiritual values, Friends had espoused three central ideas that formed the basis of their cultural and political commitments. First, they believed that all people possessed an "Inward Christ," a capacity for divine revelation that made them capable of receiving God's grace. From the Quakers' belief in humanity's spiritual equality came their emphasis on the universal priesthood of believers and their rejection of a trained or "hireling" clergy. The same conviction led Friends to accept female preachers, whom they considered as capable of divine revelation as men. Indeed, Friends thought that the preaching of women would ensure the further spread of religious truth because all inspired individuals would have the opportunity to speak. The embrace of female spiritual equality also justified the creation of women's meetings, which played a leading role in regulating the lives of female adherents. Through their meetings, women had the authority to oversee children's moral training, approve marriage partners, and help decide the distribution of poor relief to Friends in need. Although women's meetings operated under the authority of the monthly meeting and female Friends often deferred to their male counterparts, their meeting nonetheless represented an "unprecedented inclusion of females in church government" denied by other American churches.[17]

Friends' spiritual principles led to a set of distinctive cultural practices. Quakers everywhere dressed in "plain" clothing, believing they should remove all finery and ornament from their apparel for both spiritual and pragmatic reasons. According to Quaker theologian Robert Barclay, luxurious dress had "no real use or necessity," but instead revealed "a vain, proud, and ostentatious mind" unable to pursue a Christian life focused on self-denial and the inward light. Lavish clothing also highlighted superficial distinctions of social class while obscuring the divine within every person. Such dress, moreover, was wasteful, "another costly folly," in William Penn's words. Friends likewise employed distinctive speech patterns, saying "thee" and "thou" instead of the singular "you" because they sought to eliminate the taint of social class from their language and reflect the divine light within all people. Similar concerns convinced Friends that they should not remove their hats as a sign of deference. They also refused to use the traditional designations for the days of the week and months of the year, speaking instead of "first day" and "first month" because they wished to set themselves apart from a corrupt world that employed pagan names. Northern Virginia Friends retained these patterns of dress and speech up to the Civil War, helping to reinforce their sense of difference and establish visual and verbal boundaries, recognizable both to Friends and non-Friends, that separated them from the "world's people."[18]

Friends' worship patterns also marked them as distinctive. They rejected both the hierarchy and formalism of a paid ministry. Payment for ministerial services, Friends argued, cast doubt on the spiritual authenticity of the preacher. Instead, Quakers embraced the practice of silent worship, reflecting their belief in the inward light that all could cultivate. During the meeting, individual members struggled to set aside their own thoughts and desires and spoke only if the spirit within moved them. Speech, they believed, was "a faculty of the natural man, of the flesh," and thus suspect. Silence, in contrast, gave Friends the opportunity to "retire inwardly to the Measure of Grace in themselves," seeking in a communal setting the immediate divine inspiration available to all believers. Those who enjoyed what Robert Barclay called a "flood of refreshment" felt "constrained to utter a sentence of exhortation or praise," enabling those present to become "sensible of it; for the same life *in* them answers to it." Over time, Friends' meetings developed a set of settled practices. Meetings opened with a prayer, followed by a period of silent waiting punctuated by spontaneous preaching, usually by elders and ministers. Elders, who sat at the front of the meeting house facing the assembled, closed the meeting by shaking hands when they felt it had reached spiritual closure. Most contemporaries did not find this style of worship attractive, but the testimony of Quaker diarists speaks to how enriching many members found the gatherings. At its most inspired, Friends' worship became a form of communal mysticism to which all attendees had equal access.[19]

Quakers' belief in spiritual equality also led them to espouse pacifism. The Quaker peace testimony had deep roots, becoming a central component of the sect's creed shortly after its formation in mid-seventeenth-century England. Friends believed it wrong to take a human life because all individuals, even those who had not been exposed to Christianity, possessed a divinely inspired "light within" that if followed would enable them to become "children of the light." Moreover, noted Fox, "dwelling in the light takes away the occasion of wars, and gathers our hearts together to God, and unto one another." Peace was the natural consequence of following the light within. Friends' belief in the universality of the inward light also led them to embrace the golden rule: "Whatsoever ye would that men should do to you, do ye even so to them." The disciplines established by the various North American yearly meetings soon reflected these beliefs. They required Friends to eschew harsh or virulent language that might lead to violence, to refuse service in the military, and (eventually) to avoid all complicity in war-making, including taking sides or paying military taxes. The refusal of Virginia Friends to serve in the militia sparked some of the most severe repression they faced in the colony.[20]

Friends never expected their chosen path to be easy. The inward light did not reveal its truth in a moment of conversion, but instead required cultivation to ensure continuing spiritual progress. Friends believed that the outward and day-to-day symbols of spirituality—plain dress, simple and direct language, honesty, and rejection of ostentatious displays of wealth—helped reinforce and further a process of continuing revelation that for the most conscientious ended in sanctification. In a similar fashion, they celebrated industry and diligence—useful labor or a "calling"—as a sign of an individual's commitment to carrying out God's will in this life. As Quaker minister and merchant Thomas Chalkley put it, "we not only have Liberty to labour in Moderation, but we are given to understand that it is our Duty to do so. The Farmer, the Tradesman, and the Merchant . . . must certainly work, and be industrious in their Callings." Friends considered idleness "a breeder of vice" that could draw believers away from spiritual truth. Like the English Puritans who had settled in New England, Friends believed that material wealth acquired through hard work and honesty was a tangible sign of its possessors' righteous path, though the wealth that resulted from honest industry was not without its dangers. Material prosperity could engender unwarranted individual pride and distract Friends from spiritual ends and simplicity. Affluent Quakers, moreover, could misuse their wealth and spend it on frivolous material possessions. Nonetheless, by the mid-eighteenth century the leaders and elders within most of North America's Quaker communities enjoyed significant material success and embraced the concept of individual property rights.[21]

However, even if successful, sincere Friends sought to stand apart from the larger world. Quakers' practice of endogamous marriage, or marriage within the sect, helped to ensure that they remained a separate people. As Barry Levy argues, the marriage discipline played a key role in reinforcing Quaker values and practices. Endogamous marriage ensured that "every Quaker spouse was sustained by another Quaker and that every Quaker child grew up under converted parents in a sustaining, religious environment." Or as a Philadelphia Friend explained to a sympathetic French traveler, "The preservation of our society . . . depends on the preservation of the customs which distinguish us from other men." "If we should unite our families with strangers," the Quaker continued, "individuals would swerve from our usages." Friends stressed, moreover, the "nearly co-equal" role that women, as wives and mothers, played in preserving Quaker spiritual values. To them fell the crucial responsibility of influencing and regulating the marital decisions of young Quaker women. Because the law of coverture subjected wives to the authority of their husbands, the Society had "no influence" over female Friends (or their spouses) who married non-Friends. Consequently, marrying "contrary to the discipline" became the most frequent cause of disownment in the eighteenth and early nineteenth centuries, with the women's meetings responsible for disciplining wayward females. "The society subsists," concluded the Quaker informant, "only by this domestic, voluntary, and reciprocal influence." Like Quakers elsewhere, Friends in northern Virginia regulated the marriage practices, dress, language, and behavior of fellow members, and in the process they forged an exclusive and "clannish" community. Indeed, local Friends prided "themselves on being a peculiar people unto the Lord, who did not seek converts and were content to draw in upon themselves."[22]

Many of the practices and beliefs of the Quaker newcomers set them at odds with the religious and cultural values of the non-Quaker population, particularly with Virginia's planter elite. By the early eighteenth century, a small number of planter families, deriving their wealth from slavery and staple crop production, controlled the colony. Entrepreneurial in outlook, the planter elite dominated Virginia's tobacco-based economy, supplying capital and providing access to market and slave labor for most of the colony's small farmers. Planters also controlled the legal and political life of the colony, sitting as justices of the peace in each county and serving in the House of Burgesses in the provincial capital at Williamsburg. The wealthiest and most prominent among them sat on the governor's council. Eager to solidify their status within the colony yet conscious of their marginal position within the larger Atlantic world, the colony's planter elite embraced British symbols of power and wealth, building large Georgian-style homes, adopting the dress of the English elite, and purchasing a range of luxury goods from carriages to books to china. The homes and material possessions of planters reflected their genteel aspirations and the hierarchical structure of the society over which they governed.[23]

Virginia's planters also forged a convivial and male-dominated culture, marked by public occasions that helped establish personal ties among white men while simultaneously reinforcing planter authority. Meetings of the county court, militia musters, and election days served as occasions for planters to exercise their authority and good judgment as justices of the peace, officers, and candidates, respectively. Popular social occasions such as horse races became opportunities for planters to display their status through their patronage of the events while mixing with those lower in social status. Even attending Sunday services in the parish church served as a demonstration of Virginia's social and racial hierarchy. Clothed in their Sunday best, planter families traveled to church in carriages and sat in family-owned pews at the front of the church while the rest of the white community sat behind them, and enslaved blacks sat in the balcony or at the rear of the church. Planters' public authority, whether exercised in church or in the county court, derived from their control over the domestic sphere. Most planters cemented their wealth and social standing through advantageous marriages with other elite families, and Virginia courts enforced coverture and the patrilineal transmission of property. By the mid-eighteenth century, planters envisioned themselves as benevolent patriarchs ruling over their households, but the root of their power lay in their coercive control over enslaved African Americans, particularly black women, whose children were by law (written by elite planters) born into slavery. The racial and gender hierarchies of the domestic sphere, in short, served as the foundation of planter authority.[24]

Moreover, few white Virginians had misgivings about these inequalities. Even most evangelical dissenters—Presbyterians, Baptists, and Methodists who appeared in small but growing numbers beginning in the 1740s—did not question the gender and racial order that defined Virginia society and provided the foundations of planter dominance. Despite some historians' emphasis on the evangelical "challenge" to the colony's institutions, culture, and society, what remains most striking about the rise of evangelicalism is how little it changed Virginia's hierarchical social structure. Dissenters wanted to disestablish the Anglican Church, which they achieved with the 1785 passage of the Statute of Religious Liberty, but most had little stomach for radical social change. Even the Methodist clergy, who banned slaveholders from membership at the church's founding in late 1784, soon abandoned their antislavery stance after they confronted "a whirlwind of opposition" among the southern laity. By 1804, Methodist leaders had removed condemnations of slavery from versions of the church's discipline used in the South. They realized that the church would attract and retain few southern members if it censured the region's entrenched institutions and values. Likewise, despite evangelicals' emphasis on the spiritual equality of believers, their churches embraced patriarchy, expecting men to exercise authority within the household and the church. Male domination of the evangelical churches sealed their social and cultural conservatism. As historian Jewel Spangler notes, the "household heads" who controlled the evangelical churches "did so in ways that reflected . . . the patriarchal order that privileged them and subordinated slaves and other dependents."[25]

Friends had much in common with these dissenting sects. Like the evangelical dissenters, Friends sought relief from the payment of parish levies from which they gained no benefit. Possessed of their own spiritual institutions, dissenters of all stripes refused to attend services or participate in the birth, marriage, and death rituals of the established church. Aside from the nonpayment of tithes, dissenters rarely faced disciplinary action from the church vestry, the lay body that governed each Anglican parish, because their disciplinary rules imposed strict codes of behavior. Friends, like early Baptists and Methodists, eschewed the materialism and conspicuous consumption of Virginia's planters, and their plain and simple dress represented a standing (if largely silent) rebuke of the elite's cultural values. Evangelicals and Quakers also avoided the popular pastimes and social haunts of both elite and non-elite Virginians. Many dissenting clergy criticized the popular entertainments of Virginians, seeing them as signs of spiritual decline. For their part, Friends disowned members who gambled, danced, or attended the local tavern, horse races, or election-day festivities. Evangelicals and Friends also avoided drinking to excess, a common practice among Virginian men at such places and times. As historian Christine Heyrman notes, "Quakers found much to admire in the disciplinary practices" and preaching "of evangelicals," while early Baptist and Methodist ministers believed Friends worthy of emulation.[26]

But Friends went further than their evangelical counterparts in their rejection of Virginian social values and practices, choosing to adhere to their principles even though this undermined denominational growth. Quaker pacifism, a product of their belief in the inward light, led Friends to abstain from participating in militia musters and made them subject to fines and distraint of property that their fellow dissenters escaped. Friends' rejection of violence and their embrace of the golden rule led them to begin rethinking the household structure and how it might be reconstructed to instill Quaker values. By the 1760s, many Friends began to wonder about the proper treatment of servants and slaves and how they could reconcile slave ownership with the injunctions of the golden rule. Change would not, however, come quickly. Local Friends accepted the main contours of the patriarchal household—coverture and female domesticity—into the nineteenth century, even while enlarging the moral and spiritual authority of women. More immediately, most Friends tolerated slavery (and a significant number owned or hired slaves) into the 1770s. Still, Friends' desire to build households in which loving instruction and example superseded, if not entirely replaced, coercion and discipline, pointed toward a different future. Herein lay the seeds for their continuing dissent from southern social values—a dissent that set Friends on an alternative path from most evangelical Virginians, who after the disestablishment of the Anglican Church embraced Virginia's social and racial inequalities.[27]

III

Despite the cultural and religious differences between Friends and other white colonists, Quakers prospered in northern Virginia. They did so in part because before the 1760s they were not the only "outsiders" from the North in the region. Like Quakers, most newcomers traveled to the area from Pennsylvania, and few of them acted much like planters from Virginia's Tidewater. The region became, as historical geographer D. W. Meinig argues, an extension of Pennsylvania, reflecting that colony's ethnic and religious diversity. Both Loudoun County and the Shenandoah Valley were home to a German-speaking population that settled in the region in the same years as did Friends. The Germans soon established German Reformed and Lutheran churches. Likewise, a large Scots-Irish population settled in northern Virginia after 1730, establishing a Presbyterian congregation in the valley as early as 1736. In addition, Baptists and Methodists arrived in significant numbers, and a smaller population of Mennonites also settled in the valley. Some eastern Virginians, including many large planters and their slaves, settled in piedmont Fairfax and Loudoun counties in the 1740s and 1750s, but not until the 1760s and the close of the Seven Years' War did they cross the Blue Ridge Mountains into the valley. They moved west only after the British Privy Council ruled that Lord Fairfax's proprietary extended into the lower valley, and he began distributing his lands to Tidewater planters. Settling in eastern and northern Frederick County, eastern planters established large plantations employing slave labor, transforming the social and cultural landscape of the region. Before the Revolution, however, they did not settle in large enough numbers to dominate the region's social and cultural life, and outsiders still played key roles in shaping settlement patterns, particularly west of the Blue Ridge Mountains. In this culturally diverse region, Friends did not at first stand out.[28]

So diverse was the population of the lower Shenandoah Valley before the Revolution that the Anglican Church, despite its state-supported status, could establish "only a tentative toehold." When the Virginia assembly created Frederick County in 1738, it simultaneously created the parish of Frederick to extend the established church into the valley. Still, more than twenty years would pass before Anglicans decided to construct a permanent parish church in Winchester, and not until the early 1760s did a resident Anglican minister settle in the lower valley. Instead, the vestry, the governing body of the parish, decided to build a number of "chapels of ease," at which lay readers conducted services. Within a few years, many of these small structures lay in ruins, and the parish vestry was found guilty of misappropriating for their personal use over fifteen hundred pounds in tithes collected for the upkeep of church buildings. In response, in 1752 the Virginia assembly appointed a new vestry, but it continued to reflect the problems of the established church in the religiously pluralistic valley. Of the new vestry's twelve members, at least three were Quakers, and another two were German.[29]

The diversity of the population also enabled a few Friends and other respectable and wealthy non-Anglicans to assume positions within local government, particularly in the valley, despite official doubts about handing over the powers of local government to a suspect population. In 1705 and again in 1748, the Virginia House of Burgesses passed laws that required most individuals serving in county government to "repeat and subscribe the test" stating their loyalty to the crown and adherence to the Church of England. Nonetheless, the desire of colonial officials to establish effective English jurisdiction in the valley superseded such concerns, and they pressed respectable non-Anglicans into county government service, allowing Friends to serve with affirmations of loyalty. The Scots-Irish Quaker Lewis Neil was appointed a justice of the peace for Frederick County in 1743 and served as sheriff from 1751 to 1753. Similarly, in 1744 the Frederick County court granted Quaker William Jolliffe the privilege of practicing as an attorney before the court, one of only nine such individuals in the county. Quaker Isaac Parkins rose to even greater heights, serving as justice of the peace for many years and as Frederick County's representative in the House of Burgesses in 1754 and 1755. From Friends' perspective, such public service presented few difficulties. Although in the late eighteenth century Quakers began removing themselves from positions of authority within civil government because they believed such offices might require them to act in ways "inconsistent with" their "religious principles," few such restrictions existed before midcentury. Indeed, northern Virginia Friends who entered county government had as their model the colony of Pennsylvania, established by William Penn in 1681 as a "Holy Experiment" based on Quaker principles: a place where in the earliest years of settlement relative order, religious freedom, and economic opportunity prevailed.[30]

The inclusion of Quakers within local county and church government also reflected their rising social status and economic prosperity. Coming to northern Virginia in part to ensure continued economic independence, Friends' industry enabled many of them to acquire considerable wealth. Before the American Revolution, the leading Quaker families of the region—Luptons, Griffiths, Janneys, Jolliffes, and Taylors—enjoyed significant material success. Friends brought to northern Virginia the mixed-grain crop farming and improved agricultural methods of southeastern Pennsylvania, eschewing soil-depleting tobacco production. They capitalized on the growing grain markets of Europe after 1750 and helped transform the agricultural production of the region. By the 1770s, many local farmers and planters emulated the farming techniques of their Quaker neighbors in Loudoun County and the lower valley, having abandoned Virginia's traditional staple of tobacco to produce grains. Friends' contributions to local farming did not go unrecognized, and Virginians and visitors to the region praised "industrious" Quaker neighborhoods for their prosperity and successful farming methods. In 1791, Virginia resident David Stuart asserted that Loudoun County was "perhaps the best farming county in the State, being thickly settled with Quakers . . . from Pennsylvania." His comments reflected the impact of decades of Quaker agricultural practices, including the use of clover in fallow fields and deep plowing.[31]

Friends also capitalized on the processing and shipping of the region's new staple. Quakers established mills throughout the region, providing services for coreligionists and other neighbors. In Loudoun County, Jacob Janney built a mill on Goose Creek that by the early 1770s was operated by his son, Israel. The younger Janney attracted a large clientele of both Friends and non-Quakers. During the American Revolution, for example, David Griffith, a local Anglican preacher serving with the Continental Army, urged his wife to "apply to Israel Janney" for "5 or 6 Barrels of Good Flour as soon as you conveniently can." Further west in the valley, Quaker Lewis Neil settled in 1740 on four hundred acres of land on Opequon Creek, about five miles from the recently established county seat of Winchester. There he built a large grist mill and an ordinary, and launched a thriving mercantile trade with overland connections to Philadelphia and Pennsylvania. In a few years, Neil established a close relationship with Lord Fairfax, who helped the Quaker miller maintain control of his riparian rights to the Opequon in 1758. Quaker millers such as Janney and Neil enjoyed a large non-Quaker clientele because of their reputation for honesty and fair dealing. As Friends grew wealthy, they enjoyed enhanced social standing in the broader community.[32]

Many Quaker merchants prospered in a similar fashion, particularly those who settled in the port town of Alexandria, which by the 1770s had become a central collection point for the export of grains from the region. Quaker merchants such as William Hartshorne, who moved to the town from New Jersey after 1770, played a significant role in the port's growing trade. Northern Neck planter Robert Carter, for example, listed Hartshorne, who had recently dissolved a business partnership with Alexandria resident John Harper, as one of his mercantile contacts in the town in the early 1770s. Ten years later, Hartshorne retained the business of local planters, including George Washington, who advised his rent collector, Battaile Muse, to send clover seed purchased in the valley "to the care of Mr. Hartshorne in Alexandria [and] it will come safe." Many Quaker businessmen in the lower valley's major town, Winchester, also prospered. Isaac Parkins settled at the south end of the town in the 1730s. Within a few years, he built a saw mill that in December 1743 produced "1000 feet of sawn plank" for the construction of Frederick County's first court house and jail. He also built two commercial flour mills that produced for the Alexandria market. The mills made him a wealthy man and, like Neil, a business associate of Lord Fairfax.[33]

IV

Rising economic and social status during times of peace could not, however, insulate Friends from the tribulations of the Seven Years' War. The conflict between the French and their Indian allies and the English in the trans-Appalachian West had a dramatic impact on northern and western Virginia in the mid-1750s and posed the most direct challenge to Quaker values and wellbeing in the years before the American Revolution. The threat to the Virginia frontier prompted the House of Burgesses to make new demands for military service on the inhabitants of the colony. While many Virginians wished to avoid active service, the colonial government's wartime needs placed the most pressure on pacifist Quakers and created new tensions among northern Virginia's inhabitants.

After the defeat of General Edward Braddock's expeditionary force at Fort Duquesne in the summer of 1755, the Shenandoah Valley became a front line of the war. In fall 1755, Virginia Governor Robert Dinwiddie estimated that "flying Parties of Fr[ench] and Ind[ian]'s . . . have committed many barbarous Robberies [and] murder'd and carried off above 100 of our People." "Every week," he added, "brings fresh Alarms of robberies and Murders done in the back Co'[un]try." Captain Charles Lewis, marching northwest with a force of forty-one men from Winchester to Fort Cumberland in late October, described houses "entirely forsaken, and the people driven off by the Indians." Lewis reported that he "was much shocked at the havoc made by the barbarous, cruel Indians," who murdered those who did not escape and made "an entire ruin" of plantations. Although these attacks never threatened the survival of the colony, they depopulated much of the frontier and prompted the colonial government to institute a more effective military policy designed to protect the backcountry from attack and mobilize the population. Friends could not avoid being swept up in the military buildup.[34]

Prior to the war, the colony had followed lax militia recruitment policies. The militia laws of 1738 and 1755 exempted a wide variety of men from service, including "any of the persons commonly called Quakers," though the requirement that Friends supply substitutes remained a problem for them. Under the pressure of war, however, local militia officers began forcing Quakers into service as early as 1754. In Frederick County, officials jailed eight Friends who refused to serve in the militia in September, and the men remained incarcerated in Winchester for the next year. In support of their imprisoned brethren, local Quakers held a worship meeting below the windows of the jail, but armed soldiers dispersed the assembly and arrested George Hollingsworth for "disorderly meeting and assembling." The county court fined him five pounds sterling for the infraction. The coercion of Quakers grew more pronounced in 1756 when the Virginia assembly passed a new wartime measure that made no exemptions beyond hiring substitutes for draftees. Colonel George Washington, the commander of Virginia's frontier defenses along the Shenandoah Valley, confronted the problem of Quaker enlistees in 1756. In May, "a company of armed men" enlisted a group of young Friends from eastern Virginia and forcibly "carried [them] to Winchester." In June, a frustrated Washington wrote Dinwiddie for advice about what he should do with the "six Quakers" who "remain now in confinement." They would "neither bear arms, work, receive provisions or pay, or do any thing that tends, in any respect, to self-defence," Washington complained.[35]

In response, Dinwiddie urged Washington to "compel" the Friends "to work on the forts, to carry Timber, &c., [and] if they will not do [so] Confine them w'th a short Allowance of Bread and Water, till Yo[u] bring them to reason." But the imprisoned Friends would not be brought to "reason" even when faced with corporal punishment. "The Quakers," Washington replied, "chose rather to be whipped to death than bear arms, or lend us any assistance whatever upon the fort, or any thing of self-defence." According to one of the captives, local Friends "Isaac Hollingsworth and wife" and "John Hough of Farefax" meeting "came to see us . . . while we were under these afflictions." Meanwhile, the leaders of the Virginia Yearly Meeting petitioned the colony's military leaders, asking that their "youth" be reprieved from the operation of the new militia law. They also visited Dinwiddie, "pray'[in]g" that the Friends in Washington's custody "not be whip[p]ed."

Dinwiddie advised Washington in August to "use" the captives "w'[i]th Lenity, but as they are at their own Expence, I w'[oul]d have them remain as long as the other Draughts." By this time Washington, sensing the futility of coercive measures against Friends' passive resistance, had decided to release them "from the guard-house" after local Quakers vouched they would not flee. Now "at Liberty again," the former captives "got some Business among . . . friends" in Frederick County, "and by that means Supported" themselves "without Further Expense to any." By the end of the year, they had returned to their homes in eastern Virginia.[36]

Friends throughout Virginia appear to have suffered no further oppression from colonial officials during the Seven Years' War, in part because after 1758 Virginia no longer faced direct attack and pressure to raise troops fell. Perhaps more important, a large number of Friends failed to uphold their pacifist principles. Some Quakers sold supplies to the British army and profited from its presence in Virginia. In Loudoun County, Quaker Edward Thompson and his wife operated an unlicensed ordinary at the future site of Hillsboro, just east of the Blue Ridge, where they supplied members of Braddock's army with lodging and food and sold "some Liquor they call'd Whiskey which was made of Peaches" to soldiers marching west to Fort Pitt in 1755. Thompson also preached about "the great Virtue of Temperance," though the soldiers just "stared at him like Pigs." He apparently saw no contradiction between Quaker pacifist ideals and profiting from soldiers headed for the battlefield. In addition, most Friends complied with the March 1756 militia act that exempted draftees who paid a ten pound fee "to hire another man in their stead." In 1756, the Virginia Yearly Meeting noted that "Friends pret[t]y general[l]y concur in paying taxes on our estates intended for the support of war." Friends of Providence meeting, north of Winchester, violated the peace testimony because they feared an Indian attack. Unwilling to remain unprotected in their cabins, in 1755 they helped construct John Evans's "Fortification" and dwelled "therein for defence against the Indian Enemy." For this breach, Hopewell Friends discontinued the meeting in 1758. A few Friends even served in the military. Evan Rogers of Hopewell Meeting and Isaac Parkins of Center Meeting served as captains in the Frederick County militia in 1756, though they must have resigned their commissions and confessed their wrongdoing to the meeting shortly thereafter because both remained members in the early 1760s.[37]

Rogers and Parkins proved the exception, however, as most Friends honored the peace testimony enough to avoid direct fighting. And unlike their non-Quaker neighbors, many Friends remained on the frontier even during the height of the Indian attacks. For such individuals, remaining at home stood as a testament to their faith, though they counted on their reputation for fair and peaceable dealings among the Indians to protect them. The Lupton family, settled northwest of Winchester, refused to leave its home in 1757, though "Indians had killed and carried away several [people] within a few miles of their habitation." Traveling Friend William Reckitt was surprised to find that the family "did not seem much afraid." Indeed, Joseph Lupton, the family patriarch, told him that "they did not so much as pull in their sneck-string of the door when they went to bed, and had neither lock nor bar." Other Friends displayed less fortitude. Minister Samuel Fothergill reported in 1755 that "Friends beyond the Blue Mountains" have "removed, through fear of the Indians, and left their plantations and dwellings desolate." Fothergill attributed their behavior to spiritual failing, observing that "in the midst of this confusion, too few know the Rock of Defence, or have confidence towards the Ruler of heaven and earth." In fall 1757, the Hopewell meeting confirmed these reports to the Philadelphia Meeting for Sufferings, noting that eleven families—some sixty-six people—had been "driven from their habitations On acct: of ye Indian Enemy," some for "almost two years and are not likely To Get home again." Early the next year, the Hopewell meeting provided a fuller account of the losses of these families, noting that although only one Quaker family had had their home "burnt" by Indians, most lost livestock and horses and some "Household Goods." In response, the Philadelphia meeting sent fifty pounds to Hopewell Friends, which the monthly meeting distributed.[38]

In contrast to most Virginians, who sought revenge against the "barbarous" Indian enemy, local Quakers speculated about what had provoked Native Americans to "ravage and distress the Frontier Inhabitants" of western Virginia. They wondered "whether those natives . . . have not been unjustly disposes'd of those lands in some measure thro' our means." On a number of occasions, the Philadelphia meeting and visiting Friends had queried local Quakers whether they had followed the example of William Penn in Pennsylvania and obtained legal title to their land from the Indians. Pennsylvania Quakers believed that Penn's policy of fair dealing in land acquisition and trade had secured peace for the colony in its first sixty years, and they urged Hopewell Friends to follow similar practices, both to ensure peaceful relations and abide by Quaker values. In 1738, Quaker minister Thomas Chalkley had advised that Friends in the valley "do with speed endeavor to agree with and purchase your lands of the native Indians or inhabitants." Native people, Chalkley warned, "had a natural right" to "this continent of America" and could be "a cruel and merciless enemy, where they think they are wronged or defrauded of their rights." Hopewell Friends apparently took no immediate action in response to Chalkley's plea.[39]

After the Indian attacks of mid-1750s, the Philadelphia Yearly Meeting again reminded Hopewell Friends to ensure the "justness of" the "rights to the land we [Friends] in these parts are possess'd of." The committee established by the local meeting to investigate Friends' land title and respond to the Philadelphia meeting concluded that Virginia's colonial government had obtained title to the Shenandoah Valley from the Iroquois, who claimed the territory in 1744 at the Treaty of Lancaster. The Iroquois, however, had acquired the land "by having conquered the former inhabitants in war," making their claims suspect. As a result, local Friends agreed that they should write to the former inhabitants, the "Delaware and Shawanese nations," to inform them "that if they . . . can make [it] appear that they have a natural right of Inheritance in the Lands we hold, that we are willing to pay them a reasonable Consideration therefore." Still, the Hopewell meeting made this concession with reluctance, adding that they did so despite having "Lawfully purchased the Lands allready of the Several Governments, to whom the[y] Belong." Local Friends also stipulated that Indians must "convey to us their Right to the Lands we hold, and Live in Love and peace with their Brethren the English." Nothing came of the effort, and when Quaker ministers Elizabeth Wilkinson and Hannah Harris visited Hopewell in 1762, they expressed "their uneasiness with our present Situation respecting living on land not fairly" obtained from the Indians. In spite of "a willingness in the members of this meeting to take the proper steps to purchase the land," it again took no substantive action.[40]

In 1763, the Seven Years' War ended in victory for Great Britain. American colonists greeted the Treaty of Paris, which forced France to surrender its mainland North American empire, with joy. Among Friends, however, the war sparked soul searching and a reformation of Quaker attitudes and discipline throughout North America. Before the war, Friends had sometimes been lax in their enforcement of the tenets of the faith, but in the war's wake Quaker leaders and ministers worked to purify the Society by ensuring that members' behavior adhered strictly to the discipline. Eminent Friends such as Anthony Benezet, John Woolman, George Churchman, and Israel Pemberton interpreted the war and its resulting bloodshed and political conflict as punishment for Quakers' moral laxity and sinfulness. In the years since they had settled in North America, reformers argued, Friends had enjoyed material success and political influence. But in the process, they had become overly proud and lost the spiritual purity that separated "primitive Friends," the founders of the sect, from the rest of the sinful world. Only a return to first principles and a retreat from the distractions of the world, reformers believed, could achieve a thorough-going reform of society and return Friends to spiritual truth. In practice, this renunciation meant that Quaker politicians must abandon their po-litical offices, which during wartime forced Friends to compromise their adherence to pacifism. In Pennsylvania, the process began in 1756 when six Quaker assemblymen resigned from the legislature after the governor declared war against the Delaware Indians. Over the next twenty years, Friends throughout the colonies would undertake a "complete divorce" of their Society from public office. Change also meant that wealth came under more searching criticism. Reformers argued that material affluence led to pride, avarice, and ethical compromise and ultimately caused war. They called, as a result, for a return to the simplicity, reflected in dress and speech, of the early Friends and for the employment of wealth in charitable enterprises designed to aid Quakers and increasingly non-Quakers in need of help.[41]

The drive to purify the Society also produced demands to enforce more strictly Quaker practices such as endogamy, sexual continence, and sobri-ety. The efforts of reformers bore fruit in fall 1755 when the Philadelphia Yearly Meeting revised the Book of Discipline. Committed to ensuring that Friends adhere to the new discipline, reformers admonished elders and overseers "to be zealously concerned for the cause of Truth and honestly to labour to repair the breaches [in our discipline] too obvious in many places." The following year, the reformers, led by Israel Pemberton, cre-ated the Philadelphia Meeting for Sufferings, an executive body that met throughout the year to provide financial and legal aid to Friends in need, correspond with other Quaker meetings in North America and England, and explain Quaker values and behavior to the larger community. The task of purifying the Quaker community fell most directly on the monthly meet-ings, which brought minute books up to date and answered more regularly the queries of the yearly meeting, monitored the attendance of members at midweek and first day (Sunday) meetings, and established committees to renew the "ancient practice of Family Visits." These visits encouraged parents to adhere to the particulars of the discipline and inculcate Quaker values in their children. As a result of this increased diligence, in the years after 1755 the number of disownments for violations of the discipline rose sharply. Historian Jack Marietta notes that in Pennsylvania the Society disowned more than three thousand adherents between 1755 and 1776, or almost 22 percent of its membership. The most frequent violation, accounting for some 37 percent of all disownments, was marriage to a non-Quaker or failing to follow the marriage procedures of the faith.[42]

As part of the Philadelphia Yearly Meeting, Quakers in northern Virginia felt the impact of the reformers' initiatives, most directly when ministers visited the region and found local meetings in dire need of reform. English traveling Friend John Griffith experienced "a dark, afflicting time" at both the Goose Creek and Hopewell meetings, which he attributed to the "great insensibility and lukewarmness" of local Quakers. Joseph Oxley, another traveling Friend, described his meeting with Hopewell Quakers as a "gathering . . . not altogether to satisfaction." He attributed the spiritual decline to local "families . . . who had mixed themselves in marriage with those of different principles, and of near kindred." Pushed by the initiatives of the Pennsylvania reformers and stung by the critiques of visiting ministers, local Friends began a concerted effort to purify their meetings. Hopewell elders disowned 166 individuals between 1759 and 1776, a significant number in a monthly meeting that numbered no more than six hundred adherents in the latter year. As in Pennsylvania, marriage violations represented the most frequent cause for disownment, with some 56 percent of all those removed from the meeting having violated Quaker marriage practices in some fashion. Violations of Quaker nonviolence (8 percent) and gaming and dancing (7 percent) were the next most frequent infringements of the discipline, with sexual infractions and nonattendance at meeting following (both 5 percent). Hopewell Friends were not alone in this ongoing process of reform; the same process of purification took place throughout Virginia. Historian Jay Worrall estimates that Virginia meetings disowned over 20 percent of their members for delinquencies between 1763 and 1776, most frequently for marrying outside the sect or without permission of the meeting.[43]

In the drive to reform the Society, "weighty" Friends—overseers, ministers, and elders—within the various local meetings played a key role. The yearly meeting charged them with answering its annual queries about local Friends' adherence to the Society's disciplinary guidelines; they visited the homes of Quaker families in their localities to ensure the truthfulness of their responses; and they decided the fate of individuals identified as having violated the behavioral, ethical, or doctrinal standards of the Society. In most cases, overseers and elders sought to "treat" or "deal" with the offending individuals and bring them to a sincere condemnation of their "outgoing" before the meeting. They disowned those offenders who failed to display sufficient remorse for their offense. The case of Hopewell Quaker William Hoge Jr. reveals how the local meetings functioned. In March 1768, the meeting reported that he had "for a Considerable time . . . been under the Notice of the Preparative Meeting" for having "been Repeatedly Overtaken and disguised with Strong drink." In April, the committee appointed by the monthly meeting to treat with Hoge declared that they found "little hopes of amendment" in his behavior and were "Quite of the m[ind] that a Testamony might be given against him." The case was delayed, however, when Hoge, who was "very desireous of a small Tryal Further," asked for "some Longer time to try . . . to overcome his misconduct." The case dragged on for more than six months. Not until February 1769 did the meeting disown Hoge. In this case (as in others), Friends gave Hoge extended time to rectify his behavior, but ultimately the monthly meeting terminated his membership when he failed "to make Sattisfaction" and live according to Quaker standards.[44]

Within a short period of time, the strict oversight promoted by reformers became entrenched within the local meetings. With more effective mechanisms for upholding the discipline in place, Friends could monitor additional aspects of the lives of fellow members. And as the monthly meetings removed less committed Friends from membership, the more zealous had increased freedom to fulfill their spiritual callings. They soon found deficient behaviors and ethical standards that in the past Friends had accepted. Many of these reforms developed logically from Quaker values, but social and political pressures faced by the Society in the mid- and late eighteenth century convinced reformers of the need to act. Friends launched new efforts to define more strictly Quaker pacifism and convince members to leave public office. In this era, too, Friends began condemning more energetically the use of alcohol. Most famously, they initiated a campaign against slavery within their ranks and eventually in the broader society.

The enhanced influence of local leaders and the creation of an executive body in the form of meetings for sufferings created a more hierarchical church, but the Society remained responsive to the spiritual and practical concerns of individual members. Suggestions for reform and changes in the discipline could flow up from the monthly meetings or down from the yearly meeting. Regardless of the source of the reform impulse, Friends sought to forge a consensus within the group before enunciating a new spiritual concern or behavioral standard, particularly for offenses serious enough to merit disownment. Throughout the eighteenth and nineteenth centuries, Friends worked, sometimes unsuccessfully, to find compromises on controversial matters of discipline. During such internal debates, Friends frequently had to negotiate between the demands of "purists" who sought far-reaching reforms and a majority of adherents who saw little reason for immediate change.[45] The tension between those who believed Quakers should embrace various spiritual and social reforms and traditionalists who accepted the status quo would constitute a central feature of community life among northern Virginia's Friends for the next hundred years.

For Friends in northern Virginia, the period of the Seven Years' War represented the first major test of their ability to abide by the Society's spiritual commitments. Settling in the region in part to create an environment in which their principles and families could flourish, they discovered instead that Virginia's western and northern frontiers posed new moral challenges. In the midst of war, some local Friends failed to remain distinct from the world. Some served in the military or aided Virginia's military effort; others fled to the forts built by the colony's military forces. And Friends could not solve the problem of their unclear title to American Indian lands. As the Hopewell meeting noted in the 1770s, the delay resulted in part from the difficulty of discovering at "this distance of time" what "particular tribe" once "occupied these lands."[46] But it also reflected a clear reluctance of the Hopewell meeting to make the sacrifices necessary to uphold its spiritual principles. Despite establishing their own institutional infrastructure—most notably, the monthly meetings—and using it to enforce with increasing strictness the strictures of the faith, Friends were a stable and accepted group within the diverse population of northern Virginia. Friends spoke, dressed, and worshipped differently than their neighbors, but they also became integrated into the social and economic life of the region. As a result, many Friends had difficulty drawing distinct boundaries between themselves and the broader white community. In part, this confusion led Quakers throughout the colonies to embark on the "moral reformation" of their faith in the wake of the Seven Years' War. In northern and western Virginia the effort remained a work in progress into the 1770s. However, that would soon change. The pressures of the American Revolution spurred continuing reformation of the sect, including a growing repulsion toward slavery. By the 1780s, these changes would produce stark lines between local Friends and the broader community.

2

Finding a Path of Virtue
in a Revolutionary World

In early September 1777, the Revolutionary War was not going well for the new United States. The British army controlled the country's two largest ports, New York City and Philadelphia, and the Continental Army seemed unable to halt its advance. The British occupation of Philadelphia provoked widespread alarm in Pennsylvania and the Chesapeake, and the new state government of Virginia called up its militia. In Frederick County, local militia officers, following an amended state law, made no allowance for religious groups like Quakers who for reasons of conscience would not fight. On September 23, local officials drafted fourteen Friends belonging to the Hopewell Monthly Meeting into service. "With drawn swords," the American officers "pushed the Friends into rank, threatening they would have their blood if they did not comply." When the men refused "to handle any of the muskets," the officers ordered the weapons "tied to their bodies" and had the group marched to George Washington's army outside Philadelphia. The Friends refused "to partake of the provision allotted to themselves," forcing a number to drop out of the ranks "from indisposition of body" and return home as best they could. Only the intercession of Clement Biddle, a lapsed Philadelphia Quaker serving in the Continental Army, secured the release of those who made it to Pennsylvania. At Biddle's urging, Washington ordered the men freed and gave them "liberty to return home." Throughout the ordeal, Friends noted with satisfaction, the men "bore a steady testimony against all warlike measures."[1]

For northern Virginia's Quakers, such incidents became a common if sporadic feature of life during the Revolution. Many Americans viewed Friends' neutrality in the Revolutionary War as tantamount to Toryism, and they faced harassment, incarceration, financial hardships, and deep suspicion from the new state governments. In northern Virginia, the government's repression of Friends came in two waves: in late 1776 and 1777, when fighting in Pennsylvania threatened the Chesapeake, and after 1780 when the British invaded Virginia. Historians have often portrayed the Revolution in Virginia as a product of enlightened leaders who confidently led a united white population into revolt, but the experience of Friends highlights the anxieties of the state's elite and the racial and class tensions that plagued Virginia. Many of these internal conflicts resurfaced and Quakers confronted another wave of repression when the British invaded the Chesapeake during the War of 1812. In the Revolutionary and early national era, Friends faced harassment when Virginia's political leadership felt most threatened and the new nation faced its gravest military threats.[2]

Quakers' wartime experience also helped transform the Society of Friends. Since the 1750s, reforming Quakers had worked to purify the sect, codify its discipline, and in the words of English traveling minister Samuel Fothergill, divide "wheat and chaff" to separate "honest-hearted" Friends from "the worldly-minded" who opposed reformation. The Revolution accelerated the reformers' efforts. In the mid-1770s, Friends articulated more clearly and expanded the scope of their pacifist convictions, leading them to embrace a course of action that alienated them from the broader American community. Friends' suffering during wartime, moreover, convinced them to embrace a new activism that addressed a variety of social injustices, including slavery and American Indian policy. These changes transformed the Society throughout North America, including the meetings in the slaveholding region of northern Virginia.[3]

The Revolution accelerated Friends' efforts to clean their own house and generated a growing awareness that they must also work to redeem the broader society. By war's end, northern Virginia's Quakers had largely ended slave ownership among themselves. During the 1780s and 1790s they campaigned to aid newly freed African Americans and abolish the slave trade and the institution of slavery, an effort they renewed after the War of 1812. The Baltimore Yearly Meeting also tried to reimburse American Indians for the land on which the Hopewell Meeting House sat. The effort failed, but it sparked a new social concern for the Baltimore meeting: aid to and education among the Native Americans in the Northwest. The experience of war also encouraged the region's Quakers to begin enforcing more strictly the Society's rules against frivolous and immoral behavior, including the use of liquor. In response to their "sufferings," northern Virginia's Quakers, like their coreligionists throughout the United States, forged a tighter and more purified group, enhancing their identity and community. At the same time, they created for themselves an important (if often unpopular) moral role in the new American nation. How best to exercise this new role, however, remained an open question among Friends.[4]

I

The Quaker embrace of pacifism, arising from their conviction that all people were "enlightened by the divine light of Christ," first presented problems for Friends in Virginia during the Seven Years' War. After the threat to Virginia's western frontier ended in the early 1760s, Quaker attitudes toward secular government in times of peace helped ensure that colonial authorities no longer perceived the Society as a social and political threat. Friends believed that government was divinely inspired, and thus they adhered to a policy of obedience to any secular authority that did not force them to act against their conscience. As the Quaker writer Isaac Penington noted in 1681, Friends sought "universal liberty . . . to worship God," but even when governments denied them such freedoms, Penington urged his coreligionists to "be still and quiet in your Minds." "We are not," he noted, "against Magistracy, Laws, or Government, though we cannot flatter or bend to them in that which is selfish and corrupt." In eighteenth-century America, where Friends enjoyed toleration, Penington's counsel became an important component of their testimony. As the Philadelphia Yearly Meeting noted in 1755, "it is well known" that early Friends complied "with the Laws of Government under which they lived in every Case not contrary to the . . . Doctrines of our Supreme Lord." On those occasions when government violated their religious testimonies, the yearly meeting counseled members to practice passive disobedience, just as early Friends had "patiently suffered" under similar circumstances. Friends must pursue nonviolent resistance, the yearly meeting stressed, because "followers of Christ" could not use "violence to oppose the Ordinances of Magistrates." And Friends had to bear the consequences of their actions as part of a peaceful protest.[5]

Obedience to the existing government did not forestall Quaker participation in the largely nonviolent protests of the mid-1760s. Most Friends supported American remonstrations against the taxes of the British government, agreeing with their fellow colonists that only elected provincial representatives could tax them. Quaker merchants in Philadelphia participated in early nonimportation agreements, though they worked to moderate coercive enforcement tactics. When Patriots threatened violence, however, Friends began distancing themselves from the resistance movement, arguing that Americans employ less combative measures and appeal to the British conscience. When violence erupted, Friends broke with the protesters. Not only were Americans overthrowing a legally constituted government, a task Quakers believed lay in God's hands, but Patriots employed military measures to do so. Adherence to their religious testimonies demanded that Quakers take no part in the revolutionary struggle.[6]

The events of the 1760s and early 1770s left northern Virginia's Friends untroubled. They remained a curious group because of their spiritual values, but their farming acumen and their principled business practices helped restore much of the public respect they had lost during the Seven Years' War. Reflecting this shift in public opinion, in 1766 the Virginia House of Burgesses exempted Friends from military service. Quaker support for the American cause prior to 1775, in England and the colonies, also generated goodwill for local Friends. Between 1774 and 1776, the *Virginia Gazette* lauded the Society for opposing the measures of the British Parliament and for its "truly benevolent and humane" relief efforts. In June 1774, the paper reported that English Friends "have prepared a most spirited petition to the Throne" "in Defence of their Rights in the Colonies," and in August Virginians learned that "the ministry have been greatly alarmed at the conduct of the Quakers," who stood "forth to support their American brethren." As late as July 1775, the paper assured Virginians that the "Quakers of England . . . all join in one voice against the Ministry." American Quakers, the paper reported in 1774, "profess themselves ready to consent to every measure which promises to preserve the rights of Americans," though they "do not chuse to demonstrate their dissatisfaction in the noisy manner [of] less orderly . . . colonists." In May 1775 the *Gazette,* enthused with Quaker patriotism, reported incorrectly that "upwards of 6,000" Philadelphia Friends had voted to "take up arms in defence of American liberty." More accurately, the paper praised the Society for its "active" efforts to raise "contributions" for the inhabitants of Boston.[7]

In contrast, the growing Quaker opposition to slavery had a more ambivalent impact on their status in the colony. Long-held spiritual principles—the belief that the inward light resided within all people, the embrace of the golden rule, and the celebration of simplicity and industry—made slaveholding morally suspect for Friends. Still, if Quaker religious doctrines held the seeds for the rejection of slavery, few Friends acted on them before the reformers began exercising influence over the Society in the late

1750s. Only then did Friends begin a concerted effort to condemn slaveholding by their members—and only then did the issue separate southern Friends from their neighbors. Despite occasional protests from scattered meetings and individuals, in the first half of the eighteenth century many Quaker merchants participated in the slave trade, and Friends from New England to North Carolina owned slaves. Quaker merchants in Philadelphia and Rhode Island helped organize and grew rich from the Atlantic slave trade, though importing slaves became a disownable offense in 1715. These wealthy Friends, many of whom owned slaves, dominated the influential Philadelphia Yearly Meeting, which had a central role in establishing Quaker discipline. Before the 1750s, Philadelphia's Quaker merchants discouraged antislavery activities by Friends. They stopped the publication of Quaker antislavery writing and disowned abolitionists such as John Farmer, Ralph Sandiford, and Benjamin Lay who disrupted the peace and violated the discipline of the Society.[8]

Quakers living in the southern colonies found it more difficult to break their connection to slavery than did their northern counterparts. Many Friends owned slaves, often in significant numbers. In 1749, ownership of some twenty slaves made Quaker Elisha Hall the second largest slaveholder in what would become Loudoun County. Daniel Mifflin, father of Quaker abolitionist Warner Mifflin, owned close to one hundred slaves on his Accomack County plantation before he freed them in 1775, while Robert Pleasants, later Virginia's most prominent antislavery Friend, owned eighty slaves before the Revolution. Public or traveling Friends commented on the prevalence of slaveholding among southern Quakers. In 1754, Samuel Fothergill lamented that "the gain of oppression, the price of blood is upon" Maryland Friends for "their purchasing, and keeping in slavery, negroes." He added, "This very much describes also the state of Virginia." Catherine Phillips, another itinerant Friend who visited northern Virginia the same year, believed that slavery had caused much "suffering of spirit" among Friends. Although Phillips believed Friends treated their slaves comparatively well, she "could not but lament over those poor [enslaved] people."[9]

Some slaveholding Quakers defended slave ownership, often on biblical grounds. In 1757, minister John Woolman, traveling from Pennsylvania, expressed dismay when a slaveholding Virginia Friend argued that blacks descended from Cain. "Their blackness," the slaveholder claimed, is "the mark God set upon" them, adding that "it is the design of Providence that they should be slaves." Proslavery Quakers resisted alterations in the Society's slavery discipline, and before the late 1750s they succeeded in thwarting change. When Woolman attended the Virginia Yearly Meeting, he discovered that elders had watered down the query of the Philadelphia Yearly Meeting regarding slavery, making it possible for Friends to purchase slaves. Woolman lobbied against the change, but the meeting did not correct it. The interest of many Virginia Quakers in slavery ensured that prior to the mid-1750s "anti-slavery made little headway" in the colony.[10]

However, the Seven Years' War convinced many Friends of the need to initiate a thoroughgoing reform of the Society, including divorcing Friends from slaveholding. According to historian Jean Soderlund, both economic and ideological factors helped shape the direction and timing of Quaker reform. Friends who exploited slave labor—including farmers in the New Jersey and Pennsylvania countryside and Philadelphia craftsmen—reluctantly abandoned the institution. Quakers not tied to slaveholding—yeomen farmers of the New Jersey and Pennsylvania countryside and substantial Philadelphia merchants who could afford wage labor in the 1750s and 1760s—supported abolition sooner and more insistently. The groups united in the 1760s and 1770s, convinced by reformers that ending slavery would purify the Society and purge it of worldliness.[11] In 1758, the Philadelphia Yearly Meeting, the foremost meeting in America, decided to remove from positions of authority those who continued to purchase slaves and established a committee, headed by John Woolman, to visit slaveholders who refused to free their bondsmen. Over the next sixteen years the abolitionists worked to convince slaveholding Quakers to free their slaves, and in 1774 the yearly meeting resolved to disown any member who owned a slave, a policy implemented in 1776.[12]

As part of the Philadelphia Yearly Meeting until 1790, northern Virginia's Quakers began the process of disowning slaveholders within their ranks the same year. The process was complicated by the growth of the local enslaved population. In the wake of the Seven Years' War, eastern Virginians, including large planters who brought their human property with them, moved into the area, so that by 1787 over 25 percent of the total population was enslaved. Still, most local Friends had little direct association with slavery, making the effort to end slaveholding within the community somewhat easier than in Tidewater Virginia, where more Quaker masters lived. Despite the threat of disownment, reformers had to work hard to convince slaveholding Friends to free their human property. Elders concerned about the spiritual welfare of slaveholding Friends "treated" with them at length, while preparative and monthly meetings formed committees to visit members who refused to manumit their bondsmen. Traveling Friends often accompanied these committees. Itinerants Norris Jones and Sarah Harrison journeyed from Philadelphia to Virginia in 1788 and undertook the "hard laborious work" of convincing local Quakers to free their slaves. Between June 22 and June 27, Norris visited ten slaveholding Friends, eventually convincing five masters, including M. Bailey who owned twenty-two, to free over thirty slaves. "N. J." was a particularly hard case. Norris visited him twice, finding on his first visit "the most hardened spirit . . . in him that we have met with." The next day, after saying "a good deal to him," "at length the power of the Highest softened his hard heart. He came and gave me his hand and was broken even to weeping." "Miracles," Norris concluded, "have not ceased."[13]

The minutes of the Fairfax Monthly Meeting reveal the difficulty reformers had convincing slaveholders to relinquish their human chattel. As early as 1762, the Fairfax meeting cautioned member Thomas Taylor that his recent "purchase of a Negroe" was "contrary to the Judgment of the Yearly Meeting." He did not relent. Despite "having been much laboured with" over the course of the next fifteen years, he was "fixed to keep Slaves," and in November 1777 the meeting, acting at the behest of the quarterly meeting, disowned him. But the story did not end there. After the intercession of Isaac Zane Jr., a prominent local Friend, the meeting reinstated Taylor after he promised to free his slaves by 1780. The meeting exercised similar patience with other slaveholders. In 1774, it declared that slaves "have a Natural Right to freedom and Equal Justice as those of our own Color." Still, various committees appointed to treat with slaveholders noted limited progress, one reporting that only "one Friend . . . Signified to us he would" free his slaves. The problem still existed in 1778 when Fairfax Friends, at the behest of the quarterly meeting, appointed a new committee "to take some further care to obtain Manumissions" of slaves.[14]

Manumission in northern Virginia went more slowly than elsewhere in the Philadelphia Yearly Meeting because Virginia's laws made it difficult to free enslaved property. Statutes of 1723 and 1741 made it illegal for masters to free their slaves "except for some meritorious services, to be adjudged and allowed by the governor and council." The 1741 law required the re-enslavement and sale of slaves freed without authorization, with proceeds going to the local parish. The law stymied Quaker slaveholders from manumitting their human property, and a number of Virginia quarterly meetings informed the yearly meeting in 1770 that many slaveholders would free their slaves if the law permitted them. To sidestep the statutes and avoid repercussions from white neighbors who feared the presence of free blacks, some Friends treated their slaves as free people, employing "them as hired servants after they had given them their liberty." In 1778, Robert Pleasants "settled" his black population "on lands" he owned, where they lived "under" his "care, direction, and protection." His neighbors, however, worried about the prospect of independent black tenants in their vicinity and issued "a kind of threat." Pleasants responded that he had the "right to settle my own lands with Negro's, if I choose . . . so long as I support my family without charge."[15]

The Virginia meeting also urged Friends to petition members of the Virginia assembly. Pleasants asked Representative Richard Bland to "make a motion in the next Assembly to repeal the law [of 1723] which prevents a man from rewarding faithfulness with freedom for his servants." Bland did not act on Pleasants's request, though the yearly meeting reported in 1770 that some burgesses recognized the law's "injustice." Hoping to capitalize on this sentiment, in 1772 the yearly meeting sent copies of abolitionist Quaker Anthony Benezet's 1771 antislavery pamphlet, *Some Historical Account of Guinea*, to selected members of Virginia legislature, including Patrick Henry. He responded by attacking slavery as an "abominable Practice," "as repugnant to humanity, as it was inconsistent with the Bible and destructive of Liberty." The assembly and Henry did nothing, however, to repeal the 1723 and 1741 laws, reflecting widespread opposition to Quaker efforts to manumit their slaves. Still, Friends were heartened when Henry commended them for their "noble efforts to abolish slavery."[16]

Along with Henry, a small but growing number of Virginian planters shared some of Friends' uneasiness with slavery. In 1767, Arthur Lee attacked slavery, asserting that it "is dangerous to the safety of the community in which it prevails . . . destructive to the growth of arts and sciences; and . . . produces a very fatal train of vices, both in the slave, and in his master." Four years later, a writer who identified himself only as "Associator Humanus" described slaveholders as "absolute Tyrants" who hold "Numbers of poor Souls in the most abject and endless State of Slavery." Writing during the imperial crisis, he worried that Virginians' familiarity with the tyranny of slavery had made them less "strenuous in our Opposition to ministerial Tyranny." Like Thomas Jefferson, who assailed the slave trade in his *Summary View of the Rights of British America* (1774), Associator Humanus "carefully tailored" his opposition to slavery "to serve the cause of revolution." Both writers, as historian Eva Sheppard Wolf notes, "attacked the slave trade because it" enabled them to justify rebellion. In northern Virginia, the writers of the July 1774 Fairfax County Resolves adopted a similar tactic, arguing that "during our present difficulties and distress *no* slaves ought to be imported into the British colonies of this continent." Local Patriots, among them George Washington, believed that Virginians should use this moment "to put an entire stop forever to such a wicked, cruel, and unnatural trade."[17]

In the years before the Revolution the growth of elite antislavery opinion and the nonconfrontational tactics adopted by Quakers enabled members of the Society to launch a program of reform against slavery without raising widespread opposition. Moreover, their support for American protests against British imperial rule in the 1760s and early 1770s, as well as their business acumen and industriousness, generated goodwill among the broader population. In the midst of revolutionary enthusiasm, some Virginians welcomed Quaker antislavery efforts, and leading Friends linked their attacks on slavery and the slave trade to those of revolutionary leaders. Anthony Benezet had Arthur Lee's 1767 antislavery address bound to his own 1767 antislavery publication, *A Caution and Warning to Great Britain*, though he found it necessary to remove Lee's "most striking expressions least I should raise a prejudice agst. my Book."[18] In northern Virginia, local Friends were heartened by the Fairfax County Resolves attacking the slave trade. Before 1775, Friends' pacifism and antislavery convictions had not yet isolated them from the broader community.

II

Virginian (and American) opinion changed, however, when the Philadelphia Yearly Meeting issued a series of statements in 1775 and 1776 that articulated why Quakers had decided to distance themselves from the revolutionary struggle. In January 1776, Friends contrasted the "calamities and afflictions which now surround us" with the "peace and plenty" Americans enjoyed under the British crown. The address concluded that Quakers should "firmly unite in the abhorrence of all . . . measures" designed "to break off the happy connexion we have heretofore enjoyed with the kingdom of Great Britain, and our just and necessary subordination to the king." Friends intended the statement to explain their reasons for endorsing neutrality and seeking to avert a final break between the colonies and Great Britain, but Patriots understandably interpreted its praise for the British monarch as proof of Friends' Loyalism. Patriot newspapers published a series of blistering attacks on the Society, warning Quakers not to give offense by "endeavoring to counteract the measures of their fellow citizens for the common safety." Some writers wondered how a group that professed neutrality could support the monarchy. As Samuel Adams noted, "if they would not *pull down Kings*, let them not support *tyrants.*"[19]

The most withering response came from Thomas Paine, whose inflammatory and popular pamphlet, *Common Sense*, appeared the same month as the January 1776 Quaker epistle. Subsequent editions of his pamphlet appended an address to the "People called Quakers," which accused them of "dabbling in matters which your professed . . . Principles instruct you not to meddle in." Paine argued that the Society could not claim that "the setting up and putting down of kings and governments is God's peculiar prerogative" and at the same time make political pronouncements that condemned Patriot actions. To remain true to their principles, Quakers must "wait with patience and humility for the event of all public measures . . . [and] receive *that event* as the divine will towards you." Paine told Friends that their attempts to influence public opinion revealed "that either ye do not believe what ye profess, or have not virtue enough to practise what ye believe." The Society had "mistaken party for conscience," Paine concluded, and such "mingling [of] religion with politics" should "*be disavowed and reprobated by every inhabitant of* AMERICA."[20]

The following year the Society's public reputation sank further when American newspapers published a fabricated note from the nonexistent "Spanktown Yearly Meeting." The communication, allegedly found in the papers of an American officer who had defected to the British, revealed the size and location of Washington's army in Pennsylvania. Informing Congress of the letter, American General John Sullivan condemned Friends as "the most Dangerous Enemies America knows." "Covered with that Hypocritical Cloak of Religion," Friends, Sullivan argued, had "Long Acted the part of Inveterate Enemies of their Country" and "Prostituted" "their Religious Meetings . . . to the Base purposes of betraying their Country." Although Friends informed Congress and the public that the Spanktown meeting did not exist, and that no such "letter . . . [was] ever written in any of our meetings," the missive had done its damage. Many Americans believed that the Quakers posed a threat to the Patriot cause, in part because the letter appeared just as British General William Howe threatened to take Philadelphia, the new nation's capital. In Virginia, Edmund Pendleton assumed that Friends had great "hopes of How[e]'s success." The *Virginia Gazette* added to the anti-Quaker environment when it falsely reported in November 1777 that Philadelphia Friends had given "*friend* Howe a free gift of six thousand pounds on his entrance into" the city.[21]

In the face of growing hostility, the Philadelphia Yearly Meeting worked to clarify the Society's discipline and ensure that Friends throughout America remained unified, a response that only deepened anti-Quaker sentiment. As Richard Henry Lee remarked, "The Quaker m[otto] ought to be '*Nos turba sumus*' for if you attack one, the whole Society is roused." By the 1770s, reforming Friends dominated the Philadelphia meeting, and many believed that the prosperous years after the Seven Years' War had stalled the purification effort. They viewed the "calamity" of the Revolution as a punishment for the lapses of the previous decade and as an opportunity to revive the campaign. Suffering, they believed, would lead to spiritual growth and a clarification and strengthening of the peace testimony. As reformer Anthony Benezet wrote in 1778, "Let us deeply attend to a consideration of how far we . . . for want of living up to what we have and still do, so loudly profess, have contributed to the calamity wch. attends." "Has not our conformity to the world, our engagements in life, in order to please ourselves and gain wealth," Benezet asked, "begot a desire in our children to live in conformity to other people"? But such difficulties, Benezet believed, promised future redemption: "The suffering providence which now is displayed over us seems particularly calculated to bring us to our selves," and "will teach us, in future, to live more agreable to our profession."[22]

In September 1776, to ensure that Friends understood the implications of Quaker principles, the Philadelphia meeting issued instructions to its subordinate meetings, including Fairfax and Hopewell in northern Virginia, for enforcing the peace testimony in a uniform fashion. All Friends, the Philadelphia meeting stated, had to resign from positions they held within the new governments because they had been founded on violence. Friends must refuse payment of war taxes and of penalties or fines they might incur for not paying such taxes or serving in the military. Finally, they must disengage from war-related trade from which they could profit. The yearly meeting did not offer these strictures as advice; violators of these testimonies, the Philadelphia meeting stressed, could be disowned from the Society. In December, the meeting issued another epistle to fortify "weak" and "wavering" Friends, urging members to "withstand and refuse to submit to the arbitrary injunctions and ordinances of men who assume to themselves the power of compelling others." Girded by the "truth" of the inward light, Quakers could do no less than "steadily . . . bear . . . testimony against every attempt to deprive us of it."[23]

Beleaguered Friends throughout America must have found these words heartening, but they did not relieve the hardships they faced during the war years. Northern Virginia's Quakers saw firsthand the repressive nature of American measures when, at the behest of Congress, the Pennsylvania Council arrested eighteen leading Philadelphia Friends, the "Virginia exiles," marched them to the Shenandoah Valley in September 1777, and held them without charge for over seven months. Initially ordered to Staunton in Augusta County, the exiles were housed at Winchester after disowned Quaker Isaac Zane Jr.—Frederick County's assemblyman, staunch Patriot, and owner of the Marlborough Iron Works in the county—interceded on their behalf. The exiles entered the town of Winchester "peaceably" on September 29, but the next day "some turbulent persons" gathered outside their prison and "demanded" their immediate removal from the town. The officer charged with protecting the prisoners, County Lieutenant John Smith, succeeded in quieting the mob by "promising that a guard should be kept at the doors of the house" and writing to the Continental Congress and Virginia's governor for instructions about the prisoners' future. Smith's letter revealed how local attitudes toward Friends had deteriorated. "The inhabitants in this part of the country," Smith wrote, "are . . . much exasperated against the whole Society of Quakers." The negative publicity of the last few months, Smith noted, had "taught" local Patriots "to suppose these people were Tories." "I can assure you," Smith concluded, the "lives" of the exiles "will be endangered by their staying at Winchester."[24]

The presence of the exiles also endangered northern Virginia Friends. Within days of the prisoners' arrival, leading members of the Hopewell and Fairfax meetings began visiting and holding religious meetings with the prisoners, whom local authorities first housed in a Winchester tavern. The visitors soon faced threats. "Persons of an envious disposition," one of the exiles recalled, "appeared disturbed" by the visits and threatened those "staying to sit with us." Undeterred, visiting Friends decided to "risk the consequences" and remained. County residents recruited to guard the prisoners also used the opportunity to retaliate against local Friends who refused military service. They "compelled" Quaker Isaac England, who lived five miles from Winchester, to leave home and "guard over" the exiles. Although England "steadily refused to touch the musket" and said "he would not detain" the prisoners, officers would not allow him to leave for two days.[25]

Over time, the conditions of the prisoners' confinement improved, in large part because of Zane's influence, County Lieutenant Smith's indulgence, and the "truly . . . inoffensive" behavior of the exiles. Smith soon allowed the prisoners to hold regular biweekly religious services and visit

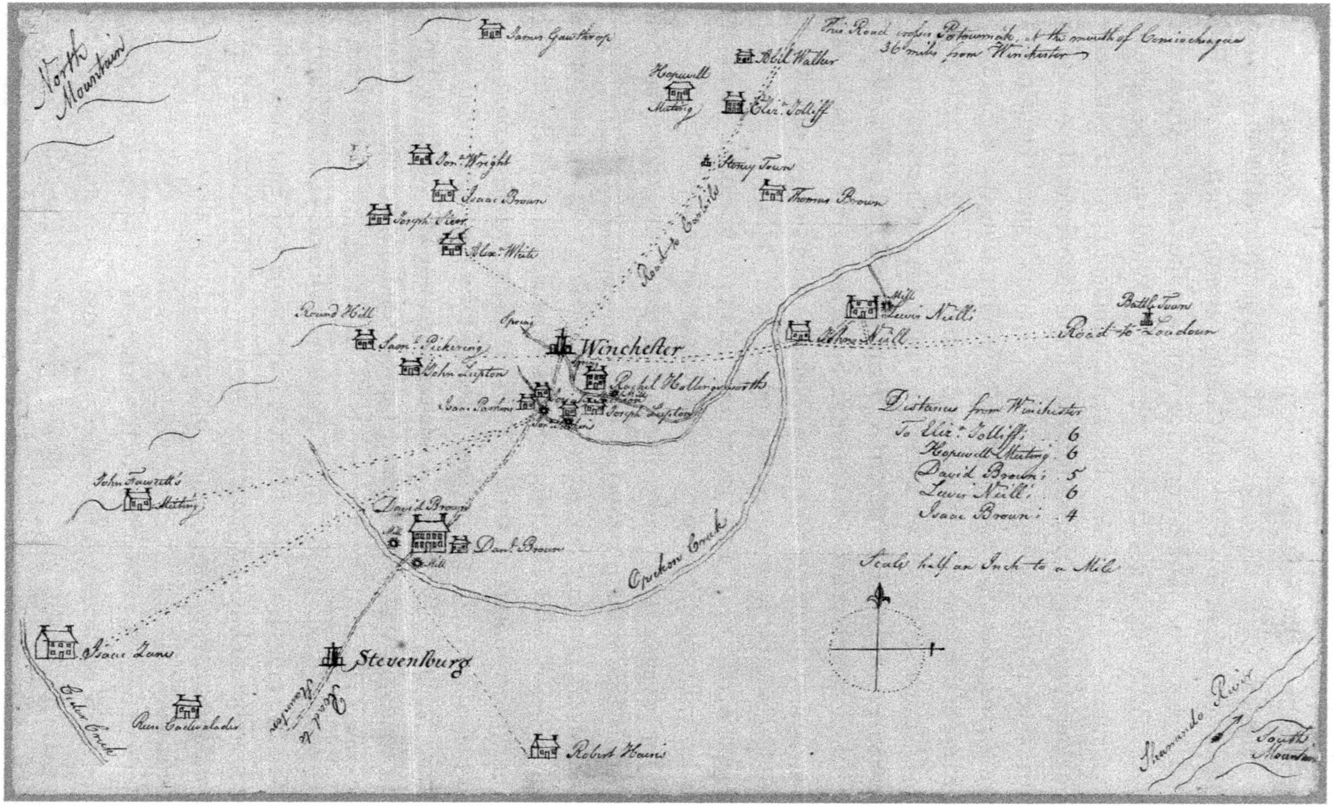

Map 2. Thomas Fisher's map of Winchester and vicinity, March 10, 1778. In Logan-Fisher-Fox Family Papers. Courtesy of the Pennsylvania Historical Society.

the homes of nearby Friends. The exiles' letters reveal how much they relied on the support and friendship of nearby Quakers. In October, Henry Drinker noted that local Friends Sarah Janney and Elizabeth Jolliffe had "been kindly to see us, justly thinking it would be a comfort to us." Some days later, Drinker reported that the exiles received "daily supplies" and "fresh provisions" from neighboring Quakers. By month's end, Drinker and two of his fellow exiles dined regularly at the home of Hopewell Friend Joseph Steer, whose "wife and Family," he reported, "have been very kind from our first coming here." Before the end of the year, county authorities permitted the exiles to move into the homes of local Friends, and Drinker reported that they "attended Hopewell Mo. Meeting." Exile Thomas Fisher's map of Winchester, completed in March 1778, reveals the prisoners' bonds to the Hopewell community. Aside from a few topographical features, he identified only the homes of Friends and local meetings.[26]

III

In April 1778, American authorities permitted the Philadelphians to return home, but not before two of them had died, a "lesson to local Friends" who refused to support the Patriot cause. But by this time Virginia Friends had "sufferings" of their own at the hands of the state government. Like American leaders in Philadelphia, Virginia's planters in 1777 feared the fate of the Patriot cause, and committees of safety subjected a number of Friends to close questioning. In Petersburg, the county committee threatened to label Quaker Edward Stabler as a traitor for refusing to support the Continental Association, the boycott of British goods that the Continental Congress had established in fall 1774. In response, some Virginia Friends, including Robert Pleasants, decided to "submit to all regulations of trade," arguing that doing so did not violate the peace testimony.[27] But Virginia's gentry worried about more than Tories and Quakers. A deeper concern lay in the Revolution's potential to unleash long-simmering class and racial tensions in the state. Planters' harassment of Quakers reflected these larger concerns.

As historian Woody Holton argues, Virginia planters reluctantly embraced revolution in part to forestall slave and class unrest. In Loudoun County, home to one of the largest concentrations of Friends in Virginia and the Fairfax Monthly Meeting, a renter's revolt erupted in 1775. As the war lengthened and the state raised more troops and supplies from an often unwilling populace, increasing class and racial tensions threatened the gentry's political control. White unrest peaked in early 1781, when a series of tax revolts swept through the state, most notably in Hampshire County in the lower Shenandoah Valley, just west of Frederick County's significant Quaker population. The Continental Congress's decision to house British and German prisoners of war in the valley after 1776 added to the unease of Virginia's revolutionary leaders. Most frightening, the Revolutionary War weakened planters' control over their slaves. During the same years that Friends worked to free their slaves, large numbers of enslaved people escaped to British lines, first after Virginia Governor Lord Dunmore issued his 1775 proclamation promising freedom to bondsmen who joined his army and again during the British invasion of the state in 1780–81. Threats to the state's independence and to slavery increased animosity toward neutral and antislavery Friends. Their repression reveals the insecurity of Virginia gentry's during the Revolution.[28]

The Loudoun riots of November 1775, sparked by an ongoing salt shortage, led to the first assault on the region's Quaker population. According to Holton, tension between landlords and tenants underlay the unrest. As a result of the land distribution policies of Lord Fairfax's proprietary, up to one third of the white heads of households in Loudoun County rented their land from large planters such as George Washington and Richard Henry Lee. A shortage of specie forced local employers and military recruiters to pay wages in paper money, but local landlords continued to demand rent payments in gold and silver. In response, tenants in Loudoun and neighboring Fauquier, led by Washington's former employee James Cleveland, refused to pay their rents unless the Continental Association lifted its nonexportation agreement (which effectively halted the flow of specie into Virginia). The disparity between wages paid to officers and common soldiers and the gentry's poor military leadership also upset large numbers of Loudoun farmers. County resident Richard Morlan warned that "he would not muster, and if fined would oppose the collection of the fine with his gun." Unrest continued into May 1776.[29] No evidence exists that Quakers, most of whom owned land, joined the revolt, but their refusal to serve or contribute to the war effort made them seem as traitorous as the rioters. County leaders may have viewed Friends' noncompliance as more dangerous, and therefore more needful of suppression, than the insubordination of the region's renters. The British invasion of eastern Pennsylvania and capture of Philadelphia in September 1777 heightened planters' anxieties and increased their efforts to suppress internal dissent, particularly among pacifist Quakers.

After fighting erupted, the state required pacifists to bear arms or hire a substitute, overturning 1766 and 1775 laws exempting them from serving in the militia. Charged with putting the new legislation into effect, Frederick County officials forcibly recruited the fourteen Hopewell Quakers in September 1777. A month later, eighteen Friends from the Fairfax meeting faced a similar fate when County Lieutenant Francis Peyton drafted them into the militia to serve with the Continental Army. Peyton released two of the men for health reasons but marched the remaining sixteen north 176 miles to outside Philadelphia, where they arrived in early November. Captive James Gawthorp "suffered much" from the ordeal, compelled by his captors to walk "with his hands tied behind him and a gun on his back." After a day in camp, the recruits were "discharged by order of General Washington" and returned home in mid-November. Throughout their "Restraint," the Quaker recruits "avoided taking any Provision" and exercised "a good degree of patience and Resignation." The strategy of passive disobedience stymied the efforts of the state to recruit pacifists.[30]

In response to Quaker tactics, the Virginia legislature changed its strategy for dealing with conscientious objectors and in late 1777 decided to excuse pacifists from service if their religious society hired substitutes. During the Seven Years' War, many Friends had found this policy acceptable, but during the Revolutionary War Quaker leaders declared the measure objectionable. The reforms within the Society had forged a more rigorous pacifist testimony that sought to avoid any complicity in war-making, and Friends refused to hire substitutes or pay fines for nonservice. Local authorities responded by distraining, or seizing, Quaker property and jailing those who owned nothing of value. The loss of property, most of it through distraint, was the biggest burden that northern Virginia's Friends faced during the war. The Hopewell and the Fairfax meetings, at the behest of the Philadelphia Yearly Meeting, each established a Committee for Suffering Cases, which detailed the ordeals of all members who suffered because of the peace testimony. By 1784, these committees reported that Friends in northern Virginia had paid almost 2,400 pounds in Virginia currency in distraints, most for refusing to hire substitutes.[31]

The state had nevertheless been slow to adopt the tactic of distraint, and not until 1780 and 1781, when the combination of external threat and internal dissent—the British incursions into Virginia that began in the fall of 1780 and a Loyalist uprising in Hampshire County in mid-1781—did local officials begin a methodical effort to seize Quaker property. By 1779, the state had seized only slightly more than 115 pounds of property from fourteen Friends in the Fairfax Monthly Meeting. The Hopewell meeting reported no distraints before that year.[32] In contrast, the 1780 British invasion of Virginia and the state's subsequent scramble for men and materials led to the widespread seizure of Quaker property and occasional forced recruitments.

Other Virginians suffered in the crisis. In 1779, the legislature empowered state officials to seize private property needed for the war effort, paying farmers in state certificates redeemable in six months. The following year Virginia imposed a draft to raise troops for the Continental Army. These measures generated widespread discontent among small farmers, who received unredeemable paper scrip for produce seized by the state and who could not afford to hire substitutes and faced the prospect of abandoning their families. In a number of locations, including Hampshire County in 1781, the state's actions sparked revolt. According to County Lieutenant Garret Van Meter, the "dangerous insurrection" began in March 1781, when the tax commissioner attempted to raise troops and collect supplies as required by "the late Acts of [the] Assembly." The leader of the revolt, John Claypole, gathered a force of close to one hundred and fifty men consisting of local draft evaders, deserters, and a few escaped British prisoners of war. In mid-June, General Daniel Morgan, who resided in Frederick County, marched four hundred soldiers into Hampshire County. In the face of this force, the revolt collapsed with only one death and the arrest of forty-two individuals. The next year the governor pardoned the insurgents. In 1781, however, with British forces under Benedict Arnold plundering eastern Virginia and threatening the state government, revolutionary leaders deemed the revolt extremely serious.[33]

The presence of British troops in the uprising pointed to another threat. Since 1777, Congress had housed British and German prisoners outside of Winchester. Many of them worked for local farm families and could easily escape into the countryside. Daniel Morgan, for one, deemed the combination of local Tories and the large number of poorly guarded British and German prisoners dangerous. Even after the defeat of Lord Cornwallis's British forces at Yorktown, Morgan remained anxious. In late 1781, he warned Washington and Virginia Governor Benjamin Harrison that the "Chain of Tories Extending thence along the Frontiers of Maryland and Pennsylvania would rather assist than prevent" the "Escape" of troops housed near Winchester. He worried particularly that the main body of prisoners was housed "in the only Tory Settlement in the County," some "five miles from Winchester." Historians place the approximate location of these barracks about four miles west of Winchester, or about two miles southwest of Apple Pie Ridge, home to the Hopewell Meeting House and a large Quaker settlement.[34]

Morgan never identified who lived in the "Tory settlement," but Frederick County had few suspected Loyalists aside from Friends. As Lieutenant John Smith noted in 1777, most local residents distrusted the patriotism of Quakers.[35] The decisions of county officials in 1780 and 1781 reflected similar doubts about local Friends. In all, 143 Quakers from northern Virginia suffered the distraint of property between 1775 and 1782 for their failure to support the war effort. The vast majority of distraints took place during those years when external and internal threats jeopardized the Patriot cause in Virginia. Of these individuals, 126 (almost 90 percent) had their property seized between November 1779 and April 1782. Friends faced, moreover, a fairly systematic repression. Approximately four hundred and fifty adult men in northern Virginia's Quaker community were subject to military service; over 30 percent of them had their property seized for refusal to serve or support the war. As the Shenandoah Valley's first historian, Samuel Kercheval, concluded, Quakers "were the greatest sufferers by the war."

Most Friends lost property in repeated seizures. Samuel Canby of Loudoun County lost over sixty pounds worth of property in six distraints between May 1780 and May 1781. In the valley, Allen Jackson suffered the biggest loss—almost ninety pounds worth of property in seven seizures between February 1781 and March 1782. Three other Friends lost over eighty pounds each. County officials did not stop with the wealthiest men. Many Friends lost small household items needed by Virginia troops. William Daniel had a pair of boots, a hat and a cheese, a frying pan and pewter plates, together valued at less than five pounds, taken from him between April 1779 and March 1781. County officials took great coats, halters, and bridles for use by soldiers. They sold silk handkerchiefs, coverlets, feather beds, and "delph dishes" at auction, often enabling "designing individuals to make profitable speculations." Most often, they took animals, wagons, and produce that American military forces put to immediate use.[36]

In the face of this extensive pressure, not all Friends honored their peace testimony. Between 1775 and 1783, the Hopewell meeting disowned seven men for "consenting to serve in the station of a soldier." Farther east, the Fairfax meeting disowned sixteen men for "bearing Arms" or "hiring a substitute and joining in the active part of the war." Most of these disownments came early in the conflict when a "martial spirit" swept the new nation and the adventure of military life appealed to young Quaker men, despite the pronouncements of the Society. Some Virginia Quakers may have decided that the Society would countenance military service because of erroneous reports that some Philadelphia Friends had joined the fighting. Although several Philadelphia-area Quakers urged their yearly meeting to support the revolutionary cause, the "Free Quakers" (as they dubbed themselves) remained a small group, and the Philadelphia meeting disowned fewer than thirty members for "enlisting as a soldier." The meetings of northern Virginia likewise disowned small numbers for military service, fewer than 6 percent of the Quaker men eligible. The vast majority of local Friends resisted the public and economic pressures to bear arms, strong evidence of the impact of Quaker reformers' efforts to purify the Society and regulate members' behavior.[37]

Reformers had more difficulty enforcing a unified policy concerning the payment of taxes in time of war, leading to some uncertainty on this question among local Quakers. For the first time in the Society's history, all Friends agreed that paying war taxes, or money collected to support the military directly, constituted a violation of the peace testimony, and the Philadelphia and Virginia Yearly Meetings made such payments grounds for removal. The majority of Friends agreed that they should pay taxes earmarked for nonmilitary purposes but disagreed whether members should pay mixed or general taxes, in which a portion of the money supported the military effort. Leaders of the Philadelphia and Virginia Yearly Meetings voiced the greatest opposition to the payment of such levies, and although the meetings worked hard to reach a consensus on the issue neither succeeded by war's end.[38]

In Virginia, the yearly meeting asked Hopewell and Fairfax Friends to send representatives to its annual gathering in December 1775 to ensure that Quakers in the province acted as one on the issue of war taxes. The meeting considered two questions: the use of "paper bills of credit that are or may be issued for the purposes of carrying on War," and "the propriety of Friends voluntarily paying or refusing to pay" a mixed tax. On the first issue, Virginia Friends followed the advice of the Philadelphia meeting and refused to accept Continental currency, making Virginia and Philadelphia the only meetings to do so. On the second issue, the payment of a mixed or general tax, the group could not agree. Four years later, largely at the behest of Quaker leader Robert Pleasants, the Virginia meeting advised Friends not to pay mixed taxes but did not make doing so a disownable offense. How many Friends in northern Virginia followed this advice is unclear.

The Fairfax committee for sufferings concluded that the matter rested with individual conscience, and the Hopewell meeting disciplined no members for paying general taxes. Still, "a considerable number of Friends" got into legal difficulties, prompting the Fairfax meeting to appoint in 1779 a committee of prominent members "to attend Court on behalf" of local tax resisters. If calls for broad tax resistance failed to generate unanimous support, the American Revolution marked the first time that Friends as a body refused to pay levies earmarked for military purposes. Quakers must not pay war taxes, Pleasants argued, because "they make us parties to the destruction, violence and confusion" caused by war.[39]

Friends also faced the problem of taking wartime loyalty oaths. Each state required that inhabitants take a test oath or affirmation in which they declared allegiance to the new government and renounced loyalty to the crown. Quakers' usual opposition to oaths, based on their belief that one should speak honestly at all times, took on added significance during wartime. In taking an affirmation, they believed, they participated in pulling down the legally constituted government and sanctioned the violence that helped create the new governments. The consequence of this Quaker scruple soon became apparent. In May 1777, the Virginia legislature passed its first law requiring an oath or affirmation from all males over the age of sixteen, penalizing those who refused with exclusion from public office, jury duty, and local courts. In October, the assembly imposed a double tax on those who refused to take the oath, and a year later raised the penalty to a treble tax. The Virginia Yearly Meeting, following the lead of its Philadelphia counterpart, directed its subordinate meetings to disown any Friend who took the oath or paid the fine. In June 1778, the Warrington and Fairfax Quarterly Meeting, to which the Hopewell and Fairfax Monthly Meetings belonged, decided that Friends should not provide accounts of their property because doing so made it easier for the state to fine those who declined to take the oath. The Hopewell and Fairfax meetings, despite internal debate, adhered to this position throughout the war.[40]

A number of northern Virginia Quakers failed to sustain this aspect of the peace testimony. The Hopewell meeting eventually disowned five members for taking loyalty oaths to the state. The Fairfax meeting faced a more serious problem. Sixteen members, including some of meeting's more prominent individuals, faced disciplinary action for either taking the loyalty oath or paying a "Fine in lieu of taking a Test." Northern Virginia Friends nevertheless disowned members less quickly for taking the loyalty oath than for other violations of the peace testimony. Reflecting this hesitation, the quarterly meeting decided that oath-takers who displayed "evident marks of their sincere repentance" and were willing "wholly to recant the Test" could return to the meeting in "full Unity." The Fairfax meeting placed offenders "under the care of the meeting," discussing the offense with them over an extended period of time in an effort to convince them of their wrongdoing. This lenient treatment worked with all but six members. Isaac Votaw was at first "not sure in his own mind that he was wrong," but the meeting kept him "under care" for almost two years until he finally admitted his "error." Likewise, William Hartshorne, whose oath-taking was first reported in 1779, came under the care of the meeting for close to four years before he acknowledged his backsliding.[41]

IV

Despite Friends' more lenient enforcement of oath-taking violations, the Society took unpopular stands in defense of its peace testimony, and members suffered economic consequences. Equally important, the adversity Friends faced during the war led them to embrace another line of conduct: giving aid to their fellow sufferers. The arrest of the Virginia exiles and the seizure of Quaker property led Quaker Warner Mifflin to consider anew the suffering of African slaves, who likewise endured arbitrary power. "I was brought," he remembered later, "into renewed sympathy with our oppressed African Brethren, who are many of them exposed to the uncontrouled power of Man." Quaker leaders shared Mifflin's concerns, and in 1779 the Virginia Yearly Meeting recommended again that Friends manumit their slaves. The Fairfax and Hopewell meetings revived their campaign, started before the war, to convince all local Friends to free their slaves. In the Fairfax meeting, a committee appointed to "treat" with slave-holding members reported regularly on its progress throughout the war and recommended the removal of two for refusing to free their human property. By 1779, Friends had emancipated enough slaves that the quarterly meeting urged the monthly meetings to establish a new committee to ensure that Friends provided aid to freedpeople.[42]

Still, Virginia law made Quaker manumissions risky. In 1780, the Virginia Yearly Meeting petitioned the state Assembly for the repeal of the 1723 law limiting manumissions. Grounded in Quaker ethics, the appeal condemned slavery as "pernicious" because it violated the golden rule. But Friends broadened their appeal to incorporate revolutionary principles, while stressing pragmatic reasons for repeal. They emphasized that slavery contravened "the natural Right of all Mankind" and the Virginia Bill of Rights, recently passed by the legislature. Friends also noted that they had taken pains to support slaves too old, sick, young, or incapacitated to fend for themselves in an effort to appease opponents of repeal who believed African Americans incapable of caring for themselves. The petition added that all Quaker manumissions remained uncertain as long as the 1723 law remained in place; local officials could seize freedpeople to discharge the wartime taxes that Quakers would not pay. Friends were pleased when the Virginia assembly "brought in and twice read" a bill affirming private manumissions. However, Friends "failed in the business" when "enemies" of the bill "took advantage of a thin House, and the absence of many members who . . . favoured it" to refer it "to the next session."[43]

Although disappointed by their failure, Quakers were not surprised by the opposition to their emancipation schemes. As the threat posed by the Revolutionary War to human property became apparent, most slaveholders viewed Friends' efforts as ill-timed at best and treasonous at worst. Whenever the British army appeared in Virginia, thousands of slaves fled to the British lines, posing a threat to the stability of the institution. Thomas Jefferson estimated that the state lost thirty thousand slaves in 1781 alone, though historians have charged him with exaggerating the figure. Still, Jefferson's numbers point to the perceptions of slaveholders who believed that the war had placed slavery under siege. As Anglican minister Jonathan Boucher noted, the war forced white Virginians to confront the fact that "we have within ourselves an enemy fully equal to all our strength."[44] In this context, Quaker racial philanthropy posed one more threat to the precarious social order of the state.

Virginia's Quakers remained undeterred in their quest to emancipate their slaves legally. After hostilities ended, in May 1782, they renewed their appeal to the legislature, requesting that Friends be allowed to follow the imperatives of their faith. They stressed again that slavery violated the natural rights celebrated by the Revolution and the state's bill of rights. The petition also reflected the broader Protestant providential tradition, shared by Friends, when it noted that "the Judgements of an offended God have been conspicuously displayed in our Country." The petitioners linked Virginia's suffering during the war directly to the existence of slavery. "We apprehend," they averred, that "the cruel sufferings of this oppressed part of Mankind hath been the chief cause of the dreadful Calamities with which we have . . . been visited." Friends achieved a measure of success when the assembly, moved primarily by revolutionary liberalism rather than Quaker warnings, enacted legislation that enabled slaveholders to free their slaves, though it refused to confirm the freedom of those blacks manumitted before 1782. Despite the law's limitations, many white Virginians opposed the act, sparking a series of petitions calling for its repeal. But the law stood until 1806 when a new statute required all manumitted slaves to leave the state within one year.[45]

The law enabled Virginia Friends to free their slaves legally, and they did so in large numbers. In the years after the passage of the 1782 act, the yearly meeting made slaveholding a disownable offense, and the Society conducted a campaign to divorce its membership from slavery. Throughout the state, monthly meetings disowned a substantial number of Friends for refusing to manumit their slaves, including thirteen families from the Cedar Creek meeting in the late 1780s and five from the Blackwater meeting in 1790. By 1796, the Virginia meeting affirmed that no member who could legally free their slaves still owned any. Even so, Friends could not free themselves entirely of slavery. The Fairfax Monthly Meeting disciplined or disowned some fourteen individuals for their ownership, purchase or sale, or hiring of slaves between 1782 and 1801, and Friend William Nicholls of Loudoun County owned slaves when he died in 1804. Likewise, slave hiring remained frequent enough among members of the Fairfax Quarterly Meeting that in 1798 it queried the Baltimore Yearly Meeting (to which it belonged by that point) for clarification about whether its members could hire enslaved people. The Baltimore meeting replied in no uncertain terms: "The practice of hiring slaves is Contrary to our Christian Testimony and Discipline," and those who violated this "sense" should be disowned.[46] Still, living in a slave-based society made it difficult for many Friends to disentangle themselves from the institution even into the nineteenth century.

Despite the difficulties Virginia Quakers faced in effecting a separation from slavery, or perhaps in recognition of them, many Friends expanded their antislavery agenda in the years after the Revolution by attempting to end it in the broader society. Into the early 1830s, Friends were the foremost white advocates of black emancipation in the new nation and among the few opponents of slavery in Virginia. In this, Quakers contrasted with most southern Methodists and Baptists, who in the post-Revolutionary years abandoned their antislavery testimonies to attract adherents. By the early nineteenth century, racial philanthropy had become the Society's most distinctive concern and a central component of its public identity, though Friends debated how best to achieve this goal. The embrace of antislavery also reflected a larger effort by Quaker leaders to secure a new civic role for the Society. For local Friends, service to the broader community became a central way to display their spiritual principles of nonviolence and respect for all humanity. It also enabled them to make a positive contribution to the new society taking shape in Virginia and the United States, despite their unpopularity.[47]

In 1778, Hopewell Friends, prompted by the Virginia exiles who attended their meetings that winter, raised again the issue of Indian lands. According to captive John Pemberton, Hopewell elders joined the exiles "in a solid conference" to consider whether the first Quakers to settle in the Shenandoah Valley had "fully satisfied" Native American claims to the land on which the meeting house sat. The committee recommended unanimously that the meeting "raise a sum," distributed by the Philadelphia Meeting for Sufferings and a committee of the Hopewell meeting, "to be applied for the benefit of the descendents of the native inhabitants" who had once resided on the land. "It becomes us as a religious society," the meeting noted, "to demonstrate that testimony of justice and uprightness which we have ever held forth." By June, local Friends had raised 665 pounds Virginia currency for the purpose, but it remained undistributed because the meeting could not determine which Indian nation had lived on the land before European settlement. The problem festered for almost twenty years as Friends debated how best to effect justice in the case.[48]

But Friends did not let the issue drop. In fall 1794, Quaker minister William Savery, attending treaty talks between the Six Iroquois Nations and the United States government at Canandaigua, New York, raised the issue with Seneca chief Cornplanter. The Tuscarora, a once-independent nation incorporated into the Iroquois alliance in the mid-eighteenth century, were present at the negotiations and claimed to have resided in the valley. However, the "ancient maps and documents" provided by the Tuscarora did not offer convincing proof that they had once resided on the Hopewell land. Friends nevertheless gave a "considerable sum" to the Tuscarora because they "had entertained strong expectations of receiving a donation," and distributed the remainder "for the service, & benifit of other Indians." The incident brought Indian concerns to the attention of the Baltimore Yearly Meeting, which in response to the "prevailing sympathy" of Friends created a permanent Indian affairs committee in 1795. The meeting entrusted the committee to raise funds for American Indians in the Northwest Territory to encourage "school education, Husbandry and the mechanic arts among them." In the early nineteenth century, the Indian committee sent Friends to live among the Indians to "instruct them in agriculture and other useful knowledge." After the War of 1812, the committee provided farming aid to the Miami and built a school at Wapakoneta, Ohio, for Shawnee and Wyandotte children. The yearly meeting's concern for Native Americans north of the Ohio River continued until the federal government began a systematic program of Indian removal in the early 1830s. Friends objected to the policy, but, seeking to avoid "giving offense to Government," the committee offered little more than "sympathy and commiseration" to the expatriated Indians. Not for the first time, Friends confronted the problem of finding effective means to achieve their goals.[49]

Aid to Indians did not increase Friends' popularity, but it did burnish their reputation for benevolence, a trait they had cultivated since the Revolution. Friends realized that if they directed their generosity toward downtrodden groups, it could help restore the good image of the Society. Thus, despite their economic problems, Friends provided aid to those who faced hardship as a result of the fighting. These efforts began almost as soon as violence erupted. In November 1775, after the British occupied Boston, the Philadelphia Yearly Meeting, to which Fairfax and Hopewell Friends then belonged, sent almost two thousand pounds Pennsylvania currency to New England for distribution to anyone who suffered because of the conflict. In April 1776, after royal governor Dunmore ordered his small military force to destroy Norfolk, local Quakers "collected . . . Provisions" for the "Use of such poor inhabitants" of the town. Northern Virginia's Quakers offered similar aid throughout the conflict. In the midst of their suffering, Friends turned their concerns outward, concurring with their brethren in North Carolina, who in 1779 concluded, "We hold it the duty of true Christians at all times to assist the distressed."[50]

After the war ended, providing aid to those who suffered remained a theme of Quaker life in northern Virginia and the nation. In the gauntlet of war, Friends achieved a new unity and strengthened their internal discipline. The conflict with Great Britain heightened the reform impulse within the Society, leading Friends to refine their pacifist testimony and accelerate their efforts against slavery. Forced by outsiders to define the meaning of their testimonies, Friends did so with vigor, disciplining and disowning those who failed to measure up. The process of purification sharpened the differences between Friends and mainstream Virginia society (and other religious groups), but it enabled the Society to forge for itself a novel role in the early republic. Once the Revolution ended, northern Virginia Quakers accepted the new state and federal governments, just as they had accepted British rule before 1776. However, by building on their wartime efforts, they, like their coreligionists throughout the nation, braced to fight for the good of the state and nation by spreading virtue as they defined it. This venture required maintaining a strong peace testimony and eliminating slave ownership among Friends. But it also inspired Friends to establish schools for poor white and free African Americans, aid and defend the interests of American Indians, campaign for an end to slavery, and aid enslaved African Americans. Out of the social tensions of Virginia and the stresses of war, Quakers discovered a new public role: a conscience for the state and the nation.[51] Over the next eighty years, this self-defined task set local Friends at odds with their southern neighbors, and often caused internal tensions as Friends debated how best to achieve their goals. But even as they pursued their agenda, Friends faced a new threat to their pacifist beliefs during the War of 1812.

V

On August 29, 1814, a fleet of seven British vessels commanded by Captain James Gordon sailed into Alexandria harbor and "arranged itself along the town, so as to command it from one extremity to the other." Located "a few hundred yards from the wharves" and houses of the town, the British squadron was "so situated that they might have . . . laid" waste to the town "in a few minutes." Gordon's force was part of a two-pronged attack on the District of Columbia. The primary British force, some five thousand men under the command of Rear Admiral George Cockburn and Major General Robert Ross, had landed at the Patuxent River in Maryland, defeated a larger American militia force at Bladensburg on August 24, and marched overland to Washington, where it destroyed most public buildings. Gordon's diversionary force had slowly sailed up the Potomac River and reached Fort Warburton, six miles below Alexandria on the Maryland side, on August 27. The fort had been designed to protect the District of Columbia from naval assault, but after a two-hour British bombardment American forces abandoned it and Gordon's force sailed to the District unmolested.[52]

Months earlier, Alexandria's town council had appointed a committee of vigilance to prepare its defenses, but the committee had not procured funding from the federal government. On August 19, the Alexandria militia was ordered across the river to Maryland to help defend Washington. It returned to the Virginia side five days later but with orders to march "into the country" across from Georgetown. Left defenseless, Alexandria's leaders sent a delegation to Gordon seeking surrender terms on August 28. Dr. Elisha C. Dick, a recently converted Friend who had repudiated a proslavery past and embraced Quaker pacifism and antislavery, joined the delegation. The next day, the British commander announced his conditions: residents must cease hostilities and deliver to the British all naval stores and ordnance, along with all available wheat, flour, tobacco, and vessels. In return, Gordon promised that his forces would not molest the town's inhabitants or destroy or enter "their dwelling houses." To avoid an attack that they believed would destroy Alexandria, town leaders capitulated.[53]

Many American newspaper editors greeted Alexandria's "degrading" surrender with "indignation," castigating the "baseness" and "cowardice" of the town's leaders. But local Friends praised the decision, seeing it as a vindication of Quaker pacifist principles. Quaker apothecary and minister Edward Stabler believed that meeting the English "in the spirit of unresisting negociation" enabled Alexandrians to escape the "outrage and pillage" visited upon Washington. In contrast to their behavior across the Potomac, British troops in Alexandria acted in a "respectful and decorous" manner. City residents lost over two hundred thousand dollars' worth of merchandise, but Stabler believed the losses would have been greater if the town had tried to defend itself. "Divine Goodness," he concluded, "produce[d] this marvellous preservation." In contrast, Alexandria Quaker John Janney lamented that "many Friends . . . took flight to the country." "The vicinity of the British army," local elders admitted, occasioned "the absence of many" members and forced the cancellation of the August 25, 1814, meeting. For Janney, such conduct revealed Friends' "want of confidence in [God]."[54]

The British occupation of Alexandria brought new pressures on Quakers. As during the Revolutionary War, Friends faced state oppression for refusing to serve in the local militia, though they also drew support they had not enjoyed thirty years earlier from some quarters. Likewise, a number of local Friends failed to abide by the Society's pacifist tenets and faced disownment. More significant, the War of 1812 again jeopardized Virginia's slave regime. The British invasion of the Chesapeake in 1813–14—and the attack on the District—panicked local slaveholders who could not prevent their human property from fleeing to the British. Contemporaries believed that two thousand four hundred Chesapeake slaves fled to the British forces, though historians estimate the number was closer to three to five thousand.[55] In an effort to reestablish social order, slaveholding Virginians used the power of the state to crack down on internal dissent. White Virginians rarely accused Friends of treason as they had during the Revolutionary

War, but they nonetheless perceived Quakers as a wartime danger because of their pacifism and opposition to slavery. The British incursion into the Chesapeake, in short, sparked a wave of repression directed at members of the Society similar to that they had experienced during the Revolution. The war reminded local Friends that they remained a people apart, and in its wake many acted with renewed conviction to uphold their principles.

The threat to Virginia Friends' pacifism began prior to the war. In 1799, the Virginia legislature—at the insistence of petitioners from Frederick, Berkeley, and Shenandoah counties in the valley—ended the release from militia duty that Quakers and Mennonites had enjoyed since 1785. The exemption, the petitioners argued, violated the rights of non-Quakers who could not escape militia duty. Such unequal treatment, they continued, tended "to destroy the harmony of neighbourhoods" and undermine "military discipline." In response, the legislature passed an omnibus militia bill in 1804 that required Friends to serve. In 1810, the Virginia Yearly Meeting, speaking for the state's entire Quaker community, petitioned the assembly for the removal of these disabilities, which, clerk Benjamin Bates noted, forced Friends to choose between "refusing a compliance with the laws of their country" or "violating what they . . . believe is . . . a law of God." The militia law, Bates concluded, contravened Friends' "liberty of conscience," which state and federal constitutions had "wisely . . . protected from the encroachment of any power in the government."[56]

Bates's petition and letter had little impact on the legislature, and Friends remained subject to state militia service. However, enforcement of these laws was spotty. While Friends in southern Virginia faced "unrelenting" pressure from county sheriffs when they failed "to muster," local officials elsewhere "were either indifferent [to] or purposely lenient with" Quakers. The minutes of the Meeting for Sufferings of the Baltimore Yearly Meeting reflected the divergent enforcement of state militia laws. In the early 1800s, the Baltimore meeting encompassed portions of Maryland, Virginia, Pennsylvania, Ohio, and the District of Columbia, making its members subject to a variety of state and federal militia laws. Some states enforced these laws with regularity. In 1811 and 1812, the Meeting for Sufferings reported that Ohio and Pennsylvania had since 1806 distrained almost eighteen hundred dollars' worth of Friends' property (on fines of just under seven hundred and fifty dollars) "for refusing to comply with military requisitions." In contrast, the meetings of northern Virginia and most of Maryland recorded no penalties.[57]

All Friends in the region felt the power of the state more fully after war erupted in 1812. In southern Virginia, county officials arrested eleven Friends of the Upper Monthly Meeting who refused militia service and jailed them in Petersburg and Norfolk. In March, Virginia militia Brigadier General Robert Taylor reported that "three Quakers have been sent down in the requisition from Nansemond [County]." The men, he noted, "refused to do duty, to furnish substitutes, or receive rations" and had been "put under guard." Taylor could not bring himself "to punish any man for a scruple of conscience" and was "at a loss to know what to do with them." But he worried about the impact that discharging the Friends might have on the local militia's already shaky cohesion and discipline. Let these forced recruits go, he worried, and "Quakerism" would "become the predominant religion in our ranks." Taylor had little to fear from sham Friends trying to avoid military service. As they had during the American Revolution, the yearly meetings urged subsidiary meetings to document all sufferings and to ensure, in the words of the Baltimore Yearly Meeting, "not to admit of any case as a suffering, which may not appear to have been faithfully borne."[58]

Liberal-minded officers such as Taylor had little desire to infringe upon the state's celebrated religious liberty, but they felt compelled to act after British ships entered Chesapeake Bay in 1813 and 1814. The British fleet posed a dual threat: it could destroy the state's ports and shipping, and its presence could foment slave unrest. "We are threatened by an insurrection of our negroes," reported Gloucester County slaveholder Nathaniel Burwell in March 1813: "ten have been apprehended and are in jail." From Lancaster County, Spencer George reported two weeks later that he had dismissed the militia to enable members to check on their slaves after "a sudden alarm among us respecting our negroes." In September, Richmond Mayor Robert Greenhow worried that "under the instigation of the British," local African Americans were planning "insurrectionary movements" and asked the governor to take precautions to protect the city. Local slaveholders also appealed to their congressional representative, Richard Brent, for federal aid. Unsuccessful in this quest, Brent reminded Governor James Barbour that the northern neck's geography left its residents "exposed to the ravages of our enemies," a consideration "more formidable" because of the region's large "negro population."[59]

The state's slaveholders had good reason for concern about their "internal foe." Seeing a chance for freedom, enslaved Virginians flocked to the British fleet. "The slaves continue to come off by every opportunity," noted one British soldier in late 1813. British officers recognized the military advantage afforded them by the presence of a large but restive enslaved population, and they encouraged slave escapes, employing runaways as guides and informants. In April 1814, Vice Admiral Alexander Cockburn, overall commander of the fleet in the Chesapeake, announced that the British would welcome "all those who may be disposed to emigrate from the United States" as soldiers or "FREE Settlers" and settle in "the British possessions in North America or the West Indies." The willingness of many escapees to bear arms for the British convinced Cockburn to train the more "intelligent fellows" for military service. Organized into the Corps of Colonial Marines in May 1814, these armed former slaves served throughout the remainder of the Chesapeake campaign.[60]

In this context, Friends' opposition to slavery and war made them deeply suspect among white Virginians. To critics, Quakers appeared little more than fellow travelers of the slaves and the British, members of a dangerous sect that menaced the social stability and military readiness of Virginia. In the lower Shenandoah Valley, Carver Willis castigated his fellow Jefferson County residents for failing to serve in the state militia and lamented "the eternal shame and disgrace" such backwardness brought to the region. "I flatter myself," he added, that "this degradation has not pervaded other parts" of the state, but is "confined to the nest of federalists (I will not say Tories) inhabiting this and a few adjoining counties." Willis certainly (though not exclusively) had in mind the prominent population of Federalist-voting Quakers in neighboring Loudoun, Frederick, and Berkeley counties. More pointedly, John Taylor of Caroline advised Virginians in 1813 not to be fooled by Friends' "amiable and peaceable" appearance. In their effort to end slavery, he warned, Quakers threatened "to plunge three-fourths of the union, into a civil war [between white and black] of a complexion so inveterate, as to admit of no issue, but the extermination of one entire party." The readiness of both men to attack Friends on the issue of race at a moment of stress revealed the sharpest divide between Quakers and white southerners.[61]

Wartime militia requisitions also sparked internal tensions among Friends, as some men of military age found it difficult to uphold the Society's peace testimony. The Hopewell Monthly Meeting, which disowned ten individuals for attending militia musters or training, faced the most acute challenge. The Goose Creek and Fairfax meetings together disowned ten men for participating in the local militia. Less clear is how many Friends faced state penalties for refusing to serve. None of the northern Virginia meetings reported "sufferings" to the Baltimore meeting during the war, but many Friends faced penalties despite the occasional sympathetic local militia officer. As former Friend Captain Thomas Gregg reported in May 1814, county officers made their first requisitions in March 1813 for men to serve six months. "Many," Gregg noted, "failed to comply with this call; some being of that . . . denomination of people called quakers." Two months later, county officials made a second demand upon many of the same individuals, who again "failed to comply." For their refusal, a "special Court Martial" fined each man ninety-six dollars per infraction. Those who could not pay were "sentenced to be imprisoned one callendar month for every five Dollars they fail to pay of the said fines." This punishment, Gregg protested, was illegal, the fines exceeding the eight-dollar sum stipulated by the state of Virginia. It also violated federal law, which stated that "no officer or private of the militia should be compelled . . . to serve two tours within the same six months."[62]

Supreme Court Chief Justice John Marshall ultimately decided the outcome of these fines after local residents, including a number of Friends, sued in federal court over the property seizures. The first case Marshall decided was that of Loudoun County resident William Meade, whom county officials jailed when Meade failed to pay a forty-eight-dollar fine assessed by a state military court after he refused to comply with a December 1813 federal requisition. Meade petitioned the chief justice in April 1815, and in early May Marshall declared the sentence "completely nugatory." The chief justice ruled that Meade had been charged and sentenced under federal law, but the court martial acted under the authority of Virginia and thus had no jurisdiction in the case. Days after the decision, Seth Smith, Goose Creek meeting's "Quaker lawyer," informed his brother that the state marshal would "return . . . the money" raised by the sale of distrained Quaker property. Friends, Smith added, planned to drop their lawsuits against the state if the marshal agreed to "pay the costs of the suits we have commenced" and reimburse all proceeds from the auction of Friends' goods. Some time passed before local officials complied with Marshall's ruling. The local sheriff refused to reimburse Smith for his brother's horse, which he had seized and sold to a local resident. Not until April 1817 did Smith obtain a monetary settlement in his favor.[63]

Friends in Alexandria, though they lived in the District of Columbia under federal jurisdiction, also benefited from Marshall's decision. In the wake of his ruling, the local sheriff "deferred the collection of most of the penalties . . . imposed" on Alexandria Friends. But this was only the latest in a series of policy changes by local authorities since 1812. In the early years of the war, Alexandria's Quakers had suffered little from military requisitions, in part because many government officials did not think the British would risk attacking a target so economically inconsequential as the District—the "sheep walk" on the Potomac, in the words of the secretary of war. When the British entered the lower Potomac in July 1813, slaveholders worried about their enslaved population, but they were reassured because "all members [of Congress] and citizens say it is impossible for the enemy to ascend the river." One Washington society woman concluded that "Our home enemy will not assail us, if they [the British] do not arrive." A year later, District residents panicked when General Ross and Admiral Cockburn entered the Potomac with a large force that included some two hundred former slaves now armed and in uniform. The Alexandria committee of vigilance urged citizens "to put their arms in best order" and directed the local militia to "be prepared, on the shortest notice for service." A week later, the committee proposed new restrictions on the town's population of "Slaves, Free Negroes and Mulattoes." Recognizing the insufficiency of these measures, Mayor Charles Simms declared August 10 "a day of humiliation, fasting and prayer." But prayer proved no more effective in stopping the British advance or pacifying local slaves.[64]

If enslaved people welcomed the arrival of the British, Alexandria's Quakers were more ambivalent. Local Friends faced a treacherous summer in 1814, and some had difficulty adhering to a path of virtue. A few local Quaker merchants became entangled in Alexandria's defense efforts when the town's two major banks offered assistance to the federal government. As the British fleet ascended the Potomac in early August, the Bank of Alexandria loaned the federal government ten thousand dollars and the Bank of Potomac another twenty-five thousand for "the erection of fortifications . . . south of Alexandria." The local newspaper praised the banks for their patriotism; however, for the Quaker merchants who sat on the boards of directors—David Lupton Jr., Mordecai Miller, and Phineas Janney—the loan illustrated the way their commercial concerns could compromise their pacifist beliefs. None of the men resigned their seats; nor did the local meeting discipline them for their apparent violation of the discipline. In contrast, the Alexandria meeting disowned two individuals who joined or trained with the local militia. As during the American Revolution, local Friends treated with some latitude those violations of the discipline they considered less egregious. Perhaps, too, the decision of the Bank of Alexandria, the wealthier of the two banks, to limit the government loan to ten thousand dollars reflected the influence of the two Quakers, Lupton and

Miller, who sat on its nine-person board. As one of twelve Bank of Potomac directors, Janney had less ability to shape the bank's decision.[65]

The meeting's elders also recognized that Lupton and Janney, both young men subject to military service, had otherwise upheld the Society's pacifist values and declined to serve or pay for a substitute when the town called up its militia in mid-July 1814. They were among eleven local Friends fined over five hundred seventy dollars for their refusal to serve. Two additional Friends, Edward Stabler Jr. and Samuel Shreve, lacked enough property to cover the cost of their fines and were imprisoned. Shreve served twenty-two days in jail, while Stabler was released after eight days when former Quaker and First Lady Dolly Madison interceded on his behalf. Deborah Pleasants Stabler, Edward's mother, and Dolly had been childhood friends in Philadelphia. The episode reveals the dangers Quakers faced for their pacifist beliefs, as well as the respect they enjoyed in some circles. Such connections enabled Friends to benefit on occasion from the support of local (and national) leaders.[66]

On September 2, 1815, after five days' occupation, Captain Gordon's fleet drew up its anchors and sailed back down the Potomac River to rejoin the main British fleet. The British took with them three brigs, three ships, and several smaller vessels filled with the produce of the town's merchants. But Alexandria residents suffered little damage to their homes or their persons. "No private dwelling was visited or entered in a rude or hostile manner," the town council reported, "nor were any citizens personally exposed to insult." Human property was a different matter. Between August 28 and September 6, fifty-four African Americans fled from their Alexandria masters and joined the British fleet, though the town council chose not to publicize these escapes. Twelve years later, the town claimed over $113,000 in total property losses during the occupation. Conciliatory tactics had enabled the town to escape wholesale destruction, but they could not ensure a quiescent slave population while the British fleet remained close. In addition to the losses, the occupation—"our degradation" in the words of one local militia officer—besmirched Alexandria's reputation for years.[67]

Friends, in contrast, believed the town council's decision to surrender wise. Their evaluation of events revealed the significant differences between themselves and most white Virginians. Pacifism helped ensure that Friends remained outsiders in Virginia, and as a result they suffered state-led repression during the Revolution and the War of 1812. In the latter conflict, the state targeted antislavery Friends in part because of its fears of slave revolt and the loss of human property. For a time, at least, white Virginians believed that Friends, like the region's African Americans, were an internal enemy that required control and coercion. When the British threat passed, state pressure eased. For many Friends, the experience of both wars convinced them to take more active measures to ensure strict adherence to the Society's discipline. Friends' suffering, such individuals believed, reflected divine displeasure with the Society's backsliding and sparked calls for renewed purity. But for all the similarities between Friends' experiences during the Revolutionary War and the War of 1812, there remained significant differences that reflected early national Quakers' altered social position. Friends suffered fewer disabilities during the latter conflict in part because the Supreme Court had removed state-imposed disabilities but also because in the intervening years Friends' pursuit of economic opportunities and civic boosterism had earned them the grudging acceptance of many white Virginians. Indeed, some Friends viewed their worldly success and the tolerance that came with it as important components of their reform efforts, reflecting an ongoing debate among Quakers over how best to improve the world. But if the peace testimony set Friends apart, their commercial activities drew them into the mainstream of Virginia life.

3

The "Worldly Cares and Business"
of Friends

In late January 1827, Thomas Irwin, "one of the oldest and most intelligent merchants" in Alexandria, passed away at the age of sixty-five. Born in Ireland, he migrated to Philadelphia in 1784, arriving in Alexandria in his mid-twenties in 1789. Two years later, he married into a respected local family and established a successful import-export firm, shipping the region's grains to Europe and importing metal goods. His business success led to civic and professional recognition. In 1803, voters elected him one of the town's four aldermen and the following year, in a reorganized municipal government, one of sixteen councilmen. Reflecting his growing local prominence, in 1806 stockholders elected him director of the Bank of Alexandria, then the town's only chartered bank. Over the next twenty-two years, Irwin held positions of regional importance and responsibility, reflecting his standing as one of Alexandria's leading citizens. But the local community also respected his character. "He was," his obituary declared, "gifted by nature with a clear and vigorous mind." As a merchant, he was "honest in his dealings and his sentiments," setting "the best example of active industry, punctuality and integrity." The practice of "uniform frugality" "guaranteed his perfect independence in conduct, thought and word." In matters of "conscience," "he was uncompromising and singularly firm," while in "friendship" he was "warm and untiring." "His course was upright," the obituary concluded, "and his end was peace." In the only overt mention of his religious faith, the notice added that Irwin would be laid to rest at "the Friends burying ground."[1]

Careful readers of the obituary could have guessed as much. Quakers celebrated the qualities attributed to Irwin, and yearly meetings in the United States and Great Britain inculcated them through regular epistles and queries. Irwin's death became another opportunity for Friends to remind themselves and the broader public of their ethical standards. He was a charter member of the Alexandria Monthly Meeting, founded in 1802, and when he married Elizabeth Janney he joined one of the most prominent extended Quaker families in northern Virginia. He also raised his six children who lived to adulthood in Quaker fashion, and all became members of the local meeting. Yet like many Quakers in northern Virginia and elsewhere, Irwin had not always abided by Friends' discipline. In 1798, the meeting reprimanded him for sharing ownership of a vessel that his partners had armed during the Quasi-War with France, and in 1816 he faced disciplinary action for "taking an oath before a Military Court," attending balls and theater in Alexandria, and his "deportment," which Friends found "inconsistent with the order of our society." Even an upstanding Quaker like Irwin found it difficult to escape the influence of the broader society.[2]

Irwin's public successes and spiritual travails reveal much about the experiences of northern Virginia's Quakers in the early national era. From social and political pariahs during the Revolution they became community leaders, respected and praised for their fair dealing and public spiritedness. They played a key role in the region's postwar economic boom—grounded in the shift from tobacco to grains—through their participation in business enterprises, internal improvement projects, and local government. The end of the Revolutionary War removed Quaker pacifism as an overt point of contention between Friends and the broader community—at least until the War of 1812. During peacetime, Friends enjoyed a largely welcoming and economically prosperous environment. The Quaker community thrived, through both natural increase and continuing migration from Pennsylvania and New Jersey. Many Friends like Irwin came south in the 1780s, drawn by the economic potential of the region and the personal and economic ties between the Quaker communities of the middle states and those of northern Virginia. Local Friends established three new monthly meetings: Crooked Run, lying south and east of the Hopewell meeting from which it split in 1782; Goose Creek in Loudoun County, which separated from the Fairfax meeting three years later; and the Alexandria meeting, created in 1802.[3]

But in Quakers' successes lay spiritual danger, as Irwin's experience reveals. As they prospered, Friends became embedded in the economic and social life of the region. Geographic concerns prompted the local meetings to separate from Philadelphia Yearly Meeting and affiliate with the Baltimore Yearly Meeting in 1790, a decision that strengthened ties with Maryland Quakers who faced similar challenges. Friends who moved to the region saw northern Virginia as their home, an identity that made it more difficult for many to remain free of the influence of the broader society. Many Quakers, including Irwin, failed to uphold consistently the Society's discipline, and even those who did not overtly violate it often became enmeshed in activities that diverged from their religious and ethical convictions. For northern Virginia Friends, economic success, growing public acceptance, and attachment to place could not resolve the tensions that arose from living in a society that violated their spiritual testimonies on a daily basis. Indeed, it only exacerbated them, complicating Friends' efforts to better the society in which they lived.

I

Economic opportunity attracted Pennsylvania and New Jersey Friends to northern Virginia in the 1780s and 1790s. In the post-Revolutionary era, the economy of the region boomed, fueled by overseas demand for local grain products. The region's shift from tobacco to wheat, which began in the 1760s and 1770s, accelerated after the Revolution, stimulating regional economic development. In part, the change reflected planters' and farmers' growing recognition that successive crops of tobacco had exhausted the region's farmland. Wheat and grains planted in a "regular and systematic course of cropping," as Quaker and German farmers had done since their arrival in northern Virginia, promised to replenish the soil and provide planters with more reliable sources of income. More important, wheat exports rose in value. Unstable and, after 1788, falling tobacco prices, coupled with a sharp rise in wheat and flour prices in the 1790s, convinced Virginians to abandon the state's traditional staple. While tobacco exports stagnated at less than four thousand hogsheads per year after the Revolution, flour exports rose consistently, from five thousand barrels in 1783 to over one hundred thousand barrels twenty years later. In 1803, Alexandria merchant William Hodgson summed up the impact of the shift on the region's agriculture: "The Lands to the Westward of this place are now converted from Tob[acc]o plantations into Farms—and in a high State of cult[ivation]. It is the finest Wheat Country in the United States."[4]

The shift in staples had a profound impact on the local economy. In contrast to tobacco, wheat spoiled rapidly in heat and humidity, requiring processing before merchants could transport it overseas. As a result, the shift to grains stimulated the establishment of new subsidiary activities, or "forward linkages," centered on processing grain for overseas consumption.

Merchants and farmers erected numerous grain mills throughout the region, prompting Tench Coxe, assistant secretary of the treasury and booster of American industry, to report in 1790 that "Virginia appears to be making a greater *progress* in merchant mills than any state in the union." Locals also processed grain into spirits and bread. In the Shenandoah Valley, numerous distilleries appeared, while in Winchester and Alexandria, the region's two largest towns, breweries produced ale for local consumption. Numerous bakeries appeared in both towns, and Alexandria-baked "biscuits" and "shipbreads" became an important export staple. The production of grains also fostered the raising of livestock, which in turn spurred the manufacture of leather goods. These various economic activities clustered at geographically favorable sites, stimulating the growth of urban places in the region and encouraging landholders to charter seventeen new towns and villages between 1780 and 1810. By the latter year, almost 20 percent of the region's residents lived in incorporated towns, where many of them—including over two-thirds of Alexandrians—worked in manufacturing enterprises.[5]

The production of bulky wheat and flour also sparked demand for an improved transportation infrastructure. A growing number of farmers and planters supported efforts to clear the region's rivers and build canals, construct improved roads, and starting in the 1830s lay out railroad lines. In the 1780s and 1790s, merchants and planters, led by George Washington, invested in the Potomac River Company, which worked to make the river navigable from the District of Columbia to Cumberland in western Maryland. The company's directors embraced an ambitious nationalist vision. They believed the Potomac watershed would link the Ohio Valley to the east, creating a commercial artery that would bind the new United States. Opening the river for navigation, local boosters believed, would transform the port of Alexandria into a commercial and manufacturing entrepôt. Technological problems and uneven water levels undermined these grand visions, but company's 1802 completion of a canal around the Great Falls of the Potomac enabled seasonal transportation of the region's produce.[6]

Continuing problems with river transportation prompted local merchants and farmers to improve the region's roads. Looking northward to Pennsylvania and the success of private turnpike companies linking Philadelphia to its hinterland, in 1802 Virginia entrepreneurs organized the Little River Turnpike Company, the first successful private road in the state. The company attracted broad local support and by 1812 had completed an improved thoroughfare between Alexandria and the Little River in Loudoun County. By the end of the decade, private companies had completed roads between the Little River and Snickers Gap and Ashby's Gap, enabling farmers in the Shenandoah Valley to transport their produce over the Blue Ridge Mountains to Alexandria on improved turnpikes. Traffic increased, with toll receipts rising from just over five thousand dollars in 1809 to almost twenty-five thousand dollars seven years later. In 1820, a traveler heading west on the road reported that it "was full from morning till long after dark." The line of "wagons conveying flour to" Alexandria "appeared to have no end."[7]

Friends played a central role in these efforts. In the years after the Revolution, Quaker merchants and millers like Irwin and William Hartshorne promoted the economic development of the region. Hartshorne migrated to Alexandria from Philadelphia in February 1774 and established a partnership with sea captain John Harper. In the early 1780s, he established his own "general hardware and all purpose store," where he sold imported manufactured goods and purchased the agricultural products of the northern Virginia countryside. As Alexandria prospered in the 1780s and 1790s, Hartshorne's business grew with it. When grain production rose in the late 1790s, he constructed a mill on the outskirts of the town on his Strawberry Hill plantation. By the early nineteenth century, the mill had become the centerpiece of his business activities. In 1803, he decided to move to his farm, as did many southern merchants turned planters. He also invested in Alexandria real estate, owning eighteen town lots by the time of his death in 1816, and serving at various times as a director of the Bank of Alexandria, which he helped found in 1792.

In addition, Hartshorne became involved in the political life of the community, a sign that he had acquired the respect of fellow citizens. In the early 1780s he was appointed street surveyor and then tax commissioner, in the latter position helping to collect taxes on slaves. In the late 1780s and early 1790s, he served as a member of the town council, overseeing the implementation of the town's ordinances controlling enslaved and free black people. In the same years, Hartshorne became a leader of the Fairfax and, after 1802, the Alexandria meetings, serving as an overseer and taking on various committee assignments. Like Irwin, he faced disciplinary action on occasion, though not for his role in the political and economic institutions that helped sustain slavery. During the Revolution, the meeting had almost disowned him for oath-taking, and in the early nineteenth century bankruptcy brought him once again to the attention of the meeting.[8]

The Thompsons, a Quaker family from Chester County, Pennsylvania, also played a significant role in the region's economic and political life.

Israel Thompson settled in Loudoun County in the early 1750s with his parents, Edward and Mary Thompson (the Quaker couple who had supplied Braddock's army in 1755). Israel purchased a farm and in 1758, along with fellow Quakers John Hough and Mahlon Janney, purchased lots in the new county seat of Leesburg. By 1775, he had established a merchant mill and a tan yard on the grounds of his Wheatland estate, and after the Revolution he shipped flour to Alexandria. His son, Jonah, moved in the early 1780s to Alexandria, where he owned a mercantile firm that imported dry goods and hardware. He also operated a flour mill in Loudoun County. Jonah became one of the town's leading merchants and entered local government, serving as councilman beginning in 1794 and as mayor in 1796–97 and 1805–8. In 1819, his fellow directors of the Bank of Alexandria elected him president. Like Hartshorne and Irwin, however, the Thompsons faced disciplinary action from the local monthly meetings. Israel ran into trouble with the Fairfax meeting during the Revolution when he took an oath of allegiance to Virginia, but after he acknowledged his wrongdoing Friends restored him to full membership. Jonah also faced disciplinary action during the Revolution for taking an oath of allegiance, but his attempts to regain full membership foundered when further breaches of the discipline—marrying a non-Quaker woman and owning slaves—prompted the meeting to disown him in 1782. As late as 1793, he attempted to regain his membership, indicating an ongoing association with the Fairfax meeting.[9]

Many local Friends emulated Hartshorne's and the Thompsons' participation in the economic and civic life of the region. Entrepreneurial-minded Quakers invested in the region's various internal improvement companies and banking institutions. Eight local Friends purchased five-hundred-dollar shares of the Potomac River Company, joining 174 wealthy slaveholding investors. Hartshorne served as director and treasurer of the company from its creation in 1785 into the late 1790s, helping oversee the company's operations, including the hiring of slave labor for construction and speculating in company shares. Another slave-hiring transportation firm, the Little River Turnpike Company, attracted Quaker investors, including Hartshorne and Alexandria merchant Phineas Janney. Hartshorne became the turnpike company's first treasurer, while Janney joined the board of directors in 1809 and became president nine years later. In 1802, Janney transferred from the Goose Creek to the Alexandria meeting, where he became a respected elder. He also operated a successful mercantile firm, specializing in imported wines and iron products. Under Janney's leadership, the turnpike company regularly paid dividends to investors—a rarity among such companies—filling his annual reports "with 'thee' and 'thou' and common sense."[10]

Friends who settled in northern Virginia carried with them Pennsylvania farming practices, growing grains rather than soil-depleting tobacco and practicing improved agricultural methods such as crop rotation. In the years after the Revolution, local Quaker farmers expanded their efforts to raise output through various agricultural improvements. In the late 1780s and early 1790s, Loudoun County miller and farmer Israel Janney began experimenting with the use of red clover and plaster of paris (or gypsum) as soil restoratives. According to his son, Daniel Janney, Israel first procured gypsum from Quaker William West of Chester County, Pennsylvania. He experimented by "sewing it on Oats, leaving some lands without its use," and found "the difference was so striking" that he began using it regularly and selling it to neighbors. Among his customers was John Binns, a farmer (and non-Quaker) who experimented with gypsum as a soil additive in the mid-1780s. In 1803, Binns published *A Treatise on Practical Farming*, which extolled gypsum, clover (which he also purchased from Janney), and deep plowing. Clover rotated with grain crops and used in conjunction with gypsum, Binns argued, helped revive heavily tilled soils and provided "the best pasture" for livestock. Janney must have realized as much; in the 1790s he traveled to "the mountainous parts of Virginia and purchase[d] cattle," which he fattened in Loudoun for both local use and the Alexandria market. Sometime before 1812, Janney introduced merino sheep to Loudoun County, obtained from his son, the Alexandria merchant Phineas Janney.[11]

Israel Janney also sold gypsum and clover to a number of Alexandria merchants, including Friends (and brothers) Daniel and Isaac McPherson, John Janney, and Elisha Janney, who stocked these items in their stores. Local Quaker farmers, among them Mahlon Janney and Thomas Smith Jr., also purchased clover seed and gypsum, though in smaller amounts. Not all local Quaker farmers accepted reports of gypsum's efficacy. George Redd of Frederick County acknowledged in an 1809 pamphlet that he lacked "knowledge of the science and chemistry" of agronomy, but he deemed the success of his "experiments" in "vivifying" his lands reason enough to publicize them. As a good Quaker, he believed his "most important duty" was to share his innovations and "render himself as useful a citizen as possible." Redd contended that salt, "properly used," had "an astonishing effect on both the stalk and grain." "In the course of three years," he noted, lands treated with salt "would produce five times as much as they" did "prior to its use." Redd's pamphlet attracted little attention, but his interest in agricultural improvement and in sharing his knowledge to assist farmers (and perhaps earn a profit) reflected common Quaker traits.[12]

The region's Quaker farmers also displayed great interest in farm machinery. In the same era that Binns composed his *Treatise*, Benjamin Bradfield, a Loudoun County Friend who had moved from Pennsylvania in the early 1790s, used northern connections to procure an "iron mould board plough" that enjoyed widespread popularity in the region. A few years later, Bradfield's neighbor and fellow Quaker Gideon Davis, "seeing the mould board and believing it too small," cast a larger version that "came into general use" among local Friends. In the 1830s, Frederick County farmer Joel Lupton invented a mowing machine and sold the patent rights to inventor Moses G. Hubbard of New York. In addition, Lupton obtained patent rights to a plow invented by John Weaver and a threshing machine invented by Chester Clark, hoping to sell the machines locally and farther west. He had a receptive market. According to Goose Creek Friend Yardley Taylor, "about 1822" Quakers in Loudoun County introduced "Horse Power Threshing Machines" that local farmers "soon generally adopted." By the 1850s, he reported, "wheat drills" were "coming into use."[13]

Agricultural innovation had a significant impact on the regional economy. After 1820, Virginia entered a long period of agricultural decline, marked by worn-out lands and widespread outmigration, but much of northern Virginia proved an exception. In 1850, Loudoun County led Virginia in "agricultural wealth," "amount of taxation," and "value of real estate." A combination of hard work and innovation enabled most Quaker farmers who stayed in the region to remain solvent—and many prospered. John Janney, who lived on the farm of his grandparents, Mahlon and Mary Taylor, in Loudoun County in the 1820s, remembered that "careful management" and the use of "Plaster of Paris," enabled the Taylors to make a "poor" 263-acre farm "quite productive." Quaker Yardley Taylor attributed the agricultural wealth of Loudoun County to the "different system of farming" introduced by Friends, which he hoped Virginia farmers would emulate.[14]

Infrastructural and agricultural improvements, however, required new sources of capital, as Quaker merchants realized. They soon became involved in running and investing in banking endeavors. Of the nine original directors of the Bank of Alexandria, chartered in 1792, two—William Hartshorne and Jonah Thompson—were Friends or former Friends. Two Quakers, Elisha Janney and Hartshorne, also served as directors of the Bank of Potomac, which began operation in 1805. Over the years, Quaker involvement in these institutions grew. Phineas Janney, after serving as director beginning in 1812, became president of the Bank of Potomac in 1825, a position he held for years. Thomas Irwin served as director of the same bank from 1818 until his death nine years later. Quakers George Taylor and John and Joseph Janney Jr. also served as directors of the bank in its first twenty-five years of operation. The Bank of Alexandria enjoyed similar Quaker involvement, with merchants Mordecai and William H. Miller (father and son), David Lupton Jr., Jonathan Janney, and James Irwin (Thomas's son) all serving on the board of directors before 1830. Local Friends also invested in and helped direct the Alexandria Marine Insurance Company, chartered by the Virginia assembly in 1798. Two of the company's original directors, merchant George Taylor and the ubiquitous Hartshorne, were Quakers, and the directors elected Hartshorne as the first president. Reflecting the ongoing importance of Quakers in the regional economy, Friends or former Friends held six of the company's fifteen directorships in 1815.[15]

II

Banks and insurance companies, turnpikes and canals, and agricultural innovation constituted important engines of economic development in northern Virginia in the early national period. Banks provided sources of investment capital for local mercantile and manufacturing firms in the region, and canals and turnpikes enabled farmers to transport their produce to the port of Alexandria. Throughout this period of growth, which lasted into the early 1820s, Friends shared in local boosterism. However, the economic exuberance of the region led a few Friends to over-extend their resources and participate in ill-fated economic ventures. The unchartered Merchant's Bank, which opened in Alexandria in 1815 and failed a year later, represented a striking example of such speculative ventures. Quakers Daniel McPherson and Peter Saunders, prominent Alexandria merchants, helped found and direct the firm. Three years later, the Alexandria Monthly Meeting reported that McPherson "was very active in originating [and] bringing into operation and conducting" the Merchant's Bank, but "managed" the institution "so incorrectly" that it "fail[ed] for a very large amount and thereby involved a great number of innocent persons in heavy losses." After an investigation, the Alexandria meeting disowned McPherson in November 1819, charging that he had "engaged in Mercantile business beyond his ability to manage," and "his creditors [had] sustained heavy losses." McPherson, the meeting concluded, had lost "sight of the intimations of Truth and christian rectitude . . . greatly to his own discredit" and to "the reputation of the society of which he was a member."[16]

The examination of McPherson's business affairs by the Alexandria meeting highlights how Quaker spiritual values and ethical practices contributed to local Friends' economic success—and public esteem—after the trials of the Revolution. The Society's deep concern for and rigorous scrutiny of "fraudulent" business activity among members reflected its concern that Friends' behavior in all realms of life express their spiritual values. Following the injunctions of Quaker founder George Fox, Friends in northern Virginia believed that the spiritual and the secular constituted a seamless whole and that their religious convictions should be manifest in their day-to-day lives. "The Lord taught me," Fox wrote, "to act faithfully two ways, viz: inwardly to God, and outwardly to man." The resulting social ethic enabled many Friends to grow wealthy. They took seriously the Protestant notion that all individuals should pursue diligently an honest "calling." Friends had a spiritual duty to be busy and active; hard work and frugality, they believed, would receive divine reward. Quakers also emphasized the need for honesty in all their transactions, both to reflect their spiritual values and maintain the reputation of the Society. As early as 1688, the London Yearly Meeting advised members that they should not "launch into trading and worldly business beyond what they can manage honourably and with reputation." One hundred and forty years later, the same meeting urged Friends to eschew "trading beyond their capital, and . . . carrying on their business by means of fictitious credit," practices Friends considered "utterly inconsistent with . . . Christian moderation and contentment." The editor of the *Alexandria Gazette*, Edgar Snowden, published the latter epistle, which he praised for its "simplicity, good sense, and peculiarity of character." Such reports enhanced Quaker merchants' reputation for fair dealing.[17]

Local Friends worried about the dangers of bankruptcy, which implied a personal weakness or failure to follow Quaker business ethics. The discipline of the Baltimore Yearly Meeting enjoined its members "frequently [to] inspect the state of their affairs" to "know whether they live within . . . their circumstances." To avoid any suspicion of personal wrongdoing, the meeting urged those who fell into debt to "submit the state of their affairs" to their creditors' "inspection" without delay and "offer . . . their property to creditors" if necessary to pay off the debt. But Friends believed such openness could not by itself sustain ethical behavior. The discipline directed overseers of local meetings to treat "seasonably" with members who appeared to live "above their means" or failed to pay their debts punctually. Further, overseers must bring the debtors' "creditors together" and mediate a settlement that satisfied the creditors and restored the debtors' reputations. Indebted Friends who failed to follow these injunctions faced disownment. Finally, monthly meetings must "carefully inquire" how financial "deficiencies have happened," and "ascertain if a fair and equal distribution of" the debtors' "property has been made." Local meetings had oversight of members' economic activity to ensure they followed practices congruent with the ethical standards of the Society.[18]

Local meetings in northern Virginia regularly exercised this authority. Although problems arose more often in the commercial town of Alexandria than in the countryside, Quaker farmers who found themselves in financial disputes with fellow Friends also faced meeting oversight. In 1785, Isaac Nichols Sr. went before the Goose Creek Preparative Meeting to complain that his neighbor and fellow Quaker Nathan Spencer refused to pay a debt owed to him. The same year Moses Farquhar of Maryland's Pipe Creek meeting lodged a complaint against George Walters of Goose Creek after the latter, "aggrieved by the Judgment" of two Quaker mediators, refused to a pay the sum they had determined. "To produce . . . Concord," the Fairfax Monthly Meeting (to which the Goose Creek meeting still belonged) reopened and settled the case some months later "to the satisfaction of the parties." Likewise, when Alexandria merchant Jonathan Myers balked at a debt-payment arrangement with merchant Joseph Janney mediated by Friends, a new committee of respected elders settled the matter to both men's satisfaction.[19]

Despite the frequent success of mediation, Quaker elders recognized its problems. Quaker minister Hugh Judge, who in 1809 became embroiled in a business dispute while a member of the Baltimore Yearly Meeting, declined a financial settlement in his favor because "unity and harmony in the society" outweighed restitution. Most dangerous, when mediation failed disputes could end up in the courts, though the discipline discouraged Friends from resorting to the law and called for the disownment of litigants who acted precipitously. In 1788, Alexandria merchant John Janney sued fellow Friend Samuel Hough for refusing to pay a "Just Debt" and was investigated by the Fairfax Monthly Meeting until he dropped the lawsuit. Eighteen years later, the meeting was less forgiving of Hough. A dispute between Hough and the estate of Thomas Taylor ended up in court after the executors complained that Hough refused to pay his debts. The Fairfax meeting granted permission to the executors to sue only after the committee assigned to mediate the dispute had "taken a good deal of pains"—some eleven months of visits—with Hough. Israel Thompson, who asked permission of the Fairfax Monthly Meeting to sue Loudoun County Friend James Dillon, faced similar obstacles from elders unwilling to see Friends turn to the law. The Fairfax meeting concluded that "the proper Methods have not been pursued in the [Goose Creek] Monthly Meeting where the Debtor resided," refused Thompson's request, and required that he solve the disagreement through mediation.[20]

The resort of local Quakers to the courts reveals that some members found the Society's dispute mediation process inadequate. But others welcomed it. Mediation enabled Quaker merchants to avoid costly and time-consuming suits before the slow Virginia courts, while many debtors found the system more forgiving. As the Baltimore Yearly Meeting urged its members, "let compassion and aid be extended to" those who face "difficult circumstances," and "manifest an honest intention" with their creditors. Such indulgence frustrated some creditors, but when Quaker businessmen faced economic difficulties, as frequently occurred in the export-driven economy of northern Virginia, they could expect to be treated with "christian charity" by Friends. When William Michener could not pay a "Just Debt" to John Sutton in January 1789, the committee appointed by the Fairfax meeting to visit him reported that he "manifested a disposition to satisfy his Creditors and proposed giving up his property for that purpose." The meeting decided that the committee "afford him [Michener] assistance" in settling his debts. Michener agreed "to give . . . his Property" to "two friends" assigned to sell the goods "in twelve months" if he could not "discharge the debts" by then. In effect, the meeting gave Michener an additional year to pay his debt to Sutton and avoid bankruptcy. The solution must have worked; in August, the meeting reported that "the Matter is now settled."[21]

Merchant William Hartshorne endured a similar financial fall and investigation by the Alexandria meeting but survived with his reputation intact. After 1800, Hartshorne faced a series of setbacks that left him on the brink of bankruptcy and sparked disciplinary action by the local meeting. Signs of his financial problems first arose in January 1800 when he placed an advert in the local paper announcing that his firm could no longer make payments to "our Creditors" because of "heavy losses" caused "by the late failures" of some business associates "in Baltimore." Compounding his problems, a year later his mill at Strawberry Hill burned to the ground. In the first months after the fire, Hartshorne believed his business would recover from the "misfortune." Writing to Frederick County planter Thomas

Massie in March 1801, he averred: "By the assistance of Providence and my Friends I hope to have my Mill rebuilt and going again in a much better situation by next Winter." Before he could recover, however, Hartshorne faced more setbacks. Soon after the fire, rains heavier than had "ever been known" caused Difficult Run, the stream powering Hartshorne's mill, to rise "near 20 feet in ten minutes." The waters broke his "Mill Race . . . in several Places," flooded his lands, and washed his cattle "from his meadow down to the tide water." Hartshorne's business stumbled on until 1807 when Thomas Jefferson's embargo, which suspended American exports and imports to and from Europe and the West Indies, closed the port of Alexandria.[22]

In 1810, worried that Hartshorne's "estate will not prove sufficient to meet all his engagements," the Alexandria meeting examined Hartshorne's business affairs. The committee appointed to investigate his finances cleared him of any personal wrongdoing, noting that his failure arose from causes beyond his control: "the payment of heavy interest for several years . . . and a considerable loss sustained . . . at the time [of] the late embargo." The committee did, however, require that Hartshorne liquidate his assets to meet the demands of his creditors. The meeting eventually reinstated Hartshorne, and though his business never rebounded, he retained the respect of fellow Quakers and the local business community. As Alexandria merchant Joseph Riddle noted, "We have not the least doubt but that he will pay all demands against him, and leave something to his family." Hartshorne "possesses," Riddle concluded, "the undiminished confidence of all good men, with whom he is acquainted." As late as 1810, shareholders elected Hartshorne a Bank of Potomac director and president of the Alexandria Marine Insurance Company. His reputation as a trustworthy Quaker survived his financial downfall.[23]

Alexandria merchant Elisha Janney's economic problems also prompted the meeting to intervene; its response cushioned his fall and enhanced the Society's reputation for ethical business practices. Janney was born in Loudoun County, the son of Jacob and Hannah Janney, charter members of the Fairfax meeting. In the early 1790s he moved to Alexandria, opened a flour and dry goods establishment, and built a flour mill on Occoquan Creek south of town. He gained enough local regard that investors elected him a director of the Bank of Potomac in 1805 and the Potomac Bridge Company in 1808. The following year, the company completed a five thousand foot span, then the longest in the U.S., across the Potomac between Alexander Island to the north of Alexandria and Washington. During these years, Janney became one of the leading members of the Alexandria meeting, serving on numerous committees and treating with wayward members. In 1809, however, he faced disciplinary action after a series of economic setbacks. The Alexandria meeting concluded that "the immediate causes" of his failure were "the embarrassments of trade . . . consequent on the embargo—and afterwards the loss of his mill by fire." But Janney also had ethical problems related to his "unguarded extension of business, on a fictitious capital, obtained from Banks" on the basis of respectable "indorsers." Procuring credit in this fashion, the meeting noted, required Janney to favor his endorsers over other creditors. The "payment of one class of creditors to the exclusion of the rest," the meeting concluded, violated the Society's "principles of justice."[24]

The meeting decided that Janney must pay off his debts by liquidating his estate, which included a wharf, two town lots, a small farm, and the "spacious 3 story brick mill house at Occoquan" destroyed by fire in 1809. But the meeting demonstrated enormous patience; a decade later, Janney had not found a buyer for the Occoquan mill seat. The meeting also required that Janney acknowledge his wrongdoing in favoring "confidential creditors." Although Friends determined that Janney acted without "fraudulent intention," the preferential treatment of one group of creditors constituted a breach of Quaker ethics. "Through indiscretion," Janney conceded, "[I] placed myself in a situation which made it difficult to do otherwise than I have done." Janney's financial problems marked the end of his mercantile career, but he remained a part of the Quaker community and fell back on family resources. In 1810, he returned to Loudoun County and became a member of the Fairfax Monthly Meeting, where he lived until his death in 1827.[25]

III

Elisha Janney's eventual reliance on family resources points to another factor that bolstered Friends' economic success in northern Virginia: the development of family networks to which merchants, tradesmen, and farmers could turn in order to get started in business, obtain technical and economic information, attract customers, raise capital for expansion, or seek aid if they fell on hard times. Friends' extended families in northern Virginia (and beyond) acted as economic support networks for Quaker entrepreneurs. The careers of many Quaker merchants, manufacturers, and tradesmen reveal how families and the Quaker practice of endogamy contributed to their success. Like all Quaker yearly meetings, the discipline of the Baltimore meeting stipulated that Friends must marry within the sect or face disownment. The marriage discipline ensured that Quaker families reinforced the Society's religious values and that Friends remained a people distinctive "from the outside world." However, marriage within the group also had economic implications and marital ties played a role in forging business links among Quakers. Friends' businesses "became a close network of concerns tied together by family relationships." Marriage within the group promoted economic alliances and contributed to Friends' business success.[26]

When William Hartshorne's first wife died he remarried Susannah Shreve, the wife of Quaker merchant Benjamin Shreve, with whom Hartshorne had business ties. The marriage to Susannah, whose assets from her first husband remained in her name, enabled Hartshorne to weather his financial collapse during the 1810s. Hartshorne's daughters, in turn, wedded three of Alexandria's leading Quaker merchants: Rebeckah married Mordecai Miller in 1792; Mary married Edward Stabler in 1808; and Sarah married Phineas Janney in 1811. For Janney, this was a second match; in 1799 he had wedded Ruth Lupton, daughter of one of the Frederick County's successful Quaker millers, David Lupton. Thereafter, Janney became one of Lupton's primary mercantile contacts in Alexandria, regularly describing market conditions in town and purchasing Lupton's flour. He also served the same function for his father, Loudoun County miller Israel Janney, reporting in 1805 that he had sold some of "father Janney's beeves" at great profit in the Alexandria market. In 1777, Lupton had also made an economically advantageous match, marrying Mary, the daughter of Isaac Hollingsworth, a Hopewell minister who speculated in Winchester town lands. Berkeley County Friend (and elder) Edward Beeson, meanwhile, must have been pleased when his daughter, Martha, wed Alexandria merchant Daniel McPherson in 1790. As a substantial farmer and miller, Beeson benefited from his direct links to the Alexandria market.[27]

Equally dense links developed between Friends' families in Loudoun County. Two of the county's prominent Quaker millers, Israel Thompson and Israel Janney, married daughters of Francis and Jane Hague, founding members of the Fairfax meeting. Janney's nuptials to Pleasant Hague linked two of the region's leading Quaker families: Israel was the son of Jacob and Hannah Janney, who with the Hagues helped establish the Fairfax meeting. Their union produced twelve children, eight of whom married into local Quaker families, including the Greggs, the Nichols, the Janneys, the Holmeses, the Govers, and the McPhersons. Young Friends sometimes had difficulty finding a suitable mate in the small Quaker community; one of the Janney's sons, Jonas, married his first cousin, Ruth Janney, in 1774 and they suffered disownment for thirteen years as a result. Still, Friends' insistence on endogamous marriage created tight family connections that afforded individual Friends economic assistance and advice.[28]

Although outmigration increased after 1800, the web of relationships and economic connections thickened in the next generation. Israel Janney, Jacob and Hannah's seventh child, had by his two wives eleven children, most of whom married Friends who lived in the region. In this generation, the Janneys linked to the Moores of Fairfax meeting (through the betrothal of David Janney and Elizabeth Moore in 1809), the Haineses of Berkeley County (Daniel Janney married Elizabeth A. Haines), and the McPhersons of Alexandria (Jonathan Janney wed Elizabeth McPherson, daughter of merchant Isaac McPherson). In 1798, Abijah, Israel's first son, married a McPherson—Jane, the daughter of John and Hannah McPherson of Berkeley County. The most prominent of Abijah's six children, Samuel M. Janney, was born in 1801. Before he launched his ministerial and antislavery career, Samuel worked in a number of mercantile and manufacturing enterprises. His early business ventures reveal how family connections enabled young Quakers to build a career.[29]

In 1815, at the age of fourteen, Samuel's family "placed" him in the "counting house" of his uncle, Phineas Janney, the Alexandria merchant and importer, where he worked as a clerk for ten years. There he met fellow Quaker Thomas Bond, an orphan from the Fairfax meeting apprenticed to an unnamed Quaker merchant—most likely Phineas Janney. In 1825, with the blessing and aid of Samuel's uncle Phineas, the two decided to open an apothecary and dry goods shop in Alexandria. A year later, Bond left Alexandria to attend medical school in Philadelphia and the pair dissolved the business. For the next few years, Janney ran his own retail shop in Alexandria, offering for sale wines and imported dry goods. In 1826, now a prosperous merchant, he married a distant cousin, Elizabeth Janney, the daughter of John and Elizabeth (Hopkins) Janney, in the process establishing another family connection that led to a new business venture.[30]

Shortly after his marriage, Janney formed a partnership with his brother-in-law, Samuel Hopkins Janney, "to build and conduct a cotton factory at Occoquan, sixteen miles south of Alexandria." For the next decade, Janney struggled to make the enterprise a success, selling his cotton to Alexandria's dry goods merchants. Despite financial aid from Phineas and other local Friends, Janney's factory failed in 1839, leaving him fourteen thousand

Figure 3.1. Portrait of Samuel M. Janney, c. 1860s. Courtesy of Swarthmore College Friends Historical Library.

dollars in debt. Following Quaker guidelines, he "laid before the overseers of our meeting and a few other Friends"—most notably his uncle Phineas—"a statement of my affairs, and asked their advice." Samuel promised to pay his debts, which he accomplished over the course of the next twenty years. He used another family resource, his wife's small inheritance of $1,450 from the sale of her father's estate, to establish a boarding school for girls, Springdale Academy, in Loudoun County in the early 1840s. Janney took each step of his early career with the advice, support, and oversight of Quaker businessmen. Raised within the Quaker community and sharing its values—in the mid-1820s he began his ministerial career—Janney garnered the trust of respected elders and community leaders. He possessed, in short, a safety net that enabled him to weather difficult financial circumstances.[31]

Local Friends of less prominence shared the economic benefits of extended family ties. When Jacob Janney, a distant relative of Samuel's, opened a store in Goose Creek in the early 1830s, he did so in partnership with his fellow Quaker Joseph Hirst. The partnership ensured that Janney had "a tolerable share of [local] custom," because Hirst, through his 1825 marriage to Charlotte Taylor, daughter of Loudoun County merchant Mahlon Taylor, had become a member of the large and prosperous Taylor clan. For a supply of goods, the pair relied on Jacob's family connections, particularly Alexandria merchants (and in-laws) Joseph Janney and Basil Hopkins, both members of the Alexandria meeting. Like Samuel Janney in Alexandria, Jacob Janney and Hirst sold wine, making their store, in Jacob's facetious account, a regular "tip[p]ling shop for the quakers." In all their business endeavors, Friends in northern Virginia practiced such mutual support. When Stephen Wilson moved to Ohio in the early 1830s he sold all his land, "at the average price of $40 per acre," to local Friends. Elisha Fawcett of the Hopewell meeting moved west in same years and could not find a buyer for his land; instead, he rented it to Quaker Nathan Lupton. When Esther Lupton put her "first rate land" near Hopewell meeting on the market, she offered it first to Friend John Purcell, who was "pretty much pleased" to pay over twenty dollars per acre. The overlapping and interlocking economic and familial relationships developed over the first hundred years of Quaker settlement in northern Virginia promoted the economic success of members, while enhancing their Quaker identity and binding the community.[32]

In addition to family ties, Quaker businessmen benefited from the Society's meeting structure, the frequent visitations of Friends throughout Great Britain and America, and the personal relationships between members of far-flung meetings. Together, these connections helped Quaker entrepreneurs develop networks that forwarded their economic endeavors. Although Quaker merchants and tradesmen did not conduct business exclusively with their coreligionists, they "relied on members of their denomination more than on outsiders" because they knew Friends followed the sect's discipline and adhered to business practices that emphasized honest dealing and eschewed speculative ventures. The religious connection, often fortified by personal links established during religious journeys or familial relations, enabled Friends to establish secure and stable business contacts in distant towns and ports. Thus, when George Drinker—of the Philadelphia Drinker family—moved to Alexandria in the 1790s and opened a retail shop, he turned to his cousin, Philadelphia merchant Thomas Cope, to supply him with goods. Twelve years later, when Drinker opened Centre Mills on Four Mile Run outside Alexandria he again turned to Cope to obtain a carding "Engine." In the intervening years, Drinker married Ruth Miller, sister of Quaker Mordecai Miller, a watchmaker and merchant, and founder of a leading Alexandria mercantile family. Through his marriage, Drinker tightened his web of relationships, adding to his Philadelphia connections a local network he utilized to advance his economic interests.[33]

Prosperous Quaker families like the Luptons and Griffiths in the Shenandoah Valley also forged geographically dispersed networks. In addition to their ties with the Alexandria business community, they developed reciprocal commercial links with Friends in Baltimore and Philadelphia that grew in importance over time. In 1807, Philadelphia merchant and Quaker Samuel R. Fisher asked David Lupton of Frederick County to collect a series of debts from local Quakers. Fisher did not know Lupton, but he did know "Our Friend Isaac Janney"—the Loudoun County miller—who had "named thee to me, as the most Suitable Person within his knowledge" to collect the debts. When Lupton hesitated to take on the task, Fisher urged him to reconsider. "Who could I get worthy of Confidence," Fisher asked, if Lupton refused. "The principal Case," Fisher concluded, "must be left to rest on some other persons," perhaps a "Lawyer . . . not much to be relied on in One's absence to get on with such Concerns." For Friends like Fisher, only a Quaker could be trusted with such tasks, though for Lupton collecting the debts was a time-consuming task. Recognizing the difficulties, Fisher offered Lupton comparable assistance in Philadelphia: "Should it be in my power to render thee any Service here—I shall be willing according to my ability." Fisher also invited Lupton to make "thy home at my house" the next time he attended the Philadelphia Yearly Meeting. Lupton's willingness to collect Fisher's debts, in short, helped to establish a reciprocal economic relationship across space, one made possible by their common religious affiliation, and that visits to the yearly meeting promised to strengthen over time.[34]

Lupton's prospective stay at Fisher's home in Philadelphia during the yearly meeting also points to the role played by the Society's meeting structure in establishing and maintaining economic and personal connections between far-flung individuals. Quarterly and yearly meetings, which regularly drew distant Friends together, contributed to the commercial success of local Quakers. As an elder of the Alexandria meeting, Quaker merchant Phineas Janney traveled frequently to Fairfax Quarterly Meeting as part of his spiritual duties, worshipping and administering the affairs of the Society with other leading Friends. While there he solidified and expanded contacts with his customers in the countryside—the farmers, millers, and small retailers upon whom his business depended. In 1804, Janney informed his father-in-law David Lupton that he would pay "the balance due thee" at "Quarterly Meeting, if nothing material turns up to Prevent." At the same time, he asked Lupton "to shew . . . to such Persons as thee thinks would be likely to have Spare Money" the recently issued articles of association for the Bank of Potomac, which Janney helped establish. At the quarterly meeting, Janney knew Lupton would find likely candidates—prosperous Friends with disposable capital—to invest in an institution that promised to pay dividends and promote the regional economy.[35]

The Baltimore and Philadelphia Yearly Meetings, in turn, enabled Janney and his fellow Quaker businessmen to maintain contacts with merchants in those cities. Between 1821 and his death in 1853, Janney attended the Baltimore Yearly Meeting as the representative of the Fairfax Quarterly Meeting on at least thirteen occasions, giving him opportunities to strengthen his contacts with the region's Quaker farmers, millers, merchants, and manufacturers. Smaller farmers also used quarterly and yearly meetings to undertake business. Joel Wright, a Leesburg Quaker, asked Frederick County Friend David Lupton to meet him at the Baltimore Yearly Meeting in 1820, where they could "settle" some outstanding commercial debts, including "Abner Chalfont[']s business." Likewise, Seth Smith of Loudoun County traveled with Phineas Janney to Baltimore in 1823 as a representative of the quarterly meeting. While there, he informed his brother Jacob Smith, he would "endeavour . . . to obtain and communicate more particular information" about the debts owed to Jacob, who had moved to Indiana some months earlier. Business affairs did not supersede the spiritual tasks assigned to Quaker overseers and elders, but for Friends like Janney, Wright, and Smith, whose beliefs required that they pursue a worldly calling, passing up such opportunities made little spiritual or business sense.[36]

For Alexandria apothecary Edward Stabler, an elder and minister of the Alexandria meeting, regular attendance at quarterly and yearly meetings along with ministerial journeys in the eastern United States provided opportunities to establish and maintain business contacts. Stabler's business success points to the various ways membership in the Quaker community boosted economic fortunes. The youngest son of Quaker minister Edward Stabler, Edward was born in Petersburg, Virginia, in 1769, where his father, an English immigrant, settled and established a mercantile firm in 1753. The elder Stabler's four surviving children all married into Quaker families.

His two sons wed daughters of Thomas Pleasants of Goochland County, Virginia, and his two daughters married members of the Hough family, one of the earliest Quaker families to settle in Loudoun County. After Edward Sr.'s daughter married he apprenticed his fourteen-year-old son, Edward, to Mahlon Hough to learn the tanning trade. In the meantime, the younger Edward's brother, after an apprenticeship with a Quaker doctor in Petersburg, moved to Leesburg, in Loudoun County, and opened an apothecary shop. In 1789, Edward moved in with his brother and learned the trade. By 1791, "he had acquired all the knowledge which could be obtained from the business of his brother," and he began looking "for a situation where he might commence business on his own account."[37]

Stabler had "no capital with which to commence business" because his father's estate had "been scattered by the disasters of the revolutionary war." As a member of a respected Quaker family, however, he did not lack resources. He turned for aid to a maternal uncle, William Robinson of Philadelphia, who loaned him one hundred pounds with which to "open a drug store in Alexandria." Once in the town, he boarded with John Butcher, a minister in the Fairfax meeting and a successful merchant, who became Stabler's economic and spiritual mentor. Butcher's example made a "powerful and lasting" impression on Stabler, who imbibed the Quaker business principles of "strict prudence and justice" and "keeping his business within the limits of his means." Such practices, Stabler concluded, "would save him from destruction" and bankruptcy. By 1794, Stabler's economic success "placed" him "in a situation to" wed Mary Pleasants, whom he had met two years earlier at his brother's marriage to Mary's sister, Deborah. Thomas Pleasants, Mary's father, quickly gave his consent to the match and "extended" to Stabler "pecuniary assistance, and the counsels . . . of experience and wisdom." Stabler's son William concluded that his father's prosperity resulted from "industry, integrity, and prudence," and "assiduous attention" to business, but Stabler's Quaker family connections clearly helped.[38]

Stabler's business thrived, along with his standing in the Society. In 1806, with the blessing of the Alexandria meeting, he made his initial appearance in the ministry, conducting his first visits to the families of Friends in Baltimore in early 1808. Possessing a "seasonable, clear, and impressive" "gift," Stabler began to "travel abroad in the service of the gospel," visiting the meetings of Friends "in the Northern, Eastern and Middle States of" the Union until his death in 1831. These visits enabled Stabler to accumulate a wide circle of acquaintances in New York and Pennsylvania. As a Quaker minister, he believed spiritual duty required him to attend the Fairfax Quarterly and Baltimore Yearly Meetings "unless prevented by paramount duty, or by circumstances beyond his control." All the while, Stabler continued to oversee his apothecary, though in March 1819 he created a partnership with his son, William. Stabler believed that he should continue his ministry while at the store. As his son noted, Stabler often found his way "opened . . . for the illustration of some important truths" while "engaged in his business." Likewise, Stabler did not abandon his commercial concerns during his religious travels, and the contacts he made during them helped him expand the business. In 1816, he thanked one of his northern correspondents for "selecting me as an agent" to oversee the sale of "his cotton on commission," and after 1819 Stabler became the exclusive Alexandria agent for medicines produced in the northern states. For Stabler and Quaker merchants like him, secular and the spiritual concerns intersected.[39]

IV

In the 1810s and 1820s, the economy of northern Virginia, following a statewide trend, began a decline that continued into the late 1840s. Economic stagnation threatened Friends' business ventures, increased the potential for disputes between members, and endangered their reputation for honesty and fair-dealing. The region's languishing population provides a measure of regional economic decline. Between 1800 and 1810, Alexandria's population grew by some 45 percent, from just under five thousand to over 7,200. In the next decade, the town's population rose by 14 percent, to slightly more than 8,200. By 1840, only forty-five more people lived in the town. Alexandria's economy had stopped growing. As the regional entrepôt before 1820, Alexandria's backwardness reflected broader changes taking place in its hinterland. Fairfax County experienced a population decline of over 30 percent between 1810 and 1830, as many white farmers and planters and their slaves moved west for better land and opportunities. Western migration also affected Loudoun County, where the population grew by only six hundred between 1810 and 1830. The story was similar west of the Blue Ridge Mountains in Frederick, Berkeley, and Jefferson counties, with only Frederick experiencing population growth. Overall, the population of the counties of northern Virginia west of Alexandria stagnated after 1810 when over eighty thousand people lived in the region; twenty years later, only 281 more people resided there.[40]

Economic growth and development in northern Virginia in the thirty years after the Revolution had been driven by the export of grains to the Iberian Peninsula and the West Indies, where the disruptions of the Napoleonic Wars opened up markets for American produce. A series of economic shocks after 1807 led to the slow decline of this trade and with it the port of Alexandria and its hinterlands. Jefferson's embargo in 1807–8 and the War of 1812 severely disrupted the town's grain trade and the local economy. In the immediate wake of the war exports grew, but the national economic panic of 1819 ended the brief recovery. As merchant Nathan Lupton explained to his father that year, "Times are very dull here and money very scarce." Alexandria's export trade had not recovered "since the Peace Establishment," Lupton continued, "and Some hundreds have been ruined by Speculation." Visitor Anne Royall reached similar conclusions in 1824. The town, she noted, had "not recovered the loss she sustained by the late war." A January 1827 fire that destroyed one hundred thousand dollars of property added to the town's woes. Economic stagnation continued in the 1830s, exacerbated by the 1837 national depression. The collapse of the once-thriving foreign grain trade had a ruinous impact on the town. By 1840, a New York visitor reported that "Alexandria's commerce has dwindled to less than the tithe of what it was." "Many of her streets," he continued, "have given a quiet resting place for the rank weed" and "blades of grass have come more frequently than the passing stranger."[41]

The town's economic doldrums resulted from more than the loss of foreign markets. First, the efforts of the region's merchants and planters to build a regional transportation network that linked Alexandria to its hinterland achieved only limited success. The Potomac River Company never succeeded in clearing the river and providing a reliable conduit for transporting produce to Alexandria. Turnpikes provided an alternative to water transport, but they remained expensive, slow, and often poorly maintained. In response, in 1827 town leaders, including Quaker merchant Phineas Janney, invested two hundred fifty thousand dollars of city funds in the Chesapeake and Ohio Canal, a still-water canal designed to connect the District of Columbia to the Ohio River. Second, after 1820 Baltimore superseded Alexandria as the primary destination for the produce of northern Virginia's farmers. In the 1790s, Alexandria's civic elite had viewed Baltimore as "a formidable rival" but one the Potomac port would soon surpass. Over the next forty years, Baltimore merchants absorbed the grain output of a broad hinterland that extended north into the Susquehanna Valley, west into Maryland, and south into Virginia, and the city grew from thirty-two thousand residents in 1800 to over one hundred and thirty thousand in 1840. Northern Virginia's farmers sent their produce to Baltimore because it offered a more reliable and lucrative market than Alexandria. As editor Edgar Snowden ruefully noted, farmers who shipped their produce to Alexandria often had to wait "two weeks" to sell "the whole, or any considerable part of their annual crop," with the result that "Baltimore prices have been generally somewhat better than ours." The consequent decline in the volume of trade also raised the price of imported goods and made Alexandria even less attractive to local farmers.[42]

Finally, construction of the Baltimore & Ohio Railroad, begun in 1827 and completed as far west as Harpers Ferry in the lower Shenandoah Valley by 1834, accelerated the shift to the Baltimore market. The construction of a branch line, the Winchester and Potomac Railroad, in the early 1830s enabled farmers as far south as Frederick County to access the B&O. The branch line attracted broad local support, including that of Quakers. Members of the Lupton family invested in the railroad, and in the 1840s—after years of complaints about the low prices they received in Alexandria—began shipping their flour to Baltimore. Many valley farmers joined the Luptons. In 1840, the directors of the Winchester and Potomac reported that their line had transported over one hundred and sixty thousand barrels of flour to the B&O and Baltimore. Alexandria's economy stagnated as it lost much of the wheat and flour trade of northern Virginia to Baltimore.[43]

Improved access to the Baltimore market pleased the region's farmers, but it did not end regional economic problems. After 1820, international outlets for American grains remained weak. Moreover, western farmers, tilling fresh soils and using the Ohio and Mississippi rivers and, after 1825, the Erie Canal to send their produce to foreign and northern markets, had a competitive advantage over their Virginia counterparts, who tilled soils worn out by decades of wasteful agricultural methods. Despite the efforts of reformers, including local Quakers, to encourage improvements, many northern Virginia farmers remained attached to soil-depleting techniques, even after the shift to grains. The reformers, moreover, provided no reliable antidote to periodic blights of rust, Hessian fly, and chinch bug that attacked the region's wheat crops. Confronted by these problems at home and the promise of bountiful lands to the west, many Virginians migrated across the Appalachians. According to the 1850 census, almost four hundred thousand white people born in Virginia lived outside the state, three-quarters of them in the Upper South and Old Northwest. Many of the migrants who headed north of the Ohio River, including a significant number of Friends, did so to escape from slavery, which they argued caused the state's economic stagnation. But most who left hoped to exploit the economic opportunities they believed lay in the West. Northern Virginians who remained, in contrast, faced declining land values, uncertain crops, and a stagnant economy.[44]

Regional economic problems placed particular stresses on the Quaker community and its web of economic, familial, and spiritual ties. The careers of Alexandria merchants Jonathan Butcher and Charles Ross reveal the customary Quaker linkage of family and commerce; they also demonstrate how business setbacks disrupted familial ties and spiritual values. While still a bachelor, Butcher—the son of merchant John Butcher, who had provided a congenial home to the young Edward Stabler—established a partnership with his brother-in-law John Paton in the late-1790s. His business prospering, he married Phebe Ross of the Hopewell meeting in 1806. When Paton died in 1819, Butcher set up his own firm and prospered despite the economic difficulties of the 1820s. In the early 1830s the overlap of family and business continued, when he took on as partner his nephew Charles Ross, the son of his wife's brother. The retail business thrived until the panic of 1837, when both men declared bankruptcy, prompting an investigation of the firm by the Alexandria meeting. Although the meeting did not criticize Butcher and Ross for the collapse of their business, it did accuse the pair of favoring particular creditors. Butcher, a charter member of the Alexandria meeting, acknowledged his wrongdoing and retained his membership. Ross refused to admit wrongdoing and compounded his infraction by marrying a non-Quaker. In early 1838, the Alexandria meeting disowned Ross; within a few months he had moved to Illinois.[45]

For Ross, business setbacks led to a broader renunciation of Quaker practices. When Loudoun County farmer and miller Jonas Potts faced disciplinary action for his economic difficulties, he too decided to give up his membership. In August 1811, Potts first appeared before the Fairfax meeting "for not complying with his engagements in payment of an Acknowledged debt due" to Quaker William Gregg. By October, Gregg had requested permission to seek recovery of the debt in the courts, which the meeting granted. Three months later, Potts became embroiled in a dispute over riparian rights with Quaker William Hough, who had dammed a local stream to supply his fulling mill and thereby reduced the flow of water to Potts's grain mill. Indebted and facing a pending lawsuit by Gregg, Potts asked the meeting for "the priviledge of instituting a Suit in Law." The meeting decided instead to appoint a committee to "inspect the cause of the uneasiness and endeavour to have the matter settled." For the next three months the committee tried to resolve the dispute; only the destruction of the dam, most likely by a spring flood, "remove[d]," in the vague wording the minutes, "the cause of complaint." Less than a year later, in early 1813, the meeting again investigated Potts for failing to pay debts. This time, the estate of Mahlon Janney requested and received permission to sue Potts for failing to pay a mortgage on land Janney had sold to Potts some years earlier.[46]

The meeting's differential handling of his case frustrated Potts. Although faced by mounting debts, he garnered little sympathy or help from local Friends, despite the injunctions of the discipline to offer support to members in such circumstances. In contrast, members of two of the meeting's leading families, the Houghs and Janneys, appeared to enjoy preferential treatment; they gained swift permission to go to court to recover debts from Potts, while the meeting denied him the same privilege. Whatever Potts thought of the meeting's actions, his subsequent history reveals a growing alienation from Quakerism. In early 1814, he was brought before the meeting again, this time "for drinking spirituous liquors to excess." Despite Potts's protestations of innocence, the meeting decided to disown him. "Considering the pains that have been taken with him and the labours that have been bestowed on him," the meeting concluded to "prepare a Testimony against him." For Potts, a history of indebtedness and disputation with Friends resulted in disownment when the meeting discovered his apparent penchant for whiskey. Potts developed a reputation for contentious and feckless behavior that, local Friends believed, made him ill-suited for membership in the religious community.[47]

A series of business disputes and arbitrations earned Goose Creek Friend Seth Smith a similar reputation in the early 1820s. Smith's troubles began after his brother Jacob moved west to Ohio in 1810 and Seth took on the task of collecting debts owed to him by Loudoun County Friends. The Goose Creek meeting would not issue Jacob a certificate of removal allowing him to join an Ohio meeting until he settled his financial affairs in Loudoun. Seth at first welcomed the meeting's mediation efforts, noting to Jacob in May 1815 that he had "obtained a judgment in thy favour" in a case against John Pancoast. However, the arbitration effort soon went awry, Seth argued, because the Pancoast "boys" gained "an advantage" when they obtained the support of leading Friends, including Israel Janney. According to Smith, during the Pancoasts' efforts to influence the outcome, "the little fellow," John Pancoast Jr., "got up and spouted away upon" the need for a rehearing of the case. "These proceedings," Smith wrote in disgust to his brother, "were so extraordinary [as] to excite my indignation and I protest[ed] against them." But the damage was done. "Several friends[,] m[ost] of whom I know to be prejudiced sp[oke] for a rehearing," which Smith eventually lost. Still, Smith remained "quite satisfied with the course I have taken." "I have no doubt," he wrote to Jacob after the affair had ended, "but friends will before long be generally satisfied I am right and that they have given way to a spirit that leads into confusion, and . . . every evil work."[48]

This experience influenced Smith's actions in November 1822 when he again faced the prospect of arbitration in his efforts to collect a two thousand dollar debt owed his brother by Isaac Brown. Although Smith initially offered to seek mediation to settle the matter, Brown "replied that he had nothing to arbitrate." Only after Smith initiated legal action did Brown appear "willing to go" before the meeting. But things did not go as Smith hoped. Brown recruited allies within the meeting, and in April 1823 "old Stephen McPherson"—who had ruled against Smith in the Pancoast arbitration—"tried to get a complaint into the meeting against me." Smith believed that "the case will be taken up in meeting against Isaac," but he remained uncertain because "friends are somewhat divided." In September, the matter remained unsettled in the local courts and the meeting, but Smith reported that "my mind has been preserved in a comfortable degree of composure amidst the disagreeable circumstances of this affair."[49]

Nonetheless, Smith remained deeply concerned what his fellow Quakers thought of his actions, asking his brother in Ohio "what do friends in your neighborhood think of it[?]" In November 1824, the matter came before the monthly meeting, which decided to disown Smith "for refusing to arbitrate agreeably to discipline" and suing fellow Friends too precipitously. Smith remained adamant that he had followed an upright course, even after his appeal failed in 1826. The quarterly meeting, he informed his brother, "confirmed the judgment" of the monthly meeting "under impressions that I know to be erroneous." But, he concluded, "I feel reconciled to the decision—because I really cannot have unity with those who have so little regard to justice as [some of] the members of the G[oose] C[reek] Meeting." Smith may have been convinced of his rectitude, but his persistent economic quarrels had by the mid-1820s earned him a reputation among local Friends as a prickly individual. As Goose Creek Quaker Jacob Janney reported after meeting Smith in 1832: "He is the same Seth yet[,] composed of a map of discordant materials."[50]

Potts's and Smith's experiences point to the broader impact on the Quaker community of the region's economic downturn: hard times increased the possibility of business-related disputes between Friends and placed significant strains on internal Quaker dispute-solving mechanisms. Moreover, outmigration sparked in part by local economic problems increased the likelihood of such disputes. After decades of growth fueled by immigration, in the 1790s the meetings of northern Virginia saw a rise in the number of people leaving, most of whom settled on lands west of the Appalachians. Pennsylvania and New Jersey Friends, many with kinship ties in the region, continued to move south until 1800. But in the 1790s, the stream of migrants moving west, which continued at a steady pace throughout the first half of the nineteenth century, began to eclipse the inward flow. Despite the arrival of ninety-five newcomers in the 1790s, the Hopewell meeting lost 142 members. Overall, the four monthly meetings in northern Virginia—Hopewell, Fairfax, Crooked Run, and Goose Creek— lost over three hundred individuals in the decade, a blow for a population that numbered no more than two thousand in the 1770s. Outmigration had the greatest impact on the small Crooked Run meeting, located in the Shenandoah Valley some fifteen miles south of Winchester. In 1807, after the departure of many of the meeting's guiding figures, including members of the Updegraff, Lupton, Taylor, Brown, and Smith families, local Friends decided to lay down—that is, to discontinue—the meeting. Those who stayed behind established a preparatory meeting overseen by the Hopewell meeting, but three years later Friends dissolved it too. Outmigration decimated the Crooked Run meeting and eliminated the Quaker presence in southern Frederick County.[51]

Large numbers of Virginians joined the post-Revolutionary westward movement, many of them settling, at least initially, in the slaveholding states of Kentucky and Tennessee. Seeking to escape from slavery, Virginia Quakers headed northwest, initially settling in southwestern Pennsylvania, where they helped set up the new Redstone and Westland meetings on the Monongahela River. Just over half the eight hundred forty removals to these two meetings between 1785 and 1810 arrived from Baltimore or Virginia Yearly Meetings; more striking, one-fifth of all removals to Redstone and Westland—168 people in all—came from the meetings of northern Virginia. For many of these migrants, the Monongahela Valley was a temporary stopping point. The 1795 Treaty of Greenville, signed in the wake of Arthur St. Clair's victory over the Ohio Indians at the Battle of Fallen Timbers, opened up the Ohio Territory to white settlement, and many southwestern Pennsylvania Friends crossed the Ohio River. They were joined after 1800 by a large flow of Friends from northern Virginia. In the Hopewell meeting "Ohio fever" began in 1802 when the ten members of the Jinkins family joined the Concord Monthly Meeting in eastern Ohio. Over the next eight years, the Hopewell meeting issued just over one hundred certificates of removal for some 315 individuals. During the following decades outmigration slowed—from 1811 to 1820 the Hopewell meeting issued sixty-one certificates of removal for just under one hundred and fifty members—but the attrition of Friends to Ohio concerned those who remained. Indeed, after a visit to the Hopewell meeting, traveling minister John Shoemaker "found Friends much exercised about their members' moving away, which had stripped their meetings."[52]

Friends had reason to worry. In addition to the demise of the Crooked Run Monthly Meeting, declining numbers forced the region's monthly meetings to discontinue more than ten (and possibly more) subsidiary meetings. Local Friends found the loss of family members and neighbors spiritually and emotionally demoralizing, and outmigration led to a variety of practical problems. Many individuals moved west so abruptly that they did not have time to settle their business affairs, particularly in a stagnant economy that depressed land prices and made debt collection more complicated. Because of his extensive economic investment in the region, Jacob Smith could not close his affairs quickly. He turned matters over to his brother Seth Smith, who soon became mired in a series of arbitrations and lawsuits that led to his disownment. Similar difficulties faced other Quaker families. John Livingston requested a certificate to move to the Baltimore meeting in 1823, but the committee appointed to look into his business affairs discovered that they were not "satisfactorily arranged." Impatient to move, Livingston left without the meeting's consent but returned a year later to settle matters and obtain a certificate to move to New York. Over the next two years, Livingston satisfied all but one of his Quaker creditors, but the one failure convinced the Fairfax meeting to "discontinue his request" for a certificate of removal. Livingston eventually tired of the process, informing the meeting in 1826—long after he had moved to New York—that he "found it out of his power to satisfy" the meeting and asked to be disowned. The meeting complied a month later.[53]

Reuben Schooley, a birthright Friend and an overseer of the Fairfax meeting, faced a similar fate when he left for Ohio in 1824 "without settling his business or satisfying his Creditors." Schooley argued that he had done no wrong because "his removal would be rather an advantage than an injury to his Creditors." And he insisted he had every intention of "paying his debts as fast as he" could. Ten years later, Schooley had still not satisfied his creditors, and the meeting decided to disown him "for his breach of discipline." The meeting acted much more swiftly to remove Isaac Holmes. "Guilty of acts which have the appearance of intentional fraud," Holmes "absconded" west "leaving several of his debts unpaid." For his "dishonest conduct," the meeting disowned Holmes. Regardless of the speed with which the meeting acted, these cases point to the persistent problems that hard times and extensive outmigration engendered within the tightly knit Quaker community of northern Virginia. Their declining numbers and consequent contraction of internal business connections made Quaker farmers and merchants more vulnerable to economic uncertainty and propelled some to expand their business contacts beyond their community. Accelerating ties with the non-Quaker world, however, threatened to the integrity of Friends' identity as a people apart.[54]

<h1 style="text-align:center">V</h1>

Recognizing no divide between the spiritual and secular aspects of life, Friends viewed their commercial and civic pursuits in the years after the Revolution as a religious duty. But the success of these endeavors also enhanced their reputation and enabled many to earn the respect of northern Virginia's white community—at least in times of peace and when slaveholders perceived few threats to the institution of slavery. Local Quaker merchants and millers joined the ranks of the region's economic and social elite, and middling Friends enjoyed public approbation for their fair dealing, respectability, and public-spirited behavior. Beyond their interest in economic development, Quakers played key roles in the founding and operation of the Alexandria Library Company in 1794 and the Alexandria Lyceum in 1834, institutions that enhanced the cultural and intellectual life of the community by introducing advanced scientific, literary, and philosophical ideas to the local population.[55]

Quaker women also received attention from non-Quakers. They earned praise for their plain dress, simplicity of manners, and seriousness of purpose that differed from the perceived frivolity and idleness of southern white women. One local poet contrasted the "jewelled out" beauty of non-Quaker women, who attended the "ball and rout," their "heads all decked with gems and curls," with the qualities of the "lovely Quaker girl," who possessed "a soul all pure and bright" and "a mind that glowed with virtue's light." Although graced with "a lily hand" and a "pretty face," the real appeal of "the Quaker girl" lay in her "kindness" and "honesty," and the "truth" that appeared in her "every look and sigh." "So boast if you will, of each lass you see," the poet concluded, "But the Quaker girl is the one for me." Another writer, only partly in jest, sexualized female Quaker dress when he concluded that their modest and plain clothing, otherwise "so emblematic of purity," gave them an air of "witchery," particularly "the snow white stocking fitted exactly to the foot that cannot be concealed."[56]

But in a slave state, such attraction posed a dangerous threat because marriage to non-Quakers could implicate Friends in slavery, as the Lupton family of Frederick County discovered. In 1811, the Hopewell Monthly Meeting disowned Isaac Lupton after they found him guilty of "committing adultery" and abandoning his first wife, Thamzin McPherson Lupton. Following Thamzin's death, Isaac remarried a non-Quaker, Margaret Compton, and after the birth of a daughter the couple received a wet nurse, "a negro girl named Celia," from Margaret's father, William C. Compton. Sometime later, Compton gave his daughter another young slave, Sam, and Celia herself gave birth to a child, perhaps fathered by Isaac. Although these slaves "continued in the [Lupton] family," Margaret claimed that she "never considered" that they belonged to her or—following the laws of coverture—"to Mr. Lupton." Reflecting his Quaker upbringing, Lupton "frequently" stated "that he never owned a negro and never would." Yet when he died indebted in 1821, five enslaved African Americans lived with the family, and his creditors sought to recoup their money through the slaves' sale. The task of settling Isaac's estate and the legal status of the five individuals (and providing for Isaac's three surviving children) fell to the executors, David and Nathan Lupton, Isaac's Quaker father and brother. Neither man owned nor rented slaves—indeed both aided local free blacks and shared antislavery sentiments—but family ties to a wayward son and brother entangled them in an extended legal battle involving the ownership of five enslaved persons.[57]

For Friends, Isaac Lupton's case provided a graphic example of the moral hazards of residing in the slave South. Friends could take comfort in earning the acceptance of white northern Virginians, but they recognized the dangers public approval and involvement in the region's social and economic life posed to their spiritual testimonies. Likewise, participation in the region's slave-based economy could draw Quaker farmers, millers, and merchants away from their ethical commitments. When Quaker minister John Comly visited Alexandria in December 1829, he found "people . . .

so indifferent, or so much engrossed with their worldly cares and business," that few attended the weekday meeting. "If Friends cannot leave their worldly business to attend meetings," wondered Comly, "how can we expect others . . . to assemble with us?"[58]

Quaker ministers throughout the United States and Great Britain had voiced similar fears for years. They worried that Friends in business would allow their worldly concerns to overwhelm their spiritual duties. But in slaveholding regions, Quaker probity faced greater challenges. Simple participation in northern Virginia's slave-based economy pushed Friends into moral compromises as their economic welfare and social standing became dependent on the production, processing, transportation, marketing, financing, and sale of the region's staples. Local Friends ended direct contact with and reliance on slave labor, but the economic pervasiveness of the institution meant they could not terminate indirect connections without undermining their economic wellbeing. Quaker millers processed the slave-produced grain of their non-Quaker neighbors, Quaker merchants stocked their shelves with products made with slave labor, and Quaker women purchased such products for domestic use. Likewise, the financial instruments issued by Quaker-financed and directed banks and insurance companies helped underwrite and expand the region's slave-based staple economy, and Quaker merchants and farmers invested in and traveled on the region's turnpikes and canals built with slave labor. Close business ties between Quaker merchants and their non-Quaker neighbors often led to friendly relations that eroded Friends' sense of themselves as a people who stood apart spiritually and socially from the larger community.

By 1808, William Hartshorne had for nearly twenty years conducted a mutually profitable trade with Frederick County slaveholder Thomas Massie, milling the planter's slave-produced wheat and grains and shipping them to foreign markets. Over time, the slaveholder and the Quaker developed a bond based on mutual respect, enough so that Massie asked a personal favor of Hartshorne. Massie explained that his son, Henry, planned to tour northern cities and wondered if Hartshorne could supply him with "letters of Introduction" to "acquaintances in" "Baltimore, Philadelphia, New York, &c." Massie wanted his son to learn from Hartshorne and his fellow Friends the virtues of honesty, diligence, and civic responsibility. For his part, Hartshorne saw no contradiction in maintaining close business and personal contacts with a slaveholding planter. Like many Friends, he believed that his interactions with non-Quakers enabled him to influence their behavior and spiritual welfare. But Friends also recognized—as

Hartshorne would a few years later during his bankruptcy—that involvement in the world represented a double-edged sword that could undermine their ethical commitments. Loudoun County Friend William Schooley saw the dangers when he apprenticed among non-Quakers. "I soon learned to delight," Schooley recalled years later, "in their vain, foolish and obscene conversation and before the expiration of my time I was as fine a fellow as any of them."[59]

Schooley redirected his spiritual path after he "broke off from my new associates" and "returned home" where he realized that God's "voice was always raised in me to warn me against evil." He concluded that the secular world's "many temptations and difficulties" imperiled Friends' ability to follow "the instructions and pointings of the spirit of truth, as inwardly revealed." Quakers' desire to remove threats from the path dictated by the inward light prompted some Friends to retreat into their community. Mary Brooke believed that only the "true unity" of Friends ensured "a Life Hid together with god in Christ which I hope will never be demolished notwithstanding all the wavering Combat that may happen here." This "wavering Combat"—the battle to find and maintain a moral path—could occur anywhere, even within the family. George Churchman, a visiting minister from Maryland, expressed pity and praise for "E. C.," whose "patient Firmness" had enabled her "to pass through" various "Trials . . . for more than 30 years past." Churchman admired E. C.'s willingness to rebuff her "beloved Father," who had "missed his way, and lost the Unity of the Faithful." Although "divers others in the Family . . . persecuted her for her firmness and plain dealing" with her father, E. C., "not flinching or leaning because of filial Affection," remained "firm and faithful" to her testimony and refused to associate with her father while he was disowned. Churchman believed that E. C.'s "firmness" played a "considerable means" in her father's return "to a State of right feeling"—that is, his acknowledgement of error and restoration to Society membership. For such Friends, the pursuit of truth and moral reform in a fallen world required they sever if necessary even the closest of emotional ties.[60]

If most Friends avoided—or like E. C.'s family opposed—such measures in pursuit of righteousness, they nonetheless recognized the dangers of living in northern Virginia. Those perils increased as Quakers earned a respected niche within white society. Even Friends who migrated west in the early nineteenth century noted the difficulty of removing from "such a highly cultivated country as" Virginia to one so "rude and uncultivated" as the Old Northwest. Ohio's supposed unhealthy climate and a longing for their former homes made some Friends "much inclined to go back to Virginia." But few returned once they moved away from slavery. As Ohio migrant John Janney put it, "I will never learn . . . to live in a slave state unless I thought some great good would result in it. My feelings in a slave state would be constantly harrow'd."[61]

Janney pointed to the moral contradictions faced by Quakers who remained in northern Virginia. By the first decades of the nineteenth century Friends enjoyed acceptance and respect from their non-Quaker neighbors, but their involvement in the region's slave-based society came at a price. The values that underlay a slave economy stood in contrast to Friends' insistence on the spiritual equality of all people, the need to eschew violence, and adherence to the golden rule. Moreover, commercial and social interaction with the white community made drawing lines of division difficult and sometimes forced Friends to compromise their ethical values. The region's wealthiest and most socially prominent Friends—those who assumed leading roles in the region's economic development or accepted positions in local government—faced the prospect of abetting the economic and legal bulwarks of slavery. Friends recognized the dangers and experienced the same "harrow'd" emotional state that drove Quakers like John Janney from the state. Instead of leaving, however, they believed their economic and civic contributions made it possible for them to act as moral arbiters of the community, the role they had embraced during the Revolutionary years. Thus, while participating in the economic and civic life of northern Virginia, Friends simultaneously conducted a series of persistent if intermittent campaigns to aid the free black and enslaved population of the state, and convince white Virginians of the economic and moral benefits of ending slavery. Before 1830, the antislavery efforts of northern Virginia's Quakers constituted the most consistent and clearest voice against slavery in the state.

4

Embracing "the Oppressor as Well as the Oppressed"

Quaker Antislavery before 1830

In April 1827, the *Alexandria Gazette* published the first of eleven articles that announced the creation of the Benevolent Society of Alexandria for Ameliorating and Improving the Condition of the People of Color and bemoaned the consequences of slavery in Virginia and the United States. In measured and deferential language, using arguments designed to appeal to the self-interest of slaveholders, the articles assailed the slave trade, lamented the economic impact of the institution, and called for the gradual emancipation and colonization of the nation's enslaved population. The conservative goals and tone of the essays typified the objectives, philosophy, and tactics of the antislavery movement before abolitionists embraced the goal of immediate emancipation in the early 1830s. The essays also reflected the strategy of antislavery Quakers, who played a prominent role in early nineteenth-century endeavors to end the institution. In northern Virginia, Friends stood at the center of efforts by local groups to dismantle slavery and aid the region's African Americans. The other essays in the series employed similar tactics. Although unsigned, the articles were written by the young Alexandria merchant Samuel Janney, who along with local Friends and likeminded non-Quakers formed the Benevolent Society to alert "the public mind" to the "pernicious effects" of slavery, "both upon the slaves . . . and the white population." Denying any "intention of interfering with the constitutional rights of slave-holders" and hoping to avoid offending local elites, "many of whom we respect," Janney argued that the impact of slavery "upon the morals, the habits, and the prosperity" of the community made it his "duty" to speak. Doing so, he believed, would "ultimately tend to the general welfare" of Virginia.[1]

For local Quakers, who since the Revolution had regarded themselves as the community's moral compass, attempting to "ameliorate" the costs of slavery remained a high priority. Although Friends became involved in other reforms—attacking the dangers of "spirituous liquors" and promoting public education—the antislavery campaign became a central component of their social concerns. Friends viewed antislavery as part of their broader economic and civic participation in the community, designed like their promotion of internal improvements, commerce, and agriculture to contribute to the welfare of the state and improve the lives of fellow Virginians, black and white. However, the same spiritual commitments that gave rise to Quaker social activism also circumscribed it. Believing that all individuals, slaveholders as well as slaves, possessed a spark of the divine—what Friends called the inward light—they eschewed language that impugned or inflamed their opponents. Instead, like most antislavery activists before 1830 they adopted tactics of moral suasion and appealed to slaveholders' conscience, believing that if cultivated the inward light could guide all individuals to embrace antislavery.[2]

In addition to these theological restraints, Friends faced external pressures that constrained their public opposition to slavery. White Virginians' commitment to slavery and fears about its stability brought Friends into conflict with the broader community and forced them to make difficult choices among their reform objectives. Participation in the local economy and civic life led many Friends to develop a deep attachment to the region—*their* region—identifying themselves as southerners and northern Virginia as home. As opponents of slavery they remained distinct from their non-Quaker neighbors, but their involvement in the region's public and commercial life implicated them in the slave economy. With only 20 percent of its total population enslaved, northern Virginia may have been in historian Ira Berlin's construction "a society with slaves" rather than "a slave society," but the Quaker experience reveals that the presence of even a small slave population had a transformative effect, reshaping all aspects of public life.[3] The large number of Quakers who emigrated from northern Virginia to escape entanglement in slavery believed that only by leaving their homes could they escape the institution. In contrast, Friends who remained could not extricate themselves from slavery's tentacles. They faced a persistent tension between their spiritual commitments and the social practices and culture of the broader community in which they lived and prospered.

This tension and the theology of the inward light compelled Friends to pursue their antislavery agenda in a deferential manner and reject the strident approach adopted by abolitionists after 1830. In the early nineteenth century, Friends' antislavery agenda garnered considerable sympathy among northern Virginia's planter elite and evangelicals. These groups worried about the practical and moral impact of slavery, and small numbers from both joined Friends in local antislavery organizations. Before 1830, northern Virginia's Quakers enjoyed a relatively tolerant environment that enabled them to pursue an antislavery agenda with little overt repression. But slaveholders' forbearance had limits. Efforts to silence Friends during moments of crisis—most notably in the aftermath of Gabriel's Rebellion in 1801—revealed the fleeting commitment of white Virginians to ending slavery and the legal and political constraints they imposed on Quaker activism.[4] These restrictions, both internal and external, shaped and circumscribed Friends' reform efforts.

I

After ending slavery within their ranks in the 1780s, Virginia's Quakers sought broader change. Robert Pleasants, a Quaker elder from the Richmond area, led the post-Revolutionary campaign. Throughout the 1780s and 1790s, he wrote to elite Virginians to convince them of slavery's immorality. He asked John Michie to reflect on the implications of the golden rule, sent antislavery pamphlets to Charles Carter of Shirley, and "rejoice[d]" when Robert Carter of Nomini Hall "freed so many [of his] slaves." In 1785, he sent an antislavery pamphlet to George Washington and urged him to free his slaves. "O remember," Pleasants wrote, "that 'God will not be mocked' and is still requiring from each of us to 'do justly, love mercy and walk humbly before him.'" James Madison, Thomas Jefferson, and St. George Tucker received similar missives. In 1790, following the lead of Pennsylvania Quakers who in 1784 established the Pennsylvania Society for Promoting the Abolition of Slavery, he organized and became the first president of the Virginia Abolition Society, cooperating with a small group of antislavery Methodists. The abolition society worked to arouse antislavery opinion in Virginia, promote the education of free black children, and, in 1795, petition the Virginia legislature to end slavery.[5]

According to Pleasants, "a considerable number of [the state's] most respectable citizens" signed the petition, which condemned slavery as "not
only a moral but political evil." Human bondage, it argued, degraded "human nature," weakened "the Bonds of Society," "discourage[d] trade and
manufactures," and imperiled the "peace" of the state. Responding to opponents of abolition who contended that inherent inferiority made African
Americans unable to participate as free people in American society, the
petition contended that the degradation of black Americans resulted from
their bondage and not from innate racial differences. "Accustomed to move
to the will of the master," the petition explained, "reflection [among blacks]
may in some degree be suspended, and reason and conviction have but
little influence on their conduct." Grounded in Quaker principles, the petition stressed the spiritual equality of all people and Christians' moral duty
to live by the golden rule, though it recognized that public opinion pre-
cluded immediate emancipation. Instead, it "humbly propose[d]" that "the
children of Slaves now born . . . be freed as they come to a proper age" and
invested "with suitable privileges, as an excitement to become useful citizens." The petition received a cold response from the Virginia legislature.
After a single reading in the House of Delegates, "further consideration was
negatived by the small majority of two votes."[6]

Pleasants's efforts had the support of northern Virginia Friends, some
of whom also backed Quaker antislavery petitions to the federal government. In 1783, the Philadelphia Yearly Meeting petitioned the Confederation Congress to end the slave trade, condemning it as contrary to "every
humane and righteous consideration, and in opposition to the solemn
declarations often repeated in favour of universal liberty." Of the twenty
Virginian Friends who signed the petition, eighteen came from northern
Virginia meetings. A committee headed by Thomas Jefferson considered
the bill and recommended that Congress urge all states that had not ended
the slave trade to do so. Congress did not act on the recommendation,
and rebuffed similar Quaker petitions in 1785 and 1786. The creation of
the new national government in 1788 prompted Friends once more to ask
Congress to end the slave trade, despite its constitutional protection until
1808. Friends from northern Virginia again joined their northern coreligionists in support of the petition. It sparked a bitter debate in Congress
between northern defenders of Quakers' right to speak and southerners
who attacked Friends as a threat to public order and defended slavery as a
positive good. Moderate Virginia politicians like George Washington and
Alexander White thought the question best avoided. "The memorial of

the Quakers (and a very mal-apropos one it was) has at length been put to sleep and," Washington predicted, "will scarcely awake before the year 1808." Congress buried all subsequent Quaker petitions against the slave trade before 1808.[7]

Friends in northern Virginia remained undeterred, their efforts helping to sustain the antislavery idealism of the Revolution that led some Virginians to question the racialist assumptions undergirding slavery. A 1790 obituary of Fairfax County's "Negro Tom, the famous African Calculator," provided a lengthy description of his mathematical abilities. Drawing on Quaker assumptions about the spiritual equality of humanity, the writer concluded that Tom proved "the genius, capacity and talents of" African Americans, while belying those who believed blacks' "supposed inferiority" fitted them for slavery. Such "sentiments," the author continued, were "as ill-founded in fact, as they are inhuman in their tendency." The trial of "Negro Moses," acquitted for murdering a brutal overseer in 1791, also elicited commentary that drew on Quaker notions of human equality. "Many Bye-Standers" argued that Moses was justified in killing his overseer because "by the laws of this country . . . a man, to preserve his own life, may kill the assailant." Such laws should "be extended to slaves," the writer argued, because blacks and whites shared a common humanity. "Have they not the same feelings, passions, and frailties that white men have?" the writer asked, and should we "suppose the more enlightened a man is the more inexcusable he is in giving way to the passions and weaknesses of human nature?" Pacifist Friends could not defend violence even in such circumstances, but in proposing that enslaved people enjoy basic legal rights the writer embraced the Society's racial values.[8]

In the 1790s, local newspapers regularly printed similar sentiments. "An Acct. of the Origin and Progress of *Slavery*," traced the peculiar institution's origins to "pirates." After "morality began to improve and enlighten the minds of men," this account concluded, only individuals without "honour" engaged in "detaining and dragging into slavery such unhappy victims as fell in their way." "A Freeman" made a more direct attack, arguing that no "*friend* to *liberty*" could "justify civil and domestic slavery upon rational and equitable principles." The writer challenged the institution's defenders to prove "that *slavery* is consistent with *human rights, free government, good philosophy, true religion*; or any other *equitable, reasonable*, or *charitable* principles in human nature, or civil society." "*Liberty*," he concluded, is "the *theme* of America! Freedom, the just due of every man!" The same year Russell Goodrich, a Yale graduate teaching at an Alexandria school, advised

Virginians to embrace "modern times" and abandon the culture of tobacco for wheat. "Let our Planters become Farmers," he argued; they would grow rich and their "improvements" spark "universal excitement." But Virginians could make this change, Goodrich continued, only if they freed their slaves, who "will never give the attention necessary for farmers."[9]

Most disturbing to the region's slaveholders, in 1795 Quakers spearheaded the creation of the Alexandria Society for the Relief and Protection of Persons Illegally Held in Bondage. William Hartshorne, the Alexandria merchant and Friend, became the group's first president. The society elected Edward Stabler and John Janney, also local merchants and Friends, the society's first and second secretaries, and Quakers made up more than twenty of the group's initial fifty members. The constitution of the society blended Quaker ethical doctrines with the natural rights philosophy of the Revolution. Echoing the Declaration of Independence, the society's constitution affirmed that "Life, Liberty, and the pursuit of happiness" were "Privileges derived from, and instituted by, the benevolent Creator and Father of the Universe, and with which he invested all nations of the earth." Only "with deepest regret," the constitution continued, could "feeling minds . . . view a coercive violation of all these privileges in . . . our African Brethren." Echoing the golden rule embraced by Friends, the constitution declared all persons "members of the same universal family." Thus "all men" must "diffuse the blessing of freedom to every part of the human race." Members of the association pledged "themselves to use all lawful means" to protect "such as are illegally held in bondage." They also endorsed educational programs designed to change "the convictions of individuals," boycotts "of all commodities . . . cultivated or manufactured by slaves," and lobbying efforts to "obtain a repeal or amelioration of the laws respecting Slavery."[10]

Slaveholders viewed the appearance of indigenous antislavery organizations as a threat to their property and an encouragement to a restive enslaved population. According to member Archibald McClean, at one of the society's first meetings local slaveholder Dr. Elisha C. Dick, who later converted to Quakerism and changed his position, barged in and "addressed us in a lengthy harangue on the . . . dangerous consequences" of the organization. The society, Dick charged, would infuse "into the Slaves a spirit of insurrection and Rebellion, which might eventually destroy the tranquility of the State." Alarm about the antislavery society spread, prompting local slaveholders to petition the state assembly. Within weeks, the assembly passed a statute aimed at "*abolishing* the *Abolition* of Slavery throughout the State of Virginia." As the act's preamble announced, the state wished to remove the "great and alarming mischiefs [that] have arisen in other states" from "voluntary associations of individuals" who deprive "masters of their property in slaves." The legislation made it more difficult for slaves to sue for freedom in local courts, stipulating that they must "obtain counsel, to be assigned by the said court, who, without fee or reward, shall prosecute the suit of such complainant." As historian Robert McColley notes, few local lawyers, dependent on the business of slaveholding planters, would willingly prosecute a freedom suit. Local Friends responded by retaining "Quaker lawyers," often coreligionists, to pursue the abolition society's interests in the courts.[11]

The Alexandria antislavery society called for the legislation's repeal, arguing that it differed from "the general *sentiments* of *justice*, and the *principles* of the *constitution*, as expressed in our *Bill of Rights.*" Freedom suits, the society noted, usually arose in the county courts where "the common court justices" who presided over the cases were "often considerable slaveholders." "Under these circumstances," the case of the "claimant must appear as clear as the sun at noon before" the justices would hear it. The legislation, as its supporters clearly intended, "destroyed almost every suggestion of hope that any person . . . can obtain liberty by due process of law." The society had no success in overturning the law, and in 1798 the assembly passed harsher legislation to discourage abolition societies in the state. The new law stipulated the death penalty for free persons who incited slaves to insurrection or murder, a ten dollar fine for those who harbored slaves without the consent of the master, and disqualified members of antislavery societies as jurors in freedom suits. With this statute the Virginia assembly identified abolitionists as "biased men . . . not to be trusted in a court of law."[12]

Still, the Alexandria society labored on, inspiring opponents of slavery in Frederick County to form their own abolition society. Headed by Quaker Richard Ridgeway, the Winchester Society for Promoting the Abolition of Slavery and the Relief of Free Negroes Unlawfully Held in Bondage began meeting in 1796. In its first statement, the society announced conservative goals similar to those of the Alexandria group. The society would not "interfere" in freedom suits involving enslaved people transported into the state, Ridgeway declared, despite a 1785 statute that freed slaves imported and residing in the state for more than a year. The society would not take "advantage of those who through ignorance of . . . the laws of this common-wealth have suffered their slaves to become entitled to their freedom." In accordance with its limited objectives, the Winchester society kept a low profile and may have ceased operation within the year. But Frederick County Friends still worked quietly on behalf of African Americans with legal claims to freedom. When "Negress Peg" sued for her freedom in the Frederick County court in 1801, local Quaker Joseph Sexton came to her defense. Peg's owner, John Harrison, had emancipated her while they lived in Philadelphia. Upon gaining her freedom, she signed an indenture with Frederick County resident Christian Hess, who moved her back to Virginia. When her indenture ended, Harrison again claimed Peg as his property. Sexton contacted a Philadelphia Friend, asking that he collect the legal documents, including Peg's manumission papers and indenture to Hess, which proved she was free. The northern Friend quickly complied, adding that he hoped the evidence would convince "the Court of Winchester . . . that Pegg is Justly entitled to her Freedom and the defendant [Harrison] be compelld to Return her and Pay sutch damages as sutch Wicked doings justly merit."[13]

In contrast, the Alexandria society maintained a high profile. In 1797, the society had sixty-two members, and between 1796 and 1801 announced its meetings in the town's newspapers. The society's annual reports to the Pennsylvania Abolition Society indicated members' efforts to improve conditions for enslaved people and free blacks in northern Virginia. In 1797, the Quaker merchant George Drinker, representing the Alexandria society at the fourth annual abolition convention in Philadelphia, reported that members aimed to "obtain legal justice for oppressed Africans" and "ameliorate their condition." The group had hired a schoolteacher and started a Sunday school for black children in December 1796. The school admitted seventeen "scholars" when it opened, a number that had grown to 108 four months later. The curriculum consisted of "orthography, reading, writing, the more useful parts of arithmetic," and "morals." "Many of the pupils," Drinker reported, "evince a strong desire and considerable aptitude for learning." In addition, the society had received twenty-six complaints over the past year from blacks illegally held in bondage, six of whom it had protected from "the law against importation." The other twenty cases were "pending" but "doubtful." The society also pursued two freedom suits in the Norfolk and North Carolina courts. Equally important, the society continued its lobbying and educational efforts among the white population. The society had prepared a petition to the Virginia assembly protesting the 1795 slave law, and it planned to issue "a new publication . . . on the subject of slavery." Drinker concluded optimistically that the treatment of slaves in northern Virginia was "less rigorous than formally."[14]

Four years later, the Alexandria society issued a less sanguine report. Although three of the five freedom suits the society had pursued in the local courts had terminated in favor of the enslaved African Americans, things otherwise looked bleak. The society declined to send a representative to the 1801 convention because it had applied its money to a freedom suit for five free blacks from Maryland whom an Alexandria resident claimed as slaves when they visited the town. Unfortunately, the black family lost its suit in the district court and were "violently wrested from their connexions," sold "to a slave driver from North Carolina," and "consigned . . . to irredeemable slavery." To add to the society's woes, the claimant, invoking the 1795 law that enabled slaveholders to sue anyone who aided a losing freedom suit, "took out a writ against one of the members of our Society who interfered" on behalf of the black family. Most disturbing, local whites forced the society to close its Sunday school, fearing literate black residents. In the face of white hostility, the society could find "no teacher of adequate merit" and had "relinquish[ed] its patronage" of the school.[15]

Gabriel's Rebellion, that "unfortunate rising of the negroes at Richmond last summer," fueled the wave of antagonism directed at the society. In August 1800, Gabriel, a charismatic and literate blacksmith hired out by his owner, planned to lead a troop of slaves into Richmond, seize the armory, and take Governor James Monroe hostage, exchanging him for their freedom. Heavy thunderstorms the evening of the planned revolt and the actions of two slaves who informed their master of Gabriel's plans derailed the assault. Monroe called out the militia, and within a few days it had rounded up over fifty suspected participants, among them Gabriel, who had initially escaped to Norfolk by ship. The state executed twenty-six convicted conspirators (including Gabriel) and transported seven others to the West Indies, while the legislature passed laws restricting the movement of slaves and free blacks. The state's punitive response reflected whites' widespread panic after Gabriel's conspiracy. It also revealed their deep uneasiness about the ongoing slave revolts and violence in Santo Domingo. In 1791, slaves on the French-held colony had risen in revolt against their masters, many of whom fled to America and spread lurid accounts of black atrocities. The unrest on the island continued until 1803, destroying the slave regime and culminating in Santo Domingo's independence. Gabriel's conspiracy, inspired by the same revolutionary idealism that led black Haitians to revolt, frightened white Virginians who were anxious about the possible extension of Santo Domingo's violence to the American South. The events persuaded most white Virginians that blacks and whites could live in peace only if the former remained in chains.[16]

In the wake of the conspiracy, Friends also came under suspicion. Gabriel's order that Quakers "be spared" because of their antislavery efforts convinced many white Virginians that members of the Society posed a threat to the slave regime and Quaker-led abolition societies had contributed to the revolt. In Alexandria, physician Elisha Dick led the attack on the society, which he believed produced "serious calamities." Writing to Governor Monroe in 1800, Dick called for "immediate legislative measures . . . to restrain if not entirely suppress the schools supported by" antislavery advocates. These schools, he argued, "are constantly inculcating natural equality among the blacks of every description[;] they are teaching them . . . the only means by which they can . . . concert and execute a plan of general insurrection." A few years later another Alexandrian concluded that though slavery was "an inveterate cancer" in society, the "peace which most men seek in retirement" "makes us rather bear those ills we have, than try experiments which we know not of." "Necessity" forced Virginians to retain slavery— and in such a Virginia, abolition societies had no place. Living under an "avowedly hostile" legislature and within a state where the "general custom gives . . . countenance to the disgraceful practice of slavery," the Alexandria society waned.[17]

By midyear it ceased to exist. Its last formal meeting took place in May 1801. In 1804, George Drinker reported that the society was "in fact dead; and I may say, I have no hope of reanimation." In addition to the backlash after Gabriel's conspiracy, Drinker identified internal divisions among members composed of "discordant materials" as a problem. The society, he noted, had allowed a few slaveholders animated by revolutionary liberalism to join, but efforts to protect enslaved people exposed the divergence between their idealism and self-interest. When the society pursued freedom suits under the 1785 law that freed slaves imported into the state and remaining a year, slaveholding members, a number of whom owned imported slaves, obstructed the group's efforts. For Drinker, only a return to Quaker principles could resuscitate the society. "Nothing will contribute to our revival," he argued, "but a more thorough conviction of a divine precept . . . to do unto others as they should do unto us." But slaveholders exhibited "a disposition to increase the measure of affliction apportioned to the poor deserted African." By 1802, Alexandria had become "a place of deposit" for slaves transported from Maryland and northern Virginia to the Deep South, and town residents regularly saw "fifty or sixty of those poor objects handcuffed and chained together, taking leave of their friends and relations, never to meet again." Sabotaged from within by slaveholding members and buffeted from the outside by legal and social pressures, the abolition society collapsed. The problem, Drinker recognized, lay in slavery's entrenchment in the economic and social life of northern Virginia. "At present," he sadly concluded, "few men" are "unpolluted by this debasing species of property."[18]

In this hostile climate, Friends faced difficult choices. As historian David Brion Davis notes, "in the contest between the internal discipline of the sect and the external discipline of the slave regime," southern Quakers "could only become apostate accommodationists, genuine subversives, or emigrants." Many made the latter choice. Virginia's economic decline after 1820 and the lure of opportunity in the West convinced many whites to leave the state, but Friends overwhelmingly settled in free states and territories north of the Ohio River, their antislavery convictions shaping their emigration decisions. Visiting northern Virginia in 1805, Quaker minister John Parrish noted that even prosperous "friends [were] leaving" and settling in Ohio as a "way of remonstrating against the abomination [of slavery]." "There is much to induce Friends of the Southern States to remove" to Ohio, noted Gerard Hopkins, a Maryland Quaker who traveled to Ohio and Indiana Territory in 1804. The land, he noted, is of "superior quality" and can "be purchased" upon "cheap and easy terms." More important, "this truly valuable country is forbidden ground to the Virginia slave-holders" because the "Constitution of Ohio" prohibits "the introduction of slaves."[19]

As Virginia Friends departed in increasing numbers, entire meetings began to disintegrate. Those who remained felt additional pressures to leave, particularly in the southern portions of the state where the population of Friends dwindled rapidly. Quaker William Walthall of Dinwiddie County remembered that by 1828 his parents found "themselves left alone as members of Friends church in a dense slaveholding community." "Realizing the danger that would attend their effort to rear their children under such circumstances," Walthall's parents "resolved to move to Ohio." Those who remained had little "hope that [the] society [of Friends] will be kept up in this land [Virginia]" as long as slavery survived. In many places the Society did not. In her 1844 visit to Virginia, minister Rebecca Hubbs recounted her meeting with "the widow" of "the late J. Butler." "The widow told me," Hubbs remembered, "that her husband sat in meeting-house alone on First-day before he died, and had frequently done so." Bereft of the social and spiritual intercourse of the meeting, which Quaker minister Samuel Janney described as the "place" Friends could best know the "will and full purpose" of God, Butler had seen his spiritual and social worlds crumble. A similar process took place in the Crooked Run Monthly Meeting, which the Baltimore Yearly Meeting laid down in 1810 after it had lost most of its members to western migration.[20]

Most meetings in northern Virginia did not face such dismal prospects, but the departure of many coreligionists and family members still produced a sense of loss among those who remained. As Ruth Lupton noted in 1836, outmigration had caused "a little revolution" among the Quakers of Apple Pie Ridge in Frederick County. The same year, William Jolliffe, another Hopewell Friend, wrote to a departed family member, "We miss you very much here[;] our meeting Looks Lonesome." Sarah Pidgeon, noting the migration of her son Edward, fretted, "I don't know how we will do without him, or he without us." Friends who remained in Virginia experienced conflicting emotions. Elizabeth Jolliffe, urged by a former neighbor to move to Ohio, had "a strong desire to go" but ultimately declined. Friends, she decided, "are becoming too restless, too fond of novelties to be satisfied long in a place," a mood she believed was "break[ing] in upon the happiness of domestic life." But as migrating Friends and traveling ministers reminded those left behind, the Chesapeake remained "clothed in sable gloom." "The effects of slavery," noted one minister after a journey through the region in 1832, "are felt and . . . seen even in Friends['] families."[21]

Friends believed that slavery sparked both the moral and economic decline of Virginia. Returning to his former Virginia home, Quaker Benjamin Ladd described how his "mind" became "[w]rapped in deep gloom" after passing "6 or 8 black people at work on the road side." The "oppressed" slaves "could not raise their heads from their work to receive my salutation" because over them stood "their oppressor," a white man who stood idly "with his arms proudly folded." For Ladd, the scene encapsulated the linked economic and moral costs of slavery in Virginia. The institution had produced a generation of proud whites who coerced and degraded African Americans and eschewed labor they believed fit only for black people. Virginia had become, Ladd believed, a "miserably impoverished country" as a result. When Friends explained why they left the state, they conflated their wish to escape the moral blight of slavery with their desire for economic improvement. Slavery's ethical consequences, they argued, lay at the root of Virginia's economic decline. As a northern Friend noted during an 1831 visit to the Shenandoah Valley, Virginia displays the "full extent of the baneful effects of slavery"; "all bears the stamp of indifference, listlessness, indolence."[22]

Quakers who remained in the state faced stark choices between accommodation and subversion. Few Virginia Friends became genuine subversives. The Society's early-eighteenth-century embrace of quietism, with its emphasis on introspection and spiritual seeking, led many members to look askance at reform efforts that reached beyond Friends into the broader world. Human vanity rather than divine inspiration inspired such campaigns, naysayers argued, while entangling members in the values and methods of non-Quaker reformers. Many Friends also came to see a conflict between their commitment to the golden rule—extending love and respect even to one's opponents—and the aggressive pursuit of social reform. Although such opposition became more pronounced after 1830, Robert Pleasants encountered resistance from some Friends in 1790 when he joined with Methodists to establish the Virginia Abolition Society.[23]

But the reluctance of some Friends to embrace an agenda of social reform beyond the Society did not make them "apostate accommodationists," as Davis argues. Some Friends, whose social, economic, and cultural commitments to the region outweighed more activist expressions of their faith, fell into this category. The minutes of the monthly meetings provide numerous examples of Friends who failed to uphold the antislavery and pacifist strictures of the Quaker discipline and lost their membership. Even the memoirs of the region's leading Friends—Samuel Janney, Edward Stabler, and Benjamin Hallowell—reveal the embrace of conservative tactics, while articulating radical implications of Quaker principles.[24] But the label "accommodationist" fails to recognize the depth of Friends' commitment to social change, and the various economic, cultural, and social pressures that circumscribed their activism. Nor does it admit the moral complexity of the choices facing southern Friends. Leaving Virginia enabled individuals to escape the moral taint of slavery, but once gone they could provide little direct aid to African Americans—both free and enslaved—who could not leave. Nor did their removal do anything to undermine the institution. Indeed, the departure of so many slavery opponents enabled white Virginians to strengthen the region's racial orthodoxy. Friends who remained, however, risked complicity in slavery and white racism—and many succumbed to the threat—but they also worked to ameliorate the lives of local African Americans and undermine slavery. Their lack of success speaks not to local Friends' moral commitment but to the entrenched nature of slavery, even in a region with a relatively small enslaved population.

The lives and decisions of individual Friends, particularly the merchants and farmers who became enmeshed in the commercial economy of northern Virginia and found neither withdrawal nor revolution viable options, reveal the problems facing the Society. Merchant William Hartshorne worked hard to mediate these two worlds, and at first glance his economic and political activities did not seem to undermine his spiritual commitments. Although in 1779 the Fairfax Monthly Meeting had queried Hartshorne for taking a loyalty oath to the state of Virginia, it restored him to full membership in 1783. Over the next twenty years, his stature within the Fairfax meeting rose and in 1802 he helped found the Alexandria Monthly Meeting, remaining a member until his death in 1816. Hartshorne led local Friends' campaign against slavery, helping to establish Alexandria's first antislavery society. In his correspondence with non-Quakers, he followed Society orthodoxy, refusing to name the days of the week and using *ye, thy,* and *thee.* As a prominent Quaker merchant, Hartshorne acquired a reputation for honesty and fair dealing. When London merchant Samuel Thorp sought an Alexandria contact, planter William Lee recommended Hartshorne, describing him as "a sharp[,] keen quaker merchant . . . who can be trusted with safety."[25]

But Hartshorne's business activities entangled him in the region's slave economy. As a merchant whose success depended on northern Virginia farmers sending their slave-raised produce to Alexandria, Hartshorne—and other local Quaker merchants—played an important role in developing the regional transportation infrastructure. In his investments in the Potomac River and Little River Turnpike companies, Hartshorne emulated Quaker entrepreneurs throughout North America and Great Britain. But in the South such firms employed slave labor. In 1785, after attempting to use white indentured servants to clear the river, the Potomac Company's directors decided to hire black slaves. Between 1786 and 1803, the company hired between a hundred and two hundred enslaved people per year. "The labour of the Potomack Company," concluded company director Thomas Johnson, "is best performed by Negroe Slaves" because overseers could exercise more control over them than "common white Hirelings" and their "services" could be "depended on in all seasons of the year." Hartshorne did not record his reaction to this decision, but he neither resigned his position as company treasurer nor sold his stock—nor did other Quaker investors. Hartshorne's investment in the Little River Turnpike Company, incorporated to build a road from Alexandria west into Loudoun County, also entangled him in the slave economy. In 1803, the company's first contractor promised "good usage to, and punctual payment for" hired slaves to build the road, a practice it continued over the next decade.[26]

Hartshorne's involvement in the Alexandria Marine Insurance Company, chartered in 1797, reveals most fully his ethical compromises. Established in response to British and French depredations on American shipping during the Napoleonic wars, the company provided insurance for Alexandria shippers and merchants who could not access their usual British or American sources. Hartshorne presided over the thriving Alexandria firm, which insured over two hundred vessels a year, including an 1809 policy for a ship carrying thirty slaves from Alexandria to New Orleans. Insured for nine thousand dollars, the slave cargo was part of the growing domestic slave trade in the early nineteenth century. Local Friends lamented the commerce in slaves centered in the District of Columbia. Five years earlier, Hartshorne's fellow Quaker and neighbor George Drinker described Friends' "shock'd" feelings when they witnessed coffles of slaves "purchased . . . here and in the State of Maryland" by "Slave dealers from the Carolinas." Still, Hartshorne signed his name to the policy, choosing worldly concerns over moral scruples.[27]

The year Hartshorne signed the policy, he faced a financial crisis. Buffeted by the volatility of the overseas grain trade, a flood and a fire that destroyed his livestock and mill, and Jefferson's embargo, which closed the port of Alexandria to overseas trade, Hartshorne struggled to keep his mercantile firm afloat. A few months later, the Alexandria meeting investigated his business dealings for improprieties, and his creditors forced him to liquidate his personal assets. The meeting ultimately acquitted Hartshorne of wrongdoing, but for the next seven years he disappeared—aside from the investigation of his business affairs—from the minutes of the meeting in which he had once figured prominently. During the same years, he supported a large family of three daughters and four sons. His youngest daughter, Sarah, did not marry until 1811 (to local merchant Phineas Janney), and his youngest sons, Pattison and Peter, remained at home until 1809 and 1814, when they moved to New York City and Baltimore respectively. The need to provide for his family shaped Hartshorne's decision to remain president of the firm, though doing so enmeshed him in slavery. It must have come as a relief when in 1810 the company's directors forced him to step down because of his financial problems.[28]

Hartshorne's experience and the story of Alexandria's first antislavery society reveal the pressures faced by Friends who remained in northern Virginia and spoke out against slavery. Quietism discouraged many Friends from participating in reform beyond the Society, but the responsibilities of supporting and establishing children often pushed activists such as Hartshorne to compromise their spiritual values. Slavery's integration into the economy and society of northern Virginia made it difficult for Friends invested in the prosperity and economic development of the region to avoid moral vacillation. Eighteenth-century Quaker reformers had recognized that wealth could undermine Friends' purity and distract them from following the inward light. For northern Virginia's Friends, the experience of individuals like Hartshorne provided a pointed lesson in how members could lose their spiritual path in a slave society. Friends' involvement in the local economy earned them toleration and even respect, but it also increased their vulnerability. Even during periods of calm white Virginians pressured them to conform to the society's values and behavior. When slaveholders saw their social order under siege, they used their political, legal, and economic power to silence Quaker activists whom they believed posed a threat to slavery. Friends' antislavery ideals survived, but for over a decade after Gabriel's conspiracy they made few public expressions of their concern. Largely silenced by the coercive slave regime established after the conspiracy and the repression of the War of 1812, Friends hesitated to act on behalf of enslaved people. Only after the war ended in 1815, and white Virginians felt a renewed sense of security, did local Friends revive their antislavery efforts.

II

William Hartshorne led the charge, inspired as much by his personal failings as by the collective faults of the local Quaker community. In April 1816, with his business concerns liquidated to pay his debts and his children all married or independent, he revived his Quaker ethical concerns, focusing on the antislavery testimony. He was not alone. After 1815, Friends throughout the region renewed their concern for the region's enslaved and free African Americans. They established new antislavery societies and spearheaded petition and education campaigns to aid free blacks, close the slave trade, and ultimately end slavery.

In early 1816, the Alexandria Monthly Meeting appointed Hartshore to a committee to investigate local Friends' adherence to the Society's testimonies on the subjects of slavery, liquor, and education. Despite his near disownment in 1810, the meeting began to entrust Hartshorne with committee responsibilities in 1814 and he soon regained his former prominence. His membership on a committee dealing with disciplinary matters reflected his restored status. The committee noted that the discipline "prohibits friends" from owning and "hiring slaves," adding that it had found no members guilty of either infraction. However, the committee argued, Friends needed to do more. "An application of the same principle renders it desireable" that when Friends "are dependent upon others for the execution of our lawful Business we should give the preference to those who . . . perform the work by free men rather than . . . employ those who . . . use the labor of slaves." Five years after the prominent New York Quaker minister Elias Hicks had published his call for Friends to boycott goods produced by slave labor, Hartshorne and his committee urged Alexandria's Quakers to separate from the larger community in which they lived. With his long public and mercantile career and consequent multiple entanglements with slavery, Hartshorne recognized the difficulty of what he proposed. Still, he exhorted Friends to take a firm stand.[29]

Hartshorne died weeks later. But local Quakers took up the cause he championed in his final months. The free produce injunctions of Quaker leaders, designed to distance Friends from the institution of slavery, helped revive the Society's antislavery campaign. Friends also responded to demographic changes in the region's African American community and the growth of the interstate slave trade. In northern Virginia as throughout the Upper South, Revolutionary and evangelical idealism prompted some slaveholders to emancipate their human property. The concurrent economic shift in the region from tobacco to less labor-intensive grain farming provided an additional incentive for whites to reduce their slaveholding, either through manumission or sale to the Deep South where westward expansion and rising cotton production sparked demand for slave labor. These changes fueled the domestic slave trade based in the cities of Alexandria, Washington, and Baltimore.[30]

Residents of Alexandria experienced these changes most fully, but they impacted all of northern Virginia. Between 1800 and 1850, Alexandria's free black population grew from 6 percent to 14 percent of the total population (from 369 to 1,409), while the enslaved population fell from 20 to 14 percent (875 to 1,382). Fairfax County followed a similar pattern; the enslaved population fell (from 46 to over 30 percent) while the free black population rose from 2 to almost 6 percent. Less dramatic changes took place farther west, but population figures followed the same trend. In Loudoun County, the free black population rose from under 2 percent (333 persons) in 1800 to over 6 percent (1,357 persons) in 1850, while the enslaved population remained steady at between 24 and 26 percent. In Frederick County in the Shenandoah Valley, the enslaved population rose slightly (from 23 to 25 percent), while the free black community more than doubled from under 2 to over 4 percent (from 453 to over 1,000 persons). This rise took place despite an 1806 state law that required manumitted African Americans to leave Virginia within a year. Attempts by the town of Alexandria to control its free black population, including an 1809 ordinance forcing all free African Americans to pay a bond of fifty dollars to ensure their good behavior and have a white resident testify on their behalf, proved ineffective. The measure also prompted a protest from Quaker town councilmen Aaron Hewes and Thomas Shreve, who declared the measure "oppressive, partial" and "*inconsistent* with the spirit of Christianity." Neither man served again on the town council.[31]

Non-Quakers had few qualms about state efforts to control free African Americans. The rising free black population worried most whites. They decided that maintaining Virginia's racial hierarchy required, as historian Eva Sheppard Wolf argues, that race rather than legal status define the social position of free African Americans. But many white Virginians feared these racial laws could not control a dangerous free black population, and they looked for additional solutions. Many concluded that colonization—the removal of free blacks to Africa or the West Indies—provided the best remedy. The Virginia legislature embraced the idea in 1816, resolving that the governor should seek federal aid to obtain "a territory upon the coast of Africa . . . to serve as an asylum for free persons of color." A year later, Charles Fenton Mercer, Loudoun County's congressional representative, helped found the American Colonization Society (ACS). Local chapters appeared in Alexandria, and in Fairfax, Loudoun, and Jefferson counties. Slaveholders dominated the leadership of these groups, but they also attracted a few Quakers. The Loudoun County chapter counted Friends Israel Janney, Mahlon Taylor, Isaac Brown, and Jacob Mendenhall among its officers. For them, colonization was a "benevolent work" that would enable free blacks to escape a repressive environment and bring Christianity and republican government to Africa. They also believed the plan would hasten "a safe, voluntary, and beneficial emancipation" of the South's enslaved population.[32]

However, most colonization supporters did not share such lofty ambitions. As the Loudoun County critic "Cassius" remarked in 1819, employing colonization to end slavery was a "visionary project." He argued that the costs of "vomiting upon the deserts of Africa two millions of our fellow creatures" would "far exceed" "ten millions [of dollars] per annum." Such expenses, Cassius asserted, revealed "the fallacy and impracticability of the scheme." He called on the county's magistrates to enforce state laws against "the oppressors of this degraded race," and on local Friends to "conquer" their "prejudices" and abandon their support for colonization. Only then would "the grand object," the end of slavery, "be accomplished." The constitution of the Alexandria chapter, echoing the national organization, confirmed Cassius's views, stressing that the society would "be exclusively directed" to peopling "the coast of Africa" with "the free people of color of the U.S." This type of colonization aimed, as abolitionist William Lloyd Garrison later charged, to protect the institution of slavery by removing a population that blurred the lines between slavery and freedom.[33]

Although Friends shared much of the racism of their white neighbors, they sincerely wanted to see slavery end. And the slave trade, which centered in northern Virginia and Maryland and often involved many of the same slaveholders who supported the ACS, offended them. Friends found particularly troubling the news that the first president of the national ACS, Bushrod Washington, had sold fifty-four "unhappy wretches" as part of a hundred-person slave coffle marched through Loudoun County in August 1821. Washington's defense of his actions—he argued he had both a "*legal* and *moral*" right to sell this "species of property"—increased Friends' consternation. Nor did they find convincing his claim that he had taken every step "to avoid the separation of families" but still had sold "three or four" married women and the parents of "five young women." Friends convinced of slavery's economic unfeasibility saw in Washington's account ample evidence to support their views. Washington claimed that he lost five hundred to one thousand dollars per year because his insubordinate slaves regularly tried to "escape . . . to the northern states." Quaker journalist Benjamin Lundy considered Washington's explanation an admission of the inefficiency "of slavery in the grain growing states" and "a most sorry excuse for so glaring an act of inconsistency."[34]

Throughout the 1820s, Lundy used the pages of his *Genius of Universal Emancipation* to attack slaveholders who embraced colonization to remove free blacks and subvert the scheme's antislavery potential. Local Friends constituted one of the most dependable audiences for Lundy's paper, which he began as a monthly in Mount Pleasant, Ohio (the destination of many western-bound northern Virginia Friends), and moved to Baltimore in late 1824. They read with concern Lundy's critique of slaveholding colonizationists—including national leaders Henry Clay, John Randolph, and Washington—whom the paper condemned "as *rank advocates of slavery*." Lundy also reported on the local slave trade, noting in July 1825 that "a traveller" near Winchester passed "five droves, or 'coffles,'" consisting of about three hundred and fifty enslaved people in all, "going to Alabama." In one of the coffles, he noted, "*twenty-four men were chained together!* Comment is useless." This "abominable 'trade,'" Lundy concluded, "is identically the same thing in principle, between America and Africa, and between Baltimore and New Orleans." Lundy's "Black List" provided a steady stream of reports about the abuse of enslaved people and the kidnapping of free African Americans by slaveholders and traders. As Lundy noted in 1826, "not a week passes without unfolding . . . the accursed practices of the heaven-daring kidnappers, and . . . the lawless, *piratical*, slaving gentry."[35]

In the summer of 1824, while traveling from Tennessee to Baltimore, Lundy held a series of antislavery lectures in Quaker communities in North Carolina and Virginia. The talks, Lundy reported, were "attended by many persons, besides members of the Society of Friends," and often prompted locals to found "anti-slavery" societies. In northern Virginia, Lundy's visit convinced about twenty Goose Creek Quakers, led by Yardley Taylor, to establish the Loudoun Manumission and Emigration Society. Like many such organizations formed in the 1820s, the Loudoun society supported voluntary colonization of free blacks, but unlike slaveholding proponents of black emigration members of the Loudoun society wanted to end slavery. According to its constitution, the society sought "to expose the evils which result from the existence of African slavery . . . in order to effect its gradual abolition," and—as Lundy began suggesting in October 1824—to "aid and encourage . . . the emigration of our colored population to Hayti." In its first public statement, the Loudoun society praised David Minge for the "philanthropic act" of "liberating and transporting his slaves to Hayti," linking the far-reaching goal of ending slavery to the conservative tactic of colonization.[36]

A month later, the society addressed the public more fully, touting, like most of the era's white antislavery advocates, conservative arguments in opposition to slavery. Signed by Yardley and Henry S. Taylor, the society's Quaker president and treasurer, the address emphasized the adverse impact of slavery on the white population. Embracing a labor theory of value, the Taylors asserted that "Labour is the great promoter of national wealth." Slavery, in contrast, "nourish[ed] indolence" and "discourage[d] industry" among both whites and blacks, constituting "a great and important obstruction . . . in the advancement" of national prosperity. Equally disturbing, the rapid growth of the slave population threatened to "endanger the future . . . security of our country." The address reminded readers that "liberty is the natural right of mankind" and "any restraint upon it . . . must in the course of time be removed" by peaceful measures or "the exercise of force." The address acknowledged that "the difference in colour" made it difficult to assimilate African Americans into white society, but the Taylors believed that enslavement forged the greatest obstacle to black equality. Slavery, the address added, had a "debasing influence . . . upon the one class" and created among whites an "arrogant and presum[p]tuous consciousness of superiority." The Taylors recognized that the country lacked the resources to remove "the entire black population of the U. States to Africa," but proposed as an alternative the "island of St. Domingo," which possessed productive soils and a republican government that welcomed former American slaves.[37]

Such conservative arguments, addressed to a white and slaveholding audience, followed the tack of most Upper South colonizationists. The address also adopted a tactic employed by Quakers since the Revolutionary era: grounding critiques of slavery in American political ideals. Slavery, the Taylors insisted, was "inconsistent with the principles of a republican government . . . that all men are created equal." Unlike most white Americans, the Taylors refused to make racial exceptions to the tenet of political equality. "However varied in colour, or intellectual endowments; however different in their habits, customs, or pursuits," the address asserted, "all are equally entitled to the enjoyment of . . . life, liberty, and the pursuit of happiness." The appeal also adopted a strident moral tone, condemning slavery as an institution "so dangerous in its consequences, and so incompatible with every principle of moral right," that it "demands the immediate exercise of those means we are possessed of, in effecting its final extinction." "What greater evil" did the nation face, the Taylors asked their readers, "than that which consigns near two millions of human beings, of an innocent and unoffending race, to the most degrading slavery—and subjects them to all the horrors of the most intolerable servitude?" Slavery, the address concluded, "is a pernicious and dangerous evil" that "cannot be justified."[38]

The expansive rhetoric, however, failed to obscure the cautious means to end slavery proposed by the Loudoun manumission society. The address captured the central dilemma faced by activist Friends in the early national and antebellum South: despite a willingness to envision fundamental social change, including legal equality for African Americans, they eschewed tactics that could produce such change and resorted instead to black emigration. They faced, of course, many obstacles to proposals beyond colonization. Slavery was deeply entrenched in the economic, legal, and political structure of the southern states, and in the first decades of the nineteenth century, Virginians embraced racialist assumptions to justify the institution. Still, Friends failed to follow the logic of their moral language to more radical conclusions, as an 1828 address by the Goose Creek society revealed. Although members of the society stressed the "evil" of slavery and its "pernicious" economic, political, and moral impacts, they would go no further than proposing slavery's "*gradual* abolition" and "the removal of our black population." Friends "lament[ed] the existence of Slavery" and "deplore[d] the consequences resulting from its continuance," but they refused to do more than issue appeals to convince "the public mind" that ending slavery would benefit the moral, economic, and political welfare of white Virginians.[39] The Quaker principle that drove Friends' social activism—the belief that all people, slaveholders and slaves alike, possessed an inward light—restrained them from more radical endeavors that might enflame slaveholders or provoke violence.

Public opinion also checked Friends. Even in the 1820s Friends faced a repressive social and legal environment, particularly in localities populated by slaveholders. In Jefferson County in the lower Shenandoah Valley, where the enslaved population constituted about 30 percent of the county's residents throughout the antebellum era, slaveholders repressed attempts to form an antislavery society in Smithfield. Inspired by the creation of a similar group in nearby Brucetown, a few Smithfield Methodists and Quakers invited Stephen Whittlesey, a Methodist cofounder of the Brucetown group, to deliver an antislavery address in June 1827. The "slavite magistrates" of the county confronted him and his local supporters at the door of the meeting house where he was scheduled to speak. "No such thing would be allowed as the formation of an Abolition Society, or the delivery of a discourse on such subject," the magistrates announced, and they threatened to arrest anyone who went forward with the meeting. Later, when Isaac Smith "a venerable preacher of the society of Friends" tried to speak in the meeting house the magistrates "broke in upon him" and "broke up the meeting." The magistrates' action demonstrated for Friends the dangers slavery posed to republican freedom and the "rank inconsistency of those who . . . are contaminated by the exercise of despotic rule!" "Liberty of speech is abridged in Virginia," a local resident concluded, and the actions of local officials "must remain an eternal blot upon our records."[40]

Such censorship was rare in the 1820s, and northern Virginia's Quakers enjoyed a relatively open political and legal environment. Many followed the lead of Goose Creek and Brucetown Friends and formed their own independent antislavery societies, a development Lundy reported excitedly. In 1824, he asserted "that the opponents of slavery are fast increasing in the south," noting the existence of forty antislavery societies in Kentucky, Tennessee, North Carolina, Delaware, and "one or two" in Virginia. By 1827, these numbers had grown to over 106 antislavery societies in the Upper South (out of 130 in the nation), including nine societies with over three hundred members in Virginia and the District of Columbia. That year, following the call of the Goose Creek society for "*an union of exertion,*" seven northern Virginia societies met in Loudoun County and adopted a "Constitution of the Virginia Convention for the Abolition of Slavery." Overwhelmingly attended by Friends, the convention appealed for an end to the "tyrannical" interstate slave trade, the gradual "extinction of slavery," and voluntary colonization of free and enslaved African Americans to Africa or Haiti. How to achieve these goals remained a more difficult matter. Despite its endorsement of colonization, the convention distanced itself from the ACS, eschewing "any direct or immediate connexion with that Society" until it "extended" its policies "to manumitted slaves." The convention instead called for a boycott of slave-produced products, support of "such candidates for public offices as are friendly to our views," and—the centerpiece of their effort—an extended educational campaign designed to convince white Virginians "of the impolicy and injustice of" slavery.[41]

The convention also sought to aid the state's free black population, calling for the removal of "legal . . . obstacles" to black education. It argued for the repeal of an 1827 state law obligating local grand juries to enforce the 1806 removal statute that enjoined manumitted African Americans to leave the state within a year or face re-enslavement. The antislavery agenda promulgated by convention delegates envisioned far-reaching political and social change, but relying on educational campaigns and established political avenues to improve the lives of blacks and appeals to the conscience of whites robbed Friends of political leverage. Recognizing the limitations of moral suasion, convention attendees embraced free produce, but slavery's entrenchment in the nation's political economy reduced the effectiveness of this option. Few Friends contemplated more radical measures, for both religious and tactical reasons. Enflaming the slaveholding and broader white population, they believed, would make their position within Virginia untenable and ensure that they went unheeded. The convention concluded that change "can only be brought about by the active and zealous promulgation of truth, communicated with courtesy of style and suavity of manner." As inadequate as such a measured response to the outrages of chattel slavery appeared to a few northern contemporaries and some subsequent historians, southern Friends believed they could go no further.[42]

The convention met again in 1828 at Winchester, though the representatives of only four local societies attended. Its address to the people of Virginia pointed to the state's relative economic decline to highlight the "pernicious" impact of slavery. The institution, the address declared, inhibited capital accumulation and population growth, undermined the value of labor and the "character" of the white population, and drove "the intermediate class which lies between the extremes of poverty and wealth" to the "free states" where they are "appreciated and their character properly respected." Slavery also "excite[d] sectional animosity" between the northern and southern states, and if allowed to fester would "weaken the bonds of the national confederation." In good Quaker fashion, however, the address asserted that any solution to the problem of slavery had to look "equally to the interest of the slave holder and the welfare of the slave." It called upon Virginia's legislators to write a new state constitution that emancipated "all slaves born after a certain date . . . upon reaching a certain age." The plan freed only the progeny of enslaved people, ensuring a "gradual" end to slavery that respected the existing rights of slaveholders. The convention also encouraged the voluntary colonization of the state's slaves. Only with the removal of the state's enslaved population, "the evil of which," the address concluded, "is almost incalculable," could Virginia enjoy "the activity of freemen" and end its economic decline.[43]

While the 1828 address still condemned slavery in strong moral terms, the convention had nonetheless issued a moderate document that appealed to white economic interests and imperiled only the future property rights of slaveholders. Members believed that they should "promote the [antislavery] cause . . . in a fair and legal manner," but this approach still angered slaveholders and created economic and political difficulties. The small Winchester society needed financial assistance from the Virginia convention after it incurred legal debts of sixty dollars while recovering Rebecca, "a colored person, entitled to her freedom," who was "kidnapped" and "sold to a southern trader." The convention's approach also alienated at least one local group, the Abolition Society of Waterford, which pulled out of the convention because it supported colonization to remove manumitted slaves rather than free blacks. Financially prostrated and facing opposition even for moderate proposals, the Virginia Abolition Convention, despite plans to gather at Goose Creek in 1829, never met again.[44]

The history of the Benevolent Society for Ameliorating and Improving the Condition of People of Color, formed in Alexandria with the assistance of Benjamin Lundy in 1827, reveals the internal and external tensions that bedeviled Quaker antislavery efforts in northern Virginia. Although dominated by Friends, the nineteen members elected a non-Quaker, Thomas Jacobs, to the presidency. The group espoused conservative goals to appeal to proslavery inhabitants of Alexandria, which Lundy described as "the very hot-bed of the Slave-factionists in the District of Columbia." "The object of the society," Quaker educator Benjamin Hallowell later noted, "was not to interfere with slavery, but to secure to the slaves their legal rights." Like the Winchester society, members of the Alexandria association offered aid to free blacks and enslaved people with legal claims to freedom that slaveholders and traders refused to recognize. Hallowell described the case of a family of thirteen Virginia slaves whose owner promised to free them at his death, but who in the meantime hired them out in Maryland. According to state law, Hallowell explained, slaves willed to be freed but hired across state lines "were *at once* entitled to their freedom." Informed of the case by Francis Scott Key, Hallowell traveled to Maryland and secured the family's liberation. In March 1828, the Alexandria society reported that it had "wrested from the grasp of the slave traders twelve people of color who have petitioned for their freedom." In 1827, the society also established a First Day school for black children, reviving the Quaker school that slaveholders had closed in 1801. By March 1828, 185 students attended the school, "one-third" of whom could read "and some remarkably well."[45]

Some members of the society believed that such limited goals did not go far enough. As Hallowell remembered, the organization "met every month (and it was a *live* society)." Among the more active members was the young Quaker merchant Samuel Janney, who believed the society should spread to "our fellow citizens more just views on the subject of slavery." In 1827, he wrote the unsigned articles in the *Alexandria Gazette* that called for the gradual abolition of slavery and stressed the adverse economic consequences of the institution. Years later, Janney recalled that he always favored "immediate and unconditional emancipation," but "knowing the prejudice against it in the minds of the people, I only asked for gradual emancipation" and the voluntary colonization of emancipated slaves. He believed that this "judicious course," backed by economic and political arguments drawn from learned and respected authorities, would appeal to rational and "patriotic" slaveholders concerned with advancing "their *present interests*," "the prosperity of their descendents," and "the community at large." Janney recognized the shortcomings of this "delicate" approach. He acknowledged that many slaveholders saw the ACS as a way to remove what they considered a dangerous free black population. But he argued that the "*effect*" of colonization would "prove beneficial to our country" by forcing discussions that encouraged "slaveholders to reflect upon the evils of slavery." He assumed "a general emancipation" would not happen without colonization because white southerners refused to let liberated slaves "remain among us." Like Quakers throughout the Upper South, Janney embraced conservative tactics he hoped would ensure a hearing among the region's slaveholders.[46]

Still, Janney's articles included a series of radical proposals that rejected notions of black inferiority and envisioned a racially egalitarian future in which black and white people lived together in peace. Moreover, as the series continued he employed moral language that castigated those who supported slavery and the slave trade and refused to consider its end. Janney believed the federal government, with its power to regulate interstate trade and legislate for the District of Columbia, possessed the authority to end the "iniquitous" and "inhuman" trade within D.C. and the nation. Congress's refusal to end the trade in the district, he believed, "poisoned" the "fountain from which the laws of freedom and equal rights are expected to flow." The slave trade, so "stained with human blood," exposed to public view the worst "cruelties" of the slave system. Janney argued that ending the "detestable traffic" would deny local slaveholders possessed of "a large number of slaves on poor land" income from "the sale of young" slaves to the Deep South. "Cut off" from "this source of profit," local slaveholders "would have to contend alone against the superior economy of free labor" and slavery would soon "be relinquished in this part of the Union." On this issue, Janney believed he could garner broad support, and the following year he composed and helped circulate a petition to Congress calling for the abolition of the slave trade and the gradual end of slavery in the District. Janney succeeded in obtaining the signatures of over one thousand district residents, including merchants, all the judges, most of the ministers, and at least twenty-six local Friends. Congress took no action; as Hallowell noted dryly years later, "the prayer it contained was not granted."[47]

More far reaching, Janney abandoned the assumptions of his age and argued for the ability of African Americans, with the proper education and training, to thrive as free people. Four of Janney's articles included brief histories, culled from the work of British antislavery activist Thomas Clarkson, of emancipated people in South America, Nova Scotia, Trinidad, Sierra Leone, and Liberia, along with an account of the efforts of Barbados slaveholder Joshua Steele who transformed his slaves into wage laborers. Janney hoped that evidence of peaceful and successful emancipation—in contrast to the widely publicized violence that accompanied the end of slavery in Santo Domingo—would convince his readers (especially liberal-minded slaveholders) that the condition of slaves in America resulted not from "the natural character of the African," but reflected "the *condition* in which he is placed." "The blame" for black "degradation," Janney argued, "attaches to those of our own nation who have reduced him [the slave] . . . to be the mere creature of another's will." Likewise, Janney lauded the efforts of local slaveholder William H. Fitzhugh, who like Quaker Robert Pleasants some forty years earlier had "settled two families of his slaves on small farms attached" to his estate, which they cultivated "as tenants." For Janney, the examples of Steele and Fitzhugh proved the Quaker axiom "that our true interest is promoted by doing 'unto *all men*, as we would that they should do unto us.'"[48]

Janney's newspaper series and the petition, despite their racially progressive notions and inclusion of "expressions so plain that they would be considered harsh," also reveal the limitations of Quaker racial benevolence. Janney remained ambiguous about where educated and emancipated African Americans would live. In his descriptions of profitable free black labor he implied that emancipated slaves could remain in America, but he accommodated white racism and the concerns of slaveholders by portraying black education as a prelude to colonization. Such tactics might have made Janney's proposals palatable to liberal slaveholders, but they undercut the moral clarity of his attack on slavery. So, too, did his decision to adopt a respectful tone, or what he later called "the meek, lamb-like spirit of Christ," in all his public communications. Janney, like most antislavery Quakers, refused to condemn the morality of slavery's defenders—except slave traders—believing that doing so increased their intransigence. His rhetorical restraint grew out of Friends' spiritual principles. Convinced that all people possessed a spark of divinity—an inward light—that could lead them to truth, Friends like Janney rejected censorious language and instead employed arguments and developed tactics designed to prick the conscience and sway the reason of slaveholders. The Quaker belief in the spiritual equality of all people mandated that activists treat friends and enemies with respect. As Janney explained in 1846, "if our love extends to all men it must embrace the oppressor as well as the oppressed"; "it is not the slaveholder . . . we assail but the system of slavery."[49]

In the late 1820s this conciliatory approach seemed promising to Friends and their antislavery allies in the Upper South, and they celebrated the progress of their cause. But the new decade dimmed their optimism. In January 1831, William Lloyd Garrison (Benjamin Lundy's former partner) began publishing *The Liberator* in Boston. Garrison called for an immediate end to slavery and condemned those who compromised with slaveholders. Eight months later, Nat Turner, a Southampton County, Virginia, enslaved preacher who claimed divine inspiration, recruited sixty fellow slaves and killed more than sixty slaveholders and their families. In retaliation, local whites launched a wave of violence that resulted in the murder and execution of over one hundred black people. Turner's revolt sparked a wide-ranging public debate over the future of slavery in Virginia. Many white Virginians, frightened by the growing black population, criticized slavery and called for its end. In the winter of 1831–32, the Virginia legislature received more than twenty petitions in response to the Southampton revolt, including nine that asked for gradual emancipation. Slaveholders in Loudoun County, worried about slavery's economic impact and the "apprehension and unquietude" that slave labor engendered in the "bosoms of those who employ it," called for "the *ultimate extinction of* involuntary servitude and the removal of a race irreconcilably antagonistic to ours."[50]

For local Friends, this response was encouraging, even if they did not share its racism. In December 1831, the Virginia Yearly Meeting petitioned the state assembly. "Our present difficulties and dangers," the petition asserted, "originated in a departure from the Laws of justice and humanity which the Creator has fixed for the government of his rational creatures." "The abolition of Slavery in this Commonwealth and the restoration of the African race to the inalienable rights of man," Virginia Friends argued, would reinstate "the laws of God" and serve "the best interests of" the state. They proposed that the legislature free all slaves born after a certain date, and that the state, aided by the federal government, "provide some territory" where manumitted slaves and free blacks could settle. Proslavery representatives tried to suppress the petition, but their efforts backfired when some members objected to such blatant censorship. Seizing the moment, slaveholder Thomas Jefferson Randolph presented a plan for ending slavery in the state. For a little over two weeks in January 1832 the assembly debated Randolph's motion, but in the end it voted, by a margin of sixty-five to fifty-eight, "that it is inexpedient for the present, to make any legislative enactments for the abolition of slavery." Over the next two years, the assembly passed statutes to strengthen slavery by removing free blacks from the state, suppressing African American religious meetings and preachers, and further restricting the rights of free blacks. In the wake of the 1832 debate, white Virginians concluded that free blacks, not slavery, provoked the unrest in Southampton and they clamped down on that population.[51]

The suppression of free and enslaved blacks soon extended to their white allies. In Alexandria, the Benevolent Society collapsed in the face of the white proslavery consensus. In the changed political environment of the early 1830s, Benjamin Hallowell recalled, Friends thought it "most prudent to suspend the meetings [of the society], and they were never resumed." In Loudoun, as John Janney later remembered, "dread overspread the country" and "slaveholding neighborhoods" organized heavily armed patrols. Janney believed them "really more dangerous than the slaves," but the show of force stifled antislavery voices. So did the decision of local newspapers to turn on Benjamin Lundy's *Genius of Universal Emancipation*. In Loudoun, the *Genius of Liberty*, which in the past had reported the activities of the local antislavery society, denounced the antislavery paper as an "incendiary publication." The statement had a chilling impact on local Friends, who distributed, read, and reprinted their views in Lundy's newspaper. Likewise, the *Alexandria Gazette*, which in 1827 had published Janney's antislavery essays without comment, now charged that Lundy and his paper had "obtained an infamous notoriety." The events of the early 1830s led most white Virginians to concur with their federal senator and congressman, John Randolph of Roanoke, who equated southern Quakers with the most zealous abolitionists of the North. "On this subject of negro slavery," Randolph declared, "I would as soon trust the Quakers . . . as any other fanatics," for "fanatics, like mad men, are on a par." Randolph concluded, "I never will suffer him [the abolitionist] to put a torch to my property that he may stake it in the blood of all that are dear to me."[52]

As they had during previous military and racial crises, white Virginians vilified their Quaker neighbors for questioning the social institutions of the state. Lundy encouraged Friends in the Upper South to "continue their efforts" to end slavery, arguing that the Southampton violence furnished "the strongest proof of the necessity of speedily putting an end to the system of oppression." As late as 1839 he "hoped that the germs of Abolitionism (though buried deep in the rubbish of apathy and self-interest) are far from being extinguished in Virginia." But few listened. "Our friends" in the Upper South, he concluded, "have evinced a disposition to let the subject rest" and their antislavery societies, begun so optimistically in the 1820s, fell "into disuse." By the mid-1830s, Lundy had stopped printing the names of his paper's Virginia-based Quaker agents, and in 1836, to ensure that no one again had the temerity to distribute similar works, the Virginia assembly passed an act "to suppress the circulation of incendiary publications." The legislation prescribed two to five years in jail for white persons "writing or circulating" tracts encouraging slaves to rebel "or denying the right of masters to property in their slaves," and jail time for anyone who subscribed to such publications. After concluding that they must protect slavery, white Virginians decided to silence all antislavery voices within the state.[53]

Turner's revolt and the rise of radical abolitionism in the North fueled a conservative backlash in defense of slavery that for a time silenced the antislavery dissent of northern Virginia's Friends, though it did not end their private efforts to aid the region's free and enslaved African Americans. Friends' attempts to find a moderate antislavery path before 1830, one that could provide justice for enslaved and free African Americans without alienating the region's slaveholders or provoking a violent reaction, had failed. Their efforts revealed the growing fault lines between white Virginians and the Quaker community. Despite the respect Friends garnered for their civic concerns and economic endeavors, their opposition to slavery set them apart. Some Quakers responded to the pressures of living in a slave society by leaving the state. As Quaker minister Benjamin Ladd noted in the early 1830s, "the bloody scene which has recently occurred in Va" will "hasten . . . Friends' migration from thence."[54] A little more than a decade later, the departure of southern Virginia's Quakers forced the few who remained to terminate their depleted yearly meeting. Many Friends in northern Virginia also left the state, but the community, clustered together in a few hamlets and neighborhoods, remained large enough to sustain its religious identity and coherence. In the face of external pressure, many of the region's Friends redirected their spiritual concerns into reforms more acceptable to the broader white society. Others turned their attention to the wellbeing of their families and religious community, which after the 1820s endured a variety of internal stresses sparked by outmigration and theological conflict. Friends did not abandon their opposition to slavery, but for those who remained in the South a public retreat in the face of external pressure and internal turmoil seemed the only viable option.

5

Internal Revolutions

The Hicksite Schism and Its Consequences

In February 1837, a visiting Quaker minister styling himself "a poor illiterate mechanic" rose in the Goose Creek Meeting House and delivered an impassioned sermon about "the present unsettled state of the Society of Friends." Ten years earlier, the Philadelphia Yearly Meeting had bitterly divided on doctrinal grounds into evangelical or "Orthodox" and "Hicksite" factions, sparking a separation in which both sides claimed to uphold Friends' ancient principles. The split soon spread to the New York, Indiana, and Ohio Yearly Meetings, becoming particularly acrimonious in the latter. In 1828, the division spread to the smaller Baltimore Yearly Meeting, to which northern Virginia's Friends belonged. Here the separation took place with relative calm because Hicksites predominated. Still, the separation left the meeting—and its constituent quarterly and monthly meetings—weakened and Friends dismayed that the Society had abandoned its quiet ways. The "mechanic" expressed the pain caused by the separation, but he also searched for explanations and solutions. The speaker was Edward Hicks, painter of multiple versions of *The Peaceable Kingdom* and cousin of Elias Hicks, the minister some blamed for the division. Employing the imagery of his paintings, Edward hoped his sermon would guide Friends' return to a peaceable state.[1]

The "Friends and friendly people" who gathered together represented, Hicks believed, "an epitome of the great family of mankind." This he divided into "four classes": "melancholy, sanguine, phlegmatic and choleric," or as in his versions of the painting *The Peaceable Kingdom*, the wolf, the leopard, the bear, and the lion. Each of these qualities, he asserted, could be used for good, but in recent years they had, when possessed by individuals "in their unregenerate state," helped produce "the present weak state of [the] Society." Melancholy or wolf-like personalities were "naturally disposed to be

Figure 5.1. Edward Hicks, *The Peaceable Kingdom*, c. 1827–1832. Oil on canvas, 17 ¾" × 23 ¾". Courtesy of Swarthmore College Friends Historical Library.

religious" and thus well represented among Friends. The same disposition, however, prompted many to "make profession of religion without being regenerated and born again." Many such "*novice*" believers had assumed leadership positions within the Society and played key roles "in the late unhappy . . . controversy." In contrast, sanguine personalities—the leopard—could be vain and boastful "libertines" who loved social intercourse and pursued the "folly and shadow of renown, called popularity." In religious groups, such individuals, the mechanic asserted, followed the "popular mania" and flocked to "religious revivals and moral reforms," thereby blowing "the flames of discord and contention." The mechanic believed few of this type existed among Friends, but where they did "they have spliced on with modern abolitionism and temperance" and caused "considerable unsettlement."[2]

Hicks also feared "cold and unfeeling" phlegmatic or bear-like personalities, "too often powerful, cruel and voracious," and lacking the appropriate "sympathy and feeling for suffering humanity." He worried about phlegmatic individuals' attraction to worldly success and "those beautiful idols of a fallen world—*wealth*, *power*, and *scholastic education*." Finally, like the lion, choleric personalities, argued Hicks, exhibited pride, arrogance, fierceness, cruelty, and ambition. Their ambition "predisposed [them] to be orthodox" and persecute those with whom they disagreed. Although cholerics included "keen-sighted, intelligent inquirers," their "self-will" led them into a "malignant, persecuting spirit." The mechanic asserted that choleric personalities dominated among Orthodox Quakers, whom he believed had sparked the separation and diminished the Society.[3]

For Hicks, individuals who failed to "deny self" and take "up the daily cross" had caused Quakers' recent travails. Only if "led and guided by a *Christ within*" would Friends once more manifest the "innocence, liberality and patience" of "the lamb, the kid, the cow and the ox." Hicks proposed a return to first principles—a rededication to the principle of the inward Christ—upon which Friends' distinctiveness lay. Only then could they avoid "the extreme orthodox" on one hand and "the extreme ultra reformers" on the other. Finding the middle way, he concluded, would enable moderates on both sides of the separation "to come together in the unity of the spirit and the bond of peace" and do good in the larger world.[4] Hicks could not ignore the social ramifications of the separation and Friends' growing involvement in the world. In the course of his sermon he attacked slavery and slaveholders, Friends' engagement with business and banking, and their pursuit of material success. He also decried abolition and radical reform. Hicks's appeal articulated the internal and external dangers faced by Friends in antebellum northern Virginia, as refracted through his own understanding of the problems.

Many northern Virginia Friends shared Hicks's concerns—even if they did not share his concern with personality. The 1828 schism generated these anxieties, as did outmigration which began in the 1790s and continued into the 1830s. Separation and migration weakened the community, diverted the attention of its leading reformers, and transformed its inner dynamics. After the schism, many Friends became preoccupied with organizational and doctrinal issues, seeking to restore peace and harmony within their community, sometimes at the expense of their concern for broader social reforms. In addition, Hicksites believed that during the split Orthodox Friends had abused the discipline—the rules and procedures that regulated Quaker life—and it weakened their desire for strict enforcement. Some Hicksites concluded that the rules of the Society, wielded as a weapon by Orthodox Friends, no longer served as a protective "hedge" that helped Friends stand apart from the world, but had become a dogmatic attachment to outward forms that hindered inward spiritual development. Similar concerns prompted some northern Hicksites to form "come-outer" congregations free from formal creeds and embrace a range of radical reforms designed to remake society. Within the Baltimore Yearly Meeting, such radicalism found little support even among the community's liberal members. In a coercive slave society, a spiritual community "that placed the right of dissent at its center" had little hope of survival. Instead, local Friends sought to avoid "the two extremes" of "orthodox formality, and sceptical ranterism," which they perceived as "the two great enemies of Christianity." But finding this moderate path remained an ongoing challenge.[5]

I

Quakers struggled to find a middle way because they never tried to remove themselves from the world even as they set themselves apart. Contemporary intellectual and cultural currents, as a result, had a deep impact on the Society. In part, the Hicksite separation of 1827–28 grew out Friends' differing responses to evangelicalism. But it also arose from the pragmatic compromises the Society had made in the late seventeenth century. To achieve toleration in England and ensure the survival of the group, Quaker leaders such as Robert Barclay and William Penn abandoned the confrontational tactics of earlier Friends and worked to codify the Society's beliefs along orthodox Christian lines. They used the hierarchical meeting structure to monitor those who preached in the name of the Society and control publication of theological works. Such efforts enabled Friends to achieve toleration in 1689. But they also changed the tone and style of Quaker preachers, from seventeenth century activists who aggressively preached to the unregenerate to eighteenth century quietists more focused on purifying the Quaker community. In this age of "Quietism," Quaker theology "began with, was structured by, and concluded with the inward light of Christ." It remained largely unchanged into the early nineteenth century.[6]

Quietism reshaped how Friends understood salvation. In the seventeenth century, Quaker preachers used revivalist methods to convert their audiences. Quietist preachers of the eighteenth century, in contrast, saw salvation (or "convincement") as a process in which the believer cultivated the "seed" of the inward Christ. By following the guidance of the light within, individuals slowly achieved "holiness"—sanctification—and became "fitted for heaven" (or justification). The various structures of Quaker life—the queries, meeting oversight, the "guarded education" of Quaker children, and endogamous marriage—helped realize the same end: the growth of the inward light as preparation for salvation. In the process, Friends reversed the traditional Christian view of redemption—justification or conversion followed by sanctification or holiness—and rejected evangelicals' emphasis on the conversion experience. Eighteenth-century Friends conceived of salvation as a progressive process attained after internal spiritual struggle.[7]

Still, a tension remained embedded within Quakerism between Friends' belief in individual revelation of the inward light and the corporate structure of the church that controlled the behavior and spiritual commitments of members. Quaker religious meetings, in which Friends sat in communal silence seeking the "leadings" of the divine light within, embraced and reflected this tension, as did the efforts of meetings at each level of the Quaker hierarchy to achieve consensus before making changes in the Society's discipline. Friends believed their meetings enabled individuals to follow their spiritual insights, but under the guidance of "weighty Friends"—the elders, overseers, and ministers—of each meeting. Quaker leaders sought to restrain "ranterism," the enthusiastic outbursts that stained the respectability of Friends in the seventeenth century. But they did not espouse doctrinal orthodoxy to stifle dissent. Despite the Society's eighteenth-century conservatism, Friends' emphasis on the inward light and the progressive nature of divine revelation allowed new ideas into the Society. Friends' slow embrace of antislavery in the eighteenth century reveals how the spiritual revelations of a few individuals could transform Quaker attitudes and behavior. When Quaker minister John Woolman came to appreciate the sinfulness of slavery, he decided he must spread his message among Friends. Only after a long campaign of moral persuasion, however, did Woolman help achieve an antislavery consensus—while providing an example to which nineteenth-century antislavery Friends pointed to justify their own tactical decisions.[8]

Still, Woolman made no doctrinal changes. He exemplified the quietism of the eighteenth century, and called on Friends to follow the logical implications of their values—particularly pacifism. The Society showed less flexibility when it came to changes in doctrine. As Quaker historian J. William Frost notes, in the eighteenth century "the whole Society stood against doctrinal innovation," despite Friends' oft-stated contention that "they had no systematic theology." Doctrinal continuity became more difficult in the early nineteenth century when liberal rationalism and evangelicalism pervaded Anglo-American culture. Quakers' openness to new ideas afforded the Society little ability to halt their spread among its members. In fact, Quakerism reflected both these currents, seeing the inward light ruled by "right reason" (in Robert Barclay's words) as the path to salvation but also accepting traditional evangelical ideas about human depravity and atonement through the crucifixion of Christ. In the era of quietism, Friends neglected evangelical notions, though they remained a part of the Society's doctrine. However, the growth of evangelicalism in the early nineteenth century and Friends' association, especially in England, with other Protestants in benevolent causes, led many members to embrace evangelical principles. Such doctrinal innovations, Friends soon discovered, caused a severe strain on the meeting structure and the goodwill of members.[9]

The fault lines of the impending split appeared in 1798 when Hannah Barnard, a minister from New York, journeyed to Great Britain on a religious visit. Traveling to Ireland, Barnard met Quaker rationalist Abraham Shackleton, who led a separation of liberal Friends in Ireland. Emboldened by Shackleton, Barnard traveled to England in 1800 where she stressed the primacy of the inward light, expressed disbelief "in the vicarious sufferings and atonement of Christ," and rejected the divine authority of the Bible. After eighteen months of wrangling, the London Yearly Meeting, anxious "to prevent the inroads of skepticism and infidelity" that Friends associated with revolutionary France, ordered that Barnard "desist from traveling or speaking as a minister" and return home. Back in New York, Barnard's monthly meeting disowned her for questioning "the authenticity of various parts of the Scriptures of Truth." Elias Hicks, the Long Island minister associated with the later split in America, opposed Barnard's disownment, but most Friends worried that she represented the radicalism and deism of the French Revolution. Politically, American Quakers supported the Federalist Party and opposed Thomas Jefferson's Democratic-Republicans and their association with French radicalism. In theological matters, the Philadelphia and Baltimore Yearly Meetings' 1806 disciplines stressed Friends' belief in the "authenticity of the scriptures" and recommended disowning those who denied the divinity of Christ.[10]

Evangelical English Friends encouraged orthodox elements among American Quakers. In the early nineteenth century, English Quaker Joseph John Gurney published doctrinal texts that raised "evangelical doctrines into unprecedented prominence." Four beliefs lay at the heart of the evangelical offensive: the sinfulness of humanity, the Bible as the primary source of knowledge about God, the divinity of Christ, and salvation through the "propitiatory sacrifice" of Christ. In America, evangelical-leaning ministers, some of them converts to Quakerism, embraced Gurney's message and sought doctrinal consensus within the Society. In 1811, English Friend Richard Phillips argued that Quakers "should have one uniform Discipline

. . . that would be binding on the society every where," and suggested that American Friends appoint delegates to attend the London Yearly Meeting. The War of 1812 halted such efforts, but in 1817 the Philadelphia Yearly Meeting debated a similar proposal and distributed it to American yearly meetings. Quietist Friends rejected the plan as an effort to impose an "aristocracy" on American Friends. The Baltimore Yearly Meeting concluded that "advantages would arise . . . from a conference of the several Yearly Meetings *on this continent*," but rejected the idea of English authority.[11]

But American evangelical Friends and their English allies continued to push for doctrinal consensus. English traveling ministers made extended visits to the United States, forcing supporters and opponents to articulate their positions. During an 1821 visit to the Ohio Yearly Meeting, English minister William Forster worried about "the sad effects which the departure from sound Christian views . . . was producing on many minds" and revived the proposal for an annual conference of Friends under English leadership. The Ohio meeting rejected the plan, but promised to revisit it the following year. The evangelical English Quaker Anna Braithwaite traveled to America three times between 1823 and 1827. During her first visit, the "regal" Braithwaite fretted about the "dangerous opinions" afloat among American Friends. In early 1824, she met Elias Hicks. His ideas, she reported, "greatly distressed me. He openly avowed his disbelief in the Divine authority of Holy Scripture—of the fall of man—of the Deity of the Lord Jesus Christ; and of the efficacy of His sufferings and death, as 'the propitiation of our sins.'" "My mind," she concluded, "is sorrowfully affected on this subject, and the widespread mischief arising from the propagation of such sentiments."[12]

American evangelicals, spurred to action by the English visitors, shared Braithwaite's concerns. Led by the Meeting for Sufferings of the Philadelphia Yearly Meeting, evangelical leaders decided in 1823 to impose doctrinal order on the Society. Philadelphia leaders worried about the impact of the debate between "Paul" and "Amicus" in the Wilmington *Christian Repository*, and tried to stop publisher Robert Porter from reprinting it. Using the pseudonym "Paul," Presbyterian minister Eliphalet W. Gilbert attacked Quakerism as "inimical to the principles of the gospel." In response, Wilmington Friend Benjamin Ferris, adopting the alias "Amicus," defended Quakers' belief in the inward light and progressive revelation, and rejected the Trinity—the idea that three distinct entities existed in one God—as unbiblical and unreasonable. Hicksite and liberal Friends approved of Ferris's efforts, but evangelical Friends, led by the clerk of the Philadelphia

Meeting for Sufferings, Jonathan Evans, believed that Amicus had "not correctly stated" Quaker beliefs. Over Evans's signature, the meeting for sufferings produced *Extracts from the Writings of Primitive Friends*, which drew selectively from the writings of early Friends to prove that Quakers held evangelical values. Evans requested that Porter insert the *Extracts* in his book. When the publisher refused, the meeting ordered ten thousand copies printed. After many Friends objected, the elders halted distribution of the *Extracts*, though they recorded its text in the minutes of the yearly meeting.[13]

Elders of the Philadelphia meeting also tried to muzzle Elias Hicks during his visits to meetings in the Philadelphia area. Evangelical Friends identified the charismatic Hicks as the most dangerous source of infidelity within the Society. A powerful speaker, Hicks attracted large crowds wherever he preached, a result, according to poet Walt Whitman, of his "powerful human magnetism" and "pleading, tender, nearly agonizing conviction." Hicks made the contest personal when he criticized wealthy elders, including Evans, for worldliness, insufficient commitment to Quaker testimonies, and abandonment of free produce. In September 1822, evangelical Philadelphia elders attempted to stop Hicks's planned visit to Philadelphia and Baltimore meetings. "Unless we can stop him here," Evans declared, "he must go on." A committee of three elders confronted Hicks in Philadelphia, but he continued southward where he found a warm greeting. Friends in Baltimore found his "gospel ministry" "edifying," while members of the Southern Quarterly Meeting, south of Philadelphia, praised Hicks for preaching "the Truths of the Gospel." After Hicks returned to Philadelphia for visits to Friends' homes, a larger group of elders questioned him about his unorthodox beliefs. And in January 1823, ten evangelical elders sent Hicks two letters accusing him of "holding and promulgating doctrines different from, and repugnant to those held" by Friends.[14]

The Philadelphia elders' actions deepened the chasm between evangelicals and their opponents. Historian Larry Ingle argues that the creation of a "Hicksite party" opposed to evangelical doctrinal conformity dated from Hicks's 1822 visit to Philadelphia. "Friends," Hicks declared, must "assert their rights, and not suffer themselves to be imposed upon" by the elders. But Hicksites did not try to reach a doctrinal consensus. Hicks represented a quietist strain, focused on the immediacy of the "indwelling Christ." He viewed true religion as experiential and mystical, and argued that salvation did not come through the "propitiatory sacrifice" of Christ but by following the "the Spirit of Truth" within. All people, quietists believed, entered the world marked by original sin and the inward divine light. Following the revelations of the latter enabled individuals to escape their sinful nature and reconcile with God. Each believer must experience a spiritual trial or crucifixion—an "inward" battle between "Satan . . . and the revelations of Christ"—before "regeneration" could occur. Hicksites' focus on the light within led them to dismiss many of the shibboleths of mainstream Protestantism. They recognized the Bible as a valuable guide and quoted from it regularly, but believed it remained secondary to the revelations of the inward light. They also rejected the doctrine of the Trinity. Religious creeds, they contended, were "dead forms" that provided no spiritual redemption.[15]

Agrarian, anti-intellectual, and antimarket themes also shaped Hicks's thought. He emphasized the need for Friends to uphold Quaker simplicity, an idea that sometimes expressed itself in suspicion of the market economy. Like his cousin Edward, the "Poor Illiterate Mechanic," Hicks praised agricultural life and disparaged market innovations such as the Erie Canal. "If the Lord had intended there should be internal waterways," Hicks pronounced, "he would have placed them there, and there would have been a river flowing through central New York." He also denounced the involvement of Chesapeake Friends in the Baltimore & Ohio Railroad and worried about the fate of Philip E. Thomas, clerk of the Baltimore Yearly Meeting and first president of the railroad. Thomas's position in the meeting, Hicks noted, was "more noble and exalted" than "such low and groveling concerns" as the railroad. After Thomas hired James P. Stabler, a member of the Sandy Spring Monthly Meeting in Maryland, to oversee construction of the first leg of the railroad, Hicks expressed his disapproval to Stabler's parents. "I conceive" the business, wrote Hicks, "principally belongs to the men of this world, but not to the children of light."[16]

Many contemporaries believed that Orthodox Friends' economic success widened the divide within the Philadelphia Yearly Meeting. Samuel Janney pointed to the "pre-eminent" "wealth and social position" of Philadelphia's Orthodox elders who gained their positions within the Society because Friends "respected . . . their wealth, intelligence, and orderly deportment." Hicksite James Cockburn also noted the "superficial and overbearing spirit" that pervaded Orthodox elders and contributed to the split. In the previous forty years, he argued, "rich and wealthy" Friends had "engaged in the pursuit and spirit of the world" and had taken "control and direction of the affairs of the society." Worldly success had made them "accustomed to lead" and "those around" them to "obey." Orthodox Friends, he concluded, had "deviate[d] from . . . the fundamental principle of the society," leaving those with "faithful minds" "deeply exercised." Historian Robert Doherty like-wise stresses the socioeconomic divide between urban, market-oriented, and wealthy evangelicals and agrarian and less wealthy Hicksites. Having achieved economic success, evangelicals wanted to make the Society a more respectable body—to transform their sect into a church—by adopt-ing mainstream Protestant orthodoxy. In contrast, predominantly rural Hicksites distrusted the market economy, embraced "noncommercial" val-ues, and sought to maintain the Society's distinctiveness. They distrusted the wealth and power of the Philadelphia elders, interpreting evangelicals' material success as a sign of spiritual backwardness.[17]

But Friends had always expressed ambivalence about wealth and the market—even while enjoying economic success—and Hicksite *and* Or-thodox preachers lamented Friends' worldliness long after the separation. When John Comly visited Hicksite meetings in Maryland and northern Virginia in 1829, he complained that "business engagements, the pursuit of wealth, and the almost universal subject of the railroad seemed so to engross the attention of . . . Friends . . . that there appears little room for subjects . . . of a religious character." "The consequences" of Friends' failure to "adhere closely" to the "plain way of living," he lamented, "are obvious in the decline of our religious society." Twenty years later, William Evans, a prosperous Orthodox leader, made similar complaints about the dangers of wealth. The rich, he lamented, develop "the love of grandeur . . . pride and self-consequence," while less affluent members feel a "temptation to fall in with the . . . opinions of rich, nominal Quakers." Friends, he concluded, need to embrace "a life of self-denial, both for our everlasting good, and for the sake of our children." In addition, little evidence exists that Orthodox Friends abandoned their sense of separation from the world in the wake of the split. Not until the 1860s did they begin to abandon their distinctive patterns of dress, speech, and disciplinary practices, including disownment for exogamous marriage. As historian Thomas Hamm notes, Friends—for all their internal divisions—remained a people apart from the world.[18]

Doherty's data also reveals that many Philadelphia-area Hicksites pos-sessed significant wealth and participated in the market economy. Almost half his sample of urban Hicksites owned more than one thousand dollars of real property, indicating little alienation from commercial life. Doherty's socioeconomic thesis also fails to account for the separations—or the fail-ure to separate—among American Friends elsewhere. Hicks's liberal allies congregated in the urban monthly meetings of Wilmington, Alexandria, and Baltimore, participating in regional economic development (and in many cases becoming wealthy). Alexandria minister Edward Stabler embraced a quietist faith and lamented Friends' excessive attention to economic matters, but he also owned a successful pharmacy. Elder Phineas Janney, a "dear" friend of John Comly's who accompanied Edward Stabler to the Philadelphia Hicksite meeting in 1828, ran a prosperous wine and iron import firm throughout the 1830s and 1840s. In the Shenandoah Valley, David Lupton and his sons thrived through a combination of commercial farming, merchant milling, investments in railroads and turnpikes, and patents for agricultural machinery. Friends like these welcomed economic development and technological innovation. Many—probably most—Hicksites disdained neither the market nor the wealth it could bring.[19]

Socioeconomic analyses also fail to explain the doctrinal diversity of Hicksites. Many Friends in northern Virginia, including influential ministers Thomas Wetherald and Edward Stabler, espoused quietism, but a significant number embraced liberal religious opinions, much to the consternation of Hicks. During a 1799 visit to the Goose Creek meeting, Hicks, like his cousin Edward nearly forty years later, fretted about the influence of Thomas Paine and the growth of "infidelity and deism among" Friends. During his 1829 visit to northern Virginia and Maryland, John Comly also encountered deist Friends. He did not, however, condemn such members but judged them on their actions. "Whatever names or terms may be used," Comly concluded, "the substance [of faith] is *good* works, as the fruit of good principles." Many Friends carried these tolerant principles west when they migrated. William Schooley, raised in the Goose Creek meeting, brought to rural Ohio the belief that Friends should accept a diversity of opinions in order to protect "the right of private judgment." Not all Hicksites shared Schooley's broadmindedness, but his tolerance represented an important strain within the group.[20]

Despite Hicks's critiques of the market and religious liberalism he found some of his strongest allies among Friends who welcomed economic development and toleration. Liberals embraced rationalist interpretations of the Bible and questioned religious orthodoxy. They looked to reason and conscience as guides, though they believed the font of both lay in the inward Christ. Baltimore Hicksite Moses Sheppard grew wealthy in the mercantile and milling business, retired early, and spent his later years investing in and directing a variety of benevolent causes. He remained a theological liberal opposed to doctrinal orthodoxy throughout his adult life, as his correspondence with Loudoun County teacher Benjamin F. Taylor reveals. Although disowned for marrying his first cousin in 1829, Taylor continued to attend the Goose Creek meeting, which he described as "dear and precious." The pair discussed scientific discoveries, the insights of liberal philosophers and theologians, and technological and commercial innovations. They condemned the "selfish, illiberal, and bigotted" "Priestcraft" of churches that elevated the Bible above modern science. When scripture conflicted with science, Taylor argued, "the scripture record" must be "interpreted in reference to the [scientific] truth ... thus established or else rejected altogether as an error originating in the mistake of the writer or translator." "Truth in science and truth in religion," he added, "will always be found consistent if bigotry, intolerance, and stupidity do not interfere."[21]

Taylor's letters echoed the sentiments of his relative and Goose Creek elder Yardley Taylor, who in the 1850s and 1860s wrote articles for agricultural and Quaker journals lauding the "benefits" of scientific farming. Taylor embraced "inductive philosophy" and "the late discoveries of the microscope." Only by careful observation, he argued, could the "laws that govern the operations of nature ... be ascertained." The application of scientific methods to the "everyday active business of life," he believed, ensured that "every department of industry [and] every business" achieved "safety, certainty and expedition, to a degree never before attained." Alexandria minister and elder Benjamin Hallowell also embraced and contributed to the scientific discoveries of his age, seeing them as part of God's progressive revelation of truth. In Alexandria, Hallowell established a successful nonsectarian school for boys that emphasized scientific and mathematical training. He gained acclaim for putting his knowledge of the natural world to work in the promotion of internal and agricultural improvements. Early in his career, Hallowell worried that his scientific pursuits interfered with his spiritual life, but as his knowledge and character "evolve[d]," he concluded that the study of nature contributed to his moral improvement. For Hallowell, God "bestowed upon" humanity a "reasoning intellect"— a rational inward light to accompany the spiritual—that enabled insight of God's handiwork and promoted ethical and moral growth. "These two guides—the Spirit of God and the Understanding or Reason," he asserted, "proceed from the same bountiful source."[22]

Many Hicksite Friends shared Hallowell's rationalist understanding of the inward light. Hallowell recalled a Philadelphia elder who rejected biblical-based dating of creation after hearing one of Hallowell's geology lectures. With "his eyes betokening the deep emotion of his soul," Hallowell remembered, the elder requested that Hallowell write a geology textbook for the local Friends school. Yet other Hicksites worried that an emphasis on science could hurt spiritual development. When Hallowell's student, William Griscom, realized that working in the school's chemistry lab conflicted with attending fifth day meeting, he asked his father for permission to miss the latter. Griscom senior urged his son to make his own judgment "enlightened by that Light that leads not into Error." But he added: "[I] would much rather thee should lose any advantages thee may have there in the pursuit of science than thee should get into the habit of neglecting meetings." The son followed his father's advice, though he noted the "small" and desultory character of the fifth day meeting, during which "we had no speaking."[23]

Hicksites, then, represented an array of economic backgrounds and doctrinal viewpoints. But they agreed on one point: they opposed elders and ministers who tried to dictate a "creed" that impeded the leadings of the inward Christ or the explorations of the rational mind. In ensuring that individual Friends retained latitude to follow the Christ within, Hicks's allies and followers believed they sustained the teachings of the Society's early leaders. Quakerism, they argued, had always embraced a "diversity of sentiment" on "secondary" points of doctrine. As Alexandria minister and Hicks ally Thomas Wetherald noted, "however diverse our opinions may be upon religious subjects, if we are under the influence of this divine and governing principle . . . which speaks in every soul," "we shall be . . . knit together" and "travail for one another's welfare in love." Other Hicksite Friends reached similar conclusions. When the Orthodox minister William Forster attended the 1825 Baltimore Yearly Meeting, he decried Hicks's teachings as "radically unsound, and subversive of the . . . essential doctrines of Christianity." Elder Evan Thomas acknowledged that Hicks might hold "some peculiar views," but he did not feel it "my place to sit as a watchman at the gate." If a preacher's message was "accompanied by the Divine influence and power," Thomas asserted, Friends need not "look critically into the exact words." Hicks, he concluded, met this test.[24]

For his part, Forster fretted over "the spirit of infidelity which reigns and almost rages in some parts of" the Baltimore Yearly Meeting and endeavored "to bear testimony" to his Orthodox beliefs. At the Alexandria meeting he concluded that Friends "seem to be very much carried off" by the spirit of "scepticism." Some local Friends agreed. Elisha C. Dick, the pro-slavery Alexandria doctor who converted to Quakerism in 1812, worried that the spread of "Unitarian doctrines" among Friends undermined faith in the divinity of Christ and the redemptive power of His crucifixion. Visits by English evangelical ministers Forster and Braithwaite emboldened Dick to condemn the meeting's leading members, including Edward Stabler and George Drinker. Among Friends of Samuel Janney's temperament, such attacks backfired. He admitted that Dick and his English allies preached "the true doctrines of Christ and his apostles," but he found their "direct and pointed" attacks "an infringement of the good order of the gospel, and of the [Quaker] discipline." He lamented the "censorious, uncharitable spirit" of Orthodox Friends, which he believed laid "waste [to] our religious Society." "I could not endure," Janney recalled years later, the "party zeal" of Orthodox ministers, and he cast his lot with Hicksites despite the diversity of their beliefs. Janney believed it more important for Friends to "live in unity and love" than dispute doctrine. Dick disagreed and resigned from the meeting in 1825.[25]

Hicksites shared little beyond their belief in the primacy of the inward light and a toleration of divergent spiritual paths. As Janney noted, "the harmony and prosperity of the Church" lay "not in the entire uniformity of religious opinions," but in "the indwelling and government of the Spirit of Christ." The Hicksites' belief that the primary source of spiritual knowledge came through the progressive revelation of the Christ within, whether conceived in spiritual or rational terms, led them to reject evangelicals' emphasis on biblical authority and the imposition of doctrinal unity. If most Hicksites had not yet embraced the broad toleration and theological modernism that characterizes most present-day Friends, they displayed greater tolerance for individual seeking than did their evangelical brethren. They disowned members for violating their disciplinary rules because they believed conduct to be the best measure of spiritual commitment. But they accepted a range of doctrinal views. Indeed, their spiritual diversity led many members to reject the Hicksite label, "unwilling," as Janney noted, "to acknowledge any other name than that of Friends."[26]

But the name stuck, enshrined during the 1827 separation of the Philadelphia Yearly Meeting. At the February 1827 quarterly meeting, evangelicals impugned the morality of Hicksites and refused to allow the Hicksite-dominated Green Street Monthly Meeting to appoint elders of its choice. John Comly, the deputy clerk of the Philadelphia Yearly Meeting, concluded that only "a separation of the two conflicting parts of the Society" could save "the whole from total wreck." After the meeting, he sought allies among reformers for "a temporary separation" and urged urban Hicksites to request membership in rural meetings where reformers predominated. The yearly meeting in April finalized the split. Prompted by British Friends, evangelicals sought an investigation of the soundness of ministers within the meeting, a move that Hicksites opposed. They countered by trying to remove Samuel Bettle, the evangelical clerk of the meeting, and nominating Comly to the post. But Bettle would not step down, prompting more acrimony. On the second day of the meeting, Comly suggested an adjournment until the two parties could reach a peaceful solution, but the meeting disregarded his proposal. The next day, Comly appealed to evangelical members to abandon their plan to judge the doctrinal soundness of the meeting's ministers, but they refused. Comly then bid the meeting "an affectionate *farewell*," followed by a majority of Hicksites who believed separation necessary to ensure the survival of the Society and their relief from evangelical domination.[27]

After the yearly meeting closed, the seceders gathered at the Green Street Meeting House to finalize an address to the quarterly and monthly meetings of Philadelphia. Asserting their faithfulness to Friends' traditional values, the seceders explained that the doctrinal division within the Philadelphia meeting had become irreconcilable because of the "oppressive" measures of the meeting's Orthodox elders. They recommended that Friends make "a quiet retreat from this scene of confusion" and that like-minded members gather in the first week of June. The address pushed the conflict into the monthly and quarterly meetings, forcing individual Friends to choose sides. The most contentious separations occurred in meetings in which minority evangelicals attempted to impose their control over the entire meeting; where evangelicals predominated they simply disowned Hicksites. Comly believed that these local battles would decide "whether arbitrary power . . . should rule the society, or . . . virtue and religious liberty of conscience . . . re-assume their rightful empire among Friends." In the weeks following the yearly meeting, evangelicals' "heavy-handed" tactics helped push many undecided Friends into the Hicksite camp. When supporters of separation met in June they proposed that a new yearly meeting gather in October. They emphasized that they did not seek withdrawal "from the Society of Friends . . . but from religious communion with those who have introduced . . . such disorders among us."[28]

Alexandria ministers Edward Stabler and Thomas Wetherald attended the October meeting, offering their endorsement of the separatists' actions. The separatists also sent an epistle to the Baltimore Yearly Meeting—the only such address it issued in 1827—revealing the support it enjoyed among Baltimore Friends. Stabler welcomed the split, seeing it as a "necessary effect" of the "powerful commotion" within the Society. "I cannot but rejoice at the present state of things," he announced in December 1827, "because

I see in it the influence of a *Power* that is stirring up the stagnant pool of religious *profession*." But as Stabler acknowledged, many Friends mourned the division, particularly after it spread to the rest of the yearly meetings. In quick succession, the New York, Ohio, and Indiana Yearly Meetings divided. During the Ohio Yearly Meeting in September, "the most turbulent . . . ever held on the American continent," fighting erupted between Hicksite and Orthodox Friends as they competed for control of the meeting house. In contrast, the New England, Virginia, and North Carolina Yearly Meetings, where evangelicals predominated, avoided internal division (at least for a time). But they could not escape taking sides in the dispute and they issued epistles condemning the Hicksite separation. The split in the Philadelphia Yearly Meeting began as a doctrinal dispute, but it had quickly exploded into an emotional contest over freedom of conscience, the exercise of authority, and control of property within the Society.[29]

<h2 style="text-align:center">II</h2>

The controversy perplexed the Baltimore meeting at its October 1827 annual gathering, providing a taste of discord to come. English minister Thomas Shillitoe, touring American meetings to expound the evangelical message, anticipated that "bonds and afflictions awaited" him in Baltimore. He objected to the meeting's answers to its queries—the questions asked each year to determine if Friends adhered to the Society's discipline—believing they had become "a mere formal matter." But he drew comfort from the thought that "Friends who remain firmly attached to our ancient principles" would reform the meeting "when [they] separated from" the Hicksite majority. Shillitoe, at least, believed a split only a matter of time. He found it "trying" to sit next to "the most conspicuous of the Hicksite preachers" from the Philadelphia and Baltimore meetings. But Shillitoe's distress peaked when "the disaffected party" argued that the Baltimore meeting should read and answer the epistle sent by the new Hicksite meeting in Philadelphia. The decision reflected Hicksites' control of influential positions in the Baltimore meeting—particularly the clerkship—which enabled them to silence those Shillitoe considered "sound members." Reports circulated that assistant clerk Edward Stabler led an inner circle of "six to eight" Friends who settled issues before they could disrupt the larger body. But their efforts did not stop a "great commotion" from erupting over the epistle. Shillitoe objected to the meeting's "illegitimate" response to the Philadelphia Hicksites.

He received in return "some rough and rather insulting usage," which he attributed to locals' prejudices against "English Friends."[30]

The conflict within the Baltimore meeting climaxed the following year, despite the attempts of some elders to avoid separation. The attendance of evangelical and Hicksite ministers from other meetings undermined their efforts, as did the debate over whether to respond to the epistles other yearly meetings sent to Baltimore. To avert a separation, Baltimore elders arrived with a "previously concerted" plan of action. When the meeting opened, the clerk, Philip Thomas, decided to read without discrimination the certificates of all visiting ministers, Orthodox and Hicksite, while Stabler, the assistant clerk, suggested the meeting refer the epistles to a committee. But three Friends objected to receiving the certificates of visitors "disowned by the Society"—that is, Hicksites. The objectors realized that the participation of Hicksite ministers and correspondence with Hicksite yearly meetings placed Baltimore Friends in that camp. Still, Baltimore elders wanted to avoid a separation. The respected elder Roger Brooke defended Thomas and Stabler, temporarily silencing the dissenters and gaining the support of a "large majority" for the proposal to delegate the epistles to committee. Orthodox Friends charged that the "rulers" of the Baltimore meeting hoped by these tactics to confine "*discussion*" and avoid open conflict.[31]

The elders' attempt to prevent a separation failed when the British evangelical minister George Jones announced that the measures taken by the meeting—admitting Hicksite Friends and referring all epistles to committee—"departed from the ancient doctrines of the Society." "I must leave the meeting," Jones continued, and "you to such choice as you have made." As Jones departed, Jeremiah Brown called out, "Thou art quite welcome to withdraw," while another attendee "opened the door" for him. Upon Jones's exit, Baltimore Friend Samuel Carey declared that the meeting had "trampled under foot" the Society's "Discipline" and he too left, accompanied by a cry of "Farewell Samuel." No Friends followed, but at day's end Dr. Thomas Worthington announced that through its decisions the meeting had "separated itself from the Society of Friends." He urged those who agreed with him "to meet together" to hold the yearly meeting "on its original foundation."[32]

The following afternoon, the committee appointed to respond to the epistles presented a draft communication for the yearly meetings and members of the Baltimore meeting. It defended Hicksite doctrines, particularly the focus on the inward light, and argued that the recent divisions arose because "those who wish to domineer over their fellow-members" tried to "impose" a "Creed" on the Society. When they failed, the epistle continued, Orthodox Friends circulated "false and high charges against" their opponents, including leading members of the Baltimore meeting. This "unexpected and unaccountable" draft sparked uproar. Critics denounced the committee for having overstepped its responsibilities and taken on a task that belonged to the entire meeting. Thomas Evans, an evangelical minister from Philadelphia, argued that the draft epistle misrepresented the history of the Society and the doctrinal basis of Friends' faith. Although committee members Brooke and Wetherald defended their actions and "a considerable number of friends approved . . . the Epistle," the meeting decided to withdraw it because some members remained "dissatisfied." Orthodox Friends believed the committee's actions revealed the willingness of Hicksite leaders to suppress "*free enquiry* and religious liberty" when it "suit[ed] their purposes."[33]

By the third day of the meeting, the elders concluded they could no longer avoid confrontation and began portraying themselves as victims of Orthodox intolerance. The epistle committee recommended that the meeting read "without reserve" all "communications" sent by Hicksite and Orthodox yearly meetings. As Baltimore elders anticipated, the Orthodox epistles produced "a feeling of deep distress" in the meeting. They contained "many heavy and grievous accusations . . . against a large body of our [Hicksite] Friends" with which the Baltimore meeting still considered itself "in full unity." The stridency of the communications enabled Hicksite elders to present Orthodox Friends as the aggressors, having departed from the "state of quietude where true wisdom resides." In contrast, Edward Stabler rose and called on Baltimore Friends to remain "calm." "Do not let us be provoked to anything like passion or recrimination," he urged, by the "unfounded" Orthodox charges. Wetherald followed Stabler. He noted the "incongruities" of the Orthodox epistles which expressed a "spirit of domination" and a "hardness (of feeling)," accompanied by "profession[s] of love." But Wetherald worried most about Orthodox threats to cease communication with meetings that corresponded with the "separatists" of Philadelphia, New York, and Ohio. A Baltimore meeting that accepted outside control over its decision making, Wetherald argued, acknowledged the "supremacy" of the Orthodox meetings. The Baltimore meeting would lose its independence and Friends "become subject to a hierarchy more despotic perhaps than was ever experienced in the Church of Rome."[34]

Local Hicksites believed the stakes in this contest nothing less than their religious freedom. Orthodox measures threatened American principles and what Hicksites considered Friends' "fundamental" article of faith: following the progressive revelations of the light "infused . . . into the soul of every individual." Although Orthodox Friends dismissed Wetherald's speech as "hyperbole," his arguments swayed the mass of the meeting. Friends appointed another committee, headed by Wetherald and Stabler, to respond to the "three friendly Epistles" from the Hicksite meetings in New York, Philadelphia, and Indiana. At this point, evangelical Friends had seen enough. James Gillingham declared that the meeting had "separated itself from the Society of Friends" and he urged those who wanted the meeting to retain "its original foundation" to gather the next morning at the nearby McKendrie schoolhouse. Hugh Balderston, treasurer of the yearly meeting, followed Gillingham, and the two proceeded to the women's meeting to repeat their proposal. Evangelical Friends concluded that only by removing themselves could they "bear a faithful testimony to the principles of the Christian religion" and remain in "brotherly intercourse . . . with other yearly meetings of Friends." Evangelicals everywhere employed comparable rhetoric, but the separation in Baltimore did not produce an "uproar or commotion" because Gillingham and Balderston asked their supporters to remain until the day's session ended. "Dignity and courtesy," reported local Friend Robert Townsend, marked the Baltimore separation.[35]

The next morning, noted one attendee, the "large congregation" of Friends who met at the appointed time "scarcely missed" "the orthodox who left us." But this sanguine account failed to acknowledge the deep scars caused by the split. Most who remained called on Friends to "live together in love and harmony," while affirming their right to exercise their judgment independently of evangelical meetings. "Each Yearly Meeting," Baltimore Friends asserted in an epistle addressed to Orthodox meetings, "constitutes . . . a body possessing . . . all the powers of self government" with neither "the right to controul the judgment nor to animadvert upon the proceedings of others." No meeting, they contended, had "the power . . . to control or prescribe rules for our conduct," particularly when Baltimore Friends had "not . . . advance[d] any new principle of Faith." Evangelical Friends, the Baltimore meeting concluded, had departed from the Society's "ancient" principles and had no right to impose their innovations on yearly meetings that abided by traditional Quaker beliefs.[36]

The meeting also revised the epistle to which the full meeting had objected and sent it to "absent" members. The division in the yearly meeting would now play itself out in the subsidiary meetings, and leading Friends wanted to present a full explanation of their position. The epistle stressed the historical independence of each yearly meeting and reiterated Friends' "great fundamental article of Faith"—"obedience to the manifestations of Divine light . . . upon the soul"—buttressed by extensive scriptural support. It also denied the two central theological charges made by Orthodox Friends—that Hicksites denied the divinity of Christ and authority of the Scriptures. The epistle reminded readers that early Friends had faced comparable accusations from "the Hierarchy [and] Politicians . . . interested in keeping up the old ecclesiastical establishment." In 1827, "the same charges are revived by some who once professed with us." Baltimore Friends could not fail to heed the message. Hicksites deserved the mantle of true Quakerism because they stood on the same "simple ground" as the revered "ancient" Friends of the seventeenth century. The meeting approved the epistle "without a dissenting voice."[37]

But as Samuel Janney acknowledged, evangelicals believed that they were "the genuine successors of the early" Quakers and that their opponents had departed from Friends' "original doctrines." Janney noted that Joseph John Gurney, the arch-evangelical who had significant "reservations" about the doctrine of the light within, "honestly believed his views to be, in all essential points, nearly the same as those of Fox, Penn, and Barclay." American evangelical Elisha Bates, the clerk of the Ohio Yearly Meeting, voiced similar certainty in *Doctrines of Friends*, his 1825 publication which contended that early Quakers embraced orthodox Christianity even while discovering the principle of the inward light. Bates's Hicksite opponents labeled his effort "a mongrel theology" that "contained and disseminated the seeds of schism." Orthodox Friends, in turn, denounced Hicks and his allies for spreading "raging waves of . . . unbelief" whose "desolating ravages" had crippled the Society. The slipperiness of language, Janney realized, compounded the conflict. Words constituted "an imperfect medium for the conveyance of thought" at the best of times, he noted, but "sacred writings" suffered from an additional problem. "The lapse of centuries . . . and the teachings of theologians" had attached to "Scriptural phrases" "meanings . . . not intended by the" original writers. Sacred words, as a result, often failed to "convey to all persons the same meaning."[38]

Janney adopted this moderate tone years after the separation took place and with distance he recognized that both sides had erred. At the time of the separation, however, he and other Friends experienced great anguish and often passionately denounced their opponents. William Schooley, a Loudoun County Friend and minister who moved to Ohio in 1815, joined the Hicksites in that yearly meeting's bitter 1827 separation. He later lamented the "fiery zeal" of his "ministry," which "was sometimes too controversial and too much tinged with the heat of party feeling." But at the time he did not hesitate, like members of the Baltimore meeting, to compare his evangelical opponents to the "bigoted and self-righteous" persecutors of George Fox. "The opposers of Fox," Schooley stated in an interview with Orthodox minister William Mott, "were as confident that they were right then, as thou art of being right now. This idea of infallibility . . . has been the cause of persecution . . . in all ages of the world and it only wants power at this time to perpetuate the same acts of cruelty."[39]

Yet the subsidiary meetings within the Baltimore Yearly Meeting did not suffer the same acrimony as elsewhere in part because Baltimore's Hicksite leaders refused to disown Orthodox Friends. Having seen the "unpleasant consequences" of such disownments, Thomas Wetherald proposed that Baltimore Friends consider those who had withdrawn "as having relinquished their rights." Such individuals could restore their membership by applying "in writing" to the appropriate monthly meeting without making an "acknowledgement" of error as required of disowned members. Baltimore Hicksites could afford such magnanimity because they had a clear majority in the meeting. Although Hicksite and Orthodox Friends disagreed over the total number of withdrawals, only two of the fifty-three representatives who attended the 1828 yearly gathering joined the Orthodox meeting. English Friend William Proctor concluded that Baltimore was "the only Yearly Meeting" in America which "as a body . . . espoused the cause of the Separatists." In all, approximately 20 percent of Friends in the Baltimore Yearly Meeting joined the Orthodox ranks. The Fairfax Quarter, consisting of rural Goose Creek, Fairfax, and Hopewell meetings, and the urban Alexandria meeting, was also dominated by Hicksites, reducing internal conflict.[40]

The minutes of the Fairfax Monthly Meeting make few references to the 1828 split beyond noting the yearly meeting's instructions for dealing with dissenting Friends. Not a single member left the meeting because of Orthodox beliefs. Conflicts that erupted in more evenly divided meetings over control of and access to Society property and records did not materialize, and Fairfax Friends took little official notice of the split. A comparable situation existed in the Goose Creek meeting, where six members, including one elder, left the meeting in 1830, according to Hicksite meeting minutes. Hopewell Friends faced a more difficult situation because some respected Friends opposed the Hicksites. The meeting decided that fifteen individuals had "relinquished their right of membership with us" for associating "in the establishment . . . of other meetings under the name of friends." The dissenters included some of Hopewell's long established Quaker families, including Griffiths, Browns, Bonds, Jolliffes, and Scholfields. Because of the dissenters' prominence and the declining number of Friends in the Shenandoah Valley, the Hopewell meeting decided to maintain contact with their Orthodox neighbors. In a rare arrangement among divided meetings, they shared the meeting house. Hicksites worshiped on Sunday morning, and Orthodox Friends met in the afternoon.[41]

Orthodox Friends found the split more traumatic. Because of their small numbers, the Orthodox Baltimore Yearly Meeting decided to "dissolve and discontinue" the quarterly meeting to which Goose Creek and Fairfax belonged. Orthodox members from Fairfax came under the jurisdiction of the Baltimore Quarterly Meeting, while the Hopewell meeting oversaw Orthodox members of the Goose Creek meeting. In 1830, the reconstituted Hopewell meeting surveyed its membership, counting eighty-one members. This represented approximately 12 percent of the nearly seven hundred Friends who belonged to these meetings before the "painful and afflicting" separation. Still, they tried not to lose heart. The number of members in the meetings, they acknowledged, was "small," but members remained "comforted . . . that as they are faithful and diligent in . . . attendance . . . an increase in strength may be experienced." Goose Creek's Orthodox Friends met first in the home of Hannah Hoge, building a small meeting house in 1836. But the meeting's future remained precarious. Orthodox minister William Evans visited the "little band" in September 1841. "We sympathized with them in their stripped state," Evans recorded, "and through the goodness of the Lord, were led to administer a word of encouragement." Within twenty years, Orthodox Friends at Goose Creek had so dwindled in number they could no longer support an independent meeting house and rented out the building.[42]

The Alexandria meeting faced a challenging time because like Hopewell it had a number of Orthodox sympathizers. The most intense debates, including the exit of leading Orthodox Friend Elisha Dick, took place prior to the separation of the Baltimore Yearly Meeting in October 1828. Still, at least eight members left the meeting in 1829 and 1830 with the "avowed intention . . . to establish . . . another meeting of Friends." In the wake of these departures, Alexandria Friends encouraged more regular attendance among the remaining members. At the last meeting for worship he attended before his death in January 1831, Edward Stabler expressed his deep "concern for members who were frequently absent from our meetings." The meeting responded in February with an epistle that expressed longstanding Quaker concerns about members' worldliness. Directed to all meeting members, the letter voiced "a godly fear" that Friends had "perverted" business affairs "from ministers to our wants into objects of devotion," and "placed [them] above God in the soul." Minister Thomas Wetherald's departure for rural Pennsylvania in 1829 also undermined the religious intensity of the Alexandria meeting, but it retained its strong Hicksite flavor while the Orthodox meeting declined within a few years.[43]

III

Dry meeting minutes fail to capture the emotional consequences of the split, even within meetings in which little overt conflict took place. Every meeting enjoyed fewer visits from traveling Friends as Orthodox and Hicksite ministers refused to venture beyond their respective meetings. This essential part of Quaker religious life, through which Friends became part of the larger religious body, suffered because of the split. When Orthodox minister Rebecca Hubbs traveled from New Jersey to the Baltimore Yearly Meeting in 1833 and 1844, she visited only "the remnant of this place," the small number of Friends who had separated from the Hicksite majority. Indiana Orthodox minister Charles Osborn also sidestepped all Hicksite meetings within the Baltimore Yearly Meeting when he visited in 1833, despite extended visits in 1811 and 1816 (including a stay in Edward Stabler's Alexandria home). Osborn lamented the "trial" faced by the scattered families of evangelical Friends who now gathered in one another's homes. Thomas Shillitoe, traveling to Hicksite-dominated Alexandria in 1829, wrote ahead to find a place he "could be safely housed." Once there, he kept to his "quarters, notwithstanding all the importunities I had, to visit here and there amongst those who had denied the faith." Orthodox minister Benjamin Ladd, who traveled back to Virginia from Ohio in 1831 and 1832, stayed with Orthodox Friends. Like Osborn, he had lodged with the Stabler family in Alexandria before the split but now lamented that "the principles of infidelity . . . have taken deep root in that place."[44]

During his celebrated 1837–40 North American visit, English evangelical minister Joseph John Gurney also distanced himself from Hicksite Friends. In November 1838, he traveled to northern Virginia. Before his stay, Gurney had "no small anxiety" about ministering in these Hicksite neighborhoods, but he found Friends "generally treated me with great kindness and respect." Hopewell, Goose Creek, and Fairfax elders allowed him to use

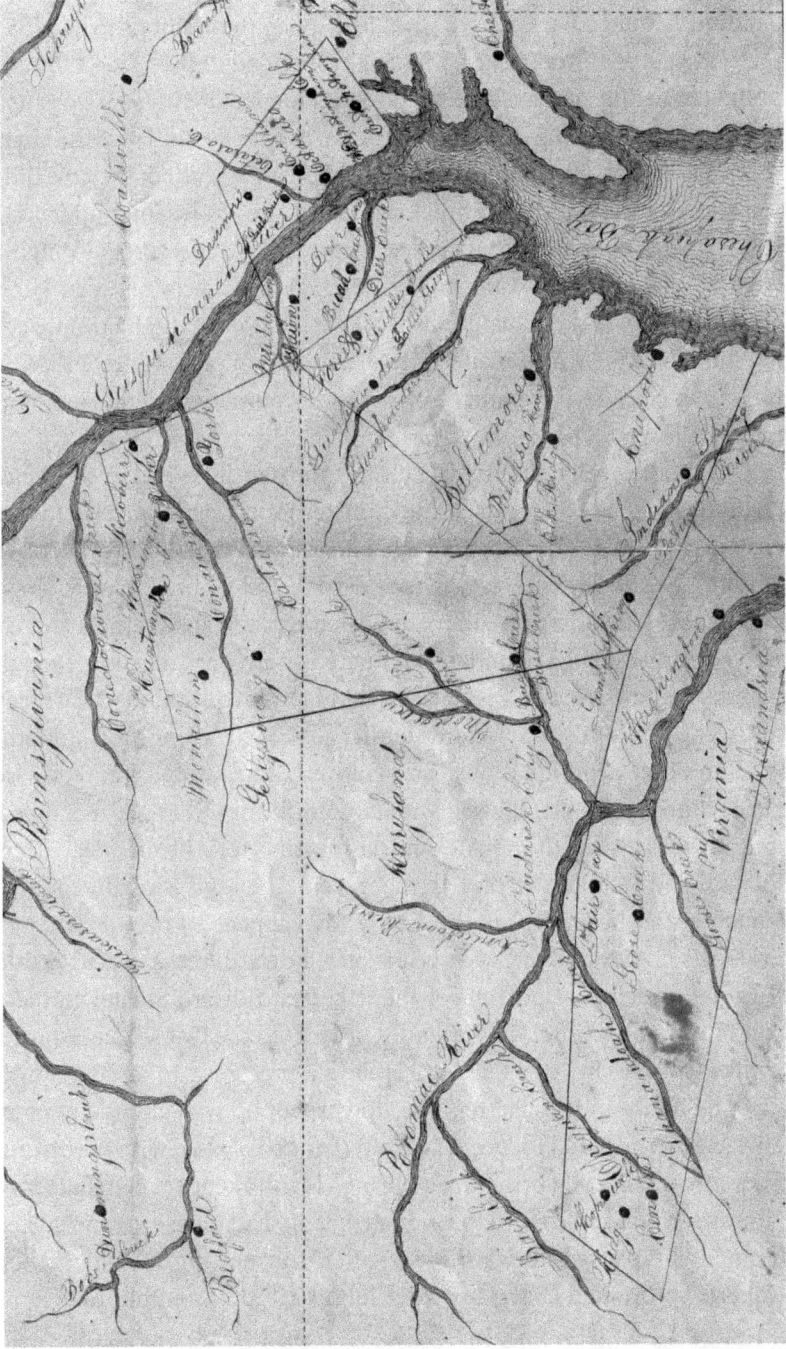

Map 3. Constituent meetings of the Baltimore Yearly Meeting of Friends (Hicksite), mid-nineteenth century. Courtesy of Swarthmore Friends College Historical Library.

local meeting houses for his appointed meetings. Local Hicksites, Gurney reported, attended his services in large numbers and listened with "attention to the scriptural evidences . . . of the divinity and atoning sacrifice of Christ." But Gurney would not attend any Hicksite services, which he believed "would have involved" him in a "compromise of principle." When the Hicksite Baltimore Yearly Meeting responded to his request for an appointed meeting with an invitation "to join them in their usual worship," he declined. By accepting the offer, Gurney argued, he would give the Hicksite meeting "a mark of religious fellowship, which the truth of the case did not warrant." Gurney never acknowledged Hicksites as Friends, applying the latter label exclusively to Orthodox members and meetings. To highlight what he saw as the *"fundamental"* doctrinal differences between Hicksite and Orthodox Friends, he published his rejection of the Baltimore meeting's invitation. He also made sure to visit and to provide "religious comfort" to the "scattered remnant" of Orthodox families who remained in the region.[45]

During their religious visits, Hicksite ministers likewise largely bypassed Orthodox Friends. When Hicksite minister John Comly traveled to northern Virginia in 1829, he made little effort to visit Orthodox meetings or families. At the Hicksite meetings at Fairfax and Goose Creek, Comly reported that "the doctrines of Truth flowed with great sweetness and ease." He visited the small, Orthodox-dominated South Fork meeting, though he noted that "few Friends" resided there and fewer still attended the meeting he arranged. Comly drew a large audience, "chiefly composed of Methodists and other denominations," and enjoyed "a heavenly favoured season." He declined visiting Hopewell with its significant Orthodox membership, journeying instead to the Alexandria meeting to visit his "dear friends" Edward and Deborah Stabler. In the wake of the separation, he found that "much social harmony and brotherly love appear to prevail among the Friends" of Alexandria. Seven years later, Edward Hicks visited northern Virginia to deliver a portrait of the deceased Edward Stabler to the Stabler family and to offer his "Friendly Advice" to the Goose Creek meeting. Unlike Comly, Hicks traveled to Hopewell, preaching to an "overflowing" meeting house in Winchester. The "townspeople" who attended, reported Hicksite Friend Sarah Pidgeon, "were very much pleased with the discourse. They said it was a real orthodox doctrine." Many attendees concluded that if Hicks's sermon reflected "Hixite doctrine," it "had been misrepresented to them." In his packed store "a few days after" the meeting, merchant Thomas Roberts confronted Orthodox elder John Griffith. "You told me," Roberts reminded Griffith, that "the Hick[s]ites did not believe in Christ. I am shure that man believes in him[;] it must be your part that does not." According to Pidgeon, the discomfited Griffith "made no reply, but hurried out as fast as he could."[46]

In part, the hostile reception Hicksite ministers received when they visited Orthodox meetings accounts for their choices. John Comly traveled through the New York and Baltimore Yearly Meetings after the split but found that few Orthodox Friends would listen to him. "Many," Comly reported in 1828 after the New York split, "have shut themselves up from intercourse or communion with those whom they once esteemed their friends." Quakers in small communities felt deeply the impact of the schism, as Samuel Janney discovered in 1833 when he accompanied New York minister Daniel Quimby on a religious visit to southern Virginia. "In his sermons," Janney reported to his wife, Quimby "steers between" the doctrines of Hicksites and Orthodox, and "no one can tell . . . which part in the society of Friends he belongs to." Still, when the pair reached the small Orthodox meetings in Richmond and Petersburg, Friends initially refused to let them attend. Richmond clerk Amos Ladd informed Quimby "that he could not consent to his holding a meeting in their meeting house as he was . . . a partisan of E. Hicks's." Quimby replied that he was "not a follower of E. Hicks or any man," but "preach[ed] the same doctrines" as Jesus Christ, "the apostles and early friends." Janney added that Quimby's sermons had the "approbation" of "Methodists, Episcopalians, and Presbyterians." How "very strange," Janney noted, that "orthodox friends should oppose him who profess to believe in the doctrines of early friends." Ladd ultimately relented, but "not many" attended the meeting and "there was not much openness to receive" Quimby's message.[47]

Janney concluded that "our side adhere[s] much more to the true *christian spirit* than those called Orthodox," though he attributed this to "the *leading members* of the orthodox party," whom he believed "have less christian charity than any other people in this land." Two years later he again confronted that uncharitable spirit. In contrast to most Hicksite meetings, Orthodox Friends disowned "separatists" even when they represented the majority of members. In the early 1830s, the Orthodox yearly meeting of Baltimore began disowning the much larger body of Hicksite Friends. Elders Joseph Townsend and Nicholas Poplin contacted Janney in late 1832 to investigate the allegation, made by Orthodox Friend Andrew Scholfield, that Janney had joined the Hicksites. Janney responded that "the charge is not correct," arguing that he held "views on doctrinal points . . . consistent with those of Geo. Fox, Wm. Penn, and Isaac Pennington." He decried the lawsuits that Philadelphia Orthodox Friends had initiated against Hicksites, seeing them as "mournful evidence that some of you have departed from the meek and peaceable spirit of the Lamb." Orthodox Friends remained unmoved by Janney's defense and disowned him some months later.[48]

Younger Friends who played no active role in the split could not escape the fallout. When Rebecca Jane Walker of the Fairfax meeting headed north to attend the Quaker boarding school in Kimberton, Pennsylvania, in the early 1830s, she confronted the split as she never had at home. Out of curiosity, Walker attended Hicksite and Orthodox meetings at Kimberton, noting the 1833 arrival of "a friend from N[ew] York" at the Orthodox meeting. "I think I have never heard any sermons that would equal this," she told her father. The minister argued that "one part" of the Society of Friends had grown "so deluded" as to "pin their faith" to the sleeves of "a few misguided men that only wished to establish a society of their own." Walker added: "I did not believe all this friend said." She also did "not like to hear" the sermons of Orthodox minister Sarah Emlen, who visited Kimberton the same year, though Walker thought Emlen "means to do good amongst us." For all her curiosity, Walker tried to stay clear of the debate among Friends. "I have never taken sides in debating parties in school . . . on topics of religion," she noted, because "I always think it is a good way to bring trouble on myself."[49]

Despite the efforts of members like Walker, the conflict remained a salient feature and a constant irritant among Friends throughout the nineteenth century. Years after the split, Orthodox and Hicksite Friends at Hopewell began worshiping at the same time, but they used the "wooden partition" formerly employed to allow men and women to meet apart to separate the meetings. Occasionally, when the Orthodox Friends had "a stranger" (a traveling minister) in their midst, they requested that Hicksites lower the "shutters," a "privilege" that was generally granted. However, when Samuel Janney visited the Hopewell meeting and asked Friends to open "the 'shutters' and doors," the Orthodox "refused." "We have never asked it since," a Hicksite Friend sadly reported in 1896, "but do not refuse them when they ask us." Still, the two groups cooperated on occasion. After the Civil War, Orthodox Friends "cheerfully contributed a goodly share" of the fifteen hundred dollars needed to repair the meeting house after Union and Confederate troops damaged it. But such collaboration remained rare, despite the declining number of Friends.[50]

IV

Such tensions wracked the Society long after the separation and moderates from both sides lamented their consequences. Among Hicksite Friends, the separation triggered internal conflict that weakened their Society. Hicksite insistence during the separation on individual conscience and the independence of meetings, led some northern and western Quakers, known as Progressive or Congregational Friends, to question the Society's hierarchical meeting structure and disciplinary rules. In response, Hicksite moderates like Samuel Janney enlarged their efforts to unite Hicksite and Orthodox Friends and bridge the divisions among Hicksites. In the 1840s, Janney traveled regularly to the North and Midwest to encourage a "unity of spirit" among Friends, and in the next decade he wrote Quaker histories to illustrate the beliefs shared by all Friends.[51] His labors encouraged conversation among moderate Friends, though they did not overcome the divide or end internal tensions. Moreover, the attention Janney and his fellow Hicksites devoted to doctrinal conflicts undermined the coherence of local meetings and distracted them from other Quaker ethical concerns.

Janney's reconciliation efforts began in 1842 when conflict erupted between Progressive Friends of the Green Plain Quarterly Meeting in Ohio, led by Joseph Dugdale, and the conservative leaders of the Hicksite Indiana Yearly Meeting. Inspired by "Garrisonian principles of equality" and Hicksite antiauthoritarianism, Dugdale and his allies in the Green Plain meeting wanted Friends to participate actively in the antislavery campaign and adopt more democratic and egalitarian forms of meeting governance. In response, the yearly meeting's conservative elders recommended dissolving the Green Plain meeting and removing four progressive ministers. Conservatives worried that Friends who allied with abolitionists would be drawn into political contests that would end in violence. They also believed activists would disturb the peace of the Society, something they wished to avoid after the tumult of the Hicksite separation. But suppressing the radicals only sparked more conflict. The Green Plain progressives refused to accept the yearly meeting's decision. They established their own meeting, arguing that it was "a settled axiom among our friends during the . . . Separation . . . that a meeting cannot be laid [down] without its own consent."[52]

Seeking peace among Hicksites, Janney arrived in Indiana in spring 1844 and met with conservatives and radicals. He called on the elders of the yearly meeting to rescind their removal of the ministers because they had not "privately labored" with them as the discipline required. After a conference with the radicals Janney convinced Dugdale to help pen a conciliatory address asking the yearly meeting to reconsider its decision to dissolve the Green Plain meeting. Janney hoped he could find a middle way and restore peace but admitted "there is no telling how it may eventuate." Over the next few years, he watched in dismay as Midwest Hicksites became more deeply divided and as similar divisions erupted in New York. Rather than submitting to the Indiana Yearly Meeting as Janney recommended, the Green Plain meeting maintained its independence. In 1848, it found allies among Progressive Friends in New York. The New York Hicksites withdrew from the Genesee Yearly Meeting after it laid down the Michigan Quarterly Meeting for "disregard [of] the injunctions of the discipline and the authority of the church." Meeting in Waterloo, the New York dissenters established the Yearly Meeting of Congregational Friends and embraced "the right of every member to act in obedience to the evidence of Divine Light, in its present and progressive unfoldings of truth."[53]

Janney opposed radicals' efforts to reshape Quaker governance, believing their promotion of extreme individualism posed as great a threat to Friends' "feeling of near unity with" one another as did Orthodox intolerance. In 1849, Janney undertook another fence-mending expedition to the Ohio Yearly Meeting, where Hicksite "reformers" called for congregational government and Friends' involvement in antislavery. After six days of debate—centering on whether the yearly meeting should accept an epistle from Congregational Friends—the reformers established their own independent body. Janney welcomed their decision. He sympathized with the radicals' political goals, but concluded that congregational government and participation in reform movements promised further schism among Hicksites. During the trip he sided with the "conservatives" of the Ohio meeting. The separation of the reformers, he concluded, "will contribute much to the peace and unity of our Society" by demonstrating to Friends "the tendency of that spirit." Upon his return to Virginia, Janney ended contact with radical Joseph Dugdale, whose actions had caused "nothing but disorder and confusion."[54]

Janney could not find a middle way with activist Hicksites, but he continued his efforts to close the breach with moderate Orthodox Friends, a task that consumed him in the 1850s. During a religious visit to a meeting house shared by Hicksite and Orthodox Friends in western Pennsylvania, he listened to an Orthodox minister. "Her sentiments," he reported, "appear to me to be very good and I could not but regret most deeply the circumstance in which we were placed." Believing he could "do something towards promoting a reunion between the two branches of the Society of Friends," Janney began writing a biography of William Penn, hoping to attract a broad Quaker audience that would recognize Friends' shared theology. Collecting evidence for the book became an exercise in building bridges to Orthodox Friends. Janney relished a visit with J. Lippincott and Alfred Cope, Orthodox Friends who shared with him "a valuable document connected with the life of Penn." During preparation of the second edition of the Penn biography, Janney met with the editors of the Orthodox *Friends' Review* to fix "any mistakes." They expressed their "full approbation" of Janney's work, and he happily concluded that "Orthodox Friends are nearly as warm in" their "commendation" as Quakers "of our branch." Janney also conversed with Thomas Evans, "one of the most influential" Orthodox ministers of the Philadelphia meeting. Janney noted that Evans received him with "great cordiality," and upon "comparing" religious views, Janney "found less difference" between himself and Evans than he "had expected." With only "a few slight alterations [Evans] agreed to my statement of the view of G. Fox on Doctrinal subjects."[55]

After receiving Janney's second book, a biography of George Fox, Evans "expressed unreservedly his deep regret at the separation which has occurred among a once harmonious brotherhood, and desired that we . . . cultivate towards each other feelings of affectionate interest." By the early 1850s, many Hicksites believed the time ripe for reconciliation because of the internal divisions among Orthodox Friends. In 1843, minister John Wilbur had led a small group of Friends, concerned by the evangelical doctrines of Joseph John Gurney and Friends' involvement in reform movements, out of the Orthodox New England Yearly Meeting. The conflict soon spread through American Orthodox yearly meetings, dividing Friends in Ohio, Indiana, and, in the early 1850s, Philadelphia. Many Hicksites believed the debate among Philadelphia's Orthodox Friends presented an opportunity to reach out to moderates in that meeting. The "difficulties among Orthodox friends," noted Philadelphia Hicksite Dillwyn Parrish hopefully, "will have the effect to make them more tolerant, and prepare some for the reception of the truth with regard to our portion of the Society."[56]

Parrish told Thomas Evans about Janney and his fellow minister Benjamin Hallowell's efforts to reach a property-sharing agreement with Baltimore's Orthodox Friends, an issue that had divided other meetings. In 1852, the Goose Creek meeting, led by Janney, proposed that Friends make "an equitable" distribution of property "according to numbers" in "those places where separate meetings have been established." Quaker meetings, the proposal noted, held property "for the common use and benefit of all . . . members," and thus "it would be right" to divide the property equitably. The Fairfax Quarterly Meeting embraced the proposal, and the Baltimore Yearly Meeting considered it in 1852. Janney held no illusions about the proposal's success. As he noted to Caleb Carmalt, the clerk of the Genesee Yearly Meeting and a fellow advocate of reconciliation, reunion could not "take place while those old persons in *both branches*, who were concerned in the separation, are living." After "solid and deliberate consideration," the committee appointed to weigh the proposal declared "that way does not open for any action on the subject by the Yearly Meeting." According to Janney, "the opposition of some elderly Friends" killed the measure. Still, moderate Orthodox Friends like Evans "appeared interested" in Janney's proposal.[57]

Hallowell and Janney also reached out to British Friends, the way paved by the positive reception of Janney's biographies. William Bennett, an editor of the *British Friend*, gave Janney's biography of Penn a glowing review, though British Quakers officially recognized only Orthodox American Friends. "We consider this new life of William Penn," Bennett opined, "incomparably the best we have met with, and quite expect it will be held the standard work by Friends" and "the public at large." "I have ever cherished the hope," Bennett wrote weeks later, "that old breeches [in the Society of Friends] may yet be healed," and he looked to works like Janney's to "help clear some things up." Not all English Friends agreed (one labeled Janney's book "dangerous" because of its doctrinal errors), but a door had opened. In early 1854, Janney started corresponding with Bennett, delighted that some British Friends welcomed his biographies. "It seems," noted Janney, "like mending one link of the broken chain by which the Friends in your country were once . . . united with us."[58]

The London Yearly Meeting's 1856 "Salutation" to American Friends of all branches appeared to Janney another manifestation of a new "liberality" among English Friends. The Baltimore Yearly Meeting for Sufferings, however, had a mixed reaction to the London missive. Despite its call for "a true restoration . . . wherever divisions or differences have existed," the salutation stressed orthodox doctrine and lamented the fate of Friends who, "beguiled by the specious appearance of a refined spirituality," had rejected "fundamental Christian truth." The meeting for sufferings declined to respond because the London meeting directed its address to individual Friends, but it permitted members to answer. Hallowell and Janney jumped at the opportunity. Their letter noted the inclusion in the London address of "a few expressions . . . which we do not approve," but they praised it as "an excellent paper" that "breathes a spirit of earnest devotion to the cause of Truth." They stressed that American Hicksites and London Friends "agree entirely in the fundamental and practical points" of doctrine—quoting extracts from Baltimore Yearly Meeting addresses to show similarities—and called on Friends to "throw the mantle of charity over the rest, as those errors which arise from different education and training."[59]

Many Friends on both sides of the Atlantic did not concur, as Janney well knew. In an editorial published in the leading Hicksite journal, the *Friends' Intelligencer*, Philadelphia elder Ann A. Townsend complained that the London Yearly Meeting had ignored the "affectionate addresses" of the Philadelphia Hicksite meeting in 1828 and 1830. She believed that "a remnant of that spirit" still remained in the 1856 salutation. No reconciliation could take place, Townsend stressed, "while certain points of doctrine"—namely, the Orthodox belief that Christ's crucifixion remained "instrumental in the salvation of man"—were "considered essential to the Christian faith." Orthodox Quakers, Townsend concluded, had "departed" from the "ancient landmark 'mind the Light,'" and only when they returned to this fundamental Quaker tenet could reunion take place. Hallowell commended Townsend's "good and logical" address, but lamented that it did not "promote that restoration of . . . Christian fellowship, which seem so essential to the full support, and spread, of our . . . religious principles and testimonies." Many British Hicksites displayed a similar lack of charity. Twice in the 1850s, Janney tried unsuccessfully to get essays published in the *British Friend*, the most liberal of British Quaker journals. In 1854, he submitted "The True Grounds of Religious Union," a call for reconciliation between British and American Friends. Three years later, the editors rejected a Janney essay that offered reasons for the decline of Quakerism in Great Britain.[60]

"Thirty years—a generation—have elapsed since the separation," noted Hallowell in 1858, but the wound remained raw for Friends. This bitterness ensured that Hallowell and Janney's efforts to find a middle way failed. (Not until the mid-twentieth century would Hicksite and some Orthodox Friends reconcile.) For local Friends, the division remained a reminder that they had fallen short of the spiritual harmony "for which Friends were once so remarkable." As Edward Hicks lamented in the Goose Creek Meeting House in 1837, when "Friends departed from the . . . spirit of Jesus," they lost their "peaceable kingdom." Friends seemed headed toward "two sad extremes": the "church of the anti-christ" for the "extreme orthodox" and "unitarian scepticism" for "extreme ultra reformers." Only by embracing "the unity of spirit and bond of peace," Hicks concluded, could "religious Friends on both sides" reconcile. Despite the efforts of Orthodox and Hicksite moderates, this middle way proved elusive.[61]

But the separation had more practical consequences. Unfolding while migration to the Old Northwest depleted northern Virginia's meetings of numbers and leadership, the split threatened the viability of small meetings. Low numbers forced Orthodox Friends to discontinue or consolidate local meetings, leaving empty meeting houses as the remnant of once-thriving Quaker communities. The numerically dominant Hicksites also suffered. Depleted membership and increased tensions with Orthodox Friends diminished community coherence and support networks. Local meetings became more dependent on "weighty Friends," the ministers, elders, and overseers who imposed Quaker discipline, provided community leadership, and offered spiritual guidance. As the minutes of the monthly meetings attest, elders and ministers such as Janney and Hallowell remained active in their local meetings. But their fixation with finding common ground and effecting reconciliation between Orthodox and Hicksite Friends distracted them from local matters and weakened their ability to sustain northern Virginia's Quaker community.

The Hicksite division also influenced Hallowell and Janney's approach to other Quaker concerns, including their long struggle against slavery. External opposition undermined Friends' commitment to antislavery. The white backlash after Gabriel's Rebellion and Nat Turner's revolt forced local Friends to drop for a time their campaign against the institution. But doctrinal discord within the Society also shaped their antislavery labors. Quaker activists like Janney and Hallowell had less time to commit to antislavery as a result of their attempts to end internal divisions. When Janney began writing his Quaker histories he abandoned his public addresses against slavery (though white Virginians' proslavery consensus in the 1850s played a central role in his decision). More profoundly, internal discord reinforced Quakers' moderate inclinations and convinced them to find a path between radical extremes. The Hicksite split taught local leaders that they must adopt a "meek, Christ-like" approach to appeal to the better natures of their adversaries. Extremism, they concluded, alienated their opponents and encouraged further division. Friends found precedent for a moderate antislavery approach in eighteenth-century Quaker quietism, but the bitterness of the Hicksite split reinforced this tendency.

Finally, the theological conflict had an impact on the internal gender dynamics of northern Virginia's Hicksite meetings. Women always possessed significant influence within Quaker governance, but the schism and its aftermath distracted male leaders and opened the door for women to play a larger role. In smaller meetings a few charismatic individuals could dominate proceedings. Samuel Janney, an effective and respected minister, social activist, and voice of reason, played such a role. Local Friends recognized the strength of his leadership from the outset of his ministry. In 1832, Jacob Janney of the Goose Creek meeting noted Samuel's appearance as "a new young preacher" at the quarterly meeting. "From his talents and superior mind," Jacob Janney noted, "he will make one of the first preachers belonging to the society if he is careful to keep in the wright track." Samuel fulfilled his early promise and by the 1850s had become the Hicksite Baltimore Yearly Meeting's foremost minister. But in midcentury, Friends began to notice his frequent absences from the community, including his failure to attend the spring 1861 Fairfax Quarterly Meeting. Janney missed that meeting to oversee the Philadelphia publication of the first volume of his history of the Society of Friends, designed like his biographies to promote Quaker reconciliation. "One young friend" wondered "whether a quarterly meeting could go on without Cousin Samuel." Janney's absence, his wife Elizabeth reported, placed a "double weight" on the only other minister in attendance, Miriam Gover. In response, she delivered "solemn and impressive sermons" to the assembly.[62] With Janney gone, Gover's spiritual authority among Friends rose, a glimpse of how the Hicksite separation impacted the position and role of women in the Quaker community.

Strengthening the Bonds of Fellowship

The Domestic and Public Lives of Quaker Women

One Sunday in July 1857, Rebecca K. Williams, the clerk of the Fairfax women's meeting, attended a particularly "favored" meeting. Minister Miriam Gover and her traveling companion, Williams's aunt, Susan Walker, had returned to Fairfax after a two-month religious journey to the Genesee and New York Yearly Meetings. "It felt pleasant," Williams reported, "to have our dear Friends Miriam and Aunt Susan to meet with us again." Gover had followed her husband Jesse Gover into the ministry in 1834, and when he died eight years later, she became Fairfax's foremost minister. Thereafter, Gover ministered regularly to a receptive meeting. "Her concerns were weighed so long and so well," Friends remembered, and she spoke "with a clearness and precision that left no doubt on the minds of her friends as to the source from whence the call emanated." When Gover traveled abroad, as she did twenty-eight times in her ministerial career, Fairfax Friends often sat in silence in their meetings, deeply missing her "practical . . . communications." When Gover died in April 1863, the meeting's heartfelt memorial praised "her labors for the cause of truth and righteousness." Williams, Gover's friend and companion, emphasized the key role she played in the meeting. "She indeed was as a mother to us all," recalled Williams, "and greatly shall we miss her words of council and the influence of her watchful waiting."[1]

The 1828 Hicksite separation and outmigration to the West eroded the cohesion of northern Virginia's Quaker community. Many "weighty" Friends departed, creating a leadership vacuum and eroding personal and economic networks that helped maintain the community's "partial isolation from the world." Friends worked hard to retain their values and meetings, but they worried how to maintain their distinctiveness in a region dominated by slavery and slaveholders. As Seth Smith, living in the town of Union in Loudoun County, noted in 1838, "the old stock of friends in this neighborhood are all gone," and in the early 1850s, Smith would leave too. By 1860, the population of the four surviving Hicksite Quaker monthly meetings in northern Virginia—Goose Creek, Alexandria, Fairfax, and Hopewell—had fallen to under one thousand people from the approximately two thousand Friends of the 1780s. In the Quaker villages of Goose Creek, Lincoln, and Waterford, Friends faced a crisis as the community structures, economic ties, and personal and religious networks that enabled them to live as a people apart from their slaveholding neighbors declined.[2]

In these circumstances, the roles of women, though always important, expanded and helped sustain the community. Women like Miriam Gover and Rebecca Williams assumed leadership positions within the Society, and by the late 1860s female Friends insisted on full equality within the meetings. Women Friends' attendance at the region's Quaker schools reflected their enhanced status. At these institutions, female Friends obtained education and employment, enabling them to participate in northern Virginia's antebellum middle class culture. Women Friends also forged a variety of informal ties that helped sustain the Quaker religious community. As male Friends' economic dependence on the broader white community grew, female networks of support became essential for preserving Friends' sense of separateness. Women's socializing, nurturing, and association building, in short, superseded men's economic networks as a source of group cohesion.[3]

Friends' doctrine and history gave women a distinctive role and status within their community, but they still could not escape the influence of southern values and practices. Quaker women, like their male counterparts, eschewed slavery and provided steady employment for northern Virginia's free black population. A few women joined efforts to aid African Americans, primarily by teaching in black schools. Unlike northern Quaker women, however, few of northern Virginia's female Friends played active roles—at least before the Civil War—in promoting progressive social causes. External social pressures and women's tacit acquiescence in southern racial values and embrace of middle class conventions constrained them. As a result, the region's Quaker women rarely crossed the divide that separated black and white, and they often treated the African American women who worked for them as inferiors. Social and theological turmoil among antebellum Quakers thus had complex consequences, both weakening northern Virginia Friends' distinctiveness while expanding leadership opportunities for women like Miriam Gover. Female Friends trod an uncertain path as they tried to sustain their weakened community and ethical concerns in the face of the South's pervasive racial and social conventions.

I

Quakers had always accorded women a special status. In the seventeenth century, Quaker founder George Fox and his wife and partner Margaret Fell reinterpreted the Pauline doctrine of female inequality laid out in 1 Corinthians and 1 Timothy. Rejecting traditional Christian doctrines, Fox and Fell viewed women and men as spiritual equals, both possessing an inward light that made them capable of divine revelation. From this source came new understandings of biblical teachings, including Paul's injunctions against women in the church. Fox argued that before Adam and Eve committed the original sin woman and man lived as equals. The fall, he asserted, gave rise to women's subordination, but the gender equality of Eden returned after believers experienced spiritual rebirth. William Penn made the same point, noting, "Sexes make no difference; since in souls there is none." Paul's injunctions, then, did not pertain to spiritually reborn Quakers and their church, but only to the unregenerate world.[4]

However, Friends' belief in women's spiritual equality failed to translate into social equality, particularly after marriage. Friends accepted the gender conventions, enshrined in religious doctrine and legal practice, of eighteenth-century English Protestants. Male Friends "insisted on" women's subordination, and few Quaker women complained about their inferior social status before the nineteenth century. In a 1676 epistle addressed to "faithful women's meetings," Fox called on women to be sober, discreet, and chaste, to love their children and husband, to be "keepers at home," and to be "obedient to their . . . husbands." Seeing women as an essential component of a Godly household, Quakers praised female Friends who embraced domestic virtue and subordinated themselves to their spouses. To protect women's status as nurturing mothers, male Friends denied women economic authority within the family and limited their participation in the marketplace. Friends' emphasis on female subordination arose in part from a desire to safeguard the Society's social respectability. Challenging existing gender relations posed a threat to Quakers' social position, and women Friends recognized that they must protect their reputation for respectability and virtue. As a result, "Quaker writings about marriage" emphasized "the necessity for a woman to be submissive to her husband."[5]

Still, the Quaker commitment to spiritual equality enabled women to widen their authority within the church and expand what was socially permissible. Most notably, Quaker women became ministers, known as "traveling" or "Public" Friends. By the late eighteenth century, ministers had a variety of functions. Usually traveling in single-sex pairs, they visited Quaker meetings around the United States and abroad to promote Friends' spiritual vitality, console the distressed, and ensure adherence to the Quaker discipline. The latter function became more important after the Society's spiritual "reformation" in the mid-eighteenth century. Traveling women Friends from distant American and English yearly meetings regularly visited northern Virginia. Between 1795 and 1813, Hopewell minister Rachel Neill recorded the visits of 139 traveling Friends to her monthly and quarterly meetings, including fifty-one women (37 percent of visitors). In 1795, English Friend Martha Routh spoke "something very Close to the Slaveholders" of the region. Four years later, Hannah Pewsey from Pennsylvania gave an "offering" to the Hopewell meeting "like the Turtle Dove." Neill found these visits enlivening in part because they reminded Friends of their distinctiveness.[6]

Northern Virginia's women spiritual leaders also visited meetings far from home, and they played a crucial role in providing moral guidance within their own communities. In 1768, Fairfax minister Sarah Janney accompanied English minister Rachel Wilson to South Carolina because Janney "had bin under an ingagement for sometime to pay a Religious Visit to the Southern parts" of the American colonies. Janney remained an active minister into the nineteenth century, traveling to meetings, speaking to non-Quaker audiences, and visiting Quaker families in Virginia and Maryland. During these visits she held impromptu services, offered advice and support, and looked for violations of the discipline. During a 1778 visit to lapsed Quaker Thomas Lewis, "some Men" whom Lewis had invited to his home "to argue with us" confronted Janney and her companions. Undeterred, Janney responded directly to her male questioners, bringing "the poor" men "to Silence." "We were," she added, "thankful for that favour." Janney thought such visits "Laborious" but "Beli[e]ved the Lord had Called us in that Service."[7]

Still, some Quaker women found speaking in public and exercising spiritual authority over men difficult. Raised among Virginian Episcopalians, "who believe in the apostolic injunction that women are forbidden to speak in churches," Harriet J. Moore reluctantly assumed the "duty" of ministering in the Society. After a lengthy struggle, Moore concluded that "strength is dispensed sufficient for every emergency." She entered the ministry in 1838, some fourteen years after she first accompanied Margaret Judge on a religious visit to southern Friends. Women born and raised within Quaker families found it easier to assume such responsibilities. Over the course of her long life, Goose Creek elder and founding member Hannah Ingledew Janney visited local Friends, advising and influencing the decisions of male coreligionists. After Isaac Nichols disinherited his daughter for dancing (a violation of the Quaker discipline), Hannah visited him. "After an hour's persuasion and argument, Isaac was well whipped" and consented to a codicil (written by Hannah) that gave his daughter an equal share of the estate. As spiritual advisors, female preachers had significant influence over Society members, with few aspects of Quaker life beyond their purview.[8]

Fox and Fell's call to forge what historian Barry Levy has called a "spiritualized household" prompted Quaker leaders, over the objections of many male Friends, to grant women a significant role in domestic and church government. Fox and Fell argued that Quaker families needed reorganization to aid parents' nurture of the inward light within their children. They stressed the need for Friends to approve the marriages of members to ensure that "spiritual leadings" superseded physical and emotional passions. Such "spiritualized" marriages between full members, they hoped, would create a domestic environment of holiness. Fox and Fell also encouraged Friends to adopt intensive methods of child raising that emphasized parents' emotional self control, tenderness, attentiveness, and firmness. Because the oversight of domestic matters usually fell to "the mothers of families," they contended that women needed to play a prominent, even authoritative role in the family. All households required a self-disciplined, holy, and rational woman to sustain Quaker domesticity.[9]

But Fox and Fell also realized that the Society needed to cultivate such women, and in the 1670s they pushed Friends to create women's meetings. "Many things women may do, and speak of amongst women," Fox explained, "are not men's business." Friends belonging to the Maryland Yearly Meeting (later the Baltimore Yearly Meeting) established the first women's yearly meeting in America in April 1677. Like men, women monitored Friends' attendance at meeting and called on members to speak and dress in "plain" fashion. They excoriated "hireling" ministers; warned members to avoid lying, slander, and falling asleep during services; called for increased love and unity among Friends; communicated their opinions and concerns to their constituent meetings; and corresponded with other yearly meetings. Women's meetings also focused on women's domestic and familial roles, believing they possessed the moral authority to promote a "deeper religiosity" and shape the behavior of their husbands and children. Female Friends called on members to extend charity to "Widows, Orphans and . . . Poor" Friends, and they collected and distributed funds to those in need, enabling them to handle money independently of men. They also promoted children's "guarded" education, though Chesapeake Quakers made little progress in establishing schools before the late eighteenth century.[10]

In the 1770s, the Baltimore Yearly Meeting Women Friends helped the Society end slaveholding in its ranks. As a domestic institution, slavery concerned women who oversaw the household and benefitted from black labor. The women's meeting felt a duty to ensure that members acted with "Justice and Equity" toward African Americans. It urged women to free the enslaved and provide moral and practical education for black people after emancipation, particularly those who lived "in friends['] families." Women believed that their domestic authority enabled them to effect change in the household. If wives stood "firm in the belief that justice is due to all men," the women's meeting announced in October 1790, they could "be instrumental in . . . convincing the unbelieving husband." The women's meeting recognized that dependent women could not legally own slaves, but they would remain bound to the institution until Quaker men freed their slaves. The campaign against slavery required a coordinated effort of women and men.[11]

Quaker women began their antislavery work in earnest in 1778 when the Baltimore Yearly Meeting decided "the time is now fully come" for the monthly meetings "to testify" against any Friend who owned, hired, or oversaw slaves. Working in concert with male Friends, the Baltimore women's meeting sought to convince "our Brethren and sisters" to give "a close consideration" of "their duty towards" enslaved and free African Americans. In 1782, the meeting reported that "encreasing Care appears to bear a Testimony against slavery," but also noted the "Deficiencies . . . respecting giving that people Suitable Learning." Three years later, the women's meeting had made progress in ending slavery among Friends but also expressed concern that "divers [women]" remained implicated in slavery because "the heads" of their "families are slaveholders." By 1790, when northern Virginia Friends joined the Baltimore Yearly Meeting, the women's antislavery campaign had met with considerable success. The women's meeting announced that members were "Clear of holding . . . Slaves . . . and some care hath been taken of those who are set free." However, the problem of wives married to slaveholders remained. A year later, the women's meeting explained that two female Friends still owned slaves, "one of which is . . . under Care, and the other . . . the Mistress only has a Right of Membership." As late as 1802, a few Quaker women still remained slaveholders because their non-Quaker husbands refused to relinquish their human property. Women Friends also lamented that members did not in all cases provide aid to their former slaves. In 1796, nine women Friends joined with six men to visit members who had free African Americans "under their care."[12]

The authority of the Baltimore Yearly Meeting Women Friends reflected the influence of female Friends in the monthly meetings, where they dealt with—and frequently disowned—women who violated the discipline or attended meetings infrequently, as well as provided charity for poor coreligionists and chose female representatives to attend quarterly and yearly meetings. The women's meetings investigated and regulated Quaker marriage practices, ensuring that both parties to a marriage were members in good standing without prior commitments. In the first decade of the nineteenth century, the Fairfax Monthly Meeting of Women Friends disowned twenty-one women for marriage contrary to the discipline (usually for marrying a non-Quaker) and another five women for fornication or bearing illegitimate children. The meeting also reinstated three women whom the meeting had previously disowned for marrying out of unity and examined thirteen prospective marriage partners seeking permission to marry. In this latter task, the groom as well as bride appeared twice before the female elders. As in other Quaker meetings, the women of the Fairfax meeting then forwarded their decisions to the men's meeting for approval.[13]

Women's meetings in northern Virginia handled the same issues as their northern counterparts, but the southern environment altered the nature of female concerns. Attending to charitable matters in the region usually required women Friends to investigate how members treated African Americans in their employ. Only once in this ten-year period, in November 1810, did women Friends believe it necessary to inspect and attend to "the necessities of the poor." However, on at least five occasions they intervened to aid local blacks or punish Friends for mistreating African Americans. In 1802, the women's meeting quickly disowned Susan Canby, who, with her husband, beat their African American serving boy so severely that he died from his injuries. Such "inhuman conduct," the women's meeting concluded, is "reproachful to our society." The women's meeting also appointed committees to "examine the situation of . . . [free blacks] among us" and reminded members of the prohibition against hiring enslaved African Americans and the injunction that Friends treat with care free blacks they employed.[14]

Within the women's meetings, female Friends learned new skills and expanded their authority and responsibility. Still, they did not enjoy equal footing with men before the 1860s. All the decisions of the women's meetings required the concurrence of male Friends who, in contrast, could act without consulting the women's gatherings. Likewise, women could not sit on the meeting for sufferings, the executive body within each yearly meeting. As early as the 1830s, some American Quaker women protested these inequalities. But only a few meetings responded to the demands of female reformers. Not until 1877 did the Philadelphia Yearly Meeting embrace the principle of full female quality. Quaker women had more success in the Hicksite yearly meetings of New York and Genesee, both home to many liberal Friends. These meetings changed their disciplines in 1838 and 1839 respectively, recognizing that men and women stood "on the same footing on all matters" and requiring both male and female branches of the monthly meetings to "obtain the concurrence of the other." Before the Civil War, only Progressive Friends—who separated from Hicksite meetings in Philadelphia, Ohio, and New York in the late 1840s and early 1850s—followed suit and "recognized" the "equality of women." Progressive Friends decided that "perfect" equality required disbanding separate meetings altogether so that men and women could "transact business jointly."[15]

Friends in the Baltimore Yearly Meeting acted more slowly. Many of the meeting's leaders judged the reformers' actions "inconsistent with good order, and due respect for the rights of others." They feared that endorsing any Progressive innovation would propel their meeting to a "confusion of tongues" and "strife, contention, and anarchy." "Friends," warned the editors of the Hicksite *Friends' Intelligencer*, must remain "on guard against" the Progressives' "spirit of assumed liberality," which "invariably" leads to "intolerance and oppression." Most Friends, they continued, "are convinced of the necessity of order and discipline in conducting the affairs of religious and civil society" and judged their long-established "system of government . . . the offspring of Divine Wisdom." Orthodox Friends' criticism of the Progressive schism in Ohio, which many attributed to Hicksite doctrines, also fed local conservatism. Too closely associated with the religious radicalism that threatened to destroy the order of the Society, women's equality found few adherents among northern Virginia's Friends.[16]

In spite of the limitations on female authority before the Civil War, Quaker women enjoyed more autonomy and influence than women of most other American religious groups. Women's meetings at all levels of Quaker governance enabled female Friends to exercise influence over both genders. They forged a culture in which women expected to have public responsibilities and men recognized female authority. And they enlarged women's organizational and leadership abilities, which some Quaker women utilized outside the meeting in reform and educational endeavors. Women's meetings, in short, served as an essential training ground for the social activism of nineteenth-century Quaker women.[17]

II

Education opened opportunities for female Friends to develop and exercise those skills. Deep-rooted Quaker beliefs about the importance of education facilitated women's access to schooling. Although some early Friends believed that reliance on the inward light and the rejection of a paid ministry made advanced education unnecessary, both Fox and William Penn stressed "liberal" learning that offered children "useful knowledge" that was "consistent with truth and godliness." Such training served as a supplement to the moral guidance that Quaker children received at home. For Penn, such "useful" learning included "mathematics, building houses, or ships, measuring, surveying, dialing, navigation," and "agriculture especially." Following Penn, Friends believed that education should offer children practical skills to promote economic success and religious training to ensure their moral welfare. Friends did not draw a sharp distinction between secular and spiritual education, convinced that becoming "a better Quaker" required training in both realms. Equally important, Friends did not draw distinctions between men and women's access to education. The domestic and spiritual responsibilities of Quaker mothers required that women have access to a "guarded" education that provided useful skills and moral training.[18]

But Friends had difficulty implementing these ideas. In the eighteenth century, most American Quakers were literate, but outside the Philadelphia region the Society established few schools before 1750. Sparse populations, recent settlement in frontier regions, lack of financial support from the yearly meetings, and unfriendly colonial administrations conspired to limit local schools. Consequently, most Quaker children learned the fundamentals of literacy and ciphering at home. The Quaker reformation of the 1750s convinced Friends to pay more attention to the schooling of their offspring. A "guarded" education, parents concluded, would shield Quaker children from the broader community and help them retain their membership. "Ought not the education and training of the youth," asked Philadelphia Friend Anthony Benezet, "be . . . the chief concern of every one that really desires the welfare and enlargement of the borders of Zion?" Prompted by Benezet, the Philadelphia Yearly Meeting, to which the meetings of northern Virginia belonged until 1790, reminded it members "of the importance of training up our youth in useful learning."[19]

Still, reformers had limited success. In 1778, a yearly meeting committee appointed to examine Friends' schools concluded that, despite the meeting's "pressing recommendations, very little has been effectually done." Widely distributed, the committee's report focused Friends' attention on the issue of education, as did the establishment of the coeducational Ackworth Boarding School by English Friends the following year. Boosters touted the benefits, curriculum, and organization of the Ackworth School, which garnered the support of the London Yearly Meeting. In 1778, the Warrington and Fairfax Quarterly Meeting, following a directive of the Philadelphia meeting, established a committee on education. A year later, it reported that all the monthly meetings had made a start, raising money (£202 by the Fairfax meeting), purchasing lots, and building school houses. They added that "a want of proper persons for School Masters in many places" hindered progress, but the region's Friends had committed themselves to building and supporting Quaker schools.[20]

In their efforts to expand education, Friends ensured that their daughters and sons had comparable access. Scholars have argued that Friends' practice of delayed marriage enabled unmarried young women to attend school longer and become teachers after graduation. But marriage and motherhood remained the expectation of most Quaker women, and Friends viewed education as the means to ensure that mothers provided moral guidance to their children. Thus, female education included domestic training, though Quaker schools also taught women the same academic subjects as men, a practice with radical implications. Rigorous schooling transformed the self-image of women Friends, who soon assumed intellectual (not just spiritual) equality with men. Educational opportunities widened Quaker women's critical and cultural horizons, and for some, opened up new careers. Historian Mary Kelley describes a similar process among middle- and upper-class American women. Encouraged by ideas of republican motherhood, more American women attended boarding schools and academies to gain the moral and civic knowledge necessary to raise republican children. Many of these women used education as a springboard to expand their participation in the nation's civic life. But Quaker women attained more public prominence than other religious women; one scholar estimates that 40 percent of women abolitionists and 15 percent of women's rights advocates were Friends. Such activity speaks to the transformative power of female education linked to Quakers' spiritual values.[21]

Among northern Virginia's Friends such changes came slowly, in part because prior to 1820 their efforts to maintain schools faltered. Although the Fairfax Monthly Meeting reported one school in 1779, it failed to remain open. In 1802, the meeting scrambled to raise funds for a new coeducational school and succeeded in 1807 at a cost of four hundred and twenty dollars. The Hopewell Monthly Meeting also had difficulty keeping open a school. A 1784 committee reported that it had purchased four acres of land, built a schoolhouse, and begun construction on a dwelling for a "school Master," but found among some Friends "a remissness" to support the effort. Nonetheless, by the 1790s Hopewell meeting oversaw two coeducational schools. Children belonging to the Goose Creek Monthly Meeting, created in 1785, attended a coeducational school taught by Quaker Philip Sharp in the 1790s, but despite efforts to raise funds in 1801 and 1802, the meeting did not build its own school, Oakdale, until 1816. Costing four hundred dollars to construct, the coeducational facility trained Goose Creek children until after the Civil War.[22]

The Goose Creek meeting's efforts reflected worries within the Baltimore Yearly Meeting that the region's Quaker youth could not obtain an education that shielded them from worldly influences. Outmigration after 1810 fueled these concerns. Friends' spiritual memoirs often describe a youthful period of engagement in the "gay" fashions of the world, followed by spiritual searching. But young Friends living in a contracting Quaker community had more contact with "the world," increasing the danger to their religious identity. Before she became a Quaker minister, the young Margaret Brown's "interesting and instructive" company drew to her "distinguished persons of both sexes" in the District of Columbia. But her "growing popularity" among non-Friends threatened to draw "her mind . . . unduly . . . from its true center." Only a teaching appointment at a Quaker school near the Sandy Spring Monthly Meeting in Maryland removed her from this "danger" and set her on a path to spiritual leadership. Likewise, minister Miriam Gover floated "thoughtless with the current" as a young woman, associating with "young people who" indulged "in much gaiety and frivolity." Only after "great conflict of spirit" did she gain "mastery" over "self" and recognize the "convictions of duty."[23]

Before he became a minister, Edward Stabler lived in Leesburg, the county seat of Loudoun County, learning the apothecary trade from his brother. In a town with few Friends and a significant slaveholding population, the young Stabler became enticed by "the attractions and dissipation of fashionable society." Only the guidance of his sister-in-law, who served as a surrogate mother during his stay in Leesburg, saved him from this "alluring danger." As a father, Stabler worried about the spiritual fate of his children. The family resided in Alexandria, home in the 1820s to a strong Quaker community, but during one of the city's periodic yellow fever epidemics he sent his daughters to the countryside where they developed "a fondness for gayety of apparel." Adopting the worldly "fashions and manners" of the Virginia elite, Stabler warned his girls, was "like . . . heaping up fuel that must at some future time be consumed by fire." A decade later, former Loudoun County resident John J. Janney tried to convince his father-in-law Seth Smith to join him in Ohio by pointing to the "evil example" of Virginia on his daughters. The "girls," Janney averred, are now at "the time of life" when "their associations and . . . ideas of moral rectitude and correct deportment will be formed." The slaveholding residents of the region, he warned, provide "few examples worthy of imitation."[24]

Such fears propelled the creation of Quaker schools. In the Alexandria meeting, Stabler wrote the 1814 report that called for establishing Quaker-run schools. Noting the "susceptible and imitative minds of" youth, Stabler stressed the "importance of securing our children" the "advantages of a well ordered education." Friends must found "select schools" "superintended by . . . the Society" and conducted by "well qualified teachers in membership with us." In response, the Alexandria meeting established separate girls and boys schools. Rachel Painter, a recent graduate from Westtown, a Quaker boarding school near Philadelphia, arrived in Alexandria in 1815 to head the school for girls. The meeting paid her five hundred dollars per year and by 1820 she taught thirty "scholars" the subjects of "Reading, writing, English Grammar and the four first rules of Arithmetic." When her school encountered financial problems in 1820, she reduced "the price of tuition" and the monthly meeting reduced her salary. Still, she thought her "prospects . . . tolerablly favourable." In 1824, Margaret Judge (later Brown) opened a school for girls, which she directed for three years.[25]

Throughout the 1790s, the Baltimore Yearly Meeting did little but encourage subsidiary meetings to establish schools. In 1815, the yearly meeting followed its own advice, collecting more than twenty-five thousand dollars' worth of pledges from the quarterly meetings to establish a boarding school. The money enabled the yearly meeting's education committee to purchase three hundred acres of land near Sandy Spring, Maryland (site of a Quaker meeting), with buildings to house sixty to eighty students. The committee anticipated that the boarding school, called Fair Hill, would accommodate only "Male Scholars," but decided in 1819 that "females should equally participate in the advantages desirable from a guarded education" and admitted girls the following year. The committee hired Friends Samuel and Anna Thomas to superintend the school, Benjamin Hallowell to teach mathematics, and Margaret Judge to instruct girls. In 1820, almost sixty boys and girls attended the school. The following year, the committee hired another woman, Hallowell's future wife Margaret Farquhar, to accommodate the rising number of female students.[26]

Rising debt forced Fair Hill to close in 1826, but Friends' interest in education remained high. Indeed, the yearly meeting had difficulty raising money for Fair Hill in part because the monthly meetings increased aid to local schools. By 1816, in addition to boys and girls schools established by the Alexandria Monthly Meeting and the coeducational institution built by Goose Creek Meeting, Fairfax supported a school taught by Friend Pennock Passmore, and Hopewell had "three schools taught by members of our Society." Many of these schools did not last long—the Fairfax school closed when Passmore left Loudoun County in 1817—but Quakers remained committed to maintaining neighborhood schools. An 1853 survey of the schools within the Baltimore Yearly Meeting revealed Hicksite Friends' support of education. The parents of Fairfax Quarter's almost three hundred children could choose between eighteen schools taught by Friends, though only the Goose Creek school was overseen by a monthly meeting. Northern Virginia Friends with the financial means also sent their children to Philadelphia-area Quaker boarding schools, including Westtown (established in 1799 by the Philadelphia meeting), Kimberton in Chester County (established in 1817), and Sharon in Delaware County (established in 1837). Fairfax Friend Rebecca Jane Walker attended a "large and pleasant" Kimberton in the early 1830s and the Griffith family from Hopewell sent their children to Westtown.[27]

But more Quaker parents put their children in the growing number of local Quaker-run schools for boys and girls. After his tenure at Fair Hill ended in 1824, Benjamin Hallowell opened a boys' school in Alexandria with the financial help of local Friends. At first, the student body consisted of the sons of Friends. But as the reputation of Hallowell's school grew, it attracted local elites, including a young Robert E. Lee, and the sons of southern politicians such as Alabama Senator Arthur P. Bagby and South Carolina Senator John C. Calhoun. To satisfy the growing demand for female education, Hallowell's wife, Margaret, opened an academy for girls over her husband's school in 1826. Samuel M. Janney also began a boarding school for girls, Springdale, in Loudoun County in 1839. In the school's first semesters, Janney enrolled the children of Friends. But Springdale soon acquired a strong academic reputation, and attracted non-Quaker students, including the daughters of slaveholders from Virginia, the District of Columbia, and Maryland, in addition to students from Ohio and Pennsylvania. Despite their varied backgrounds, the young women who attended the school developed intense emotional bonds. They became, in the words of one valedictorian, "a band of sisters" whose "endearing ties" would "decorate our hearts through long years of absence." As student Julia R. Headley noted, "I shall be very sorry when my schooldays come to finis for they have been very happy ones."[28]

Janney's young students acquired more than close emotional bonds at his school. As a minister, Janney required that all his scholars attend Friends' worship on first and fifth days unless their parents requested an exemption. "We find by experience," Janney wrote one parent, "that to break off from our secular employments in the middle of the week and to spend an hour in . . . divine worship has a salutary effect in withdrawing our affections from worldly things and promoting our spiritual growth." Still, Janney did not ignore the world. He developed a demanding curriculum for his scholars, prompting one student to complain about the "musty school books" she had to read. The course of study included traditionally feminine subjects such as drawing, painting, and needlework, but Springdale also offered a range of subjects comparable to that offered at all-male schools. Students learned the sciences, including natural philosophy, astronomy, chemistry, and physiology; arithmetic, bookkeeping, and algebra; English grammar, composition, and rhetoric, in addition to the French language; and history and geography. Compared to the curriculum offered at boys schools, Springdale excluded only classical languages and literature. As Janney noted in an 1850 advertisement, "Every effort is made to induce in the minds of the pupils a love of knowledge and desire for excellence."[29]

Janney's school had a profound impact on some students. Like Hallowell, he included practical or "experiential" learning in his teaching, using Springdale's rural setting to instruct scholars about the natural world. Students spent time outside the classroom in all seasons, conducting "walks" through the countryside. Julia Headley pursued a love of botany under the tutelage of Janney and teacher Jane S. Hewitt. "How I should love to be a naturalist!" Headley exclaimed in one letter home, attributing her interest to having "been so much in the country." Her enthusiasm inspired fellow students. After studying "beautiful insects" with Sally Ann Caldwell of Clark County, Virginia, the two women decided they "would love to study entomology"—though Headley conceded their interest was "woman-like" because the insects' "gay colours" "captivated us." Headley's stay at Springdale also sparked a concern for the mistreatment of Native Americans, while her study of the romantic poet Margaret M. Davidson, who died at the age of fifteen in 1838, prompted Headley and her fellow students to form "a literary association." Headley's fiction writing revealed the impact of her education. In one of her stories, a traveler to Loudoun County attends the Goose Creek meeting out of curiosity. The visitor had observed many "modes of worship," but never had he witnessed anything "so still yet so sublime" as Friends' silent worship. While he sat "meditating[,] a lady [rose] and delivered a few short but impressive sentences." "I confess," concluded the traveler, "for the first time I was convinced of the powers of woman!" Young women like Headley were empowered by the challenging education Janney provided.[30]

Parents seeking a demanding education for the daughters could find it elsewhere in the region. In 1846, Quaker James S. Hallowell opened the Alexandria Female Academy. James moved from Philadelphia in 1840 to teach at his uncle Benjamin Hallowell's boys academy. Two years later, when Benjamin briefly retired, James took over the school with his brother Caleb. When Benjamin returned to teaching, James opened his girls' academy, which thrived immediately, enrolling in its first year "52 scholars," who "seem pleased with us and the school." Hallowell soon expanded the building, reporting in 1858 that he had over sixty "pupils . . . and more engaged." Like Janney's Springdale, Hallowell's academy offered a range of academic subjects: "a complete English course, including Composition, Natural Philosophy, Chemistry, Physiology, Astronomy, and various branches of Mathematics." The school also offered hands-on learning with a variety of scientific apparatus, including "a superior Achromatic Table Telescope." More traditional female fare included French language classes, offered by "an accomplished French lady who resides in the Institution," and music lessons "taught by a proficient teacher."[31]

Hallowell's students, like those at Janney's school, participated in civic life and commented on the era's foremost political questions. And contemporaries praised his school, noting that "parents and guardians" will find few "more desirable situations" for their daughters. At Hallowell's academy, observed another, "the morals of the scholars will be guarded, a parental care experienced, and faithful instruction afforded." Hallowell's students also had high praise for his school. Former student Lucy P. Dorsey remembered her time at Hallowell's school fondly, even the recitations of lessons for her "dear teacher." She left school with the intellectual confidence to comment on the political questions that divided the nation—though with a female twist. "The country," Dorsey pronounced in 1860, "is in a most deplorable condition" because of the actions of South Carolina. "Isn't it a pity," she added, "that *the state* could not be treated as I once saw an obstreperous *kicking* child served—picked up and plunged head-foremost into a tub of water!"[32]

The challenging education that women Friends (and non-Friends) received in the region's Quaker-run academies improved young women's intellectual abilities and heightened their self-confidence, encouraging many to pursue professional careers that drew them into public life. Young women who attended these schools still embraced gendered assumptions about female domesticity and benevolence, and the inclusion of drawing, painting, music, and needlework in some schools' curriculums ensured that their education continued to highlight gender difference. Still, these schools changed the women who attended them. Quaker teachers began with spiritual assumptions that justified female education; their desire to produce "useful" citizens who could improve the world resulted in a practical, skills-based curriculum that made minimal distinctions between men and women. For young women Friends, the curriculum reinforced the Society's spiritual imperative to effect positive social change. Within these schools young women of all backgrounds developed the rhetorical and critical thinking skills to participate in the civic arena. They acquired intellectual self-confidence that encouraged some to become teachers, writers, and reformers.[33] But they did more. Friends' promotion of female education and contributions to the region's associational life helped forge southern middle class culture.

III

Northern Virginia's middle class—professionals, merchants, planters, and successful artisans—supported the growth of schools in the region, reflecting their embrace of republican ideals. Despite the region's slave-based economy, they believed like their northern counterparts that schools helped produced the disinterested men and republican mothers necessary to sustain U.S. political institutions. The growth of Quaker educational institutions also helped Alexandria's civic leaders promote the city and region as a cultural and educational center. Town boosters argued that "the healthiness of the town . . . the excellent society—and the contiguity to

Washington" made "Alexandria a desirable" location for schools. School promotion increased during the economic downturn of the 1820s and 1830s, when boosters identified education as a source of economic growth and a means for individuals to acquire middle class status and its cultural trappings. In 1794, Alexandrians established a subscription library "to diffuse useful knowledge" and "establish the morals of the rising generation." Forty years later and in conjunction with the library company, civic leaders created a lyceum where those who could afford the entrance fees enjoyed lectures and debates on moral philosophy, science, politics, and religion. The popularity of the lyceum's programs, "designed for the moral and intellectual improvement of the mind," convinced the institution's founders to raise money for a new building, opened in 1839. The lyceum's directors also sponsored national and state-wide educational reform efforts, sending representatives to the May 1840 and 1841 national conventions for the promotion of education, held in Washington and Philadelphia.[34]

In all these efforts, Alexandria's civic elite, like those in region's smaller towns, reflected the values of a white, urban southern middle class. In northern Virginia, Quakers played a prominent role in the creation of the middle class, endorsing and publicizing its cultural, educational, and literary (if not racial) ideals. Edward Stabler served as one of the first librarians of the library company and Friends remained active as directors and supporters of the institution throughout the early nineteenth century. In the late 1830s and 1840s, Quaker George Drinker became librarian, while four of the company's eleven directors were Friends. Quakers also played a key role in the establishment of the lyceum. Benjamin Hallowell helped found it, appealed to the town's wealthy Quaker merchants to support it, and gave frequent lectures after it opened (as did other Friends). These lectures reflected local Quakers' interest in a range of "useful" subjects, including science, history, benevolence, economic development, and moral questions. In January 1840, Quaker apothecary William Stabler delivered a medical lecture; a month later Quaker merchant George S. Hough discussed "The Progress of Events in American History." Lyceum attendees also debated weekly questions of cultural and moral significance. Friends influenced the content of these queries. The night of Hough's lecture, for example, attendees discussed a perennial Quaker dilemma: "Is a person under a moral obligation to obey a law which he deems unjust?"[35]

Local Friends' creation of schools and their promotion of educational reform and literary and cultural institutions helped Alexandria emerge as a regional cultural center. Friends brought to the region's middle class culture

Quaker notions of the appropriate roles of men and women in civic and domestic life. As Quaker historian Barry Levy argues, the domestic arrange-
ments of eighteenth century Friends became "the foundation and model"
of domestic relations among white middle class Americans in the early republic. To protect the spiritual welfare of their children, Quakers developed
the gendered assumptions—the selflessness, moral superiority, and emotional sensitivity of women—that undergirded the nineteenth century's
"cult of domesticity." Affectionate and virtuous women, eighteenth-century
Quakers and nineteenth-century Americans believed, played a crucial role
in the household. Within the confines of a warm and emotionally inviting
family circle, women inculcated virtue among their children and refined
the morals of their husbands. Spiritual imperatives—especially ensuring
that their children cultivated the inward light—propelled Quakers to this
conclusion. Political and cultural imperatives led middle class Americans
to embrace republican motherhood and the cult of true womanhood. Regardless of intent, the outcome was similar: women's responsibilities lay
within the domestic sphere, overseeing the moral welfare of their families.
The middle class culture of antebellum Virginia reflected the intersection
of Quaker domestic values and American gender assumptions.[36]

Linking femininity and virtue could have radical consequences, as the
preaching of female Friends and the moral oversight of women's meetings
revealed. More often, the gender values that underpinned nineteenth-century domesticity had conservative implications. White women sought to
reform the nation in a variety of voluntary associations, but men oversaw
their efforts and the institutions they created. White women could become
writers and shapers of public opinion, but gender conventions restricted
their occupational choices and required that they defer to men in public
debates. Women could even participate in electoral campaigns and voice
their opinions at political rallies, but only men could vote. Most important,
women could exercise moral influence within the family, but through coverture men controlled the family's property and economic destiny. Failing
to question the conventions that sustained their subordination ensured that
nineteenth century white women rarely breached the domestic "sphere."
As historian Lori Ginzberg notes, the conventions themselves became the
weapon wielded by social conservatives to control reformers who sought
improvement in women's social and economic status.[37]

Conservative gender values existed throughout nineteenth century
America, but they were most pronounced in the South, where racial and
gender hierarchies reinforced one another, and white men and many white

women embraced gender and class subordination in order to protect their racial privileges. Recognizing that their status rested on the South's interwoven gender, class, and racial inequalities, southern white women accepted their circumscribed social position in exchange for the benefits accorded them by the region's racial hierarchy. Despite her active writing and intellectual career, for example, planter's wife Louisa McCord criticized reformers who called for female equality and urged southern women to embrace patriarchy and domesticity. Slaveholding widows, who after the deaths of their husbands had economic autonomy and shouldered responsibilities normally handled by men, did likewise, supporting rather than questioning the social hierarchies of the South. Undermining female subordination, they realized, threatened to undo the social and economic power of the southern planter class to which they belonged.[38]

Friends absorbed and assimilated the nineteenth century's changing notions of domesticity and femininity, but their opinions differed in important ways. First, seventeenth-century Friends' belief in the spiritual equality of the genders led them to institutionalize women's meetings and accord high status to women preachers and elders. Friends recognized women's enhanced roles within the Society as an essential component of their distinctiveness, enabling religious women to exercise real authority over Quaker men. Women Friends also moved out into the broader world, preaching to "promiscuous" (or gender-mixed) audiences and engaging in the civic life of the region. Many non-Quaker women recognized the radical implications of domesticity and feminine morality, and embraced these cultural conventions to enter public life. They engaged in the work of benevolence, and moral and social reform, and they pursued new careers in teaching, writing, and editing. But shorn of Friends' institutionalization of gender spiritual equality, the conservative implications of the conventions limited the possibility for real change.[39]

Second, Friends rejected slavery and the racial hierarchy of the South, particularly the link between racial and gender subordination. At their most idealistic many Quakers envisioned a society of racial equality—or at least one without racial antagonism. Although never free of the taint of racial paternalism, Friends made persistent efforts to aid African Americans. While the Quaker millers and merchants who purchased slave-produced grains, the Quaker storekeepers who sold imported goods at healthy profits to slaveholders, and even the Quaker schoolmasters who taught the sons and daughters of slaveholders profited from the inequities of the southern slave economy, they also believed that free labor would promote economic development, enhance profits, and ensure social and cultural improvement for black and white. Friends also rejected the hierarchical social vision of white southerners, who identified racial and gender inequalities as inter-locked pillars of southern life. In uncoupling racial and gender subordina-tion, Friends did not see, as did white southerners, the specter of social disorder and economic collapse. Shaped by their environment and concern for social respectability, many Friends were reluctant to grant women full equality, but they remained willing to accord women greater respect and responsibilities, both within the Society and in public.[40]

Finally, Friends' unwillingness to separate the secular and the spiritual realms of life and their consequent tendency to see productive labor as a "calling" altered their view of women's labor. As historian Jeanne Boydston argues, the growth of a cash-based market economy in the eighteenth cen-tury led to a decline in the "cultural visibility" of domestic female labor. Standing largely outside the market, housework did not produce visible profit or increase the property holdings of the family. Without markers of economic value, Americans disparaged women's contributions to the household. Evangelical preachers of the Great Awakening, according to historian J. E. Crowley, sanctioned this shift in Americans' perception of productive and useful labor. Sensing moral danger in all market activity, evangelicals questioned the notion of a secular calling and emphasized instead the spiritual obligations of Christians. However, the evangelicals' attack, intended as a critique of individual greed and selfishness, had the "ironic effect" of setting profitable and self-interested labor beyond the orbit of faith while placing spiritual callings "outside the realm of material rela-tions." The redefinition of the calling transformed attitudes toward women's unpaid household work, concealing its economic relevance. Housewifery and motherhood enjoyed an enhanced ethical significance, but Americans devalued the economic significance of "women's" work. The diminished status of domestic labor marginalized the women who performed it.[41]

American culture's evolving view of domesticity and gender, associated with the rise of evangelicalism, influenced Friends. However, even Ortho-dox Friends who espoused aspects of evangelical theology eschewed reviv-alism and emotional conversion experiences. Despite doctrinal differences, all Friends continued to believe that sanctification—living a sin-free life—remained the pathway to justification (or salvation). Friends, especially Hicksites, looked to actions rather than beliefs to measure the moral worth of an individual. As a result, they infused productive labor with spiritual value, retaining the notion of the calling. Humans performed good in the world, Friends believed, when they followed the guidance of the inward light, whether this led them to careers in education, commerce, science, or housewifery. Any useful work pursued diligently had value, regardless of its economic profitability. Friends remained wary of the moral dangers of the pursuit of profit for its own sake, measuring the value of work in ethical rather than economic terms. For them, the usefulness of an individual's secular work stood as an index of their spiritual worth. Friends praised motherhood in the same idealized terms as other white Americans and they accepted society's gendered division of labor, but their emphasis on the moral dimensions of work led them to see women's work as no less valuable than men's. And they remained willing to accord Quaker women more equality within the Society and to countenance a wider range of public roles for them.[42]

IV

Significant numbers of northern Virginia's women Friends participated in the region's civic life, embraced local reform efforts, or pursued professional careers, though the South's social pressures restricted their activism. Like Quaker men, women Friends grounded their public endeavors in their faith, believing they had a spiritual duty to undertake productive work. Most women directed their energies toward the family and household, but a few stepped beyond it, frequently becoming teachers. Women began teaching in the region's Quaker schools in the early nineteenth century, though they remained few in number and Goose Creek Friend John Janney recalled "we never heard of a woman teacher" before the mid-1820s. In part, rising demand for teachers pushed women into the classroom. As Friends established more schools, even well-respected institutions like Samuel Janney's Springdale struggled to find qualified teachers. Country schools had particular difficulty attracting competent instructors. John Janney remembered that his teacher, a former student at Fair Hill, lacked the training to "take me through the [algebra] book" assigned to the class. A few years later, the Goose Creek meeting hired Martha Ann Wilson to teach its school, and throughout the 1850s it employed female Friends to teach "during the summer."[43]

Wilson taught a coeducational school, but more often women taught girls exclusively either in single-sex schools or gender-segregated classes. The separation of the genders had numerous sources, and not until the 1850s did Quaker educators consider the merits of teaching the sexes together.

Single-sex education extended Friends' practice of entrusting older women to teach domestic and child-raising skills to teenage girls. Friends believed their daughters should have "industrious habits," especially "the art and mystery of housewifery," which was "so necessary to adorn the female character." Friends' practices echoed broader cultural trends. Advocates emphasized that education prepared young women for republican motherhood and domesticity, topics that required women teachers. Gender separation also reflected fears that a coeducational environment might lead to temptation. Young male teachers, who taught briefly before moving to more lucrative professions, posed a threat to female chastity. Southern educational goals reinforced single-sex education. Middle class and elite southerners embraced female education and an expanded curriculum, but they viewed them as vehicles to transform young women into ladies. The gender-specific goals of southern education encouraged the use of women teachers and ensured that "the idea of coeducation never gained headway." To attract non-Quaker students, Quaker educators like Samuel Janney and James Hallowell conformed to the pedagogical practices of the region.[44]

But teaching also offered Quaker women a sense of independence and opportunities to enhance their intellectual life. Quaker girls deeply admired their female teachers and they became role models. After Rebecca Jane Walker's return from her Philadelphia boarding school, students kept her apprised of the changes at the school. Teacher "Aunt Margaret," M. A. Brooke informed Walker, "has left us and gone to Wilmington Boarding School." Fortunately, former student "Miss Elizabeth Biddle," whom Brooke's "love[d] . . . dearly," had taken Aunt Margaret's place. Brooke also admired her drawing teacher, Hannah Shibe, who "paints most splendidly from nature" and "understands drawing better than" their former teacher "aunt Susan." After growing close to "Misses A. and M." (Abigail and Martha Kimber), Walker developed a "notion of being teacher," excited by the possibility of a useful calling. She identified Abigail Kimber, "always in a good humour except when she has something to . . . be *mad* about," as a model to emulate. But Walker worried that such "a hard task" would not suit her because she struggled with her academic work.[45]

Like Walker, most southern white women did not pursue teaching careers prior to the Civil War. Numerous Quaker women, in contrast, embraced the opportunity to teach. When Rachel Painter returned to Philadelphia in 1830, she gave direction of her Alexandria school to her pupil, local Friend Mary Ann Talbott. After attending the Goose Creek school, Seth Smith's daughters Letitia, Kezia, and Hannah taught for a time in Loudoun

County. Letitia enjoyed and took pride in her work. "I like teaching," she noted in 1854, "though the office is a responsible one, and we sometimes have difficulties to encounter." Students who attended Springdale Boarding School also opted for teaching careers. Mary Walker Lupton taught a school in Winchester after earning high grades at Janney's institution. In 1860, a female cousin wrote to inquire how Lupton fared in her new position. Perhaps considering a teaching career herself, the cousin asked Lupton, "How many scholars has thee now?" "I would like so much," she added, "to peep in and see thee some day in school."[46]

Some educated Quaker women took their calling to teach outside the classroom, inspired by the example of female ministers who combined spiritual and social activism. When English Friend Martha Routh preached before a racially and religiously mixed Berkeley County audience in 1795, she made "some remarks concerning . . . the unjustness of the traffic" in slavery. She recognized the dangers of speaking against slavery, but used a conciliatory tone so that her message did not "lose the desired effect." She remained committed to following her inward guide and denounced slavery, even in the midst of its supporters. "I thought," she remembered, "I should not care how many slave-holders had been present." During the War of 1812, minister Rebecca Hubbs dreamed that she must visit President James Madison and speak out against the war. Virginia Friends arranged for Hubbs and her traveling companion to visit Madison's Montpelier home, and the president and his Quaker-born wife Dolly entertained the two Quaker ministers despite their message. When Quaker Lucretia Mott visited Virginia in fall 1842, she "plainly" if respectfully "rebuked" slave-holders "for the robbery and wrong they were committing on their fellow creatures." She also visited President John Tyler, urging him to emancipate the slaves.[47]

Mott acknowledged that her visit and antislavery sermons worried some "timid and fearful" "elderly Friends," but "the younger class of Friends . . . acknowledged the truth of what was said." Women were among her most receptive listeners. Visits by female ministers like Mott inspired some Quaker women to act on their spiritual beliefs and participate in benevolent reforms. Women Friends like Elizabeth Newport realized that gender enabled them to speak when men could not. At a public service held at a Maryland courthouse in 1850, Newport drew a hostile crowd when she declared that "every Christian must be an Abolitionist." But they did not act, and Newport's Quaker companions realized that "if E[lizabeth] had been a man instead of a woman, he would have been carried out of the [court] house." Alexandria Friend Margaret Judge made a similar discovery during an 1824 religious visit to Virginia and North Carolina, during which she spoke "forcibly" against slavery. But she encountered little hostility, even when she verbally "battered" "the slaveholding system" "to pieces." Non-Quaker audiences assembled in large numbers when she preached, "excited" by the "novelty of seeing and hearing a Friend, and a female, too." In contrast, "an inquisitive landlady" chastised Judge's companion, Harriet Moore, when told that Moore had left her husband and family at home. The boardinghouse owner charged Moore for the night's stay, while allowing the antislavery Judge to stay for free.[48]

But such ill-well did not quiet the women, nor did it stop female Friends from educating African Americans. In 1796, the "deeply exercised sisters" of the Baltimore Yearly Meeting urged Friends to provide "education and religious improvement" for the "neglected . . . black people" "under their care," a theme to which they returned regularly. In 1801, white threats after Gabriel's Rebellion closed the Quaker-run Alexandria First Day School, but Goose Creek Friends educated African American children alongside their own into the 1820s. Women also participated in the black education efforts of the Alexandria Benevolent Society. In September 1827, nine women met with nine male members of the benevolent society to write a constitution for a new First Day school. The group appointed Anna Stabler, eldest daughter of minister Edward Stabler, director of the female school, and George Drinker (who helped establish the 1797 school) director of the male school. Literacy, the constitution of the school noted, prepared the enslaved "for the enjoyment of freedom" and "render[ed]" "free people of colour . . . better members of society." Like the other activities of the benevolent society, the First Day school collapsed in the face of white opposition after Nat Turner's 1831 revolt. But Stabler remained a teacher. In the 1840s, she moved to Sandy Spring, Maryland, where she helped direct the Fulford Boarding School for boys.[49]

Women Friends continued efforts to teach African American children after 1831. In Baltimore, "young sisters" opened a school for African American girls in 1832, concerned about "the advancement of those oppressed daughters." In the wake of Nat Turner, the Virginia legislature raised the penalties for teaching free and enslaved blacks to read and write, increasing the dangers for Friends who supported black education. Still, in 1848 the Fairfax Quarterly Meeting petitioned the state assembly unsuccessfully for permission to educate "the free colored children in our immediate neighborhoods." Friends, the petition explained, felt a spiritual imperative to

Figure 6.1. Portrait
of Elizabeth Janney,
c. 1860s. Courtesy of
Swarthmore College
Friends Historical
Library.

educate African American children under their care, but their "religious
duty" "forbid[s] our doing any act in . . . opposition to the Laws of the
Government." Quaker men presented the petition, but the growing number
of female teachers understood its significance. Five years later, Samuel Janney's family confronted the ethical dilemma directly. When Janney closed
the Springdale school in 1852, he no longer needed to placate slaveholding
parents. The family opened a First Day school for free blacks, overseen by
Cornelia Janney, Samuel's twenty-year-old daughter. "Our school for coloured children," reported Janney's wife Elizabeth, "has been well attended."
She acknowledged that "the short time allotted" to students "to study" made

"much progress in learning" difficult, but she believed the school served an important purpose: "it convinces them [African Americans] there are some white people who feel a disinterested desire to do them good."[50]

Circumscribed by the racial and gender conventions of the South, few local Quaker women dared pursue racial benevolence farther than the Janneys. Yet if gender constrained Quaker women from pursuing the radical ends of some of their northern counterparts, it also enabled them to evade the physical threats directed at men and pursue benevolent reforms such as African American education. Quaker women's spiritual commitments pushed some to speak and act publicly, in the process challenging the region's gender and racial practices. "The Friends of Virginia," noted traveling Friend Lydia Wierman after an 1845 visit to the state, "are holding up a light in the world around them."[51] She might have added that women Friends played an integral role in Quakers' commitment to do good, notwithstanding white Virginians' hostility. But Friends also confronted internal challenges. Doctrinal division and population decline weakened economic bonds between the region's male Friends and undermined the community's wellbeing. These circumstances magnified Quaker women's status as spiritual "mothers" charged with unifying the community. The same internal turmoil, however, made them more vulnerable, less able to maintain a Quaker "hedge" against the world and resist the social and cultural values of the South.

V

The departure of Quaker families and leaders from northern Virginia after 1800 destabilized the community and disrupted economic and family ties. The first Quakers in the region patented more land than they needed and sold it to incoming Friends, usually brothers or in-laws; Quaker merchants and craftsmen provided apprenticeships and jobs to young men among their relations; and successful Quakers became sources of capital and advice. The resulting web of relationships helped bind the community and reinforce its culture and beliefs despite its outsider status in Virginia. Over time, however, the flow of Friends out of Virginia eroded economic connections. With fewer Friends able to offer aid and advice, young Quaker men attained economic independence with more difficulty, accelerating the movement of Friends from the region. Letters written by one-time Virginia residents comparing economic opportunities in the Old Dominion unfavorably to those in Ohio and Indiana encouraged the departure of ambitious young men. In the West, Virginia Friends learned, "poor people can get along much better . . . than in Va." Those who "possessed the means to start with," westerners told their erstwhile neighbors, had "many opportunities to make money."[52]

Such reports convinced many northern Virginia Friends that their future lay in the West. Numerous migrants traveled in family groups, but young men left in greater numbers than Quaker women. By 1860, adult women comprised over 56 percent of the region's three meetings, and the unbalanced sex ratio increased the number of unmarried women. The Fairfax meeting had a particularly large gender imbalance, with women comprising nearly 63 percent of the adult population, while in the Shenandoah Valley adult women made up almost 60 percent of the Hopewell meeting. Quakers placed the harmonious partnership of husband and wife at the center of their communal life. Friends' insistence on endogamous unions reflected their belief in the significance of the domestic partnership to ensure that they and their children adhered to the callings of the inward light.[53] Growing numbers of unmarried members diluted this Quaker ideal of domesticity and undermined the wellbeing of a community demoralized by the Hicksite separation. The combination of theological schism and outmigration posed a threat to community cohesion and identity. Northern Virginia's Friends faced a perilous moment.

For Quaker women, this crisis became an opportunity. Long accustomed to exercising responsibility, women reaffirmed female bonds within the Quaker fellowship, and in the 1840s and 1850s these female ties supplanted many of the community's male-dominated economic links. As historian Nancy Hewitt notes, within the "religious arena" "the disruption and decline of male authority" has often been "accompanied by the nurturance and expansion of women's power." The Quaker community of northern Virginia experienced a similar "historical moment" in the mid-nineteenth century. The repercussions of the Hicksite split and demographic decline enabled Quaker women to expand their spiritual and communal roles, just as religious women had during previous eras of "schism, division, and upheaval."[54] The enlargement of female Friends' authority followed two paths. First, women assumed additional leadership roles and exercised their moral influence more overtly. Second, women's traditional domestic duties—taking care of the sick and aged; aiding expectant mothers; providing emotional support in times of loss; and sharing information, goods, and services—took on greater significance as men's economic networks weakened.

The Fairfax meeting, smallest in the region and most affected by out-migration, witnessed this increase in women's authority. Like all monthly meetings in the Hicksite Baltimore Yearly Meeting, Fairfax chose its own elders. These individuals visited Friends within the meeting, enforced the discipline, oversaw ministers, and corresponded with the quarterly and yearly meetings. Fairfax nominated more women than men to the post. Between 1810 and 1865, twenty-eight individuals served as elders in the Fairfax meeting, including fifteen women (54 percent). More striking, the gender imbalance grew over time. In the two decades after 1810, men and women divided the duties of elder equally (seven women and eight men). After 1850, five women but only two men became elders. Transfer of responsibility to women reflected the declining number of men and placed the burden for community building on women. The meeting's corps of ministers also reflected this unequal division of labor. Of the seven ministers the Fairfax meeting recognized between 1800 and 1865, six were women. This included Miriam Gover and Louisa Steer, both of whom entered their periods of greatest activity in the 1840s and 1850s. A gender imbalance also developed within the Hopewell meeting, particularly after 1820. Women constituted 57 percent of the fifty-one individuals who served as elders between 1810 and 1865. By 1860, the division of labor among elders paralleled the gender imbalance within the two meetings.[55]

Although a more balanced gender ratio existed in the Alexandria meeting, women became elders in greater numbers than men, especially after 1840. Seventeen of the Alexandria meeting's thirty elders between 1810 and 1865 were women (59 percent), but they constituted ten of fifteen elders after 1840 (67 percent). In contrast, the Alexandria meeting enjoyed the ministry of six men over the years but only one woman, Deborah Stabler. The largest meeting in the Fairfax Quarter, Goose Creek, followed a similar pattern: a preponderance of male ministers, but a rising number of women elders who oversaw the community's daily spiritual welfare. Women represented nineteen of the meeting's thirty-four elders between 1810 and 1865 (56 percent), but the gender imbalance grew after 1840, when ten women and seven men served as elders. Five of Goose Creek's eight ministers after 1810 were women, but the meeting had no female ministers after 1847 when Sarah S. Brown died. Samuel Janney, who became a minister in 1838, was the meeting's religious leader.[56]

Overall, 56 percent of elders within the Fairfax Quarter and almost half its ministers between 1810 and 1865 were women; by the 1850s women made up almost 60 percent of the quarter's elders. As the percentage of female Friends serving as elders rose in the 1840s and 1850s, however, so did the percentage of male ministers (75 percent by 1860). This pattern looks similar to what occurred within most Protestant churches and their benevolent auxiliaries, where male ministers directed female-dominated congregations. But in the Quaker community female elders exercised great authority in the local meetings. In the years before the Civil War, women played a central role overseeing Friends' spiritual welfare and initiating new concerns. Hopewell's "exercise[d]" women sparked the 1848 establishment of a new school. In Fairfax, the women's meeting faced fewer disciplinary cases as the meeting's size declined, but its authority expanded. In the 1850s, the women's meeting investigated five couples wishing to marry and two women who married out of unity; issued certificates of removal for twenty-seven members and accepted the resignation of four more; investigated the request of one individual who wished to join the Society; and admitted the certificates of twenty-seven Friends who moved to Waterford. Women exhibited concern for Friends' treatment of local African Americans, disowning Mary Jane Hough after she hired a slave. Women Friends prepared an 1852 report describing local schools for the quarterly meeting. They also handled requests by the meeting's two female ministers to undertake religious visits to Friends near and far.[57]

Yet even with their enhanced authority women Friends could not escape entirely the South's social and cultural values. Like Quaker men, women members sought to protect the Society's—and their own—reputation for respectability. This concern helps explain the decline in the number of female ministers after 1840. As white Virginians grew intolerant of dissent, most local female Friends avoided speaking before mixed audiences or flouting the region's notions about women's proper sphere. Friends understood that their antislavery beliefs angered white Virginians; transgressing the region's gender conventions made them more suspect. When Quaker women such as Elizabeth Newport and Lucretia Mott condemned slavery to "promiscuous" audiences, proslavery whites could dismiss them as northern interlopers. Virginia Friends followed a more circumspect path. No record exists of Fairfax's Miriam Gover speaking against slavery. Her caution combined with a grandmotherly persona—physical frailty and plain Quaker dress—frequently sparked sympathy among non-Quaker listeners.[58]

Southern hostility made the prospect of public speaking daunting to most Quaker women. In December 1859, Gover asked Rebecca Williams to accompany her to the Baltimore and Warrington quarterly meetings. By the late 1850s, Williams had served as clerk of the women's meeting, as a representative at quarterly and yearly meetings, and would soon become an elder. The unmarried Williams took pride in her responsibilities, noting when she resigned the clerkship in 1857 that she had served "seven years." In February 1860, she thought herself "unqualified to fill" the "weighty appointment of elder," but accepted the post when she recalled the Bible verse, "I will make thee worthy." Gover's request, however, made Williams hesitate. Williams noted in her diary that she had "Some prospect of accompanying" Gover, "if way opens." Over the next few days Williams searched for reasons not to go. Such a journey, she pondered, "seems an arduous undertaking at this season of the year and the road so terrible." The next day, she wondered about her own abilities: "Do not feel very smart." Williams's diary then fell silent for five days. She resumed by recording, "Left home . . . in company with Miriam Gover." Williams could not refuse the request of her friend and she perceived the journey as a religious duty. Still, she found the decision emotionally trying.[59]

Few southern white women traveled without a male relative or protector, and the region's gender assumptions constrained even the most daring female Friends. In 1845, Sally Janney described the difficulty of traveling by coach and ferry the short distance from Sandy Spring, Maryland, to Alexandria. She got caught in a downpour without an umbrella and had to wait for the ferry in a Washington tavern. Her brother Frank hurried to her side when she reached Alexandria. Without his aid, she realized, "I would have been in serious difficulty." "So ended my first attempt at traveling alone," Janney wrote her sister, "Does thee think I am competent to try it again?" In 1842, Alexandria minister William Stabler fretted that the elderly minister Sarah Brown could not travel because no male Friends would accompany her. "There is a fault somewhere," Stabler added, "if a woman friend with a right concern to visit . . . shall fail to accomplish the work for want of right attendants." Stabler accompanied his wife, Deborah, and New York minister Rachel Barker on an 1845–46 religious journey to the Deep South, though "the prospect" filled him "with fear." The group faced a "stream of opposition" from white southerners who viewed Quakers "as enemies." In Wilmington, North Carolina, local Methodists "required" that Barker and Deborah Stabler "promise not to touch upon the exciting topic [of slavery]" during their services. When the women rejected this condition locals "waived" it. In Montgomery, Alabama, Methodists refused to let the women use their meeting house after a Charleston newspaper identified Barker as antislavery. The Stablers returned home safely, but southerners' hostility and women ministers' vulnerability made the prospect of their religious travel daunting.[60]

Thus most nineteenth-century Quaker women did not shoulder such public roles. Like white women throughout the nation, they remained defined by their familial and domestic roles and often earned Friends' commendation for such work. Rebecca Russell's life of service to her adopted families earned gushing praise when she died in 1888 at age 102. Never married, she worked as a domestic assistant in a number of Quaker homes, spending the last forty-four years of life with the family of Henry Stabler in Alexandria and nearby Rosslyn. Nursing the aged and the sick, helping to feed the family, visiting ministers, and Friends, and aiding in various domestic tasks, Russell earned applause for her "industry" and "unselfish devotion to duty." She was, her obituary noted, "a faithful servant of God" who proved "her faith by her works." Russell earned the highest accolades "as a nurse in sickness, comforting many by her services in times of trouble."[61] In nineteenth-century America, female selflessness signified a cultural model for northern and southern women. Among northern Virginia's Quakers, however, female sacrifice acquired greater meaning as Friends sought ways to sustain their community and identity. The attachments women forged helped bind the community, as Rebecca Williams's experience demonstrates.

Rebecca lived with her sister Rachel in Waterford, and within walking distance of her brother William and his family. She lived near the Fairfax Meeting House and rarely missed Sunday and midweek meeting. Her record of social and family visits, preparing for and attending religious meetings, correspondence and literary pursuits, domestic chores, nursing the sick and burying the dead, and supporting family survivors reveals the intersection of Quaker family, friends, community, and religious life—and the centrality of women in this convergence. Although men often joined women Friends in their visiting, and even in some domestic tasks, women engaged actively in these aspects of communal life. For Williams, social and condolence calls, and the web of kin and friends they supported, constituted a source of pleasure and an affirmation of her membership within the fellowship of Friends. "How I am blest with kind Friends," she marveled on one occasion, "more than I deserve." A gathering of Friends in her home prompted her to write: "It is very pleasant to mingle thus in a social way with friends we love." Pleasant certainly—but such contacts also helped preserve the Quaker way of life in an adverse environment.[62]

Williams's social calls included regular visits to her brother, William, his wife Mary, and their children. At least once a week, Williams walked over to her brother's house to dine with his family. And William and his family reciprocated with visits for tea and meals with Rebecca and Rachel. William and Mary's children—particular John ("Johnny") and Elizabeth ("Lizzie")—made frequent extended visits with Rebecca and Rachel who became attached to their young nephews and nieces. Rebecca and Rachel also provided child care when Mary and William visited the yearly meeting in Baltimore and when Mary shopped in nearby Loudoun County towns. Rebecca's visits to her brother's home became more frequent in July and August 1856 when William and Mary's two youngest boys, John, nearly three years old, and Edward, one year old, became ill and died within a day of each other. During these months, Williams spent most of her time with her brother's family, caring for the ill infants and providing physical and emotional support to the mother. The deaths of the infant boys came as a shock. "Severe the dispensation to his afflicted parents," wrote Rebecca in her journal, "and great the bereavement to us all." After the boys' deaths, the community mourned with the Williamses. "A large concourse of neighbors and friends" attended the funeral and Friends returned to the house after the burial. Rebecca and Rachel spent the week after the funeral with their brother and sister-in-law.[63]

The visits continued in the weeks and years that followed. Outings to Fairfax ministers Miriam Gover and Louisa Steer became part of Williams's routine in the late 1850s, as did visits to and from many members of the Gover, Janney, and Steer families. One week in June 1858, Williams had visits from sixteen Friends and relations, "all very pleasant," in addition to the weekly call from her African American washerwoman, Catherine. Williams sometimes worried that she devoted too much time to socializing and too little to spiritual concerns. "My record seems to be one of visiting and being visited," she wrote in March 1856. "I can truly say I love my friends and love to mingle with them," she continued, "but that may be a selfish love. . . . Oh, for a higher love." Other times, Williams celebrated Friends' socializing, as she did after traveling to Alexandria for the November 1857 quarterly meeting, where she dined with and saw the Stabler, Hallowell, Leadbeater, and Miller families. "This mingling with Friends is all very pleasant and sometimes proffitable," Williams concluded when she returned to Waterford, "a privilege . . . *we friends* enjoy more than any other people." Attendance at preparatory, monthly, quarterly, and yearly religious meetings provided opportunities for spiritual and secular fellowship among Friends. Williams's accounts of these visits reveal that Quakers made no distinction between the secular and the sacred. Visiting helped sustain and reinforce personal and religious bonds among a fellowship of believers.[64]

Williams's journal also reveals the central role of women in nourishing this fellowship in the 1850s. Female Friends cared for the sick and dying, both white and black, within the extended Quaker community, and with their male relations they attended the funerals of those who died. Williams repeatedly visited "little" Frank French when he lay ill in December 1854, tended "a poor, little sick coloured child" who lived among Friends in May 1856, stayed nights with a dying "Aunt Sally" the following December, and enjoyed visits from female (and a few male) Friends when a foot ailment left her "lame" in March and August 1858. Women Friends prepared food—sometimes weeks in advance—and provided housing for traveling ministers who visited local meetings and for the respected Friends who attended quarterly meetings. The influx of visitors encouraged socializing but also created headaches. Perhaps this explains Alexandria Friend Mary Lea Stabler's 1843 request to her sister that she visit during the forthcoming quarterly meeting. "I want to have some of my own folks," Stabler grumbled, "for fear some of the Goose Creekers would have to put up here—and I do not feel any interest in entertaining any of them." More often, female Friends celebrated the quarterly meetings they hosted, as when Williams noted in February 1859 that the "Quarterly [meeting] passed off very pleasantly. . . . [Had] a good share of our friends company during the time."[65]

Women Friends' sense of community extended beyond northern Virginia. Williams's journal describes an active epistolary relationship with a large number of women Friends. Faraway companions provided support for Williams and her sister—in good times and bad—and Williams reciprocated. Her epistolary friends shared spiritual and secular reading suggestions, described revelatory sermons, and sent memoirs and histories to Williams and her sister. The sisters read the books their friends recommended, helping sustain a sense of Quaker community across space. The reading Williams recorded in her diary—Josiah Gilbert's *Titcomb's Letters to Young People Single and Married* (1858), Carlo Botta's history of the American Revolution (1820–21), the novels of Charlotte Brontë, and spiritual works by Quakers and Episcopalians such as Joseph John Gurney and Susan Allibone—reveals the participation of Quaker women, even in an isolated corner of northern Virginia, in the intellectual and cultural life of the nation. The sisters, in turn, shared their literary, spiritual, and intellectual insights with local Friends, many of whom enjoyed a similar cultural engagement. The interests of Quaker women and men gave rise in 1857 to a local literary society. Led by Friends but with non-Quaker members, the society met to read locally produced fiction and essays until the Civil War. For Williams, the meetings of the society represented high points of her social calendar. Here men and women shared their thoughts about a variety of subjects—local and Virginia history, ethical and philosophical concerns, current and political events (including women's rights), even the relations between the sexes—with an appreciative audience.[66]

The role of women as producers and consumers of these literary productions highlights their importance in maintaining the Quaker community. Through their public activities women helped support the cultural and spiritual bonds of the community, while their domestic responsibilities became freighted with increasing significance. Although non-Quakers often saw male preachers as the public face of Quakerism (and in the 1840s and 1850s centered their attacks on these leaders), women helped bind the vulnerable religious group. Margaret Hallowell, wife of Alexandria schoolteacher James, believed female Friends, and especially single women, played a vital role in sustaining the local Quaker community. After an 1858 outbreak of measles, she praised her "good and useful single sister" Kate. "She seems to be in great demand," noted Margaret, and "I think . . . had better give up all idea of getting married" because she was such "a good nurse in sickness."[67] Local women Friends like Kate Hallowell embraced their traditional roles, while internal and external pressures endowed their activities with greater communal significance and enhanced women's status within the Society. Internal upheaval and social isolation shifted the burden of maintaining Quaker community to the social and family relations nurtured by women. When Friends faced growing criticism for their antislavery politics in the 1840s and 1850s, the bonds forged by women became still more important, helping to preserve the community and sustain the Society's spiritual and ethical concerns.

A "Nest of Abolitionists"

Antislavery Goals and Southern Identities

In 1860, Philadelphia Quaker Dillwyn Parrish, accompanied by fellow Friend Edward Hopper and their wives, toured Niagara Falls. While they sat on the banks of the Niagara River, "a colored man" approached the group and "enquired if" Parrish "was from Loudoun Co. Va." When Parrish replied that he was not, the stranger explained that he thought Parrish "resembled Mr. Saml Janney" of that county. Although Janney and Parrish shared little physical resemblance, Parrish was a close friend of Janney's, and after he revealed this coincidence, "a considerable conversation" soon arose between the man, Amos Norris, and Parrish's party. Norris informed Parrish that he had fled from Loudoun County in 1850 and now resided in Canada. He also introduced Parrish to Daniel Dangerfield, who had escaped from slavery in Loudoun to Harrisburg, Pennsylvania, in 1854. Using the 1850 Fugitive Slave Law, Dangerfield's owners had tried to re-enslave him, but after a celebrated 1859 trial, in which Parrish's companion Hopper played a role, the Pennsylvania court freed Dangerfield and he had moved to Niagara Falls. Parrish wrote to Janney that Norris and Dangerfield were "thriving, respectable" men, "doing well [in] every way, and . . . faithful subject[s] of the Queen." Norris wanted to contact his sister-in-law, Betsy Lambert, who "lived with" Janney when he "last heard from her." Parrish sent Norris's address to Janney and hoped that he could help the man.[1]

Norris approached Parrish and his party tentatively, but he likely decided to talk to them because of their plain Quaker dress and distinctive speech patterns. By 1860, some liberal Friends had begun to question Quakers' "external peculiarities" in dress and speech as "formalism" that placed "trivial" concerns above "personal worth and spiritual growth." But the Society's distinctive dress and speech remained symbols of identity for most Friends.

For black Americans, Friends' peculiar dress and speech served another function: it enabled them to identify white allies. As historian James O. Horton notes, Quakers acquired a "legendary" "reputation as opponents of slavery" among African Americans in the years after the American Revolution. Norris's decision to approach Parrish thus made great sense. More striking, his identification of Samuel Janney as a potential ally in his efforts to reunite his family demonstrates the impact of Janney's antislavery campaign after 1840. In the decades before the Civil War, white and black Virginians recognized Friends as foes of slavery, willing to aid free and enslaved African Americans in a variety of ways, legal and (on occasion) illegal. For allies and enemies, the region's Quakers were a "nest of abolitionists," committed to ending slavery in the state. After the Civil War, Friends' antislavery reputation grew. As a descendent of Loudoun County's Steer family reminisced in the 1940s, "no Quaker of the [antebellum] generation . . . would hesitate to enter into their [African Americans'] protection and assist in a get-away."[2]

Yet for all the repute (and, for some, notoriety) that local Friends garnered, by 1860 they had little to show for their antislavery efforts. In that year, slavery remained entrenched in northern Virginia, and their white neighbors more committed to the institution and less willing to tolerate dissent than they had been sixty years earlier. Dismayed by the South's commitment to slavery and many white northerners' apathy, some radical abolitionists criticized religious bodies, including the Society of Friends, for refusing to join their antislavery crusade. Friends, argued abolitionist Stephen S. Foster, claimed to oppose slavery, but by "electing man-stealers to fill the highest offices in the government," they "*legalize[d]*" the institution. Such hypocrisy, Foster averred, made them "more reprehensible" than "sects" who said nothing against slavery. Likewise, some historians question the image of Friends as antislavery activists. Most Quakers, argues historian Larry Gara, did little to undermine the institution of slavery. The "legend" of Friends aiding runaway slaves, he notes, reflects sloppy historical research and the actions of a few individuals (who faced criticism from fellow Friends), rather than a Society-wide commitment to helping fugitives. More recently, historian Ryan Jordan, echoing Foster, has argued that Quakers' unwillingness to participate in radical abolitionism made them the unwitting allies of proslavery politicians.[3]

In northern Virginia, a number of factors established the parameters of Quaker antislavery activism. Above all, the tolerance of the white community set limits on what Friends could safely do to undermine slavery and help enslaved people. As most white Virginians' commitment to slavery deepened in the 1840s and 1850s, they lost patience with their antislavery Quaker neighbors, who found their ability to condemn the institution circumscribed. The nature of the Quaker faith also placed restraints on antislavery activism. As the national debate over slavery intensified, Friends found that their allegiance to pacifism and antislavery often conflicted. Trying to find a path that honored both beliefs presented Friends with few good choices and produced among some individuals a sense of futility. Likewise, outmigration and doctrinal division demoralized the local Quaker community, reducing its numbers and its ability to support members facing external pressure for unpopular views. Equally important, local Friends' social and economic interaction and identification with the white community engendered racial intolerance and eroded the Society's ability to act against slavery even while it maintained an antislavery stance. Friends provided aid to northern Virginia's African American community, but local blacks recognized the parameters of that assistance.[4]

Despite these limitations, the region's Friends continued their efforts to help the black community and convince white southerners of the moral and economic damage wrought by slavery. Unable to pursue overt antislavery activities, Friends engaged in alternatives they hoped would undermine the institution and prepare for the day black Americans could be free. At Woodlawn, southeast of Alexandria, New Jersey Friends, led by Chalkley Gillingham, established a free labor agricultural colony in 1846, symbolically located on the lands of George Washington's Mount Vernon plantation, in order to demonstrate the superiority of free labor. In Loudoun County, Yardley Taylor used the southern agricultural press to promote agricultural improvement, which he believed possible only with free labor. Ministers and teachers Samuel Janney and Benjamin Hallowell promoted free school education for Virginians. An educated population, they believed, would reject slavery. Other Friends promoted regional economic development. They invested in internal improvements, new industries, and technological innovations, convinced that slavery could not survive in a modern economy modeled on the North. Slavery and white racism proved too resilient for such tactics. But as the sectional divide deepened in the 1840s and 1850s, the antislavery activities of northern Virginia's Friends helped destabilize the institution and unnerve local slaveholders who recognized its precariousness in this southern periphery.

I

In the aftermath of Nat Turner's 1831 revolt in Southampton County, northern Virginia Friends retreated from the antislavery efforts of the previous decade. Turner's insurrection posed troubling questions for pacifist Friends who discouraged slavery resistance that might spark violence. Quaker antislavery newspaper editor Benjamin Lundy blamed the bloodshed on David Walker's *Appeal to the Coloured Citizens of the World*, the "injudicious" 1829 publication that called on African Americans to use violence if necessary to end their enslavement. Walker and Turner, Lundy argued, undermined the antislavery cause in the South by convincing southerners to censor "antislavery newspapers and tracts." Friends found the rise of radical abolitionism, with its strident moral attack on slavery and the South, equally troubling. Radical rhetoric, many Quakers worried, would encourage further violence and southern intransigence. Dillwyn Parrish wondered if Friends' "peaceable principles" should lead them to question their connection "with the Anti Slavery Associations of the day." For George Truman, the concern was more practical: Would radical rhetoric undermine the antislavery cause?[5]

Quakers also had deep concerns about the impact of radical abolitionism on the character of the Society of Friends, especially after the Hicksite separations of 1827 and 1828, which adversely affected all American yearly meetings. Weakened by this doctrinal divide, Hicksite and Orthodox Friends faced a new challenge to the unity of their respective wings with the rise of radical abolitionism. Activist Quakers argued that the Society needed to take a more vigorous role in the fight against slavery. More conservative members responded that the sect had done enough and that further action would violate the peaceable principles of the Society, draw Friends into dangerous worldly associations, and encourage them to break the laws of legally constituted governments. The controversy over radical abolitionism reached its greatest intensity in the Orthodox Indiana Yearly Meeting, where abolitionist Friends led by Levi Coffin broke away in 1843 to create a new antislavery meeting. Likewise, in the 1840s Progressive or Congregational Friends in the Hicksite meetings of Ohio and New York created more egalitarian meetings to pursue their antislavery and reform agendas.[6]

Friends throughout the nation felt the repercussions of these debates. In the Hicksite Baltimore Yearly Meeting, conservatives discouraged Friends from participating in non-Quaker antislavery groups. In 1835, the meeting admonished members to "keep ourselves unconnected with the excitement now . . . prevailing in our land" and "maintain" our "meek and peaceable spirit." Four years later, the meeting reaffirmed its "earnest concern" for "the cause of the oppressed," but "caution[ed]" Friends "against entangling themselves" with antislavery "associations" that would "retard rather than promote" the abolition of slavery. Not all Friends concurred with the injunction, compelling the meeting in 1842 to warn members once more against joining abolitionist societies that employed "*political* or other means of a coercive nature." Quakers must, the address continued, support their antislavery testimony "with uprightness and integrity," but must also "be quiet, and mind our own business . . . lest . . . we bring death upon ourselves, and be the means of bringing destruction upon others." The meeting made its fear of violent results more explicit the following year, when it encouraged Friends to oppose slavery, but to do so "under the influence of that feeling which breathes peace on earth, and good will to *all* men." Members should oppose slavery independently of other groups, and convince slaveholders of its evil through example.[7]

Despite these admonitions, in the 1840s Janney resumed his antislavery activities. During the 1820s and 1830s, he had devoted his energies to directing a cotton mill with his brother-in-law and fellow Quaker Samuel H. Janney on the Occoquan River, south of Alexandria, until debt forced him to close the operation in 1839. He used his wife's small inheritance to establish the Springdale Boarding School in Loudoun County, where he joined the Goose Creek meeting. Throughout the period of financial uncertainty, Janney undertook few antislavery activities. But the success of his school enabled him to pay off most of his debts and pursue his "deep interest in the great moral reforms of his day." Quaker abolitionist Lucretia Mott's 1842 visit to the Baltimore Yearly Meeting inspired Janney's renewed activism. Before she spoke "there was much apprehension felt by many friends about her abolition views." But after "she delivered one of the greatest discourses" Janney had "ever heard," he became convinced, as did much of the meeting, "that she was on the right ground in her ministry." For Janney, hearing Mott's antislavery message was a revelation. It lifted him from the "gloom" into which his "temporal affairs" had cast him, and she emboldened him to "speak out" against slavery. Rising to speak after Mott, Janney prodded the meeting's cautious leadership to adopt a vigorous antislavery position. His "speech," Mott noted, did not correspond "with the expressions and assertions contained" in the Baltimore meeting's 1842 epistle, but "would have graced any of our anti-slavery papers." After Mott left the region, Janney renewed his public antislavery efforts which he viewed "as much my religious duty as any that I perform."[8]

Janney hoped his campaign, consisting of legislative petitions, public advocacy, and articles in a variety of Chesapeake newspapers between 1843 and 1850, would convince white southerners of the benefits of ending slavery and adopting a free labor economy. His arguments had not changed significantly since the 1820s. Janney still opposed colonization, but would accept it if voluntary and designed to end slavery. He remained certain that slavery had decimated Virginia's economy and that emancipation—gradual if necessary—would improve the material wellbeing of "oppressed and oppressor." He first directed his attention to the "arbitrary" 1806 state law that required free blacks to leave the state within a year of their emancipation. Janney wrote and circulated an 1843 petition to the Virginia legislature, signed by fifty-nine residents of Loudoun and Jefferson counties, which argued "that every man not convicted of crime has a natural right to reside in the community where he was born and that no laws can expel him without violating the principles of justice and humanity." The law also violated the rights of "the many citizens of this state" who prefer "the employment of free labour." Above all, the law hurt Virginia's economy. "The removal of whites and the expulsion of the free coloured people," the petition argued, made free labor "scarce." As a result, employers found it "difficult to procure sufficient aid in the prosecution of their business" and the state filled with "waste lands . . . impoverished by the system of slavery."[9]

Janney also called for comprehensive public education in Virginia, seeing it as an indispensable antislavery tactic. He believed a public school system would promote "anti-slavery sentiment" by eroding the white "ignorance and prejudice" that enabled slavery to survive in Virginia. He allied himself with state educational reformers and pushed in the 1840s for state-funded public schools. The 1840 census revealed high rates of illiteracy in the state, with almost one in five white adults unable to read and write. For many white Virginians, these "startling and frightening" figures exposed the state's "ignorance in strong and humiliating contrast with that of the other states." At two statewide conventions, held in Richmond in 1841 and 1845, advocates of change asked the legislature to create a public school system modeled on the proposals of northern educational reformers like Horace Mann. Janney participated in the 1845 convention. Presided over by Virginia's governor and attended by some of the state's leading politicians, the convention gave Janney an opportunity to speak before a prominent audience.[10]

Janney received a congenial hearing. Appointed to a committee of fifteen to report on common schools, Janney objected when thirteen of the members voted to retain the present system. He argued that Virginia's public schools suffered because the state did not regulate teacher quality or curriculum content. Moreover, by letting only poor children attend for free, the existing state-funded schools created class distinctions that discouraged attendance. Virginia should replace its *"pauper"* schools, Janney argued, with a statewide system of free schools for all white children, modeled on Massachusetts and New York schools. Janney prepared a minority report and took "the lead in advocating" it on the convention floor. To his surprise, the report garnered the support of three-fourths of the delegates, and the governor invited him to tea, during which Janney had "a pretty satisfactory interview . . . on the subject of Slavery." Having "unexpectedly gained so much favour among" the convention's "influential men," Janney remained in Richmond to use his newfound influence "for the benefit of the oppressed bondsmen who are shut out from the advantages of education."[11]

But Janney's success was short lived. In 1846, the assembly passed an act authorizing free schools in counties where two-thirds of voters approved them. Returning to northern Virginia, Janney delivered a series of speeches in support of free schools, but within the region only the voters of Jefferson County endorsed the plan. To Janney's disappointment, Loudoun County's electorate rejected the idea, a failure he attributed "to the influence of the slaveholders" who saw free schools "as an entering wedge for . . . the abolition of slavery." The children of wealthy slaveholders, Janney argued, grew accustomed to exercising "arbitrary sway" and learned habits of "luxury and idleness." Their teachers found them "exceedingly difficult to govern" and unwilling to do the work necessary to succeed in school. Meanwhile, the poor, suffering from slavery's debilitating economic impact, ignored education. Living in "poverty and ignorance," they "aspire[d] to nothing higher than a bare subsistence." Without hope of upward mobility, the poor had neither the resources nor saw the need for free schools. And slaveholders who could afford to educate their own children refused to pay taxes to support a statewide system. "Education," Janney concluded, "cannot prosper in a slaveholding state"; only "radical change" would extend "education to all."[12]

But Janney pursued this "radical change" through moderate tactics, seeking non-Quaker allies of education reform. In the late 1840s, he and Moncure Daniel Conway, a native Virginian and future Methodist minister, petitioned the Virginia legislature to repeal state laws that proscribed slave literacy and allowed "the arbitrary separation of [slave] families." The petition never made it to the assembly floor. Instead, Conway received a "private reply" from one the legislators asserting that "no such petition could be read in that body." The same year, Janney tried to start a Virginia-based "education and emancipation" newspaper with Leesburg editor Thomas Connolly. Baltimore newspaper editor Joseph E. Snodgrass, who credited Janney and Lucretia Mott for his conversion to antislavery, encouraged northern Virginia's Quakers to "do something . . . with your local press." While Janney wrote to northern Friends and allies for support, Connolly approached liberal-minded slaveholders, "the right kind of men" in Connolly's words, who might support the proposed newspaper. But Janney and Connolly miscalculated the temper of white Virginians. Even individuals who agreed that slavery should end believed that "the first step proper to be taken" was "the banishment of all the free Negroes." "If we would concur in this," Connolly reported, "it would make many judicious men . . . look favorably upon our scheme." Janney could have his paper only if he censored his most progressive views. "Enlightened and benevolent slaveholders" might "deplore the evils of slavery," and many agreed with Janney that Virginia would profit from "the establishment of a free school system," but they rejected Janney's attempt to use publicly funded education as a means to dismantle slavery and create a racially egalitarian society.[13]

Still, Janney and local Friends remained committed to education reform. Public schools, they believed, would undermine the racism and prejudice that undergirded slavery, spark economic modernization and agricultural improvement, and make slavery unviable and undesirable. Black education, promoted by local Friends since the 1790s when they established a First Day school in Alexandria, would prepare African Americans to make the transition from slavery to freedom and, at some future date, enable them to enjoy the rights of citizenship. Janney's education campaign exemplified Quaker antislavery tactics in the twenty years prior to the Civil War. Recognizing the dangers of their reform agenda, Friends made strategic choices about when and how to act. The early 1840s appeared to offer a good juncture for antislavery action. Ten years after Nat Turner's rebellion, white racial fears had declined but the state's economy continued to stagnate. Friends presented themselves as concerned citizens who wished to join other civic-minded residents seeking ways to reverse the state's economic, demographic, and political decline. As Janney noted to one slaveholder, "I love my native State as well as any one of her citizens" and "cannot feel satisfied to see her falling into the rear of all the rest." If Quaker reformers opted for modest methods to garner support among white Virginians, they nonetheless envisioned a radical future: a state in which free blacks lived peacefully and in relative equality alongside white southerners.[14]

II

The essays Janney published in the 1840s reflected this strategy, while publicizing the efforts of Friends to undermine slavery in the region. Friends believed that the strident rhetoric of northern abolitionists created a backlash that stiffened white southerners' resolve to protect slavery. Slaveholders could not suppress northern critics of slavery, but they could silence dissent within the South. As a result, Friends tried to avoid the taint of northern radicalism, believing that their intended audience would ignore the message if they perceived it as coming from the North. Janney insisted that his essays appear in "Southern newspapers" first. But he found it difficult to convince even sympathetic editors to print his pieces and he resorted to financial incentives. He ordered extra copies of papers and pamphlets to "gain editors over to our side," and solicited northern Quakers to pay for extra printings. Nonetheless, editors hesitated to carry his work. In 1844, the *Richmond Whig* rejected the third part of a series entitled "The Essays of a Virginian." The offending piece, editor John H. Pleasants wrote, "will not do for Va." because it proposed "that the emancipated blacks are to remain amongst us." In response, Janney sent Pleasants a series entitled "The Yankees in Fairfax Virginia," which he thought "will suit your views better." "The object," Janney explained, "is to . . . stir up our . . . people to improvement and to give a few *side blows* . . . to the system of slavery by shewing the advantages of free labour." The series, which appeared in Richmond and Alexandria papers, made no mention of black freedom. Instead, it described the settlement of northerners in Fairfax County in the 1840s and their use of free labor and improved farming methods to restore worn-out lands.[15]

In the early 1840s, farmers largely from the Hudson Valley of New York and around Philadelphia settled in Fairfax County, where they purchased and improved lands, and used the region's transportation network to market their produce in Washington, D.C. Southern reformers initially welcomed the newcomers. In an 1842 address to the Albemarle Agricultural Society, William C. Rives praised "these welcome swarms from kindred hives." "These sharp, [a]cute Yankees," he noted, recognized that the "worn-out soil of Eastern Virginia . . . offers the best opportunity of investment to the agriculturist." "We hail the advent of these enterprising strangers," noted the editor of the *Southern Planter*, for "our northern friends have read works on agriculture to some purpose!" But, Rives added, northern farmers had "one thing . . . to learn" to succeed in Virginia: "The management of slaves." Most of the newcomers did not use slave labor—and this became Janney's central theme in his essays.[16]

Janney saw the arrival of large numbers of northerners—some two hundred families consisting of over twelve hundred people before April 1847— as an opportunity to highlight the advantages of free labor over slave labor. Writing as "A Virginian" to distinguish himself from northern abolitionists, Janney opened his series by describing the "striking improvement" that had taken place "in some parts of Fairfax County." Where "neglected and overgrown" fields had once filled the landscape, now "the eye is refreshed and the heart gladdened" by "clear and enclosed" farms, filled with "green fields of luxuriant clover, and crops of waving grain." The northern farmers who settled in Fairfax County used fertilizers, crop rotation, and farming implements to produce good crops. Why, Janney pondered, could Virginians not produce the same changes in the land? The key difference, he concluded, lay in northern farmers' use of free labor. Slave labor had destroyed white Virginians' desire to work, a tendency most pronounced among the sons of slaveholding planters. They left the management of their plantations to overseers who had little incentive to improve the land and ensure its sustainability.[17]

Janney's willingness to tie the poor agricultural practices of Virginia farmers to their use of slave labor took some temerity. Quaker correspondents praised him. "I am glad to find thou art still Engaged in prosecuting thy concern," wrote George Truman of Philadelphia. "Could" Virginia but "abolish" its "slave system," he added, and "a hardy and industrious band of farmers would soon be found" to raise "the price of land fully sufficient to meet all the supposed loss" of freeing the slaves. In New Jersey, Quaker Samuel Griscom wrote to Janney that the series had "opened" "a very wide field for usefulness." Griscom produced a series of articles for the agricultural and Quaker press extolling the benefits of northern migration to Virginia. He communicated with Virginians throughout the state, and received positive responses "from about twenty different counties." He concluded that Virginia's "intelligent citizens" wanted "to encourage industrious and virtuous northern men" to settle in the state "and by enlightened free labor, redeem their soil from its present desolation." Griscom believed Friends were effective settlers because they would not be corrupted by southern values. They would avoid the "declamations or accusations" of abolitionists and instead employ the "powerful language of example" to win over their southern neighbors.[18]

One group of Quakers followed Griscom's advice. In August 1846, two New Jersey Friends, Chalkley Gillingham and Jacob Troth, purchased the two thousand acre Woodlawn estate, formerly part of George Washington's Mount Vernon plantation. The pair purchased the estate for its timber, which they harvested for the New England ship industry. But they also embraced Griscom's broader philanthropic goals. "One object in going there," Gillingham noted in his journal, was "to establish a free labour colony in a slave state." Gillingham and Troth divided the estate and sold the parcels to New Jersey and Pennsylvania Friends. By 1852, fifty-three Quaker families—over three hundred migrants in all—had settled at Woodlawn. Friends established a saw and grist mill and a store that became the hub of the commercial center of Accotink. "[We] find no difficulty in getting along without the use of slave labor," Gillingham reported after his arrival. He believed wages exerted an "encouraging" "influence" on the free black population, "elevating them to a much better condition." Local Friends, wrote one of Troth's sons some years later, reclaimed Woodlawn "not only from forest but from the 'dry rot' of slavery, in a quiet peaceable way, and without interrupting the friendly relations which existed between them and their slaveholding neighbors."[19]

The Quaker migration garnered praise—at least initially. After visiting Gillingham's saw mill and "viewing the different operations" for "some hours," one local woman "raised her hands and exclaimed, 'God bless the Yankees. I wish more of them would come here.'" In 1848, the *Alexandria Gazette* concurred that the influx of so many "industrious and enterprising" northerners "argues well for our region." Some slaveholders recognized the impact the newcomers could have. John A. Washington, the last private owner of Mount Vernon, believed that the New Jersey Friends "will produce quite a revolution in our neighborhood." Once they had established successful farms, Washington predicted that slaveholders "shall . . . be obliged to send off our slaves and have recourse to white labour for the cultivation of our lands and in our domestic employments." Washington welcomed the removal of the "ignorant slave and . . . still more degraded white population." With both groups gone, Fairfax would see the "improvement of farms, the formation of schools and a general diffusion of knowledge and morality." "In less than ten years," he added, "our lands will double in value." Washington's comments expose the distance that lay between antislavery Friends and "enlightened" slaveholders. As some northern Quakers noted, purchasing worn-out lands enabled "owners to emigrate further South with their slaves, or *sell them* to others who will transport them there." Northern settlement in the state without provision for the slaves beyond removal through colonization or sale to the Deep South fell short of Friends' antislavery goals.[20]

Despite its shortcomings, Friends pinned their hopes on agricultural improvement as an antislavery strategy. Success, they believed, would convince their white neighbors they could profit and bring economic prosperity to Virginia by ending their reliance on slavery and following Quaker farming practices. Successful innovations had the added advantage of enriching individual Friends, but few saw any contradiction in such gains as long as pursuing profit did not become their primary focus. Financial success also enabled Friends to provide aid to the free black population and prove to their non-Quaker neighbors that with appropriate incentives and training free African Americans would labor more efficiently than the enslaved. As the Baltimore Yearly Meeting had urged in 1842, southern Friends could best fight slavery through example rather than more radical means that threatened to violate their peace testimony and stiffen the resolve of proslavery whites.[21]

In the late 1840s, Loudoun County Friend Yardley Taylor pursued this course, seeking improvements in fruit cultivation so that the region's farmers could better capitalize on the growing D.C. market. Taylor's "practical" method focused on adapting northern horticultural techniques to southern climate and soils. "Only by experiment," he concluded, can farmers "determine whether" particular innovations "will suit other localities." In the 1850s, he reported his observations about locusts, tree grafting, cattle distemper, and climate. He also engaged in scientific disputes with slaveholding planters, questioning R. T. Baldwin's "shade theory" which held that all covered soils naturally rejuvenated themselves. Taylor's reputation as an agricultural expert soon rose and in June 1853 members of the Loudoun County Agricultural Society appointed him corresponding secretary. Six years later, the Virginia Agricultural Society appointed "our friend" Taylor a judge of the fruit and fruit trees exhibition at the state agricultural fair.[22] Discussions of agricultural improvement enabled Taylor to question the authority of slaveholders without repercussion while demonstrating the superiority of free labor because in practice local Friends implemented such methods without slavery.

The Quaker educator, minister, and scientist Benjamin Hallowell followed a similar strategy: promoting scientific agriculture while demonstrating its effectiveness on a farm he purchased in the Quaker community of Sandy Spring, Maryland, in 1837. He resided on the farm three months of the year, practicing what reformers called the "high pressure principle" of improvement—the heavy use of "bought manures" (plaster, guano, and lime), deep plowing, crop rotation, and free labor. Maryland agricultural improvement advocate Horace Capron visited Sandy Spring in the late 1840s and reported on "the miracles" that local Quaker farmers "had wrought" through the use of soil additives. The Methodist minister Moncure Conway visited the "beautiful and cheerful" Sandy Spring neighborhood for the first time in 1851. The community consisted of "a succession of finely-cultivated farms" that "bore witness to better culture than those in other parts of the country." In its fields worked "happy labourers,—the only happy Negroes," Conway noted, "I had ever seen." "I could tell," Conway added, "the very line on the ground where the ordinary Maryland ended and the Quaker region began."[23]

After attending the Sandy Spring meeting, Conway met "Uncle Roger" Brooke, one of the community's leaders. When Conway expressed his admiration for local farms, Brooke asked him, "can thee account for this evident superiority of the Friends' neighbourhood over the rest of this country, or of thy own [Virginia]?" "We are," added Brooke, "people of the same stock with those thee hast always known; the names of our families are old Maryland and Virginian names,—and yet thee sees a difference in our condition." Conway suggested that perhaps the Friends had settled on better land, worked harder, or practiced greater thrift. In reply, Brooke pointed to another difference: "'Has it occurred to thee that it may be because of our paying wages to all who work for us?'" "'No slave,'" he added, "'has touched any sod in any field of Sandy Spring.'" Conway's visit to Sandy Spring changed his life. As he noted after Hallowell's death in 1877, at Sandy Spring he had "sat down a Methodist preacher and rose up with faith in the inward light." His visit to Sandy Spring's improved farms also convinced Conway of the economic advantages of free labor.[24]

Hallowell designed his farm to demonstrate the superiority of free labor and improved agriculture and Virginia and Maryland farmers regularly drew on his expertise. The southern agricultural press reported his experiments "to ascertain the comparative efficacy of various Manures," and he provided advice on how to eliminate sassafras bushes, the use of guano, and methods of soil analysis. In 1853, the organizers of the Virginia Agricultural Society asked him to serve as judge of the best "written communications" on the subject of agricultural improvement. And the previous fall,

Figure 7.1. Portrait of Benjamin Hallowell. Courtesy of Swarthmore College Friends Historical Library.

the Montgomery County, Maryland, and the Loudoun County, Virginia, agricultural societies asked him to give the keynote address at their annual fairs. At both events, he stood on the dais surrounded by the counties' leading slaveholding planters, which prevented him from openly critiquing slave labor—at least if he sought another hearing or the continued enrollment of southern sons at his Alexandria school. Thus, his speeches focused on the scientific basis of agricultural improvement and the social and moral benefits of implementing better farming methods. He also echoed traditional Virginian praise for agrarian life. Sounding like a good Jeffersonian, Hallowell condemned city life as "an unhealthy and an unnatural condition of the human family." In contrast, farmers, surrounded by the "operations of the Creator," seemed "to live nearer to the Good Spirit."[25]

But Hallowell did more than flatter his listeners. Too often, he argued, southern farmers failed to exercise the proper "industry" and "economy." "The prevailing extravagancies of living," he noted, "deterred" many "young persons" from improving "the unemployed lands around us." The region's farmers must instead emulate the "*industry*," "*economy*," and "*perseverance*" of northerners. "This is the capital," he announced to his audience, "with which we should set up our children." Southern farmers needed to embrace northern models of progress: build improved roads "as they do in New England" to enhance market access and land values; mechanize farming to save labor; and invest in railroads and the telegraph to permit "business" in rural areas to be transacted with "as much readiness as it can be done in cities." In his emphasis on progress, Hallowell tapped into an important stream of the cultural life of the Upper South. But unlike the young bourgeois Virginians who simultaneously embraced economic development and slavery, Hallowell's message came with an implicit if unspoken antislavery message. He could not, as Quaker preacher Joseph John Gurney noted in the late 1830s, touch on "the subject of slavery itself . . . with any propriety." Yet he believed that the message of agricultural reform—like Quaker spiritual beliefs—"when truly received and acted on, cannot fail to undermine the system of slavery." Six years later, Hallowell linked agricultural reform and antislavery overtly. Asked to head the new Maryland Agricultural College (soon to become the University of Maryland), he accepted the post only after the trustees of the college assured him that its farm would employ "free labor only."[26]

Many Friends also saw their business affairs as an opportunity to persuade Virginians of the superiority of free labor. Since the American Revolution, Quaker merchants had invested in and promoted regional internal improvements, banks and insurance companies, and industrial and manufacturing enterprises. Business opportunities proliferated in the 1850s as Virginia's economy, after decades of stagnation, rebounded. In the Shenandoah Valley, Aaron H. Griffith directed a wool factory that his father began in 1828. By 1850, Griffith's business interests consisted of three large woolen mills employing a free labor workforce: the Brookland Woolen Factory outside of Winchester, which he owned and oversaw; a mill in Wetheredville, Maryland, that his brother, Richard, managed; and the Henry Clay Mills in Wilmington, Delaware, that his son, Isaac, directed. Griffith's factories made him a wealthy man; in 1859, he insured the Brookland mill for four thousand dollars and his home and barn (located next to the mill) for thirty-five hundred dollars. But he viewed his business enterprises as an articulation of his spiritual values, not just as a means to wealth. Friends, he advised his son, should avoid "unadvised adventures in trade or speculation" which would "jeopardize our own credit and reputation, or that of our friends." "Let the strictest moral and business probity and religious integrity," Griffith advised, "shine forth . . . in all transactions." In Virginia, this required Quaker businessmen to eschew slavery, which Griffith considered "wrong in *principle* and *impracticable*."[27]

By pursuing free labor business strategies Friends set an antislavery example that non-Quakers might emulate, while developing economic and social resources to deflect persecution. Wealthy Friends recognized that their image as honest and civic-minded citizens and businessmen helped insulate them from criticism. A commitment to commercial and civic enterprises designed to improve the wellbeing of the state, Friends believed, would permit them to express their views. In Alexandria, china merchant Robert Hartshorne Miller promoted a variety of civic and business projects while maintaining membership in the Quaker meeting. He invested in and became one of the early directors of the Alexandria Canal Company, chartered in 1830 to build an aqueduct over the Potomac River and link Alexandria to the Chesapeake and Ohio Canal. After its completion in the 1840s, the aqueduct carried coal from western Maryland to the port of Alexandria and played a central role in the town's economic resurgence the following decade. Miller purchased shares in the Alexandria and Orange Railroad, incorporated in 1848 to connect the town to the piedmont counties southwest of Alexandria, and served as a director of the Alexandria, Loudoun, and Hampshire Railroad, chartered in 1853 to construct a rail line to western Virginia's coalfields. He also helped found the Mount Vernon Cotton Manufacturing Factory in 1847, incorporated by the state at ninety thousand dollars and employing one hundred fifty wage laborers.[28]

Miller's economic investments brought him great wealth; in 1860, he reported property worth one hundred and sixty thousand dollars and ranked as the third wealthiest individual in Alexandria. He earned accolades for his role in the Alexandria Water Company, incorporated in 1850 and completed in 1852. Initiated by Benjamin Hallowell to supply clean water to the town, the project garnered the support of civic leaders but local Friends played a crucial financial role. The initial sale of the twenty-dollar shares went slowly until the "comparatively poor" Hallowell subscribed for forty shares. "The effect was electrical," Hallowell recalled. Quaker merchant Phineas Janney "doubled his subscription" and urged others "'Do thou likewise.'" Miller initially purchased five shares, eventually owning eighty-one in all, and he served as one of the company's first directors. He and two other local merchants also stood as security for the loan that enabled the city to purchase ten thousand water company shares. After Hallowell resigned in 1856, Miller became the company's president. The regular supply of clean water it provided reduced incidents of infectious disease in Alexandria and increased the efficiency of the town's volunteer fire companies. The company also provided water for many of the city's factories, including the Mount Vernon cotton mill in which Miller had invested.[29]

Hallowell took great pride in the water company, which he believed "left Alexandria better than I found it." The company's success burnished the image of Friends as civic-minded citizens. When Miller died, the local paper eulogized him as "public-spirited, and active in all that he thought would contribute to the welfare of our city. . . . His probity and honor . . . gave him a deserved influence." Miller believed that he could use this "influence" to further Friends' reform agenda, including antislavery. Although Miller did not speak publicly against slavery, he worked quietly to help African Americans. Between 1830 and 1860, he purchased and emancipated at least ten enslaved blacks, and he vouched for the free status of another eleven, many of whom his father, Mordecai Miller, had emancipated. In this, Miller followed the practice of Alexandria Quaker ministers Edward and William Stabler. They refused to participate in antislavery organizations (or even sign the Alexandria Benevolent Society's 1827 anti-slave trade petition to Congress) because they worried "political weapons" would alienate slaveholders. Together, however, the Stablers (father and son) freed eleven individuals between 1827 and 1845. Miller signed the 1827 petition, but thereafter he chose the Stablers' path. He also helped free blacks purchase homes in Alexandria. In 1815, Mordecai Miller began building rental properties on Wolfe Street for black craftsmen. After Mordecai's 1832 death, Robert continued the building—ten dwellings in all—which he sold to black families. The homes formed the basis of the African American neighborhood of "Hayti."[30]

Quaker businessmen convinced themselves they could best contribute to the antislavery struggle and uphold Friends' quietist traditions by using their social standing and wealth to aid African Americans. "The Society of Friends has been in some degree important to the world," explained minister Edward Stabler, "by exhibiting an example of the effects . . . of practical righteousness." Men like Miller worried, as Stabler had, that criticizing slavery openly would provoke a backlash among whites, hurt African Americans, and make it impossible for Friends to live according to their spiritual creed. Activists like Samuel Janney praised local Quaker merchants for their civic endeavors, recognizing that their social standing gave him latitude to pursue an antislavery agenda. When Janney's uncle Phineas died in 1853, Janney eulogized him for his support of "public improvements" in which "he always acted a leading part."[31] But Friends also realized that helping a few enslaved and free blacks amounted to little while slavery and the slave trade still flourished. Moreover, active participation in the region's economy—and identification with the wellbeing of the region's white inhabitants—jeopardized Quakers' distinct identity. Northern Virginia's Friends faced the danger, in short, of becoming more southern than Quaker.

III

The region's Friends became most aware of their identification with the South—or at least northern Virginia—when they traveled north or met northern Quakers. Many Friends who left the region for Ohio and Indiana continued to view themselves as southerners—at least for a time. The letters they composed to friends and family in Virginia reveal how attached they remained to their former home. In 1838, Mary Brown, of Logan County, Ohio, wrote her old friend and neighbor, Eliza Cowgill, about the stresses of moving west, bereft of her family and friends in Frederick County. Describing Ohio as "a fine Country," Brown lamented that "things are very different here," and that settlers had "to work almost too hard." Most disturbing was the lack of community—despite settling among Friends—when she first arrived. "When I came to this country," Brown wrote, "I felt like a Pelican in the wilderness." "An old Virginia neighbour," noted her husband Joel, "is like marrow to the bone." Seth Smith expressed his sense of loss when he left the state for Indiana in the early 1850s in trite poetry: "Farewell! O what feelings my bosom are swelling / When thinking that soon I must leave the fair scenes / Which for so many years had surrounded my dwelling / Almost ever since I had passed from my teens." Former Loudoun County resident Wilson Shepherd, writing from Illinois in 1854, asked Robert B. Smith (Seth Smith's son) to respond with "all the News about the 'Burg,'" signing his letter plaintively, "1700 miles from Union [Loudoun County]." When Smith moved to Richmond, Indiana, in the late 1850s he stayed abreast of events in Loudoun County with a subscription to the Leesburg *Washingtonian*.[32]

Northern Friends had trouble understanding southern Quakers' identification with a place that to them seemed backward. Mordecai Moore, who visited the lower Shenandoah Valley in the mid-1850s, filled his letters to his Quaker relations in Pennsylvania with disdainful descriptions of "our . . . Va. Living." His diet consisted of "poor and tough beef, no vegetables except a few peas and beets . . . something they call salad . . . [and] corn bread . . . cakes that are passable for anybody that can take the indigestible ingredients." "Our chamber and furniture," he continued, "are all in the same category." Virginia's backwardness, Moore concluded, resulted from the state's attachment to "Slavery and its infernal influence." When Quaker minister Elizabeth Newport traveled to northern Virginia in 1852 she fretted about the "cautious" testimony of local Friends who tried to dissuade her from visiting slaveholders. As an outsider, Newport recognized how the southern environment affected Friends and she implored members to remain true to their antislavery testimony. She visited individuals who "had once been members of our Society, but who at the time held slaves." John Janney, the Whig politician who in 1861 chaired Virginia's secession convention, might have received one of her calls. The son of Alexandria merchant Elisha and a cousin of Samuel Janney, John settled in Leesburg, in Loudoun County, in the 1820s to practice law (a questionable occupation among Quakers who sought to resolve internal disputes through arbitration). He broke with the Society in 1826, when the Fairfax meeting disowned him for marrying a non-Quaker. Eight years later he purchased a slave and joined the local Episcopal Church.[33]

John Janney's apostasy reminded Friends of the threat posed by living in a slave society, and ensured that meetings remained vigilant in the enforcement of the discipline despite declining membership. In 1834, the Goose Creek meeting disowned Jonah Hatcher, who married a non-Quaker and purchased a slave. Three years later, the Fairfax meeting disowned Samuel Stone after he married a slaveholding woman, and in 1841 the meeting debated whether women who married slaveholders should be disowned after it removed three women in the Hough family for having "an interest in slavery." The meeting turned for advice to respected Friends and the quarterly meeting. In August, Isaac Walker, pondered the fate of "a man" who married "out of the society," "condemn[ed] his break of discipline to the satisfaction of friends" and thus retained his right to membership, but who "in the course of events" inherited "a number of slaves" through the death of "his wife's father." "Can he," Walker wondered, "retain his right of membership according to our discipline," or "does our discipline . . . prohibit it [slave ownership] in *all* cases[?]" Walker's query reveals the dilemmas of Quakers living in a slave society. Surrounded by and often linked through personal ties to slaveholders, Friends became entangled in slavery, raising conflicts between their personal, spiritual, and community loyalties. The quarterly meeting's response to the debate, however, left little room for ambiguity: the "Monthly Meetings" must "carry faithfully into operation those parts of our discipline which relate to Slavery." The first loyalty of Quakers, the meeting insisted, must be to the faith.[34]

More often, Friends became entangled in slavery for economic reasons. The question of slave hiring remained a problem. The same factors that drove the rise of the slave trade—the shift from tobacco to grains and the resulting seasonal demand for labor—encouraged the development of a local market in hired slaves. So, too, did improvement projects, many of which employed enslaved men on a yearly basis. The Baltimore Yearly Meeting had in 1798 declared the hiring of slaves "Contrary to our Christian Testimony and Discipline" and called for the disownment of members who violated the injunction, but some Friends still erred. In 1855, the Fairfax meeting confronted a case of slave hiring by Mary Jane and Isaac S. Hough. The meeting disowned Mary Jane when she expressed no remorse, while her husband Isaac retained his membership after he acknowledged his error and promised to reimburse the enslaved man. The vast majority of Quakers did not violate the slave testimony after 1800, but working and living in a slave society made it difficult to avoid becoming implicated in slavery. After his father's death, Nathan Lupton ran a Winchester-based flour milling and mercantile business that linked Frederick County farmers to Baltimore in a network of credit and trade built in part on the labor of enslaved African Americans. Although Lupton did not own or employ slaves, the ethical dangers of his business became clear in 1843 when a creditor, "Mr. West," pressed him to repay two hundred dollars so that West could keep a slave he had purchased on credit. If Lupton did not meet the claim, one of his business associates reminded him, "we will have lost all confidence" with creditors. Accordingly, Lupton obliged West's demand.[35]

Other Friends faced similar ethical dilemmas. When Samuel Janney established his cotton mill at Occoquan in the 1830s, he found himself ensnared in the slave economy. To maintain Quaker principles, Janney employed free laborers at his mill, but like opponents of slavery throughout the nation he could not avoid using slave-produced cotton. When he moved to Loudoun County in 1839, he supplied his girls' boarding school with products produced by free labor, purchasing goods at Quaker-run free produce stores during his trips to Philadelphia. But even as headmaster of Springdale, Janney could not escape slavery entirely. The school, like Benjamin Hallowell's in Alexandria, enrolled "scholars" from slaveholding families, which provided opportunities for teaching Quaker antislavery values. But as his uncle Phineas pointed out in 1844, it also made Janney vulnerable to slaveholders. Janney's "*open opposition* to slavery," Phineas noted, posed a threat to the school's economic survival. For his part, Samuel remained resolute. Spiritual demands must trump material considerations. "When duty calls," he affirmed, "interest must not stand in the way." But determining the path of duty—one that fulfilled his responsibilities to his family, religious community, students, and spiritual principles—was difficult in a society and economy pervaded by slavery.[36]

Most Friends succeeded well enough that local African Americans recognized them as a group to whom they could turn for assistance. Friends frequently established economic and personal relationships with the region's free black population. They provided steady work for free blacks and paid good wages. In the early 1840s, Mary Lea Stabler of Alexandria paid four dollars per month for a black domestic. In 1856, Samuel Janney secured a domestic position for an African American woman, Jane Robinson, which paid a dollar a week. In contrast, most black domestics in Loudoun County "earned less" than twenty-five dollars a year. Those in Fairfax earned between twenty and sixty dollars annually in 1860. Quakers paid higher wages in part because they relied on the labor of local free blacks. Opportunities for regular work and comparatively decent wages led many free black families to settle close by Quaker communities in Loudoun and Frederick Counties. In the early nineteenth century, David Lupton rented land to Henry Wells, a free black man, for sixty dollars a year, and when Wells died Lupton administered his estate, worth over three hundred dollars. Over thirty years later, Lupton's son, Jonah, hired African American wage earners to work his farm. In Loudoun County, Quaker miller Thomas Phillips employed free black Forest Griffith, along with Griffith's wife and daughter, for one hundred and twenty dollars a year in 1846 (in addition to twenty additional African Americans between 1835 and 1858), and four years later five free blacks resided with Samuel Janney's family at Springdale Academy.[37]

Friends expressed warm feelings for African Americans with whom they lived and worked. But their relationships looked similar to those between paternalist slaveholders and their domestic slaves, reflecting Friends's absorption of the racial attitudes of the region. By the early 1840s, the Lea family of Sandy Spring had employed free black members of the Williams family for three generations. "Old Mary," noted Elizabeth Lea, had "been in the family more than 30 years." Old Mary's two sons, Ben and Tom ("both excellent and trusty servants"), and her daughter, Kitty, also worked for the Lea family. "Old Mary" had begun her service with the family in Philadelphia, and according to Lea, she remembered "what an advantage it had been to have a good bringing up" among Friends. Mary also encouraged Kitty to send her ten-year-old daughter, Mary Catherine (also Kitty), to work for the Stablers in Alexandria. The Hallowells displayed a similar regard for their black employees. Benjamin Hallowell employed "six to eight" domestics "at a time" at his Alexandria boarding school. He recalled "the comfort" he "had with the domestics," noting that Nancy Gordon Franklin, his first black employee, worked for the family for thirty-six years. Another of his longtime employees, Nathaniel Lucas, used his salary to purchase the freedom of his family and a home. The domestics in his employ, Hallowell concluded, "found a pleasant and profitable home with me and in my family."[38]

But Hallowell's remarks on training domestics also reveal his paternalism, akin to what southern slaveholders claimed for master-slave relations. Although Hallowell treated his workers with kindness and paid them punctually, his female domestics, who often headed their own households, received as little as three dollars per month. Like free black women throughout the urban South, Hallowell's employees struggled to live on such wages. On payday, he reprimanded employees for any "deficiency or dissatisfaction," or he offered practical advice, urging them to save "their money for a rainy day." Hallowell's "heart ache[d] to see" how "little the women had to save" from their low salaries, but he did not raise them. White Alexandrians, he noted, considered three to four dollars "full wages for" domestics and he would not violate the hiring practices of his southern home. The labor of black domestics also enabled prosperous Friends like the Hallowells to attain middle-class respectability and status. Living in a borderland between North and South, many Friends coupled the racial assumptions of slaveholders with a sense of middle-class identity centered on the notion of domesticity.[39]

Friends' frustrations in obtaining reliable black domestic workers reveal their assimilation of southern notions of race and class. Despite the growing population of free black women who supplied much of the domestic workforce in northern Virginia, women Friends, who oversaw the hiring of household help, complained about a shortage of good domestics. Writing from Waterford in 1847, Mary Stone reported that she had hired "a colar[e]d Woman to manage" her household "af[f]airs," but added that "girls" who "are good for any[thing]" are "hard to get in Loudo[u]n." D. G. Lea hoped that her sister Mary, living in Alexandria, would not have the same "trouble . . . getting good girls" for housekeeping "as some of us country people." From Frederick County, Lydia Lupton informed her sister in 1858 that she had managed to find "a tolerable good coloured girl" who enabled her family to "get along pretty well." Other Friends did not manage to find even "tolerable" domestic help. When Mary Moore fell ill she hired "a black nurse" to care for her and help in the household. "You would have been amused," related Moore, "to see" the woman "fussing over me." "Onlookers" found the treatment "amusing," but Moore declared it "annoying."[40]

Quaker women believed it their duty to train domestics and transform them into "reliable" and "faithful" servants. Mary Lea Stabler and her mother Elizabeth viewed Mary's oversight of the ten-year-old Mary Catherine (Kitty) as a reformation project. Before Kitty arrived, Elizabeth advised Mary "to keep a watch over" Kitty "in every respect." "Thee should always give her her meals thyself," Elizabeth continued, "she should go to bed . . . not later than 9," and "I do not think it will be proper for her to go in the street." Kitty's first days in the Stabler household went well. "We all like her very well," reported Mary, and "are quite amused with Kitty's manner of talking," providing a sample of Kitty's dialect to entertain her Maryland relations. However, when Mary suspected Kitty of telling lies and stealing she considered removing her from the household. Elizabeth responded that her daughter should "be quite strict," but added that "some of" Kitty's "family have been so valuable and honest that I would not give her up." Following her mother's advice, Mary worked with Kitty to "try to make something of her." She found that rigorous oversight worked wonders. Within weeks she reported that Kitty "is very useful to me." "I hope," Mary concluded, "to make a good servant of her yet." Mary's words illustrate the divide that separated black domestics from their Quaker employers. Although Mary taught Kitty to read and write, she could envision no future for her but that of "good servant." Condescension tinctured the affection of the Stabler family for their black domestics.[41]

The Quaker discipline—Friends' rules of conduct—ensured that members of the Society remained different from their white neighbors, but it could not protect them from imbibing some of the South's pervasive racial attitudes. Some northern Friends perceived the differences in their southern counterparts. Quaker minister George Truman concluded that southern Friends, like their white neighbors, "do not like to be interfered with by us of the North." When northerners attacked the region "in their presence," Truman observed, southern "Quakers . . . will bristle up, and become almost direct apologists for Slave-holders." Southern values did not always disappear when Friends migrated north. Mary Brown of Ohio commented wryly on a local Quaker mother, newly removed to the state from Loudoun County, who had "brought her oldest daughter up like the slaveholders. She does nothing but visit [and] play on the Piano." "How different," Brown concluded, from the training of Quaker children in the North, where youth received "a good education" that "brings them to business."[42]

Southern Friends viewed northerners' dismissal of the region with consternation. In 1842, Mary Pleasants worried that her northern relatives did not visit because they were "laughing at" and "abusing Virginia." "You would find," she exclaimed, "that Virginia is not quite so uncivilized as a good many" of you "pretend to think." Months later, when northern Friends still had not visited, Pleasants praised recent cultural and intellectual events she had attended, including debating and temperance societies, and lectures on "Mesmerism" by "de Bonneville, Mrs. Clark and several others." "I will," she concluded, "try to get to hear him—as you northerners would say." Pleasants reveals the conflicted identity of southern Friends. She defended her region by trying to convince her northern relations that Virginia participated in the latest national intellectual and cultural trends.[43] By the 1840s and 1850s, Friends had lived in northern Virginia for over one hundred years. Those who remained called the region home and praised its beauty and productivity. Like Friends elsewhere they embraced aspects of the society and culture in which they lived. Yet they remained a people apart, rejecting slavery and the violence that sustained slaveholders' dominance. As the sectional crisis deepened in the 1850s, Friends understood the extent of the difference.

IV

Before 1830, Quakers played a prominent role in antislavery efforts that sought a gradual end to slavery by appealing to the consciences of slaveholding elites and working through the legal system. However, the failure of these tactics and the popularity of colonization, with its aim of removing free blacks, prompted activists to adopt more radical approaches. Heralded by the publication of David Walker's 1829 *Appeal to the Coloured Citizens of the World* and William Lloyd Garrison's *Liberator* in 1831, abolitionists called for an immediate end to slavery, denounced colonization, and employed more strident rhetoric. Although radicals rejected violence, particularly after Nat Turner's 1831 rebellion, most Friends distanced themselves. They feared that harsh attacks on slaveholders' morals and calls for immediate emancipation would lead to bloodshed. The growing intransigence of southern slaveholders, who after Nat Turner blamed northern abolitionists for slave resistance, convinced most Quakers that radical tactics would produce anarchy and bloodshed. They also found Garrison's denunciation of the Constitution as a proslavery document and his calls for disunion dangerous, a potential source of violence and a bewildering attack on a government that ensured their religious liberty. Most Friends believed the tactics of political abolitionists, who broke from Garrison in 1839 and formed the Liberty Party the following year, little better. Using popular politics to fight slavery, they worried, would produce "coercive" measures that the slaveholding minority would resist with force. Instead, Quakers supported the Whig Party, which shared Friends' embrace of economic and moral improvement and stewardship. Northern Virginia Friends praised Whig leader John Quincy Adams who opposed slavery but distanced himself from radical abolition.[44]

In the charged political environment of the 1840s and 1850s, Friends' moderate antislavery stance, while earning the praise of politicians like Henry Clay, found little support among either abolitionists or slaveholders. Northern abolitionists grew frustrated with nonviolent tactics that did little to stop slavery's expansion. Some espoused direct action against slavery—including aid to runaway slaves and support for slave resistance—even if violence resulted. Many enslaved people living in borderlands like northern Virginia, close to the free states and the possibility of freedom, attempted escape. Reports of slave runaways proliferated in the local and antislavery press, belying slaveholders' claims of a docile African American population. Between 1817 and 1842, masters placed advertisements for some 237 runaways in Leesburg's *Genius of Liberty*, including a dramatic 1840 attempt to flee north by twenty-two slaves owned by the estate of John Marshall. The same year, the region's residents learned that Leonard Grimes, a District of Columbia free black hack driver of "good character," had helped "several slaves" escape from Loudoun County to Canada. In November 1842, a D.C. paper reported that at least one hundred runaways have "within the last month . . . clandestinely left their owners." In the fall of 1849, *The Liberator* reported that "a number of slaves" had fled from Clarke and Frederick Counties in the Shenandoah Valley, carrying "free papers so well executed" many slaveholders believed "they had been systematically supplied."[45]

By the 1850s, the flow of runaways, apparently aided by white abolitionists, had become a "Negro Stampede," convincing some slaveholders that the institution could not survive in northern Virginia. When Loudoun County planter Thomas Ellzey discovered ferrymen at Edward's Ferry on the Potomac River and brick makers from Maryland "tampering" with his slaves and assisting runaways, he concluded "that the institution of slavery along the border line of the slave and free states could, in no event, survive another generation." But few slaveholders succumbed to such fatalism. Instead, they followed the lead of South Carolina's proslavery elite and launched what historian Manisha Sinha calls a "counter-revolution" intended to silence dissent, defend slavery, and castigate abolitionists. In the 1850s, Loudoun County slaveholders rejected secession but sought "some effective means" to protect their slave property "against those internal, external, and infernal foes, who are the cause of such a large loss every year ... of runaway slaves." Such efforts reflected a broader shift in white opinion in the Upper South in the 1850s, as moderates accepted the proslavery assumptions of Deep South radicals. They condemned abolition as an attack on slaveholders' constitutional rights and a threat to the Union, praised slavery as a divinely ordained and civilizing institution, stifled dissent, and called on the federal government to protect the institution. Many slavery defenders countenanced violence to achieve these goals, viewing northern denunciations as an affront to the honor and moral standing of slaveholders and the South.[46]

Northern Virginia Friends watched this hardening of attitudes with dismay, but they believed their reputation as civic-minded citizens enabled them to continue speaking against slavery. They also hoped that living in the border South, next to the seat of the national government, would allow them to continue their antislavery efforts. Into the 1840s and 1850s the region also possessed a strong two-party political system that lessened the ability of proslavery leaders to stifle debate. Although slaveholders dominated local political life and parties, and politicians of all stripes expressed support for property rights, some whites questioned the institution's impact on the regional and state economy. In addition to Quakers, local German farmers rarely owned slaves, nor did most of the northern-born population of Fairfax County. Political contests reflected this diverse population, and into the 1850s Whigs (or former Whigs) competed successfully against northern Virginia Democrats.[47]

Northern Virginia's Whigs, however, never deviated from the South's proslavery consensus, and in 1849 local antislavery Friends discovered the limits to freedom of speech. In April, Methodist minister William A. Smith lectured at the Leesburg courthouse on black inequality and the Bible's endorsement of slavery. Four months later, Samuel Janney published a response in a local newspaper, *The Washingtonian*. Days after Janney's second essay appeared, Loudoun County's grand jury indicted him on charges of inciting slave insurrection. Some court officials refused to prosecute the respected educator, but the grand jury issued a second indictment in November and Janney's case came to trial in June 1850. Janney believed that the delays worked in his favor. His case attracted considerable attention and the judges worried about the public relations problems of prosecuting a peaceable Quaker teacher and minister. They clearly wanted his case to go away. "One of the judges came to me," Janney reported, "and said if I would only put into the form of an affidavit . . . '*that I had no intention to violate the law*,' it would have great weight with the court." Janney did so and the court "*squashed the presentment*." "So the matter ends," Janney concluded, "I think to general satisfaction." What began as a serious threat to Janney became—judged by the tone of his letters—inconsequential.[48]

In the immediate aftermath of the case, Janney paid little heed to the court's warning that he take "care and caution in meddling with the delicate question of slavery," publishing his courtroom defense, "The Freedom of the Press Vindicated." Still, the case had a deeper impact on Janney than he admitted. After his piece appeared in July 1850, he published no further antislavery essays and abandoned his public campaign. He also decided in spring 1853 to close Springdale Boarding School and in October put the building up for sale. Slaveholders' hostility to his antislavery opinions seems to have shaped his decision. In the wake of his arrest, Janney and his wife fretted about declining enrollment and began seeking more students among Friends and advertising in antislavery and Quaker journals. By August 1852, fifteen of his twenty-five students were the children of Friends. Janney sold the school to the Fairfax Quarterly Meeting, which reopened it under his direction in fall 1854 as a coeducational, all-Quaker school. "This school has been established," Janney announced in early 1855, "to promote the guarded education of *Friends' children*, consistently with our principles." In an increasingly hostile environment, Friends turned inward.[49]

In the 1850s, Janney also devoted more time to writing his biographies of Quaker leaders William Penn and George Fox. An 1849 journey to the

Hicksite Ohio Yearly Meeting convinced him of the dangers of radical-ism. The Ohio meeting was divided between reformers "actively engaged" in "the Abolition of Slavery, of Capital Punishments, war, land monopoly, and intemperance," and conservatives who "generally take no part in the Reformatory movements." "I thought I was something of an Anti-Slavery man," Janney noted, "but I would not pass for one there." He believed that radical abolitionism (or the "doctrines . . . of the Boston clique") promised "great injury to the cause" of antislavery in the South. The radicals' "new and unsound principles" were also "calculated to lay waste to the order and harmony of [the] Society [of Friends]." Janney hoped his biographies would help reconcile moderate Hicksite and Orthodox Friends, and he was pleased when they attracted favorable attention from moderate Orthodox minister Thomas Evans, whom Janney visited in Philadelphia in 1852. But moving closer to Orthodox Friends came at a cost. During the same trip, Janney met with Lucretia Mott. A decade earlier, Mott had inspired Janney to resume his antislavery campaign, but he now found his opinions "nearer to those of T. Evans than L. Mott." Mott remained "a sincere, self-sacrificing Christian," but Janney believed her radical views decreased "her power to be useful." Seeking reconciliation within the Society, Janney distanced him-self from radical Friends whom he believed posed a threat to its unity.[50]

Janney never abandoned his antislavery convictions. As he reminded his uncle Phineas, his campaign against slavery, begun in the 1820s, was grounded in his Quaker faith. "I conceive myself," he attested, "called to labour in this field . . . to do something, however small, for the relief of the oppressed." But Janney also distanced himself from radical abolitionists. His antislavery efforts, he explained, did not come "from 'those abolition-ists of the north,' as thou seems to suppose." "My pen," he stressed, "was en-gaged in this cause before the present abolition Societies were organized." Still, Janney's opinions and actions had enormous influence among Friends in northern Virginia. His decision to retreat from his antislavery campaign and heal the Society's internal divisions encouraged many local Friends to see slavery as a secondary spiritual concern.[51]

Nonetheless, Friends continued to provide assistance—within clearly defined limits—to free and enslaved African Americans who came to them for help. Little evidence exists that local Friends participated in the Under-ground Railroad. In this conservative Hicksite community, Quakers could not retain membership in good standing if they participated in aggressive and illegal measures undertaken by political abolitionists such as Wil-liam L. Chaplin in the District of Columbia—actions that violated Quaker pacifism and defied the law. Despite their history of noncompliance with legislation they considered morally suspect, Friends viewed "civil government . . . as an *ordinance of God*," and believed they must obey laws that did not violate their moral precepts. Without a civil authority, "anarchy, riot, and mob violence," which Alexandria minister Benjamin Hallowell considered "the *worst* of evils," might prevail. When "mal-administration" resulted in immoral or repressive legislation, noncompliant Friends must "patiently . . . suffer whatever might be inflicted" and seek "legal assistance for the redress of wrongs." But Friends also believed they lived, despite the moral atrocity of slavery, in a "favored land," where an "enlightened" government bestowed "religious liberty" and provided its citizens with "higher privileges" than the "people of any former age." The liberty they enjoyed to speak "truth" put more "responsibility" on them "to be a disciple of him [Christ] who was meek and lowly in heart, who went about continually doing good." Friends had a heightened responsibility, in short, to emulate Christ and uphold "all truth."[52]

Quakers found balancing these injunctions—opposing war and slavery while living under governments that sustained both—a difficult proposition. Most local Friends concluded that their "peaceable" testimony enabled them to provide financial and legal assistance to African Americans seeking freedom or reuniting families trapped in slavery. After Janney abandoned his public advocacy of antislavery, he helped at least two African American families purchase their freedom. In 1852, he and eleven other Friends secured a twelve-hundred-dollar loan for Wilson Anderson, a free black man, so that he could purchase his enslaved wife and four children from Virginia Blincoe, who threatened to sell them and separate the family. Three years later, Janney traveled south to Warrenton to purchase the freedom of a young girl, Eliza Robinson, and her disabled mother, Jane, from a Fauquier County slaveholder after Philadelphia Quaker Jane Johnson took an interest in the girl. Janney explained to Johnson that the region's Friends "are often called on to aid" local slaves who wished "to buy their freedom." Many such individuals save "a little money or have near relations who aid them," and many local slaveholders, concerned about the vulnerability of their slave property, "will take much less than their market value." Still, "the means" of local Quakers "are not adequate to the demand."[53]

Janney suggested that northern abolitionists might more effectively fight slavery by using antislavery southerners as "faithful agents" to purchase "young persons, and especially . . . females." Such a scheme would force "the whole Union" to "share the burden" of ending the institution. The tactics of northern abolitionists, he added, only "excited" and "exasperate[d]" southern slaveholders who then stifled antislavery southerners. Janney accurately described the deepening crisis engendered by slavery in the 1840s and 1850s, even if his solution held little promise of success. On the borders of the South, defenders of slavery worried about the future of the institution, their fears heightened by an apparent rise in fugitive slaves, the activities of a biracial antislavery community in the District of Columbia, and strident abolitionist calls to end slavery. These threats prompted northern Virginia's proslavery forces, led by Democrat and John C. Calhoun acolyte R. M. T. Hunter, to return Alexandria to Virginia in 1846 to protect the slave trade of the city.[54] The same anxiety over the future of the institution in the borderlands prompted Loudoun County slaveholders to lash out at Janney in late 1849 and a few years later against Quaker Yardley Taylor.

Taylor achieved acclaim for his promotion of agricultural improvement and his 1853 topographical map of Loudoun County. But Taylor's description of the county also revealed his antislavery politics. Taylor reserved his greatest compliments for the non-slaveholding areas of the county where, he argued, the use of free labor dramatically increased output. County residents knew of Taylor's antislavery politics since 1824, when he helped organize the Loudoun Manumission and Emigration Society. By the 1850s, local slaveholders labeled him "the chief of the abolition clan in Loudoun." Taylor cemented his antislavery reputation in March 1856 when local Friends criticized slavery during a meeting of Goose Creek Literary Society. The evening began innocently enough. Formed by local Friends in 1851, the literary society met in the Quaker school house. At its March meeting, the society offered the following question for discussion: "'*Resolved*. That we do endorse the nomination of Millard Fillmore by the American Party.'" Taking the negative side, Francis H. Ray, a New York Friend recently arrived in Loudoun to teach at the Springdale Boarding School, "strongly opposed" Fillmore because he had signed "the odious and unconstitutional Fugitive Slave Law" and supported the extension of slavery into the territories. The local Democratic press reported that during his speech Ray "was prompted by an old man with a broad brim white hat . . . the veritable Yardl[e]y Taylor."[55]

In response, slaveholders John Simpson and James R. Trayhern expressed their astonishment that such "Black Republican" and "Abolitionist" "sentiments should be uttered on Southern soil." In a ninety-minute rebuttal, Trayhern announced that Ray ought to return "to the North, and mingle with Fred. Douglass and Lucy Black*wool* Stone." "The South," he added, "was no place for the expression of such sentiments." When members of the predominantly Quaker audience cried out, "He has the liberty of speech," Trayhern responded that Ray had "*entire* freedom of speech upon Virginian soil," if he would "speak *right*." The editor of the Leesburg *Democratic Mirror*, Josiah B. Taylor, "thinking to make some Capital for his party," reported the debates as a "Black Republican Meeting in Loudoun." The editor warned white residents that Friends held "insurrectionary" principles whose "*essential* nature" aimed "at the destruction of both property and social peace!" "Has the monster of abolition," he asked, "grown to such proportions as to flap its dark wing over . . . the South?" Southerners could not silence northern fanatics, but they must "not suffer . . . in silence" such "insult and endangerment from within."[56]

Other Virginia papers, including the Alexandria *Virginia Sentinel*, picked up the story. Warning that "treason stalks abroad," the press denounced Ray as "the devil incarnate on earth," and warned him "to beware of those potent arguments—tar and feathers, and personal violence." The paper called on "the good people of Loudoun" to "protect the South from the injurious consequences of this domestic treason." The press coverage sparked "indignation meetings" that denounced Ray and his fellow Quakers. Days later, a local committee of slaveholders visited the schoolteacher and warned him to leave the state "upon pain of personal violence if" he refused. Ray soon departed. But his coreligionists left in the state faced "deep seated and almost incurable prejudices" among local whites, who believed that the "incendiary doctrines of northern fanaticism" had entered Virginia through the "auspices" of local Friends.[57]

Taylor earned slaveholders' animus because during the debate he denounced the 1850 Fugitive Slave Law as contrary to "higher law." Weeks later, he acted on these principles, aided the escape of a fugitive slave, and faced legal charges. In a subsequent interview with a local slaveholder, Taylor "admitted that a runaway slave came" to his house, that he fed the man, and gave him an introductory "letter to a friend in Pennsylvania." But he also believed himself "innocent of" breaking the law, arguing that he had acted "in conformity with the principles" of his faith, extending aid like the Good Samaritan to an individual in obvious need. The angry slaveholder denounced Taylor's actions as a "Monstrous!" violation of state law, but the Loudoun County court did not convict him. Taylor believed that by not seeking out the fugitive he had found a way to reconcile his principles and Virginia law. He added that Pennsylvania Friends "complained of" him because he was "not accomplishing quite as much as they have a right to expect." Taylor's assistance to the runaway pushed the definition of "passive" resistance and represented the outer limits of Quaker philanthropy and slaveholder tolerance in northern Virginia. But Taylor's reputation for civic involvement and agricultural improvement helped him escape without legal consequences.[58]

He did not, however, escape public censure. In July, a broadside addressed to Taylor insulted his appearance—"a square built, heavy set, hugely footed, not very courtly figure of an old man"—and warned him of "gross delusion" if he believed he could "preach . . . incendiary doctrines with impunity." The broadside focused on Taylor's history of antislavery activity and his denunciation of the Fugitive Slave law at the March meeting. "The principle of moral and positive laws," the writer lectured, "is the same and the obligation rests upon us to obey one as the other. . . . The Bible, morality, and patriotism, all alike unite in enjoining it as a solemn duty which every man owes to the government." Convinced that Taylor abetted runaways, the writer castigated him for his management of the local "affairs of the Underground Railroad Company." He reminded Taylor that he lived "in the South," or at least "in a *quasi*-Southern county," making it "not quite so propitious a point for the prosecution of your philanthropic labors, as if the entirety of your surroundings were anti-slavery." In northern Virginia, Taylor could not undertake his "assaults upon Southern institutions" without repercussions. The broadside served a variety of purposes—a public shaming, a lecture on southern values—but above all it made clear the dangers that Taylor and his fellow Quakers faced if they did not desist from their antislavery activities.[59]

Local slaveholders' denunciation of their Quaker neighbors reveals how vulnerable they felt as the sectional crisis deepened. They insisted that all the region's white residents embrace slavery and southern "interests." Local antislavery Friends experienced firsthand the extent of the change. Before the 1850s, they had received a generally respectful hearing among their white neighbors by presenting themselves as patriots who sought a gradual end to slavery because of their deep attachment to the state and desire to restore its economic and political stature. The rising political tensions of the late 1840s and 1850s curtailed the ability of Quakers to voice safely their alternative vision of Virginia. Located on the border between slavery and freedom, northern Virginia's slaveholders recognized the fragility and worried about the fate of their peculiar institution. Thus, they worked to silence all internal dissent, including that of local Friends. In effect, the region's slaveholders turned south, linking their fate to that of the Deep South, even if they did not yet embrace secession.

Facing these dangers, Friends did not abandon their commitment to antislavery or their efforts to aid local African Americans in the 1850s, though they eschewed confrontational paths. Yardley Taylor continued to promote agricultural improvement in the southern press until after the Civil War commenced. Friends in the Shenandoah Valley employed free labor in factories and on their farms. Chalkley Gillingham oversaw the growth of a thriving free-labor community at Accotink, centered on the Woodlawn meeting. Samuel Janney carried on promoting black education, supporting his daughter Cornelia's school for free blacks in Loudoun County and becoming a trustee for a proposed school for free black girls in Washington, D.C. Benjamin Hallowell promoted free labor on his Maryland farm and at the fledgling University of Maryland, but confronted by white racism in Alexandria he also gave limited support to colonization efforts. Friends' challenge to slavery, in short, always remained within the boundaries defined by their spiritual beliefs and regional economic and social connections. The same factors that made their activism possible—their spiritual principles and social ties—also constrained it. In the face of their white neighbors' intractable defense of slavery, Friends' options narrowed and they faced the practical limitations of their antislavery approach. In the fall of 1859, John Brown's raid on Harpers Ferry raised the specter of civil war and presented northern Virginia Friends with the greatest spiritual dilemma and physical threat they had yet faced. Over the next six years, they would learn what it was like to live "in the Lion's mouth."[60]

"The Union Forever"

Northern Virginia Quakers in the Civil War

In December 1859, Mary S. Lippincott, a Philadelphia Quaker teacher and minister, learned that Friends in "Louden County" believed "they will be ordered to leave the State." Six weeks earlier, John Brown had launched his raid on Harpers Ferry, hoping to foment a slave revolt. The U.S. military had crushed the raid, and the state of Virginia had tried and executed Brown and those captured with him, but white Virginians feared further abolitionist raids. Reports of escalating slave escapes and resistance—especially the burning of the barns and crops of jurors who convicted Brown—stoked white unease. In response, more Virginians embraced secession. In Shepherdstown, located just west of Harpers Ferry, a newspaper reported that the town's residents, "from the editor down to the *devil*, have spent several days of this week in shouldering our muskets in defense of Southern Rights." As the *Richmond Whig* noted, "recent events have wrought almost a complete revolution in the sentiments, the thoughts, the hopes of" white Virginians. Even "the oldest and steadiest conservatives," who had once "scoffed at the idea of a dissolution of the Union as a madman's dream," now believe "that its days are numbered."[1]

Although Virginia's militancy declined after Brown's execution, its virulence worried Friends. Southern fanaticism, grounded in the defense of slavery, posed a threat to Friends' antislavery testimonies and the continued wellbeing of their community. They possessed a strong attachment to the state, but their spiritual commitments led them to break with the vast majority of white Virginians, who in the spring of 1861 opted for secession and war. Just as they rejected slavery—in part as a product of their rejection of violence—northern Virginia Friends eschewed secession. "Friends," stated the Loudoun County meetings in fall 1861, have "always borne a testimony against war . . . abstaining from all kinds of military services and patiently suffering the penalties that ensued. This testimony . . . is in accordance with the example . . . of Christ and especially with his Sermon on the Mount." "We deem it our religious duty," Friends concluded, "to take no part in [this war]; and to abstain from every act that would give aid in its prosecution."[2]

Individual Friends, however, did not always follow the Society's official pronouncements. The vast majority of Quakers were committed to the Union, which they perceived as the source of their religious liberty. As the war continued and northern war aims included ending slavery, Friends' Unionism became more overt. Yet for Friends, embracing the Union cause presented a moral dilemma: supporting the Union war effort compromised their peace testimony, a central component of their faith. Friends throughout the northern states confronted this same moral quandary. As Abraham Lincoln told Quaker minister Eliza P. Gurney, "Your people have had, and are having, a very great trial. On principle, and faith, opposed to both war and oppression, they can only practically oppose oppression by war." For Friends in northern Virginia, resolving "this hard dilemma" posed an ongoing and dangerous challenge.[3]

Over the course of four years of war, the local Quaker community, often living in a no man's land over which neither Union nor Confederate forces exercised complete authority, experienced the theft and destruction of property by both armies. They faced arrest, imprisonment, and conscription by hostile southern military authorities. They suffered the attacks, reprisals, and hostility of secessionist neighbors. And they confronted various guerrilla and partisan bands—most notoriously Lieutenant Colonel John S. Mosby's 43rd Virginia Cavalry—that terrorized and punished local pro-Union populations, disrupted communications and transportation facilities, and confiscated property and foodstuffs at will. Friends experienced what historian Mark Grimsley calls "the hard hand of war" long before the North's military leadership abandoned its early "rosewater" treatment of southern civilians and embraced tactics designed to undermine the morale of the white South.[4] Despite their Unionism, Friends often suffered with their southern neighbors during punitive Federal campaigns. The threat of arrest and conscription fell on male Friends, forcing many to flee the region for Maryland or western Virginia. Quaker women who remained faced many difficulties but played a key role in maintaining their community's integrity. Like their Confederate counterparts, they employed gender conventions to elude the worst depredations, express political opinions, and articulate displeasure (and occasional approbation) with the war's political and military leaders. Women's response to war helped transform Friends' adherence to and interpretation of the peace testimony and their disciplinary standards. From war emerged a more permissive and individualist Quakerism.

I

John Brown's attack on Harpers Ferry in October 1859 left the thousand Friends who resided in northern Virginia conflicted. They denounced his actions while sympathizing with his goals and worried about the national and personal repercussions of his violence. "I fear," wrote minister Samuel Janney, that Brown's raid "will produce excitement and alarm through the state and may do much harm." Despite periodic repression, slaveholders usually accepted Quakers' presence because they had earned a reputation as civic-minded *southerners* committed to the prosperity of the region. As Shenandoah Valley resident Mary Hollingsworth pronounced after a fall 1860 visit to a Friends meeting, "The society is doubtless a good one." The Hopewell meeting had disowned Hollingsworth's father, David, in 1831 for hiring a slave and marrying a non-Quaker and the family had thereafter joined the local Episcopalian Church. But Hollingsworth still praised Friends' "testimony against war" and the Society's enforcement of "economy, punctuality, veracity and perseverance" among its members. "In purity and simplicity," she concluded, "the Society of Friends will compare favorably with any number of professing Christians."[5]

Although many locals shared Hollingsworth's high opinion of Friends, Brown's raid exacerbated the racial fears of white southerners who identified local Quakers as suspect, in part because Brown associated with Friends and sometimes received their assistance. In the 1840s, Brown had entered business and socialized with Quakers in Jefferson County, Ohio. In December 1857, Brown and ten of his recruits wintered a few miles outside the Quaker community of Springdale, Iowa, where friendships developed between Brown's followers and some meeting members. Brown returned to Iowa again in early 1859, accompanied by eleven slaves he had rescued from Missouri. During the escape, Brown and his party hid in Springdale for two weeks, bringing national attention—and among southerners notoriety—to his Quaker allies. More damning, two Springdale Friends, Edwin and Barclay Coppoc, joined Brown at Harpers Ferry, highlighting Brown and the Quakers' common views. They shared, for example, an ethic of plainness. Contemporaries commented on Brown's humble style of living and dress. For paranoid Virginia slaveholders, such similarities made local Friends a suspect group because they also voiced antislavery beliefs like those that prompted the Coppocs' "acts of murder and rapine." More discomfiting to Friends, Brown justified his violence by citing Quakers' spiritual touchstone, the golden rule. "The Bible," Brown stated during his trial, "teaches me that all things whatsoever I would that men should do to me, I should do even so to them." "I endeavored," he continued, "to act up to that instruction." Friends rejected Brown's reading of the golden rule, seeing it instead as the basis for their repudiation of violence. In the panicked weeks after Brown's raid, however, few white southerners found Friends' interpretation convincing, concluding that they threatened the region's proslavery orthodoxy.[6]

To confront perceived internal and external threats, in late 1859 white Virginians formed militia and volunteer companies and vigilance committees, creating a state of "undeclared martial law" in northern Virginia. A wave of black unrest, including arson and the poisoning of farm animals—sparked, whites believed, by northern provocateurs—prompted local officials to arrest outsiders and local blacks, and led to calls for the enslavement of free blacks. Officials stifled free speech, charging postmasters and recipients of northern papers with distributing "incendiary documents." Some residents, particularly the large number of northerners in Fairfax County, believed Virginia in "a state of anarchy" and prepared "to leave." "We are," concluded another white Virginian, "in the midst of a Reign of Terror."[7]

Friends experienced firsthand the repressive measures of the "John-Brown year." A Washington court found Quaker Daniel Breed guilty of "using language . . . calculated to excite slaves to insurrection" during a private conversation. He escaped jail time "by giving bond for two thousand dollars to keep the peace for a year." In February 1860, Mary Lippincott traveled south to attend the Fairfax Quarterly Meeting. She reported that the meeting "was unusually large" because many non-Quakers "wanted to hear whether or not Friends would have anything to say about John Brown." But Quaker speakers, Lippincott reported, made "no allusion to [John Brown] or to politics." "We desire," she stressed, "nothing but to persuade men to be Christians." Likewise, Friends in Frederick County, reported J. W. Griffith, "mind their own business." "None . . . are so reckless as to be willing to accompany a John [Brown] in his efforts to free the Negroes." Friends believed that only by maintaining their principles of Christian pacifism and extending goodwill toward all people (even proslavery "madcaps"), could they pursue their ethical concerns. In the tense post-raid atmosphere they had little alternative—at least if they wanted to remain in Virginia.[8]

Not all Friends agreed. Some called on their coreligionists to denounce the proslavery militants. J. Richards, writing from the relative safety of Baltimore days after Brown's execution, urged Quakers in northern Virginia to "speak out!" "Don't be frightened by Gov. Wise and the soldiers!" A few northern Friends viewed Virginia Quakers' response to southern intransigence as moral compromise. Rhode Island Quaker Rebecca Buffum Spring believed Friends in northern Virginia lacked moral fortitude. She traveled south in November 1859 to join Lydia Maria Child, who had received permission from Virginia's governor to visit Brown in jail. Spring hoped Friends could help her find Child, but they would not. "I [will] have nothing to do with it," local Friend David Howell huffed. "Let her [Child] stay in her own country and mind her own business." Spring reminded Howell that had John Woolman, the Quaker minister most responsible for Friends' antislavery testimony, still been alive he would have helped her. "I don't care what John Woolman would" do, replied Howell, "I know David Howells wouldn't." "Muttering about dangerous times," Howell saw a "shocked" Spring to the door. Howell "trembled," remembered Spring: "his lips were blue, his face twitched nervously. I was sorry for him."[9]

Spring believed Howell failed to uphold his Quaker principles, but she refused to acknowledge the powerful social pressures southern Friends confronted. Spring's gender and class enabled her to travel in Virginia. Emboldened by her faith, she praised Brown and his antislavery principles during her brief stay in the state. But she could return to her northern home after she offended white southerners. Friends like David Howell, unless they planned to uproot their lives and families, did not have this option. By leaving, moreover, they could no longer serve as antislavery examples to their white neighbors and employers of local African Americans. In the months after Brown's raid, Friends made a strategic decision to lie low, but they did not abandon their antislavery or pacifist beliefs. What Spring and some northern Quakers interpreted as moral compromise, northern Virginia Friends viewed as necessary for the survival of the community. Quaker leaders urged their coreligionists "to maintain this testimony against slavery," but also to "be watchful, lest we be leavened into . . . action contrary to our professed principles." Or as Samuel Janney put it, "I trust we shall . . . bear our righteous testimonies against all evil without allowing the least animosity to prevail in our hearts against any of our fellow creatures."[10]

Northern Virginia Friends had faced this balancing act between radical ends and limited means—and between their antislavery and pacifist principles—since they first embraced an antislavery path in the late eighteenth century. But the rise of aggressive abolition and its culmination in Brown's raid heightened their dilemma. Friends believed they must hold steadfast to their intertwined spiritual and political commitments—pacifism and antislavery. Adhering to these beliefs, however, left local Quakers with few allies in the months after Brown's raid. Sharing a sense of southern identity, they felt ill at ease among radical northern Friends who praised Brown as "a faithful old . . . martyr," a "noble confessor," and a "moral hero." Although they shared the antislavery commitment of northern abolitionists, they believed such tactics self-defeating, a trigger for southern resistance. Moreover, northern radicalism endangered southern Friends. Thus, they were glad to see the Brown hysteria decline in 1860 as more moderate voices reasserted their influence on Virginia politics. Old Whigs in particular called for border-state cooperation to fight northern and Deep South extremism that they believed threatened to tear apart the Union and jeopardize Virginia's social peace and racial hierarchy. Friends welcomed such moderation after the ascendency of secessionists in the months after Brown's raid. Nonetheless, many white Virginians identified them as suspect "Yankees" whose rejection of slavery posed a risk to the state. As the nation headed toward Civil War, northern Virginia's Friends occupied a political no man's land.[11]

II

For all their unease, Friends found the presidential election of November 1860 reassuring. Because of voter intimidation, only a few Friends and recent northern immigrants cast their ballots for the antislavery Republican Party. They gave Lincoln scattered votes in Alexandria, Fairfax, Loudoun, and Frederick counties. More important, a majority of the region's voters indicated their antisecessionist views by supporting John Bell's Constitutional Union ticket. In the weeks after Lincoln's election Friends reported "much unsettlement," but even after the secession of the seven Deep South states between December 1860 and February 1861 the region's voters elected antisecession delegates to Virginia's convention, called on February 13. Disowned Friend John Janney led Loudoun County's delegation, and the convention elected him to preside. Over the next seven weeks, the convention turned back secessionist proposals, though the unionism of many of the delegates remained "conditional" on Lincoln's willingness to forswear the use of force against the seceded states. The tenuousness of many of the delegates' unionism became clear on April 12 when South Carolina's troops opened fire on Federal vessels attempting to supply the Union garrison at Fort Sumter in Charleston harbor, and Lincoln responded by calling up seventy-five thousand volunteers to put down the rebellion. Five days later, on April 17, the Virginia convention voted eight-eight to fifty-five to secede. In the May 23 referendum that followed, a majority of northern Virginia's voters agreed, though reports of intimidation marred the poll.[12]

The vote revealed the ideological isolation of the region's Quaker community. A significant number of voters throughout northern Virginia voted against secession, but pockets of Union support usually centered in Quaker-dominated communities. Over three quarters of the voters in Fairfax County voted for secession, but at the poll at Accotink local Friends pushed the vote against secession to over 80 percent. When a local secessionist told John W. Deavers that he "would be taken in the woods and hung" if he did not vote for secession, Deavers replied that he "would die for a good cause." At the Quaker-dominated Waterford poll in Loudoun County just under 90 percent of the voters rejected secession, in a county where close to 70 percent supported it. "The election," Quaker Rebecca Williams noted, "pass'd off quietly here," but elsewhere in the county "whole troops, non-residents, have been taken to the polls . . . to vote for disunion, and union men have been intimidated." In Frederick County, where 81 percent of voters embraced secession, Friends worried about their future in Virginia. As a Winchester newspaper reported, "There is now . . . one party in Frederick county—and that party, for the South."[13]

Virginia's secession, and the Confederacy's decision to locate its capital at Richmond, just one hundred miles south of Washington, D.C., ensured that northern Virginia became "the main theater of the war." Long a political borderland between North and South, northern Virginia now became a military borderland between the Union and Confederate armies. Beyond its political and strategic importance, northern Virginia and the Shenandoah Valley constituted some of the richest agricultural land in the state, and control of its resources, both sides believed, would prove crucial to winning the war. The Union's military leadership concluded that the valley served as a "granary of the Confederacy," a breadbasket that fed General Robert E. Lee's Army of Northern Virginia and supplied horses for his cavalry units. The region's civilians were caught in the crossfire and from the war's outset faced depredations by both sides. Union military leaders' decision in 1863 and 1864 to adopt harsher tactics against the South's civilian population in order to undermine the Confederate war effort increased suffering in the region. These "hard war" tactics impacted the region's civilian population, whether loyal or disloyal.[14]

The political, strategic, and economic importance of northern Virginia made it contested ground throughout the war. Outside the garrisoned town of Alexandria and the ring of Federal forts that soon surrounded it, neither side exercised complete hegemony. Nominally under Federal control after Colonel John W. Geary entered with his 28th Pennsylvania Volunteer Infantry in February 1862, Loudoun County remained subject to Confederate occupation and attack throughout the struggle. In the war's early years, Colonel Elijah White's 35th Virginia Cavalry operated in the county. During Lee's invasions of Maryland and Pennsylvania in September 1862 and July 1863, units attached to the Army of Northern Virginia marched through the area. In the last years of the war, Mosby's partisans wreaked havoc against Unionists and Federal troops. Confederate and Union forces clashed over the lower Shenandoah Valley until fall 1864, the rotating occupations exacerbating civilian suffering. Historians estimate that Winchester changed hands over seventy times during the war. Even most of Fairfax County, just miles from Washington, remained disputed ground into 1864. Federal advances southward brought more stability to the county, but the battlefield woes of the Army of the Potomac and the ability of Mosby and other Confederate partisans to strike deep behind Federal lines kept its civilian population uneasy.[15]

Northern Virginia Quakers' anxieties rivaled those of any of the region's civilians. As Unionists, Friends faced the loss of property and freedom whenever Confederate troops entered their neighborhoods. A popular ballad praising Mosby began, "Colonel Mosby's last order I'm glad to relate / A tenth of the grain from the Quakers to take." The chorus returned to the same theme: "Oh, Colonel Mosby, the Quakers' hard fate / Is pretty hard to relate." But Friends fared little better when Union troops entered the region. Federal soldiers and officers often made no distinction between Unionist Friends and non-Quaker civilians. Despite occasional attempts to protect Friends, Union soldiers confiscated their foodstuffs and supplies, commandeered their meeting houses for army use (often resulting in great damage), and during Major General Philip Sheridan's burning raids of fall 1864 destroyed their barns and produce alongside that of other civilians.[16]

Local Friends experienced five distinct—though overlapping—depredations during the war. In the first months, southern officials conscripted young Quaker men for service in the Confederate army—and they did so in periodic waves throughout the war. Friends responded by escaping north to Maryland or west into the Appalachian Mountains, or by passively resisting. In the war's opening days the Quakers at Woodlawn, southeast of Alexandria, "felt . . . in great danger, our families exposed to the marauding and merciless soldiers" of the Confederacy. Woodlawn Friends, "being of northern birth" and "likely objects of their [Confederate] vengeance," decided to move "most of the families" north of Washington, D.C. So did many Alexandria Friends, including schoolteacher Caleb S. Hallowell, who moved to Philadelphia. Minister Chalkley Gillingham stayed for a few days with "my old friend" Benjamin Hallowell, the Alexandria school teacher and scientist, who had already moved north with his family to his Sandy Spring, Maryland, farm. A few days later, most of the Woodlawn Quakers proceeded north to New Jersey, along with a stream of "refugees flying from the Southern Army." Gillingham and his family decided to stay in Carroll County, Maryland, living in the home of Quaker Nathan Haines, where they could "watch the progress of events in Virginia." After Federal troops occupied Alexandria on May 24, Gillingham and his sons returned. The Union line "did not extend a mile south of Alex.," however, and the family had to "live outside the U.S. government" until mid-October when Federal soldiers inhabited the Quaker meeting house at Woodlawn. Until then, Gillingham and those Friends who ventured back to their homes were subject to continual alarms from "scouting parties of rebel troops." Even after Federal troops occupied Woodlawn, Quakers remained near the front lines and military "encounters" took place "in sight of" them for the first two years of war.[17]

In Loudoun County, a "reign of terror" erupted in late June 1861, as Confederate units drafted local Friends and other Unionists into the militia. In two days in mid-July, over fifty Friends ran to Maryland, though "several squads of men" did not make it, driven back by "Confederate pickets." In her diary, Rebecca Williams reported the departure of many Quaker young men "to keep from being press'd into the [Confederate] army." By July 16, "above two hundred Union men" had gone "over to Maryland." Attendance at the meeting fell "in consequence of so many of our men having left." Williams also noted that Quaker Rachel Ann Means wanted to cross into Maryland to discover the fate of her non-Quaker husband, Samuel. A prosperous Waterford miller and staunch Unionist, Samuel Means fled Virginia in early July to escape enlistment in the Confederate army. When he left, local secessionists took twenty-eight horses, two wagons, forty-two hogs, and "large quantities" of flour and meal from his farm. In retaliation, Means helped lead Colonel Geary's Federal troops into Loudoun in February 1862, and four months later he formed an independent cavalry unit, the Loudoun Rangers. Minister Samuel Janney understood the dangers facing Quaker men, but at first hesitated to send his only surviving son Phineas out of the state. By August 1862, Phineas had moved north, largely at his mother's urging. In leaving, Phineas joined some one thousand Loudoun County Unionists who fled in the first year of the war.[18]

The distance between Frederick County and Maryland and the Shenandoah Valley's uncertain military situation made Hopewell Friends' escape to Union lines more difficult. The Confederacy controlled the lower valley in the early days of the war, leaving Unionists largely "defenseless" until February 1862 when Federal troops, led by Major General Nathaniel Banks, invaded. Over the next two and half years, control of the valley alternated between Union and Confederate forces. Federal troops withdrew from all but the northern border of the valley in June 1862, after a series of defeats at the hands of Major General Stonewall Jackson's much smaller Confederate force. They re-entered the valley in January 1863, led by Major General Robert Milroy, only to flee in June 1863 during Lee's Gettysburg campaign. A small Federal force marched into the valley once more in April 1864, but retreated before a larger Confederate army commanded by Lieutenant General Jubal A. Early, who then invaded Maryland and threatened the outskirts of Washington (including the Quaker community at Sandy Spring). Only after Sheridan took command of the Federal forces in the valley in August 1864 did the Union establish firm control, though Mosby's raiders remained an irritant until the war's end. The unstable military situation made life difficult for all civilians. "How little those who are away from the seat of war," wrote Quaker Lydia Lupton in June 1863, "know of the feelings and the alternate hopes and fears which we are made to partake of." "Oh what a state of things," added Quaker Harriet Griffith, "what a trial we have to bear."[19]

While the lower Shenandoah Valley remained in Confederate hands, military officials employed "conscript hunters" to enlist all able-bodied white men in the county militias or Confederate army. A number of Friends got swept up in these enlistments. In July 1861, Harriet Griffith reported that recruiting officers "had come after" her uncle Robert Griffith and other Quaker men, forcing them to work "out on the breastworks" defending Winchester. Most male Friends, however, escaped the region. "The boys," Griffith wrote days later, "were preparing to go away; they got clothes and money ready." On August 1, she reported that "Uncle Robert has gone to Maryland with a great many others." Friends heard that their fleeing male relatives "had all got over the river safely, but have heard nothing more of them." The experience, Griffith noted, prompted "many tears at meeting." Over the next three years, the tides of battle dictated the movements of northern Virginia's young Quaker men. Whenever Confederate troops controlled the region there was a "general skedaddling" by Unionists; they returned when Federal troops occupied the lower valley. Diarist Mary Lupton, a member of the Hopewell meeting, noted the return of Quaker "refugees" to Winchester in late December 1862 after "the Yankees" occupied the town. Following the June 1863 Confederate victory at the second battle of Winchester, she recorded that Quaker "refugees [had] got along safely across the river." Jubal Early's July 1864 offensive again sent young male Friends fleeing north. Lupton reported that her brothers "Edward and Hugh soon fixed up . . . and met with Wilson, David, Tillie, Joe, Joel, and others at [the] Loup. Joel, Jr., rode [off] about an hour and half after they had gone."[20]

While most young Quaker men in the Shenandoah Valley fled north to Maryland, others escaped into the mountains of western Virginia. In this they followed many Mennonites, fellow pacifists who by 1862 had established what amounted to an "Underground Railroad" of "pilots" and "depots" for transporting their young men away from Confederate recruiters. No evidence exists to suggest that Friends and Mennonites coordinated their escapes—though the two churches together petitioned the Virginia and Confederate governments for relief from conscription and arrest—but Friends knew that the option of western flight existed. During the war's early months, Quaker John D. Wright remained at the home of his father Jesse Wright, which was situated "for a long time between the picket lines of the opposing forces." Although subject to conscription after Virginia and the Confederate Congress passed conscription laws in March and October 1862 respectively, John eluded capture for some time. When he concluded that his father's home "was no longer a safe place" he headed west into the Appalachians—and not a moment too soon. "As he reached a hill-top overlooking his home," he saw Confederate soldiers "entering the house in search of him."[21]

Greater dangers faced the mostly older Friends who remained in their homes. Friends tried to adhere to the principles enunciated by the Society, embracing neutrality, accepting "whatever civil government is established over us," and enduring the "penalty" authorities doled out for "non-compliance" with its laws. They also followed the counsel of the Baltimore Meeting for Sufferings (Hicksite), which expressed sympathy for refugees who fled, but advised members "to remain quietly at their homes" attending "peaceably to their own ordinary and proper business." Joseph Branson, whose sons went north to Maryland in July 1861, remained on his farm throughout the war. "His house is always open to the wayfarer," one contemporary noted, "be he Yank or Reb." Quaker Jesse Wright followed a similar tack: opening his house and extending hospitality "to all . . . comers." He concluded that a neutral path would enable him and his property to survive the war. As a northern visitor noted in 1864, "wisdom had taught" such men "caution and the value of silence," and the need to keep political "opinions . . . locked within" their "breasts."[22]

Despite such precautions, Friends' Unionist sentiments made them subject to arrest, particularly when Federal troops threatened Confederate control and secessionists suspected Friends of aiding them. In March 1862, while Banks's Union troops threatened the Shenandoah Valley, Stonewall Jackson arrested twenty-one Unionists, including seven Hopewell Friends, and marched them to Harrisonburg, seventy miles up the valley. Quaker Job Throckmorton, described by the Confederate provost marshal as a "harmless man," contracted typhoid fever and died in custody in Harrisonburg. A second Friend, Mordecai Bean, died months later after his captors transferred him to a Richmond prison. They were the first Virginia Friends to die for their beliefs since the seventeenth century. Confederate authorities also arrested Samuel Pancoast, a Quaker merchant, for collaborating with the enemy after he transported salt across the Potomac into the valley. According to Unionist Julia Chase, authorities believed he used his "few pigeons" as "carrier doves" to send "messages [north] to the injury of the Southern Confederacy." Pancoast spent two years in jail. In late October 1862, rebel soldiers arrested Quaker cotton manufacturer Aaron Griffith after the Confederate postmaster opened a personal letter in which he complained that pro-southern sympathizers had harassed him and stolen his property.[23]

Friends east of the Blue Ridge also faced the prospect of arrest. In November 1861, after his return from the Baltimore Yearly Meeting, Samuel Janney faced detention for entering the North without the permission of Confederate authorities. The intercession of a Confederate family whose daughter had attended Janney's Springdale school secured his release. In August 1861, Confederate authorities arrested John B. Dutton, a leader of the Waterford meeting, and two other Friends after a number of raids of northern Loudoun County by Federal forces. Believing that Unionists had served as scouts and spies for the Federal sorties, Confederates rounded up suspected civilians. They held Dutton in a Manassas military jail for two weeks before he obtained his release. Shortly after a second arrest, he escaped to Maryland. In 1863, members of the 35th Virginia Cavalry arrested Friends William Williams and Robert Isaac Hollingsworth, prominent members of the Fairfax meeting, in retaliation for the detention of two southern civilians by Union troops. Taken to Castle Thunder in Richmond, they remained imprisoned until November, when Williams caught smallpox and Confederate authorities released them into the custody of Richmond Quaker John B. Crenshaw. The two men returned to Waterford on Christmas Day. Confederates arrested at least twenty-four northern Virginia Friends between 1861 and 1864, some more than once. The sporadic nature of the arrests belies claims of a systematic Confederate policy to repress local Friends, but the constant threat of detention left the Quaker community uncertain of its future and for much of the war bereft of men.[24]

The third difficulty faced by Friends was the loss of corporate property. Confederate and later Union troops occupied the Society's meeting houses, often doing great damage. The Winchester (Centre) Meeting House did not survive the war, as Confederate and Union soldiers and townsfolk sequentially destroyed it. In the summer of 1861, the Confederate army used the meeting house as a hospital, leaving it "in a pretty good condition." When Federal troops arrived in Winchester in March 1862, they "demanded the key and took possession." "Friends," the Hopewell meeting reported, "never used it afterwards." A year later, after two Federal occupations, only the walls of the meeting house remained standing, and during the summer "Citizens of the town" tore them down and took the bricks. No more than a "small portion of the foundation wall" remained and Friends estimated it would take three thousand dollars to replace the building. In Alexandria, Federal troops commandeered the Quaker meeting house, using it as a hospital after June 1862. The dwindling number of Alexandria Friends had to gather "at a private house" for worship until late 1864.[25]

Woodlawn Friends had to share their worship space with soldiers at various points during the war. When Federal troops extended their lines southeast of Alexandria in November 1861, they occupied the meeting house, making it the "headquarters of their Pickett guard." Thereafter they frequently denied Friends access to the building, and worship services took place in Friends' homes. At other times, Federal troops allowed Friends to meet for worship in a portion of the building, amidst "the munitions of war." The soldiers, Chalkley Gillingham reported, usually "behaved them-selves" but on other occasions they "talked and went out considerably" during Friends' worship. They also damaged and left the meeting house in disarray. In early 1863, troops began using the meeting house as a field hospital, forcing Woodlawn Friends to meet in the homes of members. Fairfax Quakers faced a similar situation in 1861 and 1862, worshipping among Confederate troops who occupied their meeting house. Among an assemblage of soldiers and weapons, Friends met in silence, ignoring the "titter[s]" and "amused whisper[s] of some of the . . . soldiers," until the elderly Miriam Gover, the meeting's leading minister, rose to speak. In a feeble voice, she "prayed that the wings of peace might be spread over" a "once prosperous and happy land, and for the strangers that were that day gathered in" the meeting house. Soon, remembered one Friend, "loud sobs broke from strong men and great tears forced themselves down . . . sun-burned cheeks." Friends celebrated this small victory, but as Rebecca Wil-liams noted, Confederate troops left a trail of dirt and destruction behind.[26]

Friends fretted about the property damage, but they found more dis-turbing the disruptions to their spiritual life caused by Confederate and Union troops. Although soldiers never occupied the Hopewell Meeting House, the unstable military situation impeded the attendance of Friends, often reducing meetings to five or six people. The arrest and death of Job Throckmorton—taken by Confederate soldiers while he journeyed to meeting—highlighted the dangers. Virginia Friends found it difficult to attend quarterly and yearly meetings when they had to cross military fron-tiers. In Waterford, Rebecca Williams grieved that the Confederate occu-pation of Loudoun prevented members of the meeting from participating in the 1861 yearly meeting. Living on the Union side of the military divide, Woodlawn Friends could not attend the Fairfax Quarterly Meeting. Still, Chalkley Gillingham reported that Woodlawn Friends failed to meet for their twice-weekly religious services only "once or twice" during the war, despite the "interference" of fighting men. Hopewell Friend Lydia Lupton expressed for many the importance of these meetings. "There are a few of us," she noted, "that love to meet together," even in the face of "so much tumult."[27]

Individual Friends also suffered property losses because of Confeder-ate impressments. Quaker communities feared the arrival of Confederate troops who took whatever food, livestock, and supplies they needed. In the war's first months, Chalkley Gillingham reported that "rebels" continu-ally "alarmed" Woodlawn Friends, "coming into the neighborhood and carrying off men, horses, waggons and provisions." The arrival of Federal troops lessened the threat, but whenever they departed, as they did in July 1863, the community faced harassment from "[Confederate] Guerrilla bands roving about, stealing horses and colored men." For the first eleven months of the war, Loudoun County Friends suffered more serious depredations. One Friend reported in September 1861 that "between six and seven thousand horses and one thousand waggons had been carried away" by Confederate troops, "as well as all the Crops." "Soldiers passing constantly," noted Rebecca Williams in August, "raviging the countryside of horses, fruit and almost everything." Loudoun Friends heard that Quakers in the Shenandoah Valley were "much oppress'd by having . . . their horses and other property press'd." The long struggle for the valley ensured that such confiscations lasted throughout the war. One day in fall 1862, Mary Lupton noted that "22 rebels have been here today [and] 13 got dinner." That night, she reported: "Eight more . . . honoured us with their presence, if honor it be." A week later, she recorded that "Forty-seven [rebels] here today. . . . They were in the spring house [and] got some milk."[28]

Manufacturing enterprises in the Shenandoah Valley also suffered from war's devastation. During Aaron Griffith's 1862 imprisonment local rebels confiscated "his horses, harness, and much personal property" for "government and personal use." They also stole cloth from his Brookland mill and transferred its machinery to the mill of a Confederate neighbor. As long as the family remained at Brookland, outside of Winchester, they faced threats from Confederate soldiers and partisans. In January 1864, after "a company of rebels" broke Griffith's "door open and threatened to blow his daughter's brains out," the family moved to Winchester. They feared "to stay any longer" in the countryside where residents knew "not what an hour may bring forth." "Soldiers," reported traveling minister Elizabeth Comstock in December, had "stripped" this "ancient and wealthy family" "of all they had," and they survived on Union army rations. By war's end, Griffith estimated his property losses as a result of Confederate confiscations at over twenty-three thousand dollars.[29]

Property damage rose in 1864 and 1865, when Mosby and his partisan brigade, along with other irregular Confederate units, conducted guerrilla war behind Union lines. Mosby began operations in northern Virginia in early 1863. Using hit and run tactics, Mosby's men attacked Union supply lines, railroads, and isolated units. They became an irritant and distraction for Federal troops in the region. Mosby's daring, his successes, and the failure of Federal troops to stop his small cavalry force made him a folk hero within the Confederacy. Mosby drew a large portion of his force from northern Virginia, and local southern sympathizers housed, fed, supplied, and helped hide his men from Federal troops. Contemporaries soon dubbed southern Loudoun and northern Fauquier counties, "Mosby's Confederacy." Unionists, in contrast, labeled his battalion an "infernal band of freebooters" and Mosby a "rebel highwayman."[30]

In its first months of operation, Mosby's "guerrilla cavalry" limited their sorties "to combatants only." However, as Confederate military hopes waned, Mosby's men altered their tactics and confiscated the property of Unionists. Local Quakers' "profitable farms" made an inviting target. In May 1864, Mosby's "inhuman rebels," in the words of one Friend, entered Waterford "and appropriated to their own use several horses and two wagons loaded with corn, belonging . . . to Union citizens. They also visited the tannery of Asa M. Bond, and arrested thirty-five dollars worth of leather." During the attack on Point of Rocks, Maryland, in July 1864, which locals later dubbed the "Great Calico Raid," Mosby's men looted Quaker John Dutton's store. Dutton lost his entire stock during the raid, as did fellow Waterford resident (and lapsed Quaker) Samuel Gover. Throughout early 1864, the Woodlawn community also suffered from attacks by Confederate irregulars. "Parties . . . of Robbers, Highwaymen and Horse thieves" "infest the country all around," bemoaned Chalkley Gillingham, "robbing houses of money and everything of value they can lay their hands on."[31]

In Loudoun, Mosby's confiscations climaxed in early 1865 when he ordered one of his detachments to take "one-tenth part" of the Quakers' "grain, forage and bacon" and send it south into Fauquier County, Mosby's base. Confiscation, claimed Mosby's surgeon, Aristides Monteiro, provided the "only method" of "reasonable certainty" to make recalcitrant Friends pay taxes to the Confederate government. Small detachments of Mosby's men appeared at wealthy Friends' homes, including Samuel Janney's, where they stayed the night guarding three Unionist conscripts. One of Janney's Goose Creek neighbors, "Mr. R. T___ " (likely Richard Henry Taylor, son of Yardley Taylor), objected loudly when Monteiro and his squad of ten descended on his "well-tilled and comfortable farm" to take the Confederate tithe and food and lodging. Monteiro expressed surprise that a member of this "gentle sect" should display "such electric sparks of anger" to the demand for property. The "fat and robust" Friend "foamed at the mouth, stamped his feet," and "promised to die before he would" comply with the soldiers' demands. After Monteiro informed him that the band "had no especial objection to his dying," the "infuriated Quaker" retreated. The incident revealed how four years of war had aggravated the divide between Friends and their neighbors. By 1865, many white southerners dismissed them as hypocritical and disloyal outsiders.[32]

Friends also suffered at the hands of their ostensible allies, the Federal troops stationed in northern Virginia. The large number of Union troops stationed in and around Alexandria early in the war often resorted to foraging. "Wherever" Federal troops camp, Chalkley Gillingham reported, "devastation follows in their train." The soldiers on Quaker R. F. Roberts's hundred-acre farm west of Alexandria "destroyed every fence" for firewood. Other civilians suffered the loss of their "dwellings" through destruction or occupation. In Loudoun County, Samuel Means's Unionist Loudoun Rangers, like their Confederate counterparts, lived off the land, usually enjoying the support of the region's Unionist population. However, their actions sometimes raised the ire of Friends like John Dutton who protested the confiscation of the family horse, Harry, by Means's cavalry in spring 1863. Likewise, the Unionist Quakers of Hopewell noted "that depredations were . . . committed, and property destroyed by the federal armies during their alternate occupation of our Valley."[33]

"Passive" and "active" Union measures intended to neutralize Mosby's cavalry resulted in the greatest problems for Friends. Among its "passive" tactics, the Union blockade of the Potomac, designed to stop the movement of people and flow of goods to southern partisans, most affected Quakers. Without passes, Friends had difficulty traveling across the river to visit religious meetings and relatives. The many Quaker women who remained in Virginia struggled, like their Confederate neighbors, to obtain foodstuffs and clothing. In spring 1862, Federal treasury officials established three points of entry across the river to enable Unionists to obtain goods "for family consumption." Seeking to capitalize on the trade, Waterford Quakers John Dutton and Amasa Hough Jr. established stores on the Maryland side of the river, and in late 1862 Samuel Janney sought permission to import goods for sale into Loudoun County. His request went nowhere because military officials sought tighter trade restrictions. In January 1864, after Mosby conducted a raid on a Union cavalry unit camped at Loudoun Heights above Harpers Ferry, the military closed all trade across the river until June, when it allowed avowed Unionists to purchase family goods only.[34]

Quaker civilians suffered more from the "active" measures adopted by the Union military. In August 1864, Lieutenant General Ulysses S. Grant, the new general-in-chief of the Union armies, ordered Phillip Sheridan, commander of the Union army in the Shenandoah, to send a division into Loudoun County "to destroy and carry off the crops, animals, negroes, and all men under fifty years of age capable of bearing arms." Grant reasoned that "male citizens under fifty can fairly be held as prisoners of war, not as citizen prisoners" because if they were "not already soldiers, they will be made so the moment the rebel army gets hold of them." Grant made only one exception to his order. Informed that Loudoun County's Quakers were "favorably disposed to the Union," he ordered Sheridan to exempt "these people . . . from arrest." Sheridan "endorsed" Grant's "programme in all its parts, for," he noted, "it was time to bring the war home to a people engaged in raising crops . . . to feed the country's enemies." In Loudoun County, Grant's order led to the August arrests of ninety-four "rebel sympathizers." But the Federal dragnet ensnared Union men as well, including "several" Friends. Samuel Janney, who feared the Federal action would spark Confederate retaliation, secured the Quakers' release and those of some other Union men. Sheridan informed Janney that Loudoun residents "must not complain" about bearing their "share" of "the burdens imposed by this war."[35]

Northern Virginians experienced greater burdens as Sheridan sought to destroy the region's agricultural output. He focused first on the Shenandoah Valley. In October 1864, Sheridan reported that his army had "destroyed over 2,000 barns filled with wheat, hay, and farming implements; over seventy mills filled with flour and wheat; have driven in front of the army over 4[,000] head of stock, and have killed and issued to the troops not less than 3,000 sheep." In late November, he set his sights on Loudoun, ordering Major General Wesley Merritt's cavalry to burn barns and mills, and carry off livestock, forage, and foodstuffs. On the morning of November 29, Goose Creek Friend Carrie Taylor saw "smoke rising all around us from our neighbor's barns, stock yards, and corn fields." The "Yankees," she realized, "had come to burn up everything but the houses." They made little distinction between friend and foe, destroying the property of Unionists and Confederates alike. When the Union troops arrived at Taylor's home, the family "begged" them to leave their horses and livestock, to no avail. "Oh, what destruction there is in the neighborhood," lamented Taylor. She claimed "Union people have fared the worst." Federal officers did not make a tally of the destruction in Loudoun, but Merritt estimated it in the "millions." Loudoun County Friends estimated their losses at more than one hundred ten thousand dollars.[36]

Civilian suffering in northern Virginia, which climaxed in the late 1864 "burning raid," helped alter the relationship between Confederates and Unionists. Although political loyalties rarely changed, civilians on both sides focused on survival and sought aid where they could find it—even from their ostensible enemies. In contrast to other regions of the occupied South, civilian foes developed a "tentative toleration" that led occasionally to mutual aid. But more than shared suffering, which occurred in other southern regions, accounts for civilian cooperation across the partisan divide. In northern Virginia, in contrast, the Quaker population was large and respected enough to shape civilian relations across enemy lines. Friends' antebellum reputation for goodwill and civic engagement, and their willingness to feed and extend medical aid to starving and wounded Confederates, helped promote toleration between civilian foes. In addition, Quakers' rejection of violence ensured that Confederates did not see them as a military threat—in contrast to Unionists in other parts of the borderland South.[37]

As a result, Friends received help from unexpected quarters. When Confederate authorities arrested John B. Dutton in 1862, secessionist Frank Myers, later a captain in Elijah White's 35th Virginia Cavalry, helped obtain his release. Dutton's daughter, Mollie, pronounced Myers "very kind indeed." After Confederate troops arrested William Williams and Robert Hollingsworth in 1863, secessionist neighbors—planters William B. Lynch, Charles Ball, and Thomas M. Edwards—visited Confederate officials in Richmond to appeal for their release. They argued that Williams and Hollingsworth "were Virginians, held for others who did not" want them jailed. "If the authorities wanted hostages for citizens of the Confederacy being held . . . by the Yankees," they added, "they could go to the enemy's country to get them." Although Friends bemoaned the Confederate allegiance of our "*once* cherished . . . neighbors," the mutual suffering of war and their religious beliefs led them to seek rapprochement with the rebels. Samuel Janney, who used his influence with Union authorities to obtain the release of Confederates, concluded that Friends played a significant role in ensuring that northern Virginia did not descend into the violence that plagued Missouri and east Tennessee. Local Friends' "example," he believed, "had a salutary influence in tempering the asperity that always attends" war.[38]

III

Quaker women played a central role in extending aid to civilians and combatants in the war. In its early months, women from Goose Creek and

Waterford contributed "bread and vegetables" to the Confederate hospital at Leesburg. Their Hopewell counterparts sewed caps for Confederate volunteers and filled "haversacks" with food as they headed off to Bull Run. In the fall 1862 aftermath of Antietam, Quaker women in Loudoun and Frederick Counties fed—sometimes under protest—Confederate and then Union troops. Rebecca Williams treated sick and injured soldiers at a temporary hospital established in Waterford. In the Shenandoah Valley, Quaker women fed and treated Confederate soldiers as they retreated south in July 1863 after Gettysburg. Although Hopewell Friends begrudged the demands of soldiers from "the *upper crusts* of the *confederacy*," they gave to the "poor fellows" who appeared at their doorsteps. The women of Winchester exhibited the greatest willingness to extend aid across the wartime divide. As the battle for the valley transformed the town into "a regular shuttlecock" between "the contending armies," its "female inhabitants" grew "familiar with the bloody realities of war." The town became "one vast hospital" as its churches, hotels, and homes accommodated between four and six thousand wounded. According to one visitor, all the town's women were "turned into hospital nurses and cooks." Both Confederates and Unionists catered to their wounded first. While serving in the Army of the Shenandoah in August 1864, Rutherford B. Hayes noted that the "Union families" of Winchester "took our wounded off the field and fed and nursed them." Throughout summer and fall 1864, Quaker Harriet Griffith visited the town's hospitals on a nearly daily basis. She and other Friends fed and tended the "poor wounded men" when the Union army abandoned the town to the Confederates and patients became "prisoners."[39]

The provision of aid to wounded troops by the Unionist women of Winchester became more systematic in September 1864 when the United States Sanitary Commission, the northern voluntary association established in 1861 to provide aid to soldiers, sent representatives to the valley after Sheridan's army. Sanitary commission members organized the town's more than forty hospitals into seven districts and deputized seven of the town's "most estimable Union ladies," including Friends Harriet Griffith and Martha Sidwell, to oversee them. Between September and December, when the Union military removed the last of the wounded from Winchester, Griffith and her fellow "loyalists" visited the hospitals under their oversight every day. Sanitary commission officials, soldiers, and townspeople commended them for their efforts. Henry Root, a surgeon with a New York regiment, praised Winchester's "glorious Society of Unionist" women who sacrificed "their personal comforts" to "aid our sick and wounded soldiers." The women's "humane and generous" aid to "Confederate wounded" "deeply impress[ed]" even "bitter" Winchester secessionists, and sanitary commission agents met "respect and gratitude" "everywhere" they traveled in the region. Winchester Confederate Laura Lee concurred. "The Yankees," she marveled, "certainly are wonderfully indulgent and considerate about our wounded."[40]

But not all local women—and not all Friends—exhibited such magnanimity toward the enemy. Northern Virginia's status as a no man's land forced some women to become participants in the conflict. As the region descended into a war of occupation, marked by the hit-and-run attacks of Confederate partisans and Federal "hard war" tactics designed to crush civilian support networks, the domestic sphere became a scene of war. The dependence of partisan units on the support of local households politicized women's domestic responsibilities and transformed them into accomplices. Confederate women who provided food, clothing, shelter, and emotional support for southern partisans helped resist Federal occupation. Unionist women, with Quaker women at the forefront, embraced similar roles on behalf of Federal units. U.S. troops commented on the friendly welcome and aid they received in Unionist neighborhoods, with Quaker-dominated Waterford—"a good Union town"—getting special notice. Stephen Weld, an aide-de-camp to Union Major General John F. Reynolds reported in July 1863 that he "stayed at Mr. Hough's house" and "lived on the fat of the land." He praised the "merry maidens of the place" who cheered and waved the "starry flag" and gave Federal troops water as they marched through town.[41]

Like their Confederate counterparts, Quaker women embraced nineteenth-century gender conventions, expected enemy troops to honor these values, and lambasted men who did not. Despite the public prominence of a few female preachers, Quaker women celebrated their role as moral guardians of the family, and men and women alike viewed the gendered conventions of their households as a source of middle class respectability. Women's plain garb and their administration of the Quaker discipline within the women's meetings served as a display of the moral seriousness of their domestic lives. And while women preachers violated American gender conventions by speaking publicly, they adhered closely to the conventions of dress and religious piety. Deemed competent by virtue of their gender and morality to guide the domestic sphere and regulate their coreligionists' lives, northern Virginia's women Friends rarely questioned the antebellum gender and legal conventions that constrained them. Instead, they accepted notions of female dependence and expected male protection and support.[42]

The war did not shatter the era's gender conventions, even as it pushed women into novel roles and responsibilities. Regardless of political affiliation, southern women deployed the values that constrained them in peacetime to defy their enemies. Confederate women facing Union occupation and Unionist women living in divided regions of the Confederacy believed that "the armor of gender would protect them" and keep their domestic space inviolate. The absence of fathers, husbands, and sons made southern women vulnerable to attack by enemies and thrust upon them the responsibility of defending and supporting their households and communities. They had to raise crops without the labor of men and they had to provide for their families in a time of scarcity and inflation. Women tried to defend their property and livestock from the depredations of hostile neighbors, enemy troops, and parties of foraging soldiers and partisans. When localities descended into guerrilla war, women's domestic tasks became vital components of the war effort. Facing parallel experiences, southern Unionist women and Confederate women living under Union occupation responded in similar ways, employing gender conventions to manipulate, undermine, and express contempt for their enemies.[43]

Although northern Virginia never descended into the savagery of other southern regions, women Friends still confronted the depredations of regular and irregular Confederate soldiers. During Robert Griffith's three-month 1863 exile north of the Potomac, a Confederate officer confronted his middle-aged sister at gunpoint, demanding that she give up her horse. "I do not propose to give up my horse," she responded defiantly, and "cannot be robbed of many years." She added an appeal to southern gender conventions: "Shoot if that is the way with you Southern gentlemen, who so boast of your chivalry." Confronted by a Unionist woman who deployed the South's patriarchal values, the southern officer had little choice but to ride on, leaving the horse in Griffith's possession. Other Confederate soldiers found themselves nonplussed when confronted by Quaker women. The men from Elijah White's cavalry sent to arrest Fairfax Quaker Asa M. Bond in August 1863 failed, recalled the unit's historian, "owing to" their "inefficiency." More accurately, they found themselves undermined by the patriarchal traditions southerners claimed to defend. When they tried to enter the house, Bond's two daughters beat the soldiers with "broomsticks and rolling pins," symbols of female domesticity. Convinced that such weapons would not suffice, one of the daughters ran next door and rang a large bell;

she then fired off two shots from a revolver. Confronted by female defiance and unwilling to use the force necessary to subdue the sisters, the soldiers retreated.[44]

In the Shenandoah Valley, Harriet Griffith's 1864 confrontation with "the rebel raider" John Mosby revealed how southern honor conventions protected Quaker women. Griffith and a male cousin borrowed a horse and buggy from the Union quartermaster in Winchester to visit her grandfather in the country. Outside of town, the pair spotted Mosby charging toward them. Griffith "took the reins" and ordered her cousin, an adolescent subject to physical assault and possible conscription, into the back where he remained hidden from Mosby's men. After telling Mosby her name and destination, the colonel asked, "Are you the daughter of Griffith, the Union man?" Shielded by her gender, Harriet replied, "My name is Hattie Griffith," and "I am the daughter of Aaron Griffith, and proud to say that I am a Union girl." By 1864, Mosby had become a southern "folk hero," an outnumbered but successful defender of the region who used daring means to undermine the Yankee invasion of the South. As a chivalrous upholder of southern honor, Mosby could not employ violence without provocation against a dependent white woman. He led Griffith's horse into a nearby field and "told her that if she would remain quietly there, not a hair of her should be hurt, for he honored her bravery." He left her under guard while he "transact[ed]" some "private business, which was to rob a Union family." Upon his return, Mosby led Griffith's horse back to the road, "told her he hoped she would get home safely," and left her in possession of the borrowed horse and carriage.[45]

A few Quaker women offered more than verbal defiance to secessionists and the Confederate army. Winchester schoolteacher Rebecca M. Wright served as an informant for Sheridan in September 1864. Seeking more information before he launched an assault on Jubal Early's Winchester-based army, Sheridan turned to African American peddler, Tom Laws, who had permission from the local Confederate commander to enter Winchester to sell vegetables and who offered to carry information for the Union general. Sheridan also learned that Wright "might be willing" to provide "the position of Early's forces." On September 15, Wright discovered that Early had sent an infantry division and artillery battalion east to Petersburg to reinforce Lee's army. Early's force in Winchester "is much smaller than represented," Wright informed Sheridan, adding that she took "pleasure" in aiding the Federal cause. Laws carried Wright's note out of Winchester on September 16. With concrete information in hand, Sheridan moved against

Figure 8.1. Portrait of Rebecca M. Wright, c. 1860s. Courtesy of Swarthmore College Friends Historical Library.

Early and three days later defeated him at the battle of Winchester. The gender and racial assumptions of Confederates had played a significant role in their defeat, blinding them to the threat posed by dependent white women and black men.[46]

Hours after the battle, Sheridan visited Wright in her schoolroom, where he wrote the dispatch announcing his victory. His decision attested to the Unionism of the town's Friends and the crucial role of Quaker women in helping him. It also suggests how school teaching helped facilitate women Friends' activism, giving them the self-confidence to contribute to the

Union war effort. Like their Confederate counterparts, Quaker women based their wartime partisanship on recognized gender conventions, but their activities pushed beyond accepted boundaries. Friends had long accepted women teachers, but Wright used the independence afforded to her by the classroom to aid the Union. She received both accolades and censure. In 1867, Sheridan sent Wright a gold brooch, watch, and chain for her "courageous and patriotic" contribution. She wore them proudly, but when neighbors discovered her benefactor, many insulted her in the street and ostracized her family. Fearing for their safety, the Wrights moved to Philadelphia in 1868.[47]

Like Wright, young Quaker women throughout northern Virginia embraced the Union cause and pushed the boundaries of acceptable female—and Quaker—behavior. In May 1864, Elizabeth (Lizzie) and Emma Eliza (Lida) Dutton and Sarah Steer began publishing a pro-Union newspaper, the *Waterford News*. The three came from Unionist families and had participated in Waterford's Literary Society before the war. Sarah Steer, the daughter of Samuel L. and Harriet Steer, was twenty-six when she began editing the paper. Her father had fled to Maryland early in the war. The Dutton sisters—aged twenty-four and nineteen in 1864—were the daughters of John Dutton, the Waterford merchant who moved to Maryland after Confederate authorities arrested him twice. From his store at Point of Rocks, Dutton had easy communication with Baltimore, where Charles C. Fulton, the editor of the Republican *Baltimore American*, printed the young women's newspaper. The *Waterford News* garnered attention in the North after John Schooley, a Waterford resident and volunteer in a Maryland regiment, sent the first two issues to Lincoln.[48]

Recognizing the newspaper as a "hazardous undertaking," the editors employed the era's gendered language and conventions to provide themselves with a measure of protection. They also used these cultural assumptions to mock Confederate women. In June 1864, the editors reported that "the 'chivalry'"—that is, Mosby's Rangers—"have visited several of their beloved 'sisters in the faith,' and kindly taken from them their 'carriage horses' to use in their guerrilla pilgrimages." They used the same gendered gibes against Quaker men who failed to fulfill their obligations. Bachelors who reveled in their "*single blessedness*" received reminders that during wartime a wife could help save both property and person: "When Mosby comes, his fate he [the bachelor] rues / And sighs—*Oh! for a wife to save my shoes*." And when a large pothole appeared in Waterford's main street, the editors called on the "ladies" of the town to gather "at their first opportunity" to fill it. "Fearful [that] the gentlemen will get their feet muddy, the ladies will try and remedy it." When their mockery failed to prompt "the gentlemen" to action, the editors warned "all young ladies . . . not to let their heart's devotion rest on young men who are so lost to the spirit of chivalry *once* the boast of Virginia's sons."[49]

A number of the editors' columns, particularly editorials, adopted a thoughtful tone to weigh in on a variety of political subjects: Union soldiers' right to vote, the 1864 federal election (a ringing endorsement for Lincoln and Andrew Johnson), the treatment of rebels at war's end (a call for leniency for all but Confederate leaders), and a defense of Sheridan's scorched earth policy in Loudoun County. Yet the editors couched their statements in deferential language. Anticipating complaints from readers who might look askance at young women participating in the region's civic life, the editors assured the public that "we are not believers in women's rights, literally speaking." They insisted that they acted only out of their "great interest in the affairs of our country," their desire to help advocate "the union of *States* and *freedom* of persons as well as opinion." They reminded readers that their paper had a single aim: "To cheer the weary soldier, and render material aid to the sick and wounded." To fulfill the latter goal, the editors sent all proceeds from the paper to the U.S. Sanitary Commission, raising a thousand dollars from the first two issues alone.[50]

The editors added another ingredient to the mix: throughout the paper's life, they emphasized their love of Virginia while linking this identity to Unionism. "Every true Virginian," they announced in their inaugural issue, boasts of "our banner"—the stars and stripes—and "never falter[s]" in their "stand for the Union." Or as another columnist noted in early 1865: "The pride of the 'Old Dominion' rules too strongly [in] the hearts of her sons and daughters to bow in *submission* to her *foes*." All "*truly* loyal" Virginians, the editors asserted, must support the "principles of unity and *freedom*" associated with the state. Wartime conditions gave the three young editors the opportunity to reshape the political and public life of northern Virginia. Like women who entered the public sphere as writers, editors, and reformers in the antebellum period—and in the process expanded women's civic opportunities—the editors of the *Waterford News* wrapped themselves in political opinions and cultural values acceptable to their readers to enlarge the boundaries of the woman's sphere.[51]

When the war ended and the men of the community returned, the editors' subversion of gender roles largely came to an end. The Dutton sisters ended their public dalliance, married Union veterans, and moved away from

Figure 8.2. Quaker-supported Freedmen's School, Camp Todd, Virginia, 1865, similar to those established by Friends in northern Virginia. Pencil sketch by Emily Howland. Courtesy of Swarthmore College Friends Historical Library.

Waterford. But Sarah Steer continued to push gender boundaries, teaching in the local freedmen's school until 1870. She reflected women Friends' desire to do good through education, training African Americans in the skills they needed to succeed as free people and helping to forge better relations between the races. In April 1862, Philadelphia-area Hicksite women began sending clothing and aid south to needy freedpeople. Two years later, they joined with Hicksite men in the Friends' Association for the Aid and Elevation of the Freedmen. The association purchased clothes, books, and medical supplies for the freedpeople. It also hired teachers who traveled south to establish schools for African Americans. In Virginia, the association hired over twenty teachers who directed fifteen schools in Fairfax, Loudoun, and Prince William counties where local Friends, though devastated by four years of war, provided aid. Between thirty and eighty students (depending on the season) attended Sarah Lloyd's school at Woodlawn, located east of Alexandria. The students heard lectures by Chalkley Gillingham and had evening "penmanship" classes from local Friends. When Lloyd fell ill in late 1868, a "faithful friend" from the Alexandria meeting took her place until she recovered. At Goose Creek, Elizabeth Janney, wife of Samuel, donated a small lot and building materials for a black school, and the association hired Isabella Skillman of New York to teach classes for fifty-plus students.[52]

Most of the northern teachers stayed in Virginia only a few years, but Sarah Steer never left. She took over the Waterford school in early 1866 and it grew rapidly. In early 1867, she had to turn away more than ten children who wanted to attend. A new building, paid for by the association and local African Americans, and constructed by Waterford's black men, enabled her to increase the size of the school from thirty-eight students in 1867 to nearly seventy, three years later. Her curriculum focused on reading and writing, geography, and arithmetic, and she opened a First Day school in August 1867 for adults who could not attend school during the week. She also instructed women in sewing one afternoon a week to enable them to turn the "calico" sent south by the association into wearable clothing. Steer believed "this useful branch of learning" inculcated habits of industry and diligence, as did the temperance society she persuaded her students to form. She also encouraged her adult male students to vote, proudly noting in November 1867 that "the colored men of this district came up nobly. Every one voted right, notwithstanding the adverse influences brought to bear upon" them.[53]

Steer sought to make her black charges independent. She took great pride in hiring and training a forty-year-old black assistant, Ann E. Gross, whom she paid seventy-five cents a week. Steer hoped that Gross would take her place when the association ended its support of the school, but she died in the summer of 1867, much to Steer's sorrow. After Gross's death, Steer hired new assistants, one of whom moved to Philadelphia in 1870 to attend high school and "qualify herself for a teacher." She also helped tutor local black minister, Henry Carrol, whose "application to study, and general deportment as a pupil" had "a good effect in the school." Like the Quakers who formed the association, Steer sought to cultivate black leaders, while providing her students with the skills they needed "to rise above the condition of *dependence* they have so long occupied." In her letters to the association Steer highlighted the promptness with which black parents paid their half of her twenty-dollar salary each month and supplied her with coal and other supplies for the school. She also praised the African American community's desire to keep the school open with a black teacher after the association ended its support in April 1870. After five years of teaching, Steer believed "there is a decided improvement in the condition of the colored people" of Waterford. Friends and blacks praised her work and when the school closed Steer felt "quite proud of" it and her students' accomplishments.[54]

But she also felt "sorry to give" the school up. She had good reason to regret its closing. Designed to help local blacks achieve "self-dependence," the benevolent work at the school became the means by which Steer, for a time, overcame her personal and economic dependence and claimed a role in the civic life of the region. Ironically, Steer's success in promoting black self-reliance undermined her independence. In 1869, the Philadelphia association began to replace its white female teachers in northern Virginia with African American instructors. A year later, the state of Virginia established a free school system, absorbing the seven surviving Quaker-founded schools in northern Virginia and hiring African Americans as teachers. Thereafter, the Philadelphia association, no longer able to raise sufficient funds, reduced the money it directed to the region. For Steer, the end of the school meant a retreat into the quiet life of the Waterford Quaker community, her days as a participant in the public sphere at an apparent end.[55]

But women's wartime activities had a lasting impact—at least among Quakers. Women Friends had long exercised influence within the governing bodies of the Society, but they made gains after the war. In 1870, the Hicksite Baltimore Yearly Meeting, acting at the insistence of the quarterly meetings, allowed women to sit on the representative committee, the re-named meeting for sufferings, through which men alone had overseen the affairs of the Society. The yearly meeting also made the men's and women's meetings equal in authority. Friends embraced new roles for women, particularly in medicine and education. The 1864 establishment of coeducational Swarthmore College through the combined efforts of Hicksite Friends in Philadelphia, New York, and Baltimore (including Benjamin Hallowell), provided expanded educational opportunities for women. While most southern white women worked to contain the cultural changes wrought by war, Quaker women promoted a loosening of gender conventions within their community.[56]

IV

Northern Virginia Quakers' embrace of the Union cause weakened their commitment to the impartiality required by the peace testimony. Since the American Revolution, Friends had asserted that pacifism lay at the core of their spiritual beliefs, and that they must "be peaceable ourselves, in word and actions." "Our conduct and deportment" must "in every respect . . . carefully avoid every thing that would encourage a war-like spirit in ourselves, or in any manner would go to the support of War." In 1861, meetings across the region reasserted their commitment to the "ancient" peace testimony. But Friends in northern Virginia and throughout the nation had difficulty avoiding "party feeling" before a slaveholding republic committed to the violent defense of its oppressive labor system. "The Society of Friends as a body," acknowledged Samuel Janney, "remained true and loyal to the Federal Union." The vast majority of Friends did not fight, but confronted by a war that promised to end slavery and transform the South they found genuine neutrality harder to achieve.[57]

Having long identified as Virginian, a small number of Friends, mostly residing in Alexandria, became Confederate partisans. "A few families," Janney conceded, "allowed their sympathies with the Southern people to lead them astray." "The Friends of Alex.," reported Chalkley Gillingham, "are carried away with the spirit of the Southern rebellion." By June 1862, they had stopped holding religious meetings. How "doleful for Friends to become rebellionites," lamented Gillingham. Alexandria's wealthiest Friends, part of the town's business and civic elite, had opposed secession in early 1861. But when Virginia voted to leave the union and Federal troops "invaded" Alexandria, leading Friends, including Robert H. Miller, "went with the state" and refused to take the federal oath of allegiance. Another "Secesh Quaker," William Stabler, greeted Rochester Friend Julia Wilbur "very coolly" when he learned that she had come to Alexandria to work among the town's contraband population. Identified as Confederates, the "Queer" Quakers of Alexandria—as Wilbur labeled them—suffered under Federal rule. In response to Lee's June 1863 invasion of Pennsylvania, Alexandria's Union provost marshal ordered all residents who refused to take the oath transported into the Confederacy. Fearing for his health and property, Miller turned to his son, Francis, "a strong Union man," to obtain a reprieve (though it proved unnecessary when Union officials rescinded the order after Gettysburg). Miller's prominence made him an attractive target for Federal reprisals. In October 1864, in response to Confederate attacks on Union trains traveling west from Alexandria, Union military authorities ordered the town's leading secessionists, including Miller, to ride exposed on the train engines. Only the intercession of a relative enabled Miller to escape the edict.[58]

The Quaker community mourned the decisions of their secessionist brethren who in the contest between their southern and religious identities chose the former. But declension from a strict adherence to Quaker principles afflicted most Friends in the region. The death and suffering caused by the war and its disruption of slavery led many to abandon any pretense to neutrality and a few to abandon their peace testimony. From the war's opening days, Loudoun Friends expressed disdain for the Confederacy and "the crazy secessionists" who threatened to destroy the nation. In Alexandria, at least eight Quakers took the oath of allegiance, contrary to the Quaker discipline, and joined the Alexandria Union Association, a pro-Union political organization. Despite their pledge to remain "passive" under Confederate rule, Friends in Loudoun, Fairfax, and Alexandria provided some of the three thousand seven hundred-plus votes that elected Francis H. Pierpont governor of the restored Union government of Virginia in May 1863. Pierpont's Alexandria-based administration produced a new state constitution in February 1864 that served as the basis for Virginia's postwar government, ending slavery and creating public schools for the state's white children. Quaker John Hauxhorst of Fairfax County played an active role in the convention, while Friend William Hough served as janitor.[59]

Others went beyond political involvement and offered aid to the Union military, much as Rebecca Wright had done. In early September 1862, Quaker refugees Amasa Hough Jr. and Samuel Steer re-entered Loudoun County to assess the strength of Confederate forces. When they discovered two Confederate regiments marching on the Federal garrison at Berlin, they hurriedly returned to Maryland to warn the Union forces, accompanied by sixteen local African Americans seeking freedom. In response, Confederate authorities ordered cavalry units and partisans to control the flow across the Potomac of "traitors" who carried "news to the Yankees" in exchange for "blood money." In early 1864, after repeated Confederate raids on the Woodlawn neighborhood, residents established a watch and armed themselves. The peace testimony discouraged Friends from joining these defense efforts, but Chalkley Gillingham conceded that "our sons do and we cannot prevent it." After another Confederate raid in July, Quaker youths pursued the small band of raiders, cornering and forcing them to abandon the horses they had stolen. Gillingham explained that Friends had not joined the army and acted "merely to keep off robbers." But elsewhere in the region Quaker men volunteered for military service. In fall 1861, John Dutton's son, James, headed to Alexandria and joined the town's union association. He later joined a Union cavalry unit, returning to his family in early 1865 after being wounded.[60]

Dutton's decision reflected a broader wartime change within the Quaker meetings of northern Virginia. The war's growing death toll, the suffering

Confederate troops inflicted on the Quaker community, and the transformation of the Union war effort into a crusade against slavery led the majority of Friends to abandon the pretense of neutrality. "The reelection of Lincoln," wrote John Dutton in 1864," "will show the people of the South that we intend to put down the rebellion; to be one country. . . . The whole *Union* and nothing but the *Union* is the determination of the *people*." Such sentiments, uttered by the community's respected ministers and elders, assuaged the consciences of young Friends who fought for the Union. Ambivalent statements by the yearly meeting reinforced Friends' partisanship. The meeting for sufferings, which in previous wars had provided guidance in disciplinary matters, failed to issue clear directives after 1861. In 1863, a divided meeting could do no more than appoint a committee "to extend . . . advice and assistance" to any members "brought into difficulty" by "military operations." In part, the meeting's unwillingness to issue a uniform policy reflected the different conditions facing Friends. Maryland Friends debated how to respond to the Union draft, and benefitted from the lenient treatment federal authorities generally accorded religious noncombatants. A December 1863 war department circular directed that those who refused to bear arms or pay the fee for reasons of conscience should "be put on parole" by the local provost marshal. Despite this provision, a number of young Quaker men joined "the ranks of the warrior," as the Baltimore Hicksite meeting acknowledged in 1865.[61]

Friends in northern Virginia, negotiating the demands of two combatants, faced a greater threat to their peace testimony. In spring 1861, two young Quaker men, seized by war fever, joined militia companies and faced disciplinary action from their meeting (both retained membership after acknowledging their error). At least one Friend, Thomas F. Miller of the Fairfax meeting, joined Mosby's cavalry, suffering disownment in 1866 for his decision. Only one other Quaker, Kirkbride Taylor of the Goose Creek meeting, joined the Confederate military. In contrast, at least eleven Friends, including some who fled into Maryland to escape Confederate conscription, joined the Union army. Of these, seven joined the Loudoun Rangers, the cavalry unit established by Samuel Means in 1862 to defend Loudoun's Unionist population and supply intelligence to Federal forces. But the unit's military ineptitude hurt its ability to recruit, and it never reached the four full companies Means envisioned.

Nine of the fifteen local Friends who joined military units voluntarily left or were disowned by their meetings during or shortly after the war. Although meetings sometimes disowned these individuals for disciplinary breaches other than violating the peace testimony, military service led to their alienation from the Quaker community.[62]

In contrast to previous wars, however, meeting minutes provide an unreliable guide to military service, reflecting the broader changes the war effected within the Quaker community. Monthly meetings struggled to restrain Unionist zeal, especially among young women and men. The handwringing of the Hicksite yearly meeting in the face of this challenge forced it to fashion a more flexible disciplinary policy in fall 1865. The war's "extraordinary circumstances," the meeting conceded, had subjected Friends "to a severe test" and many had been "carried away by the current of popular enthusiasm." Friends could not overlook "past offenses" of the peace testimony entirely, but a strict enforcement policy might destroy the local meetings. As Baltimore Friend Joseph J. Janney noted years later, "There were not enough members who were entirely innocent to pronounce judgment on the alleged violators." Consequently, the yearly meeting directed monthly meetings to appoint a committee of "judicious Friends" to accept the "voluntary acknowledgements" of delinquents. When the committee deemed this verbal confession "satisfactory," the matter ended "without reporting the names of the individuals." Consequently, the meetings recorded only those Friends who failed to express regret for their military service, and did not document those whose Unionist sympathies led to violations of the peace testimony's call for neutrality. When confronted by the conflict between their peace testimony on the one hand and the combined weight of antislavery and nationalism on the other, Hicksite Friends of the Baltimore Yearly Meeting—like Friends throughout the nation—sided with the latter.[63]

The contrast between Friends' lenient treatment of Civil War infractions of the peace testimony and their handling of such cases in previous wars reveals their retreat from rigorous enforcement of the discipline. Non-Quakers noticed the changes. Union victory sparked a wave of partisanship among Quakers. "Their is great Rejoicing with the Union People," noted one disgruntled Confederate. Samuel Janney "Had the Old Gobelar killed and Invited Many of his Union Friends to Eat and be Merry." William Tate "Shut him Self up in a room and Laughed his Fill." Other Friends sought to redress Confederate confiscations or punish secessionists. Benjamin Birdsall traveled "to Upperville to haul the Corn away that Mosbys Men impressed." Henry S. Taylor believed that "the Secesh aught Never to be allowed to vote again" or "hold any office of any kind." Moncure Conway, the antebellum admirer of local Friends, found their wartime partisanship disturbing. He believed that Friends forgot "their peace principles" when they interpreted the war as "God's agency for ending slavery" and saving the nation. "How merely academic," he lamented, "are the most radical peace principles when a flag demands blood."[64]

Conway overstated the extent of Friends' backsliding. Despite strong Unionist sentiments, few Friends endorsed bloody measures in the face of the war's suffering and death toll. Still, their failure to enforce the peace testimony reflected an important shift in the Quaker community. Like Protestants throughout the North, Friends interpreted the war as God's punishment for the sin of slavery and part of a divine plan to bring liberty to America and the world. "The wisdom, goodness, and power" of the "Almighty Being," explained the yearly meeting in 1863, "permits the passions of man to work out their own chastisement, and brings forth . . . results that cannot be foreseen by human wisdom nor frustrated by human depravity." If the war had been the means through which an "inscrutable" God had ended slavery and saved the Union, Friends' failings during the conflict left them less certain of their capacity to enforce their disciplinary rules with rigor. "It is not our place," noted the meeting, "to judge others who may believe themselves called to pursue a different path from that in which we walk." Instead, all Friends had "a Christian duty" to deal "with offenders in the spirit of meekness and love." "The first object" in treating with wayward members, the 1864 meeting reminded members, "is the restoration of the diseased member to health rather than its separation from the body." A year later, the yearly meeting urged members "to be tender towards all who . . . violate[d] our precious testimonies." The Civil War represented a watershed for Friends during which the emphasis of their faith shifted from communal conformity to individual autonomy. In casting the hallowed principles of peace and antislavery into conflict the war helped undermine Friends' moral certainty and encouraged them to embrace more fully the individualistic components of their spiritual beliefs.[65]

Change did not arrive overnight nor did Quaker communalism vanish. But a shift appeared nonetheless. In 1865, the Baltimore Yearly Meeting decided that parents and masters of apprentices should no longer be held responsible for their dependents' violations of the peace testimony. The consequences of such infractions now fell on the individual. Likewise, Friends' enforcement of the marriage discipline became more lax in the 1860s, as meetings stopped disowning Friends who married non-Quakers. Concerns about the Society's falling membership prompted this decision, as did the rising status of women's meetings. A more visible change affected clothing choices. "Young Friends," noted Mary Hollingsworth, "have taken decided grounds in favor of popular styles of cutting broadcloth and other vanities." "The drab era of Quakerism," she concluded, "was drawing to a close." The rapprochement between the region's Hicksite and Orthodox Friends, led by Samuel Janney and Benjamin Hallowell, also reflected the softening of moral certainty. Hallowell believed that salvation did not depend on joining Friends' "*outward religious organization*," but rather on individuals embracing "the Spirit of God in their own hearts." Emphasizing themes first sounded during the Hicksite split, Hallowell argued that within Quakerism "no room exists . . . for sectarianism, or prejudice against race, class, or caste." In this atmosphere, Progressive Friends like Joseph Dugdale, who left the Hicksites in the 1840s, found a welcoming environment. Chalkley Gillingham pronounced Dugdale a "spirited minister" who offered "exceedingly appropriate and solemn" remarks during an 1865 visit to northern Virginia.[66]

Despite these changes, Friends' lives after Appomattox returned to many of their prewar patterns. Most resumed their agricultural, civic, and business pursuits among a sometimes hostile but usually tolerant non-Quaker population. Over the years, the wartime tensions that divided the white population dissipated, as a dwindling number of Quakers turned their social concerns toward Native Americans in the West. Still, Friends' Civil War experience exposed the limits of southern unity and the fragility of the Confederacy, particularly on its borders. Little wonder that Confederate President Jefferson Davis refused to grant Quakers an exemption from Confederate conscription laws. Instead, he lamented that "within the limits of the Southern Confederacy" there existed "a body of people unwilling . . . to fight" and "die in defense of their country." Such internal dissent, he realized, posed a threat to his vision of an independent southern nation. As historian William Freehling argues, "anti-confederate southerners" helped undermine the Confederate cause and promote Union victory.[67] While most Friends did not take an active role in the fighting, they strongly opposed slavery and secession. Their rejection of the Confederacy's central values—slavery, racism, and the violent defense of its "rights"—constituted a rebuke to antebellum southern society as most white southerners conceived it. While insisting on their southern identity, Friends—and foremost among them female Friends—modeled a different set of southern values bereft of patriarchy and racism.

Epilogue

Conflicting Paths of Virtue in Nineteenth-Century America

"Doing good," writes columnist Nicholas Kristof, "is harder than it looks." The Quakers of eighteenth- and nineteenth-century northern Virginia would have concurred. For over one hundred years, they worked to implement their Christian principles in their daily lives, both as a sign of the power of the inward light and as an example that their non-Quaker neighbors might emulate. Friends' work ethic, principled and honest business procedures, and concern for civic improvement and regional economic development earned them the appreciation and respect of many white Virginians, who recognized them as public-spirited members of the community. For their part, Friends developed a deep attachment to northern Virginia, viewing themselves as southerners distinct in outlook and attitude from northern Quakers. Friends' long residence in, contributions to, and identification with the region enabled them to speak publicly to a range of issues that white Virginians would not have tolerated from northern interlopers. Still, the region's Quakers remained outsiders, instantly recognizable by their dress and speech, and distrusted for their pacifism and vision of racial and social justice. The sense of difference became most pronounced during times of war and rising political tension when white Virginians demanded unity. At such moments, Friends faced their most difficult ethical and tactical challenges. Their peaceable principles required that they behave and speak in ways that lessened the possibility of conflict, but the heightened vigilance of white Virginians ensured that if they voiced or acted on their beliefs, they could engender the violence they sought to avoid. Silence and the peace that it might bring, however, meant compromising their broader agenda of social and racial justice. Underlying Friends' antebellum efforts to realize justice in the South was the question of means and ends that confounded all nineteenth-century reformers.[1]

While a growing number of northern abolitionists concluded that the moral injustice of slavery required the use of violence, local Friends eschewed it for reasons of conscience and self-preservation. Some chose to depart Virginia despite their attachment to the state because they believed that only by leaving the South could they protect their antislavery testimony from compromise and enjoy the economic benefits of a free labor economy. But in leaving they abandoned their ability to extend direct aid to free blacks and enslaved Virginians, and their removal did nothing to undermine the institution of slavery or change the social and cultural values of the region. Those who remained embraced a variety of tactics—from antislavery declarations and petitions to the promotion of a free labor economy through northern immigration, economic development, and agricultural improvement—but they recognized by the 1850s how little their efforts had achieved. When the Civil War erupted and the institution of slavery began to collapse, local Friends confronted the dilemma of whether violence could achieve a greater social good. Like many northern Protestants, they interpreted the war as a reflection of God's will, part of His divine plan to end slavery and redefine the meaning of American liberty. But Friends remained deeply distressed by the violence and suffering necessary to achieve these goals. Their belief in progressive revelation through the inward light had produced a sense of confidence that the ways of God might eventually become knowable to humanity. The war, in contrast, produced an uncharacteristic sense of fatalism in the face of God's "inscrutable" will.[2]

In the war's immediate aftermath, northern Virginia's Quakers renewed their outreach among African Americans, contributing money, supplies, and teachers for black schools throughout the region. They also continued to employ blacks, offering them, as they had before the war, comparatively generous wages and treatment. But by 1870 leading Friends no longer focused on the achievement of African American equality in the South. Despite growing racial oppression and violence in Reconstruction Virginia, Friends reduced their efforts on behalf of the black community. A variety of factors contributed to their inaction. In the wake of the war, Friends feared another wave of westward migration that threatened the survival of their community. More important, Friends worried that continued social and cultural isolation would make them the targets of their white neighbors' violent efforts to restore the old racial hierarchy. Already suspect for their antislavery and Unionist opinions, many Friends concluded that they must reconcile with the region's white population, even if that meant ending aid to local blacks. Some Friends went further, abandoning their antebellum calls for racial justice and imbibing the racism of the postwar era. In their later recollections, some Friends aped the attitudes of the broader society, criticizing "old-time, primitive negroes," and treating their dialect, folklore, and behavior as a source of humor. Other Friends, like their white neighbors, reminisced fondly about the faithfulness of African Americans during the antebellum and Civil War eras. The violence of the war had ended slavery, but some Friends concluded that perhaps God's plan for racial justice, at least in the postwar climate, extended no further.[3]

Instead, in the late 1860s and early 1870s, many Friends directed their attention toward another longstanding but less prominent social concern: the fate of Native Americans. Quakers in seventeenth-century Pennsylvania established a reputation for fair and peaceful relations with the Indians; during the American Revolution, Hopewell Friends tried to identify and reimburse the original owners of the land on which their meeting house sat. The effort helped spark within the Baltimore Yearly Meeting a new interest in the plight of Native Americans, and in 1795 the meeting created a committee devoted to Indian concerns. Led by Philip E. Thomas between 1808 and 1865, it focused attention on the plight of Natives in Ohio until the early 1830s. In 1839, the committee responded to a request of the northern meetings to help the Seneca, part of the Iroquois nation, protect their land claims in upstate New York. Baltimore's Hicksite Friends initiated a concerted effort to "civilize" the Seneca, establishing schools, promoting agriculture, and teaching Indian women European domestic skills. Most important, they helped the Seneca obtain permanent title to fifty-two thousand acres in western New York, along with a federal annuity.[4]

After the Civil War, the violence sparked by the migration of whites into Indian land west of the Mississippi renewed Friends' concern. In 1867, Hicksite Friends from six yearly meetings met in Baltimore and produced a memorial that called for "a liberal and just policy" to stop bloodshed and save Indians from "ultimate extermination." The Friends' proposal sought to "civilize" the Indians by offering them tenure to "fertile tracts of well-watered country" and the supplies and education necessary to their success as farmers. Orthodox Friends met in Baltimore two years later. After their conference, they met with president-elect Ulysses S. Grant, as did Hicksite Friends. Two weeks later, Grant's advisor Ely S. Parker, a Seneca Indian trained in Quaker schools, sent identical letters to the Indian committees of both Baltimore yearly meetings asking them to suggest Friends who would serve as Indian agents. After some hesitation, both groups endorsed the proposal. Hicksites took charge of six agencies in Nebraska—the northern superintendency—appointing Samuel Janney to oversee a population of approximately six thousand Native Americans. As noted by Benjamin Hallowell, the secretary of the meeting's Indian committee, when Friends "were invited" into this "wider field of usefulness, they did not feel at liberty to refuse to enter it."[5]

Janney served two years as superintendent, joined by his brother Asa and Jacob M. Troth of the Alexandria meeting, both of whom worked as agents. Expanding their public roles, women also played an active part in the Quaker effort in Nebraska. Janney's daughter, Cornelia, ran an Indian school, as did Asa's daughter Cosmelia. Asa's second daughter, Thamsin, dispensed medicines to local Indians. Baltimore Friends continued to support Grant's Indian "peace policy" after Janney's 1871 departure, donating more than sixty thousand dollars to the Indian nations living within the northern superintendency. Friends began to withdraw in the late 1870s, after President Rutherford B. Hayes abandoned Grant's peace policy in response to renewed violence in the West and the steady erosion of public support. Friends took pride in their efforts among the Indians, but doing good west of the Mississippi hindered their ability to advance racial justice at home. In following their concern for Native Americans, they neglected the freedpeople of Virginia at a crucial moment—when white conservatives began to "redeem" the state of Republican rule and reestablish the racial hierarchy of the antebellum era.[6] Oppressive racial policies in the South and West and growing indifference in the North multiplied human suffering and left Friends with difficult choices. Many continued to act as exemplars of a more humane America, extending aid as they could and speaking out when possible. But they could and would not coerce Americans to follow them. And with every choice they made, they faced the dilemma of abandoning other ethical concerns.

For their efforts, Friends earned both acclaim and denunciation. When President Grant announced his Indian peace policy he praised Quakers, voicing what had become by the 1870s a common sentiment among Americans. Friends "are known," observed Grant, "for their opposition to all strife, violence, and war, and are generally noted for their strict integrity and fair dealings." But some disagreed. A Baltimore newspaper conceded that "there are many honest and upright Quakers, but there are just as many dishonest men in that Church as in any other." "When vices strike a . . . Quaker," the paper continued, "he is the hardest rascal that can be found." Such distrust had long existed in the United States, particularly before and during the Civil War among southern slaveholders whose wealth depended on the exploitation of black Americans. But Friends also faced condemnation from fellow reformers. Prior to the war, many Garrisonian abolitionists had viewed Quakers' refusal to join antislavery societies and their willingness to participate in the political system as a failure to abide by their principles. As growing numbers of abolitionists embraced more aggressive tactics in response to slaveholders' intransigence and the Compromise of 1850, the Society of Friends fell increasingly out of step with the abolitionist movement, even while they remained committed to their antislavery testimony.[7]

Historians of the abolition movement have not ignored Friends' contributions to it, but they have privileged the most radical abolitionists in their accounts, even while disagreeing about whether Garrisonians, political abolitionists, or African Americans stood at the vanguard. Certainly, in recent years historians have tended to deemphasize the significance of moderates, including political abolitionists and Friends. For scholars the moral blight of slavery stands in bold relief. As a result, they have studied most fully those individuals who embraced militant measures, condemned slavery in striking terms, and came closest to enunciating modern notions of racial justice. Scholars studying the movement before 1830 have thus paid significant attention to Quakers who stood at its forefront before the rise of immediatism; after 1830, however, Quakers and other moderates attract less notice. The reform leaders of the antebellum era require such study, but so do the moderates (however defined) who constituted a majority within the antislavery movement. Understanding why antislavery garnered support so slowly among an American population that espoused the values of evangelical spiritual equality and Enlightenment egalitarianism requires that scholars give more consideration to the motives and values of moderates who for a variety of reasons—beyond the racism of white Americans—declined to embrace the uncompromising approach of militants. In most accounts, the triumphs of the Civil War—the destruction of slavery and the unification of the nation—overshadow its human costs. But the history of the battle against slavery, and the Civil War that led to the institution's demise, should remind us that radical tactics, even in the pursuit of the most moral aims, can have unintended and even tragic consequences.[8]

Even while Friends embraced the results of the war—the end of slavery and the opportunity to turn their efforts toward another oppressed population—they recognized its immense human sacrifices. Their abhorrence of violence had helped sustain their testimony against war and their hope that slavery could be ended by peaceable means. But throughout the antebellum era, they faced the question confronted by all reformers: Social justice, but by what means and at what cost? Southern Friends' contemplation of and answer to this question reveals how moral values can clash. Many nineteenth-century activists, including the Garrisonians and Progressive Friends, believed in a "single divine Truth." They were convinced that the achievement of one social reform would lead to a broadened definition of human rights and democracy that would remove all fetters to individual freedom. For radicals, in short, the pursuit of slavery's demise represented the first step in a series of social and cultural reformations that would collapse all social hierarchies and inequalities and produce a democratized and egalitarian Christian polity. But reformers' sense of moral urgency, and the tenacity of both their northern and southern foes, pushed many of them to contemplate aggressive and violent tactics. In attempting to eliminate slavery, the nation's most egregious evil, many radicals hesitantly accepted another: the possibility of violence on an unprecedented scale.[9]

This is far from concluding that the Civil War was wrong or immoral (even Friends ultimately accepted it as the inexplicable if tragic work of God). Instead, the saga of northern Virginia's Friends should encourage all those who seek progressive social change to examine and question, constantly and rigorously, how best to achieve the end of social justice. As political philosopher Isaiah Berlin has noted, in the weighing of ethical goals lays the essential measure of the life morally conducted. For those who seek progressive social change, the dilemma of means and ends—of balancing the moral necessity to achieve certain goals against the danger of unintended consequences—should remain at the heart of every decision, as it did for Friends in northern Virginia. "We can only do what we can," writes Berlin, "but that we must do, against difficulties." Guided by their inward light, Friends tried to do what they could for the oppressed, hoping to achieve their vision of the moral society by means that caused as little violence, spiritual and physical, as possible. As Samuel Janney wrote, Friends seeking a "practical piety" remained ever mindful of the consequences of their actions, believing that they could only be "useful in . . . society" if they balanced the "Spirit of Truth" against the need to "sympathize with" their fellows, especially with those "whose spiritual vision" had "not yet fully prepared [them] for the reception of truth."[10] We live in a world fraught with conflict borne of people's incapacity to empathize with their fellows. In such a world, Friends' tolerance and compassion for humanity, with all its limitations, retains its relevance and significance.

Notes

Abbreviations

AA	*Alexandria Advertiser*
ADA	*Alexandria Daily Advertiser*
AF	*American Farmer*
AG	*Alexandria Gazette*
AH	*Alexandria Herald*
AL	Abraham Lincoln
ALSC	Alexandria Library Special Collections
AMM	Alexandria Monthly Meeting
ASP	*American State Papers*
BH	Benjamin Hallowell
BMS	Baltimore Meeting for Sufferings
BSV	*Baltimore Saturday Visiter*
BYM	Baltimore Yearly Meeting
BYMWF	Baltimore Yearly Meeting Women Friends
CCHS	Chester County Historical Society
CMM	Crooked Run Monthly Meeting
CVSP	*Calendar of Virginia State Papers*
DNI	*Daily National Intelligencer*
ECQC	Earlham College Quaker Collection
FAPF	Friends' Association of Philadelphia for the Aid and Elevation of the Freedmen
FHL	Friends Historical Library, Swarthmore College
FI	*Friends' Intelligencer*
FMM	Fairfax Monthly Meeting
FMMWF	Fairfax Monthly Meeting Women Friends
FQM	Fairfax Quarterly Meeting
FR	*Federal Republican*
GL	*Genius of Liberty*
GMM	Goose Creek Monthly Meeting
GUE	*Genius of Universal Emancipation*
GW	George Washington
HCQC	Haverford College Quaker Collection

HF	Hopewell Friends
HJRA	*Horticulturist and Journal of Rural Art and Rural Taste*
HMM	Hopewell Monthly Meeting
HMMWF	Hopewell Monthly Meeting Women Friends
HRL	Handley Regional Library, Winchester, Virginia
HSP	Historical Society of Pennsylvania
IHS	Indiana Historical Society
LC	Library of Congress
LV	Library of Virginia
MHR	Maryland Hall of Records
NCPEUS	National Convention for the Promotion of Education in the United States
NE	*National Era*
NEYM	New England Yearly Meeting
NI	*National Intelligencer*
NWR	*Niles Weekly Register*
NYT	*New York Times*
PAS	Pennsylvania Abolition Society
PF	*Pennsylvania Freeman*
PMS	Philadelphia Meeting for Sufferings
PYM	Philadelphia Yearly Meeting
RW	*Richmond Whig*
SCB	*Sanitary Commission Bulletin*
SEP	*Saturday Evening Post*
SMJ	Samuel M. Janney
SP	*Southern Planter*
TBL	Thomas Balch Library
TF	*The Friend*
TL	*The Liberator*
UV	University of Virginia
VC	*Virginia Centinel*
VCC	Virginia Constitutional Convention (1864)
VG	*Virginia Gazette*
VHS	Virginia Historical Society
VMHB	*Virginia Magazine of History and Biography*
VS	*Virginia Sentinel*
VYM	Virginia Yearly Meeting
WFQM	Warrington and Fairfax Quarterly Meeting

Prologue: Quakers Living in the Lion's Mouth

1. SMJ to Isaac T. Hopper, December 15, 1844, in SMJ, *Memoirs*, 88.

2. Account of SMJ's arrest based on SMJ, *Memoirs*, 97–106; John Janney to SMJ, September 28, 1849, February 25, 1850; and SMJ to Phineas Janney, March 14, June 16, 1850, SMJ Manuscripts, FHL. See also Hickin, "Antislavery in Virginia"; Hickin, "Gentle Agitator," 183–86; and Eaton, *Freedom-of-Thought*, 135–37.

3. BH, *Autobiography*, 275.

4. "Letter from Lydia Wierman," *PF*, November 20, 1845 (my thanks to Deborah Lee for this citation).

Chapter 1. Friends Come to Northern Virginia

1. Fothergill to Mary Pemberton, December 4, 1754, and Fothergill to Susanna Fothergill, December 13, 1754, in Crosfield, ed., *Memoirs*, 164, 166; Catherine Phillips, *Memoirs*, 101.

2. For accounts of the rise of the Society of Friends in England, see Barbour, *Quakers in Puritan England*; Ingle, *First among Friends*; Bacon, *Quiet Rebels*, 9–24. On English religious movements during the 1640s and 1650s, see Hill, *World Turned Upside Down*.

3. Hening, ed., *Statutes*, 1: 532–33; 2: 48, 49–51, 165–66, 180–83, 246–47. Worrall, *Friendly Virginians*, 1–66; Horn, *Adapting*, 56–57, 394–99; Weeks, *Southern Quakers*, 7–8, 13–49; Rufus Jones, *Quakers in American Colonies*, 265–95, 306–307, 317–19, 334–38; Carroll, "Quakerism on the Eastern Shore," 170–89; and Carroll, ed., "Robert Pleasants," 3–16.

4. McIlwaine, ed., *Journal of House of Burgesses*, 2: 431, 433; 3: 78–79; 6: 9, 268; Hening, *Statutes*, 3: 171, 298; 5: 16–17. On Friends and the Anglican Church, see John K. Nelson, *Blessed Company*, 281–83.

5. Gragg, *Migration*, 29, 30, 41; Fawcett, "Quaker Migration," 102–108; Mitchell, *Commercialism and Frontier*, 149–50; Hofstra, *Planting of New Virginia*, 81–84; Hofstra, "'Extention of His Majesties Dominions'"; and McIlwaine, Hall, and Hillman, eds., *Executive Journals*, 3: 549–50. On competency, see Vickers, "Competency and Competition."

6. HF, *Hopewell Friends History*, 12–16; McIlwaine, Hall, and Hillman, *Executive Journals*, 4: 229, 347; and Hofstra, *Planting of New Virginia*, 29–31, 100–102.

7. Gertrude E. Gray, comp., *Virginia Northern Neck*, 1: 131, 139, 140, 142, 143, 144, 145, 146, 147; 2: 1, 3, 4, 5, 9. Worrall, *Friendly Virginians*, 131–32; Janney and Janney, *Ye Meetg Hous Smal*, 6–12 (although these sources report different totals for Janney's land purchases).

8. Levy, "'Tender Plants,'" 240–65; and Levy, *Quakers and the American Family*, 58–61, 81–82, 127–37, 236–48 (quotation 241).

9. *VG*, November 17, 24, 1738. See also "Quakers' Petition." John K. Nelson, *Blessed Company*, 283, 286, 451n12; Hening, *Statutes*, 6: 88–90. On Anglican geographic weakness, see Spangler, *Virginians Reborn*, esp. 9–42; and [Hodge], "Davies's State of Religion," 171.

10. Hofstra, *Planting of New Virginia*, 19, 116–25, 131 (quotation), 174–75; Mitchell, *Commercialism and Frontier*, 22–24; Kercheval, *History of Valley*, 41.

11. Longenecker, *Shenandoah Religion*, 15; Hofstra, *Planting of New Virginia*, 18, 34, 131–33; Charles Lewis, "Journal," 208; Morrison, ed., *Travels*, 2: 31–32; Cresswell, *Journal*, 47–49; Gragg, *Migration*, 41, 49.

12. James, *People among Peoples*, 5–59; Barbour, *Quaker Crosscurrents*, 19–24; and Beeth, "Outside Agitators," 19–95.

13. James, *People among Peoples*, 5–16; Bauman, *For the Reputation of Truth*, 231–34; Larson, *Daughters of Light*, 30–34; Frost, *Quaker Family*, 3–5; Levy, *Quakers and the American Family*, 78–80 (quotation 78).

14. James, *People among Peoples*, 5–16; Beeth, "Outside Agitators," 96–288; Beeth, "Between Friends," 108–27; Larson, *Daughters of Light*; Frost, *Quaker Family*, 3–5; Marietta, *Reformation*, 74–77.

15. HF, *Hopewell Friends History*, 21, 40–49, 70–92; Worrall, *Friendly Virginians*, 124–27, 130.

16. Hinshaw, *Encyclopedia*, 6: 463–65; Janney and Janney, *Ye Meetg Hous Smal*, 13–20.

17. For a detailed discussion of Quaker theology, see Frost, *Quaker Family*, esp. 10–63. See also Tolles, *Meeting House*, 4–11; Larson, *Daughters of Light*, 16–23, 30–34 (quotation 31); Levy, *Quakers and the American Family*, 78–80, 193–230; and Soderlund, "Women's Authority."

18. Barclay, *Apology*, 534; Penn, *Some Fruits of Solitude*, no. 73; Tolles, *Meeting House*, 8, 125–27; Larson, *Daughters of Light*, 25, 346n1; Lapsansky, "Past Plainness," Frost, "From Plainness to Simplicity," and Garfinkel, "Quakers and High Chests," in Lapsansky and Verplanck, eds., *Quaker Aesthetics*, 1–40, 65–69, 376; Frost, *Quaker Family*, 192–97.

19. Larson, *Daughters of Light*, 4, 17–18, 185; Levy, *Quakers and the American Family*, 12; Bauman, *Let Your Words*, 7 (first quotation); Barclay, *Apology*, 354; Frost, *Quaker Family*, 35–40; and Garfinkel, "Quakers and High Chests," in Lapsansky and Verplanck, *Quaker Aesthetics*, 71–72.

20. Fox, quoted in Hamm, *Transformation*, 2; Fox, quoted in Tolles, *Meeting House*, 9; Brinton, *Religious Philosophy*, 5–7; and Peter Brock, *Pioneers*, xi–xvi.

21. Tolles, *Meeting House*, 51–62 (Chalkley p. 56); Frost, *Quaker Family*, 30–47, 196–206; Marietta, *Reformation*, 98–105, 306n5; Levy, *Quakers and the American Family*, 141–44.

22. Larson, *Daughters of Light*, 30–34, 133–42, 224–27; Levy, "'Tender Plants,'" 245–47 (quotation 246); Levy, *Quakers and the American Family*, 71–80, 132–33, 193–230; Brissot de Warville, *New Travels*, 222 (quotation); Marietta, *Reformation*, 6–7, 10–13, 61–66; Stevenson, *Life in Black and White*, 15–18, 24–25; Janney and Janney, eds., *John Janney's Virginia*, 4 (quotation).

23. For useful studies of the colonial Virginia and its planter elite, see Kulikoff, *Tobacco and Slaves*; Emory Evans, *'Topping People'*; Morgan, *American Slavery*, 295–387; Kamoie, *Irons in the Fire*; and Isaac, *Transformation of Virginia*.

24. Isaac, *Transformation of Virginia*; Breen, *Tobacco Culture*; John K. Nelson, *Blessed Company*, 64–65, 187–94; and Kathleen M. Brown, *Good Wives*, esp. 247–373.

25. On evangelicalism as a challenge to Virginia's social and cultural values, see Isaac, *Transformation of Virginia*, and Gewehr, *Great Awakening in Virginia*. On the evangelical retreat from antislavery and embrace of patriarchy, see Heyrman, *Southern Cross*, passim (quotation 24); Spangler, *Virginians Reborn*, passim (quotation 163); Mathews, *Slavery and Methodism*, 3–61; and Essig, *Bonds of Wickedness*.

26. See Isaac, *Transformation of Virginia*; and Heyrman, *Southern Cross*, esp. 26, 142–45, 154–56, 195 (quotation 142).

27. On Quaker domesticity, see Levy, *Quakers and the American Family*; and Frost, *Quaker Family*, esp. 76–79, 140–42.

28. Meinig, *Shaping of America*, 159–60; Longenecker, *Shenandoah Religion*, 15–29; McMaster, "Religion, Migration, and Pluralism"; Poland, *Frontier to Suburbia*, 25–29, 39–49; Mitchell, *Commercialism and Frontier*, 9–13, 27–31; and Bliss, "Tuckahoe in New Virginia."

29. Hofstra, *Planting of New Virginia*, 50–55, 184–86; Longenecker, *Shenandoah Religion*, 21 (quotation); Hening, *Statutes*, 6: 258–60; John K. Nelson, *Blessed Company*, 282–94; Brydon, *Virginia's Mother Church*, 2: 68–138. The three Quakers were James Cromley (or Crumley), Lewis Neil, and Isaac Parkins; see Meade, *Frederick Parish*, 15–16.

30. Hening, *Statutes*, 3: 288–91, 5: 206. For Quaker affirmations allowed in various contexts, see Hening, *Statutes*, 3: 298, 4: 354, 5: 206, 489, 6: 49, 261, 7: 549. Hofstra, *Planting of New Virginia*, 160–66; Norris, ed., *Lower Shenandoah Valley*, 71–73, 198–99 (Neil); Jolliffe, *Jolliffe Family*, 61–62 (Neil and Jolliffe); HF, *Hopewell Friends History*, 18–19 (Parkins); BYM, *Discipline of Yearly Meeting 1806*, 25 (quotation); Tolles, *Meeting House*, 10–28; Rufus Jones, *Quakers in American Colonies*, 417–22, 459–74.

31. Richards, ed., "Stuart's Report," 289; Janney and Janney, eds., "Israel Janney's 'Ledger B,'" entry for John Binns, Folio Y, VHS; Gouger, "Northern Neck," 79–81. On the Chesapeake's agricultural transformation, see Lewis Cecil Gray, *History of Agriculture*, 2: 581–83, 606–608; Craven, *Soil Exhaustion*, 66–108; Klingaman, "Significance of Grain"; Clemens, *Atlantic Economy*, 168–205; and Crothers, "Projecting Spirit," 47–83, 318–20.

32. Janney and Janney, "Israel Janney's 'Ledger B,'" VHS; Griffith to Hannah Griffith, December 17, 1778, David Griffith Papers, VHS; Jolliffe, *Historical Account*, 176–79; HF, *Hopewell Friends History*, 169, 204–205. On Friends' reputation for honesty, see Raistrick, *Quakers in Science*, 42–48; and Walvin, *Quakers*, 61–79.

33. Carter, "Merchants and Mills," 246; GW to Baittaile Muse, August 22, 1785, in Fitzpatrick, ed., *Writings of GW*, 28: 235; HF, *Hopewell Friends History*, 18–20, 166–77.

34. Titus, *Old Dominion at War*, 73–108; Dinwiddie to Sir Charles Hardy, October 18, 1755, in R. A. Brock, ed., *Official Records*, 2: 251; Charles Lewis, "Journal," 208 (quotations), 209, 211, 214–15. See also, Kercheval, *History of Valley*, 68–108.

35. Hening, *Statutes*, 5: 16 (1738 law), 6: 531 (1755 law), 7: 14–17 (1756 law); HF, *Hopewell Friends History*, 187–88; "Narrative of the Conduct and Sufferings of Some Friends in Virginia, 1760," in Peter Brock, "Colonel Washington," 21; GW to Dinwiddie, June 25, 1756, in Fitzpatrick, *Writings of GW*, 1: 394.

36. Dinwiddie to GW, [June], August 19, 1756, in R. A. Brock, *Official Records*, 2: 434, 481; GW to Dinwiddie, August 4, 1756, in Fitzpatrick, *Writings of GW*, 1: 420; "Narrative of the Conduct and Suffering of Some Friends," in Peter Brock, "Colonel Washington," 24–26. Weeks, *Southern Quakers*, 174–76; Peter Brock, *Pioneers*, 42–44.

37. Fairfax Harrison, ed., "With Braddock's Army," 312–13; John T. Phillips, *Historian's Guide*, 305–306, 326–27; Hening, *Statutes*, 7: 15–16; Letter of Edward Stabler, October 20, 1756, in Peter Brock, "Colonel Washington," 18; "To the Friends of the Meeting for Sufferings in London," July 1756, in VYM minutes, May 28–30, 1757, MHR; HF, *Hopewell Friends History*, 57–58, 116; Worrall, *Friendly Virginians*, 157; HMM minutes, July 23, 1759 (Rogers), and February 6, 1764 (Parkins), FHL; Hinshaw, *Encyclopedia*, 6: 440, 428. The HMM minutes between 1735 and 1759 are not extant.

38. Reckitt, *Account of the Life*, 61 (a "sneck" was the latch of a door or gate); Fothergill to Susanna Fothergill, November 6, 1755, in Crosfield, *Memoirs*, 219–20; HF, *Hopewell Friends History*, 118–20.

39. HF, *Hopewell Friends History*, 121, 113–15. Chalkley letter reproduced in Kercheval, *History of Valley*, 46–47; see also James, *People among Peoples*, 80–81. For traditional views of Penn's "benevolent" Native American policies, see Rufus Jones, *Quakers in American Colonies*, 495–508; and Tolles, "Nonviolent Contact." For recent views that see Penn's policies as part of "a great colonization effort," see Hinderaker, *Elusive Empires*, 88–90, 101–105; Francis Jennings, "Brother Miquon," in Dunn and Dunn, eds., *World of Penn*, 195–214; and Merrell, *Into the American Woods*, 28–38.

40. HF, *Hopewell Friends History*, 121–22; HMM minutes, April 5, 1762, FHL.

41. Marietta, *Reformation*, esp. 32–72, 97–128, 150–68; James, *People among Peoples*, esp. 141–92; Larson, *Daughters of Light*, 198–231; Tolles, *Meeting House*, 234–39. On Benezet and Woolman, see Jackson, *Let This Voice*; and Slaughter, *Beautiful Soul*.

42. Marietta, *Reformation*, 6–7, 54–58 (quotation 54); James, *People among Peoples*, 170–76; Kelsey, "Early Disciplines."

43. Griffith and Oxley, *Journal of . . . John Griffith*, and *Joseph Oxley's Journal*, in William Evans and Thomas Evans, eds., *Friends' Library*, 2: 455, 5: 424. Hopewell figures from HMM minutes, 1748–1776, FHL, supplemented by HF, *Hopewell Friends History*, 75, 496–501. Worrall, *Friendly Virginians*, 183–86.

44. James, *People among Peoples*, 7–11, 171–76; Marietta, *Reformation*, 73–81. HMM minutes, March 7, April 4, June 6, December 5, 1768, February 6, 1769, FHL.

45. James, *People among Peoples*, 16–22.

46. SMJ, *History*, 3: 440.

Chapter 2. Finding a Path of Virtue in a Revolutionary World

1. Gilpin, *Exiles in Virginia*, 181; Mekeel, *Relation of Quakers*, 264.

2. For an older, "consensus" view of Virginia's Revolution, see Selby, *Revolution in Virginia*. For recent scholarship that emphasizes class and racial divisions in Virginia, see Holton, *Forced Founders*; and McDonnell, *Politics of War*. See also Eckenrode, *Revolution in Virginia*, esp. 232–60. For local studies of Quakers in the Revolution, see Thorne, "North Carolina Friends"; Sappington, "North Carolina and the Non-Resistant Sects"; Oaks, "Philadelphians in Exile"; White, "Friends and the Coming of the Revolution"; Tiedemann, "Queens County, New York Quakers"; and Guenther, "A Crisis of Allegiance."

3. Fothergill to John Churchman, March 1756, and 1759, in Crosfield, *Memoirs*, 252, 367.

4. James, *People among Peoples*, esp. 240–334; James, "Impact of Revolution"; Marietta, *Reformation*, 222–79; and Bauman, *For the Reputation of Truth*, 159–83.

5. Fox, in Hamm, *Transformation*, 2; Penington, *Works*, 326–27; PYM, in Mekeel, *Relation of Quakers*, 2–3, 9n5; James, *People among Peoples*, 243; Peter Brock, *Pioneers*, xi–xvi. See also BYM minutes, October 13–18, 1806, FHL. Northern Virginia's Friends joined the BYM in 1790.

6. Mekeel, *Relation of Quakers*, 1–83; Peter Brock, *Pioneers*, 141–44.

7. Hening, *Statutes*, 8: 242–44; *VG*, February 10, June 9, August 4, September 29, 1774, May 18, June 16, July 7, 29, 1775.

8. Soderlund, *Quakers and Slavery*, 17–18, 32–86, 145; Drake, *Quakers and Slavery*, 1–47; David Brion Davis, *Problem of Slavery in Western Culture*, 306–16, 483–84; Wax, "Quaker Merchants"; Gary, "Economic and Political Relations," 169–84; and Nash, "Slaves and Slaveholders," 253–54.

9. Stevenson, *Life in Black and White*, 17; Drake, *Quakers and Slavery*, 75–76, 83; Fothergill to James Wilson, November 9, 1756, in, Crosfield, *Memoirs*, 282–83; Catherine Phillips, *Memoirs*, 101, 70.

10. Woolman, *Journal of the Life, Gospel Labors and Christian Experiences, of . . . John Woolman*, in William Evans and Thomas Evans, *Friends' Library*, 4: 345–47; Worrall,

Friendly Virginians, 145–51; Beeth, "Outside Agitators," 422–27. See also Weeks, *Southern Quakers*, 199–201; and Gary, "Economic and Political Relations," 185–87, 218–19.

11. The origins of Quakers' antislavery efforts has sparked a lively scholarly debate focused on the relative weight and interaction of economic interests and religious doctrine; see Soderlund, *Quakers and Slavery*, 112–77; Frost, "Origins"; and Nash, "Slaves and Slaveholders," 253–54. For an interpretation that emphasizes ideology, see Marietta, *Reformation*. For one scholar's evolving response to the question, see David Brion Davis, *Problem of Slavery in Western Culture*, 291–332, 483–93; David Brion Davis, *Problem of Slavery in Revolution*, 213–54; and David Brion Davis, *Inhuman Bondage*, 126–27, 230–49, 256. See also Drake, *Quakers and Slavery*, 48–84; Tolles, *Meeting House*, 24–28, 234–39; and James, *People among Peoples*, 1–2, 103–68, 216–39. For forums on this issue in *Quaker History* and *The Southern Friend*, see Marietta, "Egoism and Altruism"; Soderlund, "On Quakers and Slavery"; Beeth, "Historiographical Developments"; White, "Quaker Historiography"; Soderlund, "Response"; Chu, "Recent Developments"; and Beeth, "Methodology."

12. Soderlund, *Quakers and Slavery*, 98–103; Drake, *Quakers and Slavery*, 48–84. The NEYM disowned slaveholders after 1774; New York Friends followed suit in 1776. The Baltimore, North Carolina, and Virginia Yearly Meetings testified "their disunion" with slaveholders in 1778, 1781, and 1784, respectively, though the Virginia meeting did not make slaveholding a disownable offense until 1788.

13. Gary, "Economic and Political Relations," 191; Worrall, *Friendly Virginians*, 152, 229–30. On the growing enslaved population of northern Virginia, see Crothers, "Projecting Spirit," 36–37, 54.

14. FMM minutes, June 26, July 31, 1762, October 25, November 22, December 27, 1777, February 28, March 28, April 25, May 23, 1778 (Taylor); August 27, 1774 (statement against slavery); July 25, 1778 (lack of progress), FHL.

15. Hening, *Statutes*, 4: 132, 6: 112; VYM minutes, June 1770, MHR; Catherine Phillips, *Memoirs*, 70; Pleasants to Joseph Lewis, July 29, 1778, Pleasants Letterbook, MHR.

16. VYM minutes, June 1772, MHR; Worrall, *Friendly Virginians*, 225; Albert, "Protean Institution," 168; Weeks, *Southern Quakers*, 204–206; Henry to Pleasants, January 18, 1773, in Brookes, *Friend Anthony Benezet*, 443–45. See also Pleasants to Robert Bolling, January 10, 1775, Pleasants Letterbook, MHR.

17. Lee, *Extract from an Address*, 1; *VG*, July 18, 1771 (Associator Humanus), August 4, 1774; Wolf, *Race and Liberty*, 1–38; Albert, "Protean Institution," 116–20, 165, 178–82.

18. Benezet, *Caution and Warning*; Benezet to Robert Pleasants, April 8, 1773, in Brookes, *Friend Anthony Benezet*, 301; Wolf, *Race and Liberty*, 12.

19. PYM pronouncements, January 5, 24, 1775, January 20, December 20, 1776, in Gilpin, *Exiles in Virginia*, 282–93; see also, *VG*, March 2, 1775. Samuel Adams, in Mekeel, *Relation of Quakers*, 93–96, 136–40 (quotation 138); and Peter Brock, *Pioneers*, 144–47.

20. Paine, in Foner, ed., *Thomas Paine*, 54–59.

21. PYM testimony, October 4, 1777, and Sullivan to Congress, August 25, 1777, in Gilpin, *Exiles in Virginia*, 57–59, 61–62, 299; Sullivan to John Hancock, August 24, 1777, in Mekeel, *Relation of Quakers*, 173–74; Pendleton to William Woodford, September 13, 1777, in Mays, ed., *Letters of Edmund Pendleton* 1: 223; *VG*, November 14, 1777.

22. Lee to Patrick Henry, September 18, 1777, in Paul H. Smith, Gephart, Gawalt, Plakas, and Sheridan, eds., *Letters of Delegates to Congress*, 7: 637 ("we are a multitude";

my thanks to Jane E. Calvert for citation); Benezet to James Pemberton, January 28, 1778, in Brookes, *Friend Anthony Benezet*, 326–27; Marietta, *Reformation*, 251–79.

23. Mekeel, *Relation of Quakers*, 162–63; Peter Brock, *Pioneers*, 147–48, 189–90; PMS, December 20, 1776, in Gilpin, *Exiles in Virginia*, 291–93.

24. Pemberton, *Life . . . of John Pemberton*, in William Evans and Thomas Evans, *Friends' Library*, 6: 293, 288–89; John Smith to John Hancock, October 1, 1777, in Gilpin, *Exiles in Virginia*, 163. On Isaac Zane, see Moss, "Isaac Zane." On the Virginia exiles, see Gilpin, *Exiles in Virginia*; Oaks, "Philadelphians in Exile"; and Mekeel, *Relation of Quakers*, 173–88.

25. Pemberton, *Life . . . of John Pemberton*, in William Evans and Thomas Evans, *Friends' Library*, 6: 293; Gilpin, *Exiles in Virginia*, 172.

26. Smith to Hancock, October 1, 1777, in Gilpin, *Exiles in Virginia*, 163; Drinker to Elizabeth Drinker, October 4, 14, 17, 23, November 4, and December 10, 1777, in Henry Drinker Letters, HCQC.

27. Longenecker, *Shenandoah Religion*, 53; Stabler to Israel Pemberton, May 16, 1775, Pemberton Papers, HSP; *VG*, February 11, 1775; Henrico Quarterly Meeting, February 2, 1775, in Mekeel, *Relation of Quakers*, 103.

28. Holton, *Forced Founders*, 85–88, 175–84; McDonnell, "Popular Mobilization"; and "Class War?" On the social tensions in Revolutionary Virginia, see Isaac, *Transformation of Virginia*; Isaac, *Landon Carter*; Breen, *Tobacco Culture*; Kathleen Brown, *Good Wives*; and Kulikoff, *Tobacco and Slaves*. On black unrest, see Frey, *Water from the Rock*, 53–56, 63–64, 143–71; and Quarles, *Negro in American Revolution*, 19–32, 115–19, 111–33, 140–42. On prisoners in the Shenandoah Valley, see Miles, "Winchester Hessian Barracks"; and Knepper, "Convention Army," 137–266.

29. Holton, *Forced Founders*, 175–88 (Morlan quotation 181); McDonnell, "Popular Mobilization," 970; Bliss, "Rise of Tenancy."

30. Hening, *Statutes*, 8: 242; 9: 34, 139; "Narrative of the Sufferings of Members of the HMM," August 2, 1778, and "Narrative of . . . the Sufferings of Members of the FMM," August 25, 1779, PMS, Misc. Papers, FHL; George Crosfield Sr. to George Crosfield Jr., 1778, in Crosfield, *Memoirs*, 289.

31. Hening, *Statutes*, 9: 345; 10: 261–62, 314–15, 334–35, 360–61, 417–18; FMM minutes, December 27, 1777, and HMM minutes, January 5, 1778, FHL. For financial losses, see "An Account of Sufferings in the FMM," August 28, 1779; "An Account of Friends Sufferings in Loudoun County," May 26, 1781; "An Account of the Sufferings of Friends Belonging to FMM," August 25, 1781; "An Account of the Sufferings of Friends Belonging to the FMM," February 23, 1782; "An Account of Friends Sufferings Belonging to . . . HMM," September 3, 1781; and "An Account of Friends Sufferings Belonging to HMM," May 30, 1782, in PMS, Misc. Papers, FHL.

32. "Account of Sufferings in the FMM," August 28, 1779, PMS, Misc. Papers; and "Account of the Sufferings of Friends at FMM," September 21, 1780, PMS, Minute Book, both FHL.

33. McDonnell, "Popular Mobilization," 974–81; McDonnell, "Class War?" 337–39; Van Meter to Thomas Jefferson, April 11, 14, 20, June 16, 1781, Van Meter to Thomas Nelson, July 28, 1781, and Peter Hog to Thomas Nelson, August 2, 1781, in Palmer, McRae, Colston, and

Flournoy, eds., *CVSP*, 2: 28–29, 40–41, 58–59, 163–64, 262–63, 284–85. See also Eckenrode, *Revolution in Virginia*, 246–48; and Graham, *Life of General Daniel Morgan*, 378–81.

34. Morgan to GW, November 25, 1781, GW Papers, American Memory, LC; Morgan to Harrison, December 11, 1781, in Palmer, McRae, Colston, and Flournoy, *CVSP*, 2: 646–47; Miles, "Hessian Barracks"; and Barton, "Revolutionary Prisoners of War," 41–42.

35. Smith to John Hancock, October 1, 1777, in Gilpin, *Exiles in Virginia*, 163.

36. For this and previous paragraph, see "Account of Sufferings in the FMM," August 28, 1779; "Account of Friends Sufferings in Loudoun County," May 26, 1781; "Account of the Sufferings of Friends Belonging to FMM," August 25, 1781; "Account of the Sufferings of Friends Belonging to the FMM," February 23, 1782; "Account of Friends Sufferings Belonging to . . . HMM," September 3, 1781; and "Account of Friends Sufferings Belonging to HMM," May 30, 1782, all in PMS, Misc. Papers, FHL; Kercheval, *History of Valley*, 148. According to McDonnell, *Politics of War*, 415–16, Loudoun County officials arrested and fined "approximately 125" Friends for refusal to serve in the military.

37. HMM and FMM minutes, 1775–1783, passim, FHL; *VG*, June 16, 1775; Mekeel, *Relation of Quakers*, 131–32, 283–93; Worrall, *Friendly Virginians*, 194–96, 203.

38. Mekeel, *Relation of Quakers*, 192, 266; Peter Brock, *Pioneers*, 167–69, 171–72.

39. Epistle of Virginia Friends to PMS, December 22, 1775; Epistle of the PMS to the VYM, March 25, 1776, in PMS Minute Book; Letter from the VYM and FMM Regarding the Payment of War Taxes and Use of Continental Currency, December 22, 1775, PMS Misc. Papers; and FMM minutes, May 22, 1784, February 27, 1779, all in FHL; Worrall, *Friendly Virginians*, 196, 217–18; Peter Brock, *Pioneers*, 168–69, 172–73; Mekeel, *Relation of Quakers*, 150–51, 192; Pleasants, in Archer, "Quaker's Attitude," 179.

40. Peter Brock, *Pioneers*, 162–64; Mekeel, *Relation of Quakers*, 189–90, 193, 271–72, 336; Hening, *Statutes*, 9: 281–83, 351, 549; WFQM minutes, June 22, 1778; and FMM minutes, March 23, 1782, FHL.

41. HMM minutes, September 4, 1780–November 3, 1783, passim; FMM minutes, March 27, 1779–February 22, 1783, passim, both FHL.

42. Mifflin, *Defense of Warner Mifflin*, 17; Peter Brock, *Pioneers*, 212; FMM minutes, March 25, 1775–September 28, 1782, passim, FHL.

43. Albert, "Protean Institution," 171–73; Quaker Petition, November 29, 1780, Early Virginia Religious Petitions, LC; Virginia General Assembly, House of Delegates, *Journal* (1780), 32, 38; Pleasants to Benezet, February 1781, in Brookes, *Friend Anthony Benezet*, 437 (quotation).

44. Frey, *Water from the Rock*, 53–56, 63–64, 68, 143–71, 222n22; Jefferson to Alexander McCaul, April 19, 1786, in Jefferson Papers, American Memory, LC; Boucher, *Reminiscences*, 134. See also Holton, *Forced Founders*, 133–63. On Jefferson's numbers, see Pybus, "Jefferson's Faulty Math."

45. Quaker Petition, May 29, 1782, Early Virginia Religious Petitions, LC; David Brion Davis, *Problem of Slavery in Revolution*, 197; Hening, *Statutes*, 11: 39–41; Wolf, *Race and Liberty*, 32–35. See also Albert, "Protean Institution," 210–65; and Schmidt and Wilhelm, "Early Proslavery Petitions." For the 1806 law, see Shepherd, ed., *Statutes 1792–1806*, 3: 251–53.

46. Beeth, "Outside Agitators," 426–31; Weeks, *Southern Quakers*, 212–13; FMM minutes, June 26, 1782–June 7, 1801, passim (fourteen individuals); FQM minutes, December

18, 1797, March 9, October 15, 1798, FHL; Janney and Janney, *Ye Meetg Hous Smal*, 61 (Nichols).

47. James, "Impact of Revolution," 369–77. On most evangelicals' abandonment of antislavery, see Heyrman, *Southern Cross*; Spangler, *Virginians Reborn*; Mathews, *Slavery and Methodism*, 3–61; and Essig, *Bonds of Wickedness*.

48. Pemberton, *Life . . . of John Pemberton*, in William Evans and Thomas Evans, *Friends' Library*, 6: 294; HF, *Hopewell Friends History*, 123–24; SMJ, *History*, 3: 440–41.

49. Savery, *Journal of the Life . . . of William Savery*, in William Evans and Thomas Evans, *Friends' Library*, 1: 354, 363–66; HF, *Hopewell Friends History*, 124; BYM minutes, October 12–16, 1795, October 28–30, 1833, FHL; Gerald Hopkins, *Mission*, 6 (quotation), 121–98; Swatzler, *Friend among the Senecas*, 135–37. On Northwest Indian Removal, see Bowes, *Exiles and Pioneers*.

50. Mekeel, *Relation of Quakers*, 294–313; *VG*, April 13, 1776; FMM minutes, March 25, 1775–September 28, 1782, passim, FHL; Thorne, "North Carolina Friends," 339 (quotation).

51. James, "Impact of Revolution," 377–82.

52. Pitch, *Burning of Washington*.

53. Capture of the City of Washington, Doc. No. 13: Report from the Corporation of Alexandria, in *ASP: Military Affairs*, 1: 589–96; *AG*, September 8, 1814. For Dick, see SMJ, *Memoirs*, 10–11; and AMM minutes, February 12, 1812, FHL.

54. For press attacks, see *NI*, September 1, 1814; *Richmond Enquirer*, August 31, September 14, 1814; *AG*, September 8, 13, 15, 17, 1814; and Skivora, "Surrender of Alexandria." William Stabler, *Memoir of Life of Edward Stabler*, 55–56; Janney to Micajah Crew, September 28, 1814, in Worrall, *Friendly Virginians*, 314; AMM minutes, August 25, 1814, FHL.

55. H. Clay to R. King, May 10, 1825, in *ASP: Foreign Relations*, 6: 342; Cassell, "Slaves of the Chesapeake Bay"; George, "Mirage of Freedom"; and Whitfield, *Blacks on the Border*, 32, 37.

56. Frederick County Petitions, November 11, 1796 (ten), December 8, 1797; Shenandoah County Petitions, November 11, 21, 1796; Berkeley County Petitions, November 9, 1796, all in Early Virginia Religious Petitions, American Memory, LC; VYM and Bates, *Memorial of . . . Friends*, 5–7. See also *FR*, May 31, 1813; *NWR*, February 25, 1815, November 30, 1816; and Peter Brock, *Pioneers*, 221–23.

57. BMS minutes, February 2, 1811, February 1, October 12, 1812, FHL.

58. Hinshaw, *Encyclopedia*, 6: 127; Taylor to James Barbour, March 21, 1813, in Palmer, McRae, Colston, and Flournoy, *CVSP*, 10: 211; BMS minutes, February 4, 1815, FHL; Epistle from the FQM to GMM, February 20, 1815, SMJ Manuscripts, FHL.

59. Report of Gov. James Barbour to the Council of State, May 12, 1812, Burwell to Barbour, March 30, 1813, George to Barbour, April 9, 1813, Greenhow to Barbour, September 8, 1813, and Brent to Barbour, February 11, 1814, in Palmer, McRae, Colston, and Flournoy, *CVSP*, 10: 137, 217, 223, 234, 279, 300; Proclamation of Vice Admiral Alexander Cockburn, April 1814, in Weiss, "Corps of Colonial Marines," 89n6.

60. Robert B. Taylor to Barbour, June 27, 1813, Palmer, McRae, Colston, and Flournoy, *CVSP*, 10: 234; Robert Barrie to John Borlase Warren, November 14, 1813, and Proclamation of Vice Admiral Alexander Cockburn, April 2, 1814, in Weiss, "Corps of Colonial Marines," 89n5–6.

61. Carver Willis to James Barbour, May 21, 1812, in Palmer, McRae, Colston, and Flournoy, *CVSP*, 10: 147; John Taylor, *Arator*, 127. On Quakers' Federalist sympathies, see David Brion Davis, *Problem of Slavery in Revolution*, 326.

62. HF, *Hopewell Friends History*, 516–18; GMM minutes, October 5, 1812, September 30, 1813, March 30, April 27, 1815; FMM minutes, April 28, June 2, 1813, June 29, November 2, 1814, February 1, December 27, 1815, FHL; Gregg to James Barbour, May 18, 1814, Palmer, McRae, Colston, and Flournoy, *CVSP*, 10: 331–32; Worrall, *Friendly Virginians*, 283. A gap exists in the minutes of BMS between November 6, 1813 and February 4, 1815, and local meetings supplied no documentation about Friends who made "indirect payment of fines or other military demands."

63. *Meade v. Deputy Marshall of Virginia District* (circa May 1, 1815), in Johnson, Cullen, and Hobson, eds., *Papers of John Marshall*, 8: 85–89; *FR*, June 2, 1815; Smith to Jacob Smith, May 16, July 2, August 6, 1815, April 15, 1817, in Clarence Smith Papers, IHS.

64. AMM minutes, August 3, 1815, FHL; Secretary of War John Armstrong, in Green, *Washington*, 60; Margaret Bayard Smith to Jane Kirkpatrick, July 20, 1813, in Hunt, *First Forty Years*, 90–91; John W. Epes to James Barbour, July 17, 1813, in Palmer, McRae, Colston, and Flournoy, *CVSP*, 10: 261; *AG*, July 30, August 9, 11, 1814.

65. Report from the Corporation of Alexandria, *ASP: Military Affairs*, 1: 592; *AG*, November 4, 1813, January 20, August 18, 1814; AMM minutes, December 23, 1813, FHL.

66. AMM minutes, July 21, 1814, FHL; Worrall, *Friendly Virginians*, 283.

67. Report from the Corporation of Alexandria, *ASP: Military Affairs*, 1: 592; *AG*, September 8, 1814; *GUE*, December 23, 1826; Thomas Prosser to James Barbour, August 29, 1814, Palmer, McRae, Colston, and Flournoy, *CVSP*, 10: 379–80. Data on slave escapes from Alexandria provided by John McNish Weiss, personal correspondence, September 13, 2007.

Chapter 3. The "Worldly Cares and Business" of Friends

1. *AG*, January 29, February 2, 1827; *AA*, February 14, 1803, March 7, 1804, January 21, 1806. See also T. Michael Miller, *Artisans and Merchants*, 1: 226–27, 2: 344; T. Michael Miller, *Portrait*, 12, 185.

2. Hinshaw, *Encyclopedia*, 6: 752; FMM minutes, March 24, April 23, July 28, 1798, AMM minutes, December 26, 1816, February 20, 1817, FHL.

3. Crothers, "Projecting Spirit"; Wolf, *Race and Liberty*, 1–84; Albert, "Protean Institution," 116–209. Hinshaw, *Encyclopedia*, 6: 589, 609–14, 725–28; Gragg, *Migration*, 25–45.

4. GW to Arthur Young, August 6, 1786, November 1, 1787, in GW, *Letters*, 8, 11–12 (quotation); Strickland, *Observations*, 45–52; Hodgson to Samuel Thorp, October 4, 1803, Hodgson Letterbook, LV; Crothers, "Projecting Spirit," 58–102, 468–89. See also Lewis Cecil Gray, *History of Agriculture*, 2: 606–609; Craven, *Soil Exhaustion*, 66–108; Clemens, *Atlantic Economy*, 168–205.

5. Crothers, "Projecting Spirit," 58–102, 232–309; Hirschman, *Strategy*, 98–119; Carville Earle and Ronald Hoffman, "Staple Crops"; Coxe, *View of United States*, 303.

6. Crothers, "Projecting Spirit," 103–67.

7. Ibid., 168–231; Hills, "Origins of West End," 109 (quotation).

8. Sketch of Hartshorne's life based on *AG*, 1784–1816, passim; *AA*, 1797–1806, passim; T. Michael Miller, *Artisans and Merchants*, 1: xxiii-xxvi, 191–93; Hinshaw, *Encyclopedia*,

6: 503, 746–47; FMM minutes, March 27, 1779, February 22, 1783, May 26, 1792; AMM minutes, April 26, July 26, 1810, FHL.

9. Costantino, *Quaker of the Olden Time*; T. Michael Miller, *Artisans and Merchants*, 1: xxvi–xxix, 2: 184–85; FMM minutes, July 24, October 23, 1779, February 24, 1781, September 28, November 23, 1793, FHL; Hinshaw, *Encyclopedia*, 6: 573.

10. Crothers, "Projecting Spirit," 135–37, 202–19, 490–515; Hinshaw, *Encyclopedia*, 6: 364, 511, 521, 530, 560, 573, 668; *AG*, March 31, 1827; Fairfax Harrison, *Landmarks of Old Prince William*, 2: 564–65, 577 (quotation). See also George Rogers Taylor, *Transportation Revolution*, 27–28.

11. Daniel Janney to N. F. Cabell, January 2, 1854, Yardley Taylor to N. F. Cabell, January 11, 1854, Nathaniel Francis Cabell Papers, LV; Binns, *Treatise*; Janney and Janney, "Israel Janney's 'Ledger B,'" Folio Y (1), and 255, VHS; Phineas Janney to David Lupton, January 18, 1805, Lupton Family Papers, VHS. See also True, "John Binns," 36–38; and Poland, *Frontier to Suburbia*, 76n29, 76n32, 90–91.

12. Janney and Janney, "Israel Janney's 'Ledger B,'" Folio Y (1), 255, VHS; Redd, *Late Discovery*; Hinshaw, *Encyclopedia*, 6: 435.

13. Taylor to N. F. Cabell, January 11, 1854, in Cabell Papers, LV; Chester Clark to Lupton, November 6, 1830, and John Weaver to Lupton, July 24, 1834, Lupton Family Papers, VHS; Cartmell, *Shenandoah Valley Pioneers*, 453. See also Lewis Cecil Gray, *History of Agriculture*, 2: 792–800.

14. Craven, *Soil Exhaustion*; Lewis Cecil Gray, *History of Agriculture*, 2: 909–15; Lynn Nelson, *Pharsalia*, 51–68; Janney and Janney, *John Janney's Virginia*, 16, 72; Yardley Taylor, *Memoir of Loudoun*, 21–22.

15. Crothers, "Banks and Economic Development"; Crothers, "Commercial Risk"; T. Michael Miller, *Artisans and Merchants*, 1: 19–21, 320–21; and T. Michael Miller, *Portrait*, 20–22, 238–39.

16. *AG*, May 19, 23–26, 1815, May 20, 1816; T. Michael Miller, *Artisans and Merchants*, 1: 311, 332, 2: 100; AMM minutes, January 22, February 26, August 20, September 24, 1818, June 24, July 22, September 23, November 25, 1819, FHL.

17. Fox, in Rhoads, *Business Ethics*, 3; Walvin, *Quakers*, 29–79 (1688 quotation 32); Frost, *Quaker Family*, 196–206; *AG*, February 13, 1827. See also Raistrick, *Quakers in Science*; Tolles, *Meeting House*; and Windsor, *Quaker Enterprise*.

18. BYM, *Discipline of Yearly Meeting 1806*, 106–11, BYM, *Rules of Discipline 1844*, 89–94.

19. FMM minutes, January 22, March 26, May 28, 1785, November 24, 1787, January 26, 1788, FHL.

20. Judge, *Memoirs*, 312–13; FMM minutes, December 27, 1788, May 23, June 27, November 24, 1789, April 28, 1792, May 5, 1805, April 26, 1806, FHL; BYM, *Discipline of Yearly Meeting 1806*, 11–15; BYM, *Rules of Discipline 1844*, 9–13.

21. BYM, *Discipline of Yearly Meeting 1806*, 39–41, BYM, *Rules of Discipline 1844*, 91; FMM minutes, January 24, February 23, April 7, July 25, August 22, 1789, FHL.

22. *AG*, January 30, 1800; *AA*, March 5, 1801; *Times* (Alexandria), March 6, 1801; Hartshorne to Thomas Massie, March 10, 1801, Massie Family Papers, VHS; Phineas Janney to David Lupton, June 21, 180[?], Lupton Family Papers, VHS.

23. AMM minutes, April 26, July 26, 1810, FHL; Riddle to Hartshorne Jr., [March] 1801, Joseph Riddle Letterbook, LV; T. Michael Miller, *Artisans and Merchants*, 1: 21, 320.

24. T. Michael Miller, *Artisans and Merchants*, 1: 234, 2: 43–44; *AA*, September 13, 1804; *AG*, May 27, 1809; Hinshaw, *Encyclopedia*, 6: 518, 754; AMM minutes, October 21, 1809, November 26, 1810, FHL.

25. *AG*, June 30, November 24, 1809, May 16, 1810, May 28, 1811, June 1, 1812, June 21, 1819; AMM minutes, October 26, December 21, 1809; FMM minutes, May 30, 1810, FHL; Hinshaw, *Encyclopedia*, 6: 754.

26. BYM, *Discipline of Yearly Meeting 1806*, 41–54; Levy, "Tender Plants"; Frost, *Quaker Family*, 150–86 (quotation 158). On Quaker family networks, see Walvin, *Quakers*; Tolles, *Meeting House*, 119–21; Levy, *Quakers and the American Family*, 96–100, 153–89, 236–48; and Price, "Great Quaker Business Families," in Dunn and Dunn, *World of Penn*, 363–99.

27. Hinshaw, *Encyclopedia*, 6: 264, 415–16, 507, 746–47, 757–58; Janney to Lupton, January 18, 1805, May 27, 1815, Lupton Family Papers, VHS; HF, *Hopewell Friends History*, 170–71, 265, 295; *VC*, June 10, 1789.

28. Costantino, *Quaker of the Olden Time*, 33; Janney and Janney, "Israel Janney's 'Ledger B,'" vi, VHS; Hinshaw, *Encyclopedia*, 6: 499–500, 660–61.

29. Hinshaw, *Encyclopedia*, 6: 661–63.

30. SMJ, *Memoirs*, 1–52; Hinshaw, *Encyclopedia*, 6: 758, 472, 731; *AG*, September 15, 1827.

31. SMJ, *Memoirs*, 1–52; SMJ to Phineas Janney, September 17, [1842]; SMJ, "Memoir of Phineas Janney, 1852," both in SMJ Papers, LV.

32. Jacob Janney to Mary Janney, November 24, 1832, FHL; Hinshaw, *Encyclopedia*, 6: 651, 749, 756; T. Michael Miller, *Portrait*, 189–90.

33. Frost, *Quaker Family*, 203–204; Raistrick, *Quakers in Science*, 45–46; Walvin, *Quakers*, 69; Drinker to Cope, May 26, 1793, July 18, 1805, in Cope-Evans Family Papers, HCQC; Hinshaw, *Encyclopedia*, 6: 738, 766.

34. Fisher to Lupton, January 28, July 23, 1807, November 6, 1809; and Lupton to Fisher, October 13, 1809, in Lupton Family Papers, VHS.

35. Janney to Lupton, August 10, 1804, Lupton (Bond) Family Papers, FHL.

36. BYM minutes, 1821, 1823–24, 1826, 1829, 1832, 1836, 1839, 1842–43, 1845–47, FHL; Wright to Lupton, July 17, 1820, Lupton Family Papers, VHS; Seth Smith to Jacob Smith, September 10, 1823, Clarence Smith Papers, IHS.

37. William Stabler, *Memoir of Life of Edward Stabler*, 13–20; Hinshaw, *Encyclopedia*, 6: 510–12.

38. William Stabler, *Memoir of Life of Edward Stabler*, 20–29; T. Michael Miller, *Artisans and Merchants*, 1: 54; Hinshaw, *Encyclopedia*, 6: 479, 735.

39. William Stabler, *Memoir of Life of Edward Stabler*, 39, 42, 44–45, 63, 82, 89–90, *AG*, March 1, 27, 1819, January 7, 1840.

40. T. Michael Miller, *Artisans and Merchants*, 1: xix; *AG*, November 17, 1841; Historical Census Browser, UV. In 1810, 80,353 people lived in the region (excluding Alexandria); in 1830, just 80,634 did so. Including Alexandria, the figures rise to 87,580 in 1810 and 90,400 in 1830.

41. Peterson, "Alexandria Market"; Galpin, "Grain Trade," 424–26; T. Michael Miller,

Portrait, ix, xv-xvii; Lupton to David Lupton, April 23, 1819, Lupton Papers, FHL; Royall, *Sketches*, 106, 111; *AG*, January 23, October 1, 1827, February 29, 1840.

42. Crothers, "Projecting Spirit," 146–52; Littlefield, "Potomac Company"; Sanderlin, *Great National Project*, 45–60; *AG*, October 3, November 13, 1827, September 23, 29, 1840, March 24, 1845; Historical Census Browser, UV; Browne, *Baltimore*.

43. Browne, *Baltimore*, 141–42, 152, 154; and John Lauritz Larson, *Internal Improvements*, 90–91, 230–33; *AG*, February 4, 1840, August 16, 1842; Jonah Lupton Receipt, August 3, 1831, Joel Lupton Receipt, July 22, 1831, Charles A. Gambrill to Nathan Lupton, January 28, 1843, in Lupton Family Papers, VHS; and Orndorff and Co. to Nathan Lupton, November 26, 1842, Lupton Papers, FHL; Seth Smith to Jacob Smith, September 28, 1842, April 21, 1843, in Clarence Smith Papers, IHS.

44. On Virginia's antebellum agricultural stagnation, see Craven, *Soil Exhaustion*; Lewis Cecil Gray, *Agriculture*, 2: 909–915; Lynn Nelson, *Pharsalia*, 51–68; Stevenson, *Life in Black and White*, 25–29, 175–86. On the economic impact of slavery, see *AG*, May 22, 1827; Genovese, *Political Economy*; and Fields, *Slavery and Freedom*. On migration, see Lynch, "Westward Flow"; Schwarz, *Migrants*, 7–11; Philyaw, *Virginia's Western Visions*, 121–47; and Fischer and Kelly, *Bound Away*, 202–11. For regional crop blights, see *GL* (Leesburg), May 20, 1817; *AH*, June 28, 1819; and *AG*, June 2, 1827, April 8, 1840. For declining land values, see Elisha Fulton to Jacob Smith, April 15, 1821; and Seth Smith to Jacob Smith, July 6, August 25, 1824, December 22, 1826, March 3, 18, 1827, in Clarence Smith Papers, IHS.

45. T. Michael Miller, *Artisans and Merchants*, 1: 54; T. Michael Miller, *Portrait*, 47–48; Hinshaw, *Encyclopedia*, 6: 735, 774; AMM minutes, June 22, August 24, December 28, 1837, January 18, February 22, 1838, FHL; *AG*, September 29, 1827.

46. FMM minutes, August 28, October 2, 30, 1811, January 29, February 26, April 29, 1812, January 27, 1813, FHL. A fulling mill cleaned, shrank, and thickened cloth.

47. FMM minutes, February 2, March 30, 1814.

48. Seth Smith to Jacob Smith, February 28, 1810, April 16, May 16, July 2, August 6, 1815, in Clarence Smith Papers, IHS; GMM minutes, March 30, August 3, 30, November 2, 30, 1815, FHL.

49. Seth Smith to Jacob Smith, November 13, 1822, April 16, 28, September 10, 1823, in Clarence Smith Papers, IHS.

50. Seth Smith to Jacob Smith, October 8, 1823, November 10, 1824, June 12, 1825, May 18, 1826, in Clarence Smith Papers, IHS; GMM minutes, November 11, 1824, January 13, March 17, May 12, June 16, July 14, October 13, 1825, March 16, 1826; FQM minutes, February 21, 1825, February 20, 1826; and Jacob Janney to Mary Janney, November 24, 1832, all in FHL.

51. Gragg, *Migration*, 41, 93–94; Weeks, *Southern Quakers*, 269, 272–73; Hinshaw, *Encyclopedia*, 6: 589; CMM minutes, December 1, 1798, March 1, 1800, May 2, 1801, November 30, 1805, August 2, 1806, FHL.

52. Specht, "Mixed Blessing," 50–51, 146n82, 206–24; HF, *Hopewell Friends History*, 436–49; Worrall, *Friendly Virginians*, 263–71 (quotation 267).

53. Meetings discontinued between 1790 and 1830: Back Creek, Smith's Creek, Lower Ridge, Middle Ridge, and Mount Pleasant (Frederick County); Mill Creek and Bullskin (Berkeley County); Gap (or Potts) and Leesburg (Loudoun County); Southland and Culpepper (Culpepper County); and Stafford (Stafford County). See T. Chalkley Matlack

Quakeriana (1934), books 15, 17, 19, HCQC. FMM minutes, June 11, 1823, January 14, March 10, August 11, November 10, 1824, January 12, February 12, 1825, November 15, December 25, 1826, FHL.

54. FMM minutes, April 11, August 11, 1824, September 10, November 12, 1834, October 14, 1835 (Holmes), FHL.

55. BH, *Autobiography*, 129; Seale, *Alexandria Library Company,* 1–17; *AG*, February 5, 1821.

56. *AG*, January 18, 1827, July 31, 1840. On female Quaker dress, see Caton, "Aesthetics of Absence," in Lapsansky and Verplanck, *Quaker Aesthetics.*

57. HF, *Hopewell Friends History*, 330; HMM minutes, November 7, 1811, February 6, March 5, 1812, FHL. Depositions of Wm. S. Compton, Margaret Lupton (nee Compton), and Mary Gallagher, n.d.; Deposition of Margaret Lupton, March 27, 1824; Depositions of Ruth Thomas, Barbara Hutzlars, Thomas Clark, and Mary Light, November 6, 1824; and Barton and Williams Petition to Frederick County Superior Court in Case of *Hoge, et al. v Nathan Lupton, et al.*, n.d. [c. 1842], all in Lupton Family Papers, VHS.

58. Comly, *Journal*, 451, 454–55.

59. Thomas Massie to William Hartshorne, April 24, 1808, Massie Family Papers, VHS. On the Massie family, see Lynn Nelson, *Pharsalia.* Schooley, ed., *Journal of William Schooley*, 12.

60. Schooley, *Journal of William Schooley*, 13–14, 58; Brooke to Sarah Janney, n.d. [c. 1790], and Churchman to Mahlon Janney, November 9, 1798, in Janney Family Papers, FHL.

61. Joel Brown to Eliza Cowgill, December 31, 1839, Walker-Conard-Cowgill Family Papers, FHL; Janney to Seth Smith, July 17, 1846, Clarence Smith Papers, IHS.

Chapter 4. Embracing "the Oppressor as Well as the Oppressed": Quaker Antislavery before 1830

1. *AG*, April 30, May 28, 1827. The other articles appeared on May 7, 14, 22, June 22, 27, 30, July 4, 10, 21, 1827. For SMJ's authorship, see SMJ to Phineas Janney, December 25, 1844, SMJ Manuscripts, FHL.

2. See Frost, *Quaker Family*, 10–63; Ingle, *Quakers in Conflict*, 3–61; and Hamm, *Transformation*, 2–3, 122–24.

3. Ira Berlin, *Many Thousands*, 7–14, 105–108. See also Einhorn, *American Taxation*, esp. 6.

4. See Wolf, *Race and Liberty.*

5. Pleasants to John Michie, December 4, 1787, to Charles Carter, August 17, 1790, to Robert Carter, October 8, 1791, to GW, December 11, 1785, to James Madison, June 6, 1791, to Thomas Jefferson, June 1, 1796, February 8, 1797, and to St. George Tucker, May 30, 1797, in Pleasants Letterbook, MHR. See also Worrall, *Friendly Virginians*, 227–28, 243–44; McColley, *Slavery*, 156–59; David Brion Davis, *Problem of Slavery in Revolution*, 196–97; and Albert, "Protean Institution," 176–78. For antislavery among Baptists, see Scully, *Religion*, 109–19.

6. Minutes of the Third Convention of Abolition Societies [1796], in American Convention *Minutes*, 1: 72; Johnston, "Antislavery Petitions," 671–73. See also Albert, "Protean Institution," 176–79.

7. Quaker Petition to the Continental Congress, October 4, 1783, in Bruns, *Am I Not a Man*, 493–501; Worrall, *Friendly Virginians*, 237–38, 240–42; Drake, *Quakers and Slavery*, 92–95, 100–13; Knee, "Quaker Petition"; GW to David Stuart, March 28, 1790, in Fitzpatrick, *Writings of GW*, 31: 30. See also Jordan, *White over Black*, 325–35; Boller, "Washington, the Quakers," 85–88; and Boller, "George Washington," 78–79.

8. *AG*, December 9, 1790, January 2, February 17, 1791. For a contrary view, see ibid., February 10, 1791.

9. *AG*, May 12, November 17, February 10, 1791, February 9, November 8, 1792.

10. Archibald McClean to William Rogers, February 15, 1796, PAS, reel 11, HSP; *AG*, April 12, 16, 1796; *AA*, August 29, 1797. See also Jordan, *White over Black*, 359–60; and David Brion Davis, *Problem of Slavery in Revolution*, 196–99, 209–10, 213–32.

11. McClean to William Rogers, February 15, June 6, 1796, PAS, reel 11, HSP; Shepherd, *Statutes 1792–1806*, 1: 363–64; McColley, *Slavery*, 159–61. On "Quaker lawyers," see HF, *Hopewell Friends History*, 182.

12. *AG*, May 5, 1796; Petition of the Alexandria Abolition Society to the Virginia Assembly, 1796, in Netherton and others, *Fairfax County*, 210–11; Shepherd, *Statutes 1792–1806*, 2: 77–78; McColley, *Slavery*, 161.

13. Minutes of the Fourth Convention of Abolition Societies [1797], American Convention *Minutes*, 1: 132; *AG*, April 16, 1796; Hening, *Statutes*, 12: 182 (1785 law); Hinshaw, *Encyclopedia*, 6: 437; HF, *Hopewell Friends History*, 182; Thomas Harrison to Joseph Sexton, July 29, 1801, Sexton Family Papers, LV.

14. *AG*, June 9, 1796, February 23, 1797; *AA*, August 24, 1797, February 22, August 30, 1798, September 28, 1799, February 28, 1800, May 7, 29, November 27, 1801; Minutes of the Fourth Convention of Abolition Societies [1797], Minutes of the Fifth Convention of Abolition Societies [1798], American Convention *Minutes*, 1: 128–30, 133–36, 164.

15. Minutes of the Seventh Convention of Abolition Societies [1801], American Convention *Minutes*, 1: 240–43.

16. Egerton, *Gabriel's Rebellion*; McColley, *Slavery*, 107–13; Aptheker, *Slave Revolts*, 218–26, 235–39; Jordan, *White over Black*, 375–402; Shepherd, *Statutes 1792–1806*, 2: 279–80, 300–301, 326.

17. Egerton, *Gabriel's Rebellion*, 49, 51; Dick to James Monroe, September 26, 1800, in Palmer, McRae, Colston, and Flournoy, *CVSP*, 9: 178; *AA*, March 30, 1803; Minutes of the Seventh Convention of Abolition Societies [1801], American Convention *Minutes* 1: 240–43.

18. *AA*, May 29, 1801; Minutes of the Tenth Convention of Abolition Societies [1805], American Convention *Minutes*, 1: 371–76; Drinker to Joseph Bringhurst, December 10, 1804, PAS, reel 12, HSP; Drinker to Thomas P. Cope, July 18, 1805, Cope-Evans Family Papers, HCQC; Jordan, *White over Black*, 400, 320.

19. David Brion Davis, *Problem of Slavery in Revolution*, 207–208; "Notes on a Deputation to Congress," Diaries of John Parrish, HCQC; Gerald Hopkins, *Mission*, 34–35. See Schwarz, *Migrants*, 6, 81–84; Fischer and Kelly, *Bound Away*, 288–90; Weeks, *Southern Quakers*, 245–85; Worrall, *Friendly Virginians*, 265–71; Hamm, *Transformation*, 13–15.

20. Autobiographical Notes by William B. Walthall, LV; Benjamin W. Ladd to Elizabeth Ladd, May 14, [c. 1830], Ladd Family Papers, ECQC; Hubbs, *Memoir*, 111–12; SMJ to Rebecca Janney, September 13, 1851, SMJ Papers, LV; Hinshaw, *Encyclopedia*, 6: 589–608.

21. Lupton to Joel Lupton, May 15, 1836, Lupton (Bond) Family Papers, FHL; W. Jolliffe

to Eliza Cowgill, June 24, 1836, Pidgeon to Eliza Cowgill, August 17, 1836, E. Jolliffe to Eliza Cowgill, August 21, 1836, Walker-Conard-Cowgill Family Papers, FHL; Elizabeth [?] to James Emlen, February 4, 1832, Emlen Family Papers, FHL.

22. Benjamin Ladd to Elizabeth Ladd, c. 1830, Ladd Family Papers, ECQC; Abby A. Cope to Emma Cope, June 29, 1831, Cope Family Papers, FHL. See also Wolf, *Race and Liberty*, 196–229; Fischer and Kelly, *Bound Away*, 207–11; and Susan Dunn, *Dominion*, 31–60.

23. On quietism, see Rufus Jones, *Later Periods*, 1: 32–103; Hamm, *Quakers in America*, 29–30; and Frost, *Quaker Family*, 30–47. Pleasants to James Pemberton, June 19, 1790, and Pleasants to Samuel Bailey, July 23, 1790, Robert Pleasants Letterbook, MHR.

24. William Stabler, *Memoir of Life of Edward Stabler*; SMJ, *Memoirs*; and BH, *Autobiography*.

25. FMM minutes, March 27, 1779, February 22, 1783, April 24, 1802, FHL; Hinshaw, *Encyclopedia*, 6: 746. See Hartshorne's correspondence with Thomas Massie in the Massie Family Papers, VHS; and letters in the Hartshorne Family Papers, HCQC. William Lee to Samuel Thorp, April 15, 1793, William Lee Letterbook, VHS.

26. Crothers, "Projecting Spirit," 85–87, 134–36, 214–15, 490–515; Fairfax Harrison, *Landmarks of Old Prince William*, 2: 564–65.

27. Crothers, "Commercial Risk"; Insurance Policy No. 2157, Marine Insurance Company of Alexandria Insurance Policies, VHS; Drinker to Joseph Bringhurst, December 10, 1804, PAS, Reel 12, HSP. On the domestic slave trade, see Gudmestad, *Troublesome Commerce*; and Tadman, *Speculators*.

28. AMM minutes, November 23, 1809, September 22, 1814, FHL; Hinshaw, *Encyclopedia*, 6: 746.

29. AMM minutes, April 25, 1816, FHL; Elias Hicks, *Observations*. See also Nuermberger, *Free Produce*.

30. On free blacks in the Upper South, see Ira Berlin, *Slaves without Masters*, 15–107, 135–81; Fields, *Slavery and Freedom*; Whitman, *Price of Freedom*; and Stevenson, *Life in Black and White*, 166–205. On the D.C. slave trade, see Pacheco, *The Pearl*, 15–47; Bancroft, *Slave Trading*, 12–66; Gudmestad, *Troublesome Commerce*, 35–61; and Ridgeway, "Peculiar Business."

31. Overall, the free black population of northern Virginia grew 232 percent between 1800 (1,562) and 1850 (5,188), while the total population rose 9 percent (85,561 to 93,224); Historical Census Browser, UV. Shepherd, *Statutes 1792–1806*, 3: 252; Guild, ed., *Black Laws*, 111–12 (1837 amendment); *AG*, August 19, 1809, June 11, 1811; T. Michael Miller, *Artisans and Merchants*, 1: xxx–xxxiii.

32. Wolf, *Race and Liberty*, 130–61; Egerton, *Charles Fenton Mercer*, 161–96, 237–55; Guild, *Black Laws*, 99; Colonization Society of Loudoun, Virginia, *Address*, 3, 8; *GL*, May 2, 16, 1820; *AH*, August 18, 1819; *AG*, June 25, 1819, December 5, 1823. See also T. Michael Miller, "Out of Bondage"; Stevenson, *Life in Black and White*, 280–81; Poland, *Frontier to Suburbia*, 142–46; and Burin, *Slavery and the Peculiar Solution*.

33. *GL*, June 1, 1819; *AG*, December 5, 1823; Garrison, *Thoughts*. See also Wolf, *Race and Liberty*, 101–103, 162–79, 199–206, 242–47; McGraw, "American Colonization Society"; Egerton, "Its Origin"; and Waldstreicher, *Perpetual Fetes*, 302–308.

34. *NWR*, September 1, 1821 (quoting the *GL*, August 21, 1821), September 29, 1821; *GUE*, October 1821. See also Gudmestad, *Troublesome Commerce*, 6–8, and Bancroft, *Slave Trading*, 15–16.

35. *GUE*, August 1, 1823, December 1824, March 1824, July 1825, July 29, 1826. The "Black List" ran between July 1821 and March 1831. See also Thomas Earle, ed., *Benjamin Lundy*; and Dillon, *Benjamin Lundy*.

36. Thomas Earle, *Benjamin Lundy*, 22–23; *GUE*, October 1824, June, September, October 8, 1825. See also Poland, *Frontier to Suburbia*, 143–44; and Stevenson, *Life in Black and White*, 281.

37. *GUE*, July 4, November 5, 1825.

38. *GUE*, November 5, 1825. For contrasting accounts of southern antislavery, see Degler, *Other South*, 13–96; Harrold, *Abolitionists*, 9–25; Stampp, "Fate of Southern Antislavery"; Finnie, "Antislavery Movement"; Stewart, "Evangelicalism"; Allen, "Southern White Critics"; and Hickin, "Antislavery in Virginia."

39. *GUE*, August 11, 1827, May 3, 1828.

40. *GUE*, May 5, July 14, 1827; Historical Census Browser, UV.

41. *GUE*, October 1824, November 25, 1826, March 31, September 29, October 14, 1827, April 26, May 3, 1828; Thomas Earle, *Benjamin Lundy*, 209, 211, 214, 218.

42. *GUE*, May 3, 1828; Guild, *Black Laws*, 103. For abolitionist critiques of Quakers, see Foster, *Brotherhood of Thieves*, 61–62; see also Jordan, *Slavery and the Meetinghouse*. On northern abolitionists' embrace of immediatism, see Newman, *Transformation*, 86–175; and Stewart, *Holy Warriors*, 33–49.

43. Virginia Convention for the Abolition of Slavery, *Minutes* (1828), 1–2, 7–12; *GUE*, September 28, 1828; Thomas Earle, *Benjamin Lundy*, 226. The Loudoun, Bruce Town, Winchester, and Apple-Pie Ridge societies sent fifteen members to the 1828 convention; all but one were Friends.

44. Virginia Convention for the Abolition of Slavery, *Minutes* (1828), 11, 3, 5–6, 2. On divisions within the Upper South's antislavery movement, see Finnie, "Antislavery Movement," 337–42.

45. *GUE*, August 25, 1827, March 1, 1828; BH, *Autobiography*, 109; SMJ to Dillwyn Parrish, June 4, 1875, and "Rules for the Government of Friends First Day School," September 13, 1827, SMJ Manuscripts, FHL.

46. BH, *Autobiography*, 110; SMJ, *Memoirs*, 28–33; *GUE*, March 1, 1828; *AG*, April 30, 1827. The articles also appeared in the *GUE*. See also Hickin, "Antislavery in Virginia," 461–65. Quakers Moses Sheppard of Baltimore, Nathaniel Crenshaw of Hanover County, Virginia, and Benjamin Coates of Philadelphia never abandoned their support of colonization, believing "Liberia afforded the only asylum" where the "free colored race . . . enjoy real freedom and happiness"; Sheppard to Franklin Anderson, January 9, 1841, Moses Sheppard Papers, FHL. See also Forbush, *Moses Sheppard*; Worrall, *Friendly Virginians*, 355–58; and Lapsansky-Warner and Bacon, *Back to Africa*.

47. *AG*, June 22, 1827; *GUE*, February 2, 9, March 1, April 26, 1828; Thomas Earle, *Benjamin Lundy*, 221; SMJ to Phineas Janney, December 25, 1844, and SMJ to Dillwyn Parrish, June 4, 1875, SMJ Manuscripts, FHL; BH, *Autobiography*, 110. See also Hickin, "Antislavery in Virginia," 461–65; and Jenkins, *Edward Stabler*, 45–61. For reprints of the petition and signatories, see U.S. Congress, *Journal*, 23rd Cong., 344; and *NE*, March 29, 1849.

48. *AG*, June 27, 30, July 4, 18, 1827. On Fitzhugh, see also *GUE*, July 28, 1827.

49. SMJ to Phineas Janney, December 25, 1844; and SMJ to Gideon Frost, November 3, 1846, SMJ Manuscripts, FHL; *AG*, July 18, 21, 1827; SMJ, *Memoirs*, 11. For similar Quaker

sentiments, see Schooley, *Journal of William Schooley*, 112; and Hubbs, *Memoir*, 88. Drake, *Quakers and Slavery*, 114–66; and Jordan, *Slavery and the Meetinghouse*, 22–23.

50. Masur, *1831*, 9–62; Oates, *Fires of Jubilee*; Mayer, *All on Fire*, 117–26; Johnston, "Antislavery Petitions," 682–84 (quotation); Alison Goodyear Freehling, *Drift toward Dissolution*; Wolf, *Race and Liberty*, 197–234, 242–47; Wyatt-Brown, *Southern Honor*, 402–34; and Eaton, *Freedom-of-Thought*, 30, 89–215.

51. Quaker petition, in *TF*, December 31, 1831; Wolf, *Race and Liberty*, 230 (quotation); Guild, *Black Laws*, 106–108; Masur, *1831*, 48–62.

52. BH, *Autobiography*, 110; see also SMJ to Dillwyn Parrish, April 6, 1875, SMJ Manuscripts, FHL; Janney and Janney, *John Janney's Virginia*, 94; John Randolph in Virginia State Convention, *Proceedings and Debates*(1829–30), 858.

53. *GUE*, September 1831, December 1831, January 1834, March 8, 1839; Thomas Earle, *Benjamin Lundy*, 247; Guild, *Black Laws*, 199–200.

54. Ladd, in Worrall, *Friendly Virginians*, 349.

Chapter 5. Internal Revolutions: The Hicksite Schism and Its Consequences

1. Edward Hicks, *Little Present*, reprinted in Edward Hicks, *Memoirs*, 263–365. See Ford, *Edward Hicks, His Life*, 132–35; Ford, *Edward Hicks: Painter*, 85–88, 94–97; Weekley, *Kingdoms*, 54–64; and Worrall, *Friendly Virginians*, 359–60. On the Hicksite-Orthodox split, see Ingle, *Quakers in Conflict*; Doherty, *Hicksite Separation*; Hamm, *Transformation*, 12–36; Forbush, *Elias Hicks*, 111–288; Barbour, *Quaker Crosscurrents*, 100–45; and SMJ, *History*, 4 (pt. 2): 1–347.

2. Edward Hicks, *Little Present*.

3. Ibid.

4. Ibid.

5. Isenberg, *Sex and Citizenship*, 93 (first quotation); Edward Hicks, *Little Present*, 90 (second quotation). See Wahl, "Congregational or Progressive Friends"; Wahl, "Longwood Meeting"; Densmore, "Dilemma of Quaker Anti-Slavery"; and Densmore, "Be Ye Therefore Perfect." On Hicksites and radical reform, see Hamm, *God's Government Begun*, xxi–xxiii, 31–56, 195–210, 216–17; and Jensen, *Loosening the Bonds*, 151–52, 185–92, 195; and Jordan, *Slavery and the Meetinghouse*. On the discipline as "hedge," see BYM, *Discipline of Yearly Meeting 1806*, 3.

6. Larson, *Daughters of Light*, 23–26, 34–39; Tolles, *Meeting House*, 5–6; Frost, *Quaker Family*, 25, 40, 45 (quotation); Hamm, *Quakers in America*, 13–30. For the classic exposition of Quaker beliefs, see Barclay, *Apology*.

7. Hamm, *Quakers in America*, 30 (quotation); Frost, *Quaker Family*, 14–19, 32–33; Isichei, *Victorian Quakers*, 16–19. See also SMJ, *History*, 4 (pt. 2): 10–80.

8. James, *People among Peoples*, 3, 6–22; Ingle, *Quakers in Conflict*, 3–4; Rufus Jones, *Quakers in American Colonies*, 136–46; Barbour, *Quaker Crosscurrents*, 4–7, 19–24; and Frost, *Quaker Family*, 3–5. On Woolman's antislavery efforts, see Woolman, *Journal of the Life, Gospel Labors and Christian Experiences, of . . . John Woolman*, in William Evans and Thomas Evans, *Friends' Library*, 4: 333–50, 365–80 (quotation 333); Soderlund, *Quakers and Slavery*; and Slaughter, *Beautiful Soul*.

9. Frost, *Quaker Family*, 40, 16; Isichei, *Victorian Quakers*, 3–16; Ingle, *Quakers in Conflict*, 10–37, 65–80; Hamm, *Transformation*, 20–28; and SMJ, *History*, 4 (pt. 2): 81–87.

10. Barbour, *Quaker Crosscurrents*, 102–103 (first quotation); SMJ, *History*, 4 (pt. 1): 7–39 (quotations 36, 39), (pt. 2): 94–96; Forbush, *Elias Hicks*, 118–22, 195; and Ingle, *Quakers in Conflict*, 9–12. BYM, *Discipline of Yearly Meeting 1806*, 19, 27–28, 64, 101–102.

11. Rufus Jones, *Later Periods*, 1: 285 (first quotation); Isichei, *Victorian Quakers*, 3–9; Hamm, *Transformation*, 20–23; Ingle, *Quakers in Conflict*, 11–14, 20–21, 31–33, 78–80; Forbush, *Elias Hicks*, 136–42, 228; SMJ, *History*, 4 (pt. 2): 74–76 (quotation 76); [PYM (Orthodox)], *Declaration Respecting Those Who Have Separated*, passim (quotation 9); [William Davis], *Narrative*, 18–23 (quotations 19, 18).

12. Ingle, *Quakers in Conflict*, 30–37, 96, 127; Forbush, *Elias Hicks*, 220–27; SMJ, *History*, 4 (pt. 2): 174–79; Seebohm, ed., *Memoirs of Forster*, 1: 328; [William Davis], *Narrative*, 21–22; Braithwaite, ed., *Memoirs of Anna Braithwaite*, 49–50, 118, 139–40.

13. Ingle, *Quakers in Conflict*, 19–20, 81–121; SMJ, *History*, 4 (pt. 2): 227–29 (quotation); Forbush, *Elias Hicks*, 198–201, 218–19; PMS, *Extracts from Writing of Primitive Friends*. See also Gilbert and Ferris, *Letters of Paul and Amicus*.

14. Reynolds, *Walt Whitman's America*, 37–40; "Elias Hicks," *SEP*, January 4, 1823; Ingle, *Quakers in Conflict*, 39–40, 104–19; Forbush, *Elias Hicks*, 128, 161–63, 210–16; SMJ, *History*, 2 (pt. 2): 214–26; Cockburn, *Review of Causes*, 68–79.

15. Ingle, *Quakers in Conflict*, 41–45, 80–95, 112 (quotation); Forbush, *Elias Hicks*, 191–202; SMJ, *History*, 4 (pt. 2): 104–39; Elias Hicks, *Journal*, 122–23, 158; Gould, trans., *Sermons by Wetherald and Hicks*, 54–55, 71, 83, 98–99, 100–101, 104, 108, 113–14 (quotation), 155, 195–96, 199–200, 202–203, 208–209, 227 (quotation), 243–44, 246, 249; Comly, *Journal*, 395–97 (quotation); William Stabler, *Memoir of Life of Edward Stabler*, 182–84 ("The Atonement"). For Orthodox Quaker beliefs, see "The Society of Friends," *SEP*, July 28, August 4, 11, September 1, 22, 1827. See also Holifield, *Theology in America*, 320–27.

16. Hicks, in Forbush, *Elias Hicks*, 280–81; Hicks to Deborah and James Stabler, June 28, 1829, in Wilbur, *Life and Labors*, 98–99; Ingle, *Quakers in Conflict*, 46–51. See also Elias Hicks, *Journal*, 276–77; and [William Davis], *Narrative*, 29.

17. SMJ, *History*, 4 (pt. 2): 237–38; Cockburn, *Review of Causes*, 53–59; Doherty, *Hicksite Separation*, 33–66. See also Ingle, *Quakers in Conflict*, 23–24, 46–52. But see also Hamm, *Transformation*, 16–17; and Forbush, *History of BYM*, 64.

18. Comly, *Journal*, 454–55; Charles Evans, ed., *Journal of William Evans*, 560–61; Hamm, *Transformation*, xiii, 36–97; Hamm, *Quakers in America*, 43–54; and Tallack, *Friendly Sketches*, 17–25. For the decline of plainness, see Frost, "From Plainness to Simplicity," in Lapsansky and Verplanck, *Quaker Aesthetics*, 29–37; and Isichei, *Victorian Quakers*, 25–43, 61–65, 144–65.

19. Doherty, *Hicksite Separation*, 43; William Stabler, *Memoir of Life of Edward Stabler*, 95–96, 98, 102–103, 306, 308; AMM minutes, March 20, 1828, FHL; Comly, *Journal*, 451; "Memoirs of Phineas Janney, 1852," in SMJ Papers, LV; "A Sketch of the Life and Character of the late Phineas Janney, of Alexandria, Va.," *NE*, August 24, 1854. For the Luptons, see "A Copy of the Personal Estate of David Lupton, Decd., [c. 1822]"; Joel Lupton Patent Materials, various dates; J. W. Hand to Joel Lupton, April 10, 1839; Abner Williams to Nathan Lupton, January 30, 1843; Walter W. W. Bowie to Joel Lupton, March 13, 1853, all in Lupton Family Papers, VHS; Cartmell, *Shenandoah Valley Pioneers*, 452–54.

20. Elias Hicks, *Journal*, 70–71; Comley, *Journal*, 453–54; Schooley, *Journal of William Schooley*, 53–58, 108, 124–25; Hamm, *God's Government Begun*, 31–87, 162–65.

21. Forbush, *Moses Sheppard*; Benjamin F. Taylor to Moses Sheppard, February 2, April 28, July 3, 1846, July 16, 1848, Moses Sheppard Papers, FHL; Hinshaw, *Encyclopedia*, 6: 710.

22. Yardley Taylor, untitled, *FI*, April 28, 1855; Yardley Taylor, "How Wood Is Formed," *HJRA* 14 (August 1859), 346; Yardley Taylor, "Glimpses of Science—No. 1," *FI*, April 27, 1861; BH, *Autobiography*, 89–90, 209, 229–30. See also BH, "Evolution—Darwinism," *FI*, February 10, 1877, 810–12. On reason as part of the inward light, see Forbush, *Elias Hicks*, 196; and Ingle, *Quakers in Conflict*, 44, 57, 118, 132.

23. BH, *Autobiography*, 146–47; William W. Griscom (son) to William Griscom (father), October 5, 19, 1850, William Griscom to William W. Griscom, October 11, 1850, in William Wade Griscom Family Correspondence, FHL.

24. Schooley, *Journal of William Schooley*, 57–58 (quotations); SMJ, *History* 4 (pt. 2): 17–18, 172; Gould, *Sermons of Wetherald and Hicks*, 29–30, 40–41, 54–55, 104, 243–44, 296 (quotation); [William Davis], *Narrative*, 37–38.

25. Seebohm, *Memoirs of Forster*, 2: 36–37; Braithwaite, *Memoirs of Anna Braithwaite*, 122, 132–33; SMJ, *Memoirs*, 17–21. On Dick, see Hinshaw, *Encyclopedia*, 6: 738.

26. SMJ, *History*, 4 (pt. 2): 347, 180–81; BH, *Autobiography*, 317–27. In contrast, see Ingle, "A Ball that has Rolled."

27. Comly, *Journal*, 294–333 (quotations 303, 309, and 327); Ingle, *Quakers in Conflict*, 160–200; SMJ, *History*, 4 (pt. 2): 236–69. For an Orthodox view, see Charles Evans, *Journal of William Evans*, 106–108.

28. Comly, *Journal*, 333–67, 626–32 (quotations 335, 628, 629, 632); Ingle, *Quakers in Conflict*, 199–213.

29. William Stabler, *Memoir of Life of Edward Stabler*, 122–23 (quotation), 140; Comly, *Journal*, 342; Ingle, *Quakers in Conflict*, 214–46; Forbush, *Elias Hicks*, 240–74 (quotation 269); Hamm, *Transformation*, 15–20.

30. Shillitoe, *Journal of the Life . . . of Thomas Shillitoe*, in William Evans and Thomas Evans, *Friends' Library*, 3: 399–400; Ingle, *Quakers in Conflict*, 226–27. The minutes of the BYM gave little sense of the turmoil, reporting only that the committee appointed "to prepare Essays of Epistles . . . to which this [meeting] corresponds" completed their task "so far as way might open"; see BYM minutes, October 29–November 1, 1827, FHL.

31. "Baltimore Yearly Meeting," *TF*, November 22, 1828; W. and R. S. "A Narrative," typescript, 1–3, FHL; BYM minutes, October 27–31, 1828, FHL; SMJ, *History*, 4 (pt. 2): 308.

32. "Baltimore Yearly Meeting," *TF*, November 22, 1828; W. and R. S., "A Narrative," 3–5, FHL; [William Davis], *Narrative*, 24–25; SMJ, *History*, 4 (pt. 2): 309.

33. W. and R. S., "A Narrative," 7–11, FHL; "Baltimore Yearly Meeting," *TF*, November 22, 29, 1828.

34. BYM minutes, October 27–31, 1828, FHL; W. and R. S., "A Narrative," 11–16, FHL; SMJ, *History*, 4 (pt. 2): 309–11.

35. BYM minutes, October 27–31, 1828, FHL; W. and R. S., "A Narrative," 14–18, 21, FHL; "Baltimore Yearly Meeting," *TF*, November 29, 1828; SMJ, *History*, 4 (pt. 2): 311; Forbush, *History of BYM*, 66.

36. W. and R. S., "Narrative," 18, FHL; BYM minutes, October 27–31, 1828, FHL.

37. BYM minutes, October 27–31, 1828, FHL; W. and R. S., "Narrative," 18–19, FHL.

38. SMJ, *History*, 4 (pt. 2): 181, 170, 7–8. On Gurney's doubts about the inward light, see Isichei, *Victorian Quakers*, 7 (quotation); and Hamm, *Transformation*, 21. Bates, *Doctrines*;

Good, "Elisha Bates"; Schooley, *Journal of William Schooley*, 58–59; Charles Evans, *Journal of William Evans*, 83.

39. Schooley, *Journal of William Schooley*, 64, 56.

40. BYM minutes, October 27–31, 1828, FHL; W. and R. S., "Narrative," 20–22, FHL; "Baltimore Yearly Meeting," *TF*, December 13, 1828; Ingle, *Quakers in Conflict*, 245; Proctor, quoted in Forbush, *Elias Hicks*, 274. At the time of the split, Orthodox Friends claimed one hundred and fifty withdrawals while Hicksites counted forty-six. An 1865 estimate produced by the Baltimore Orthodox and Hicksite meetings agreed on a "relation" of "about one to four"; SMJ, *History*, 4 (pt. 2): 346.

41. FMM minutes, December 12, 1828; GMM minutes, August 12, October 14, 1830; HMM (Hicksite) minutes, June 10, September 9, 1830, FHL; SMJ, *History*, 4 (pt. 2): 343; HF, *Hopewell Friends History*, 142. Janney and Janney, *Ye Meetg Hous Smal*, 87, report that eight families left the Goose Creek meeting.

42. "A List of Members of Hopewell Monthly Meeting after the Separation in Society in 1828," in HMM (Orthodox) Register of Births, Deaths, and Membership, FHL; HMM (Orthodox) minutes, July 7, 1830, FHL; Janney and Janney, *Ye Meetg Hous Smal*, 87; Charles Evans, *Journal of William Evans*, 230. Population estimate from Worrall, *Friendly Virginians*, 342; and "Statistics of Goose Creek Monthly Meeting, Loudoun County, Virginia," *FI*, June 18, 1859.

43. AMM minutes, March 19, April 23, May 21, July 23, 1829, February 18, June 24, 1830, February 24, 1831, FHL; Hinshaw, *Encyclopedia*, 6: 790.

44. Worrall, *Friendly Virginians*, 359; Hubbs, *Memoir*, 85, 107; Osborn, *Journal*, 23–28, 145–47, 368–69; Shillitoe, *Journal of the Life . . . of Thomas Shillitoe*, in William Evans and Thomas Evans, *Friends' Library*, 3: 470; Benjamin Ladd to Elizabeth Ladd, n.d. [but before 1828], May 17, 1831, July 23, 1832, in Ladd Family Papers, ECQC.

45. Gurney, *Journey in North America*, 248–58; Gurney, *Letter to Followers*, passim (quotation 4); Worrall, *Friendly Virginians*, 365–66.

46. Comly, *Journal*, 448–51; Ford, *Edward Hicks, His Life*, 132–35; Sarah Pidgeon to Eliza Cowgill, September 2, 1837, Walker-Conard-Cowgill Family Papers, FHL.

47. Comly, *Journal*, 398; SMJ to Elizabeth Janney, November [?], 22, 28, 1830, SMJ Manuscripts, FHL.

48. SMJ to Elizabeth Janney, November [?], 22, 1830, SMJ to Joseph Townsend, December 18, 1832, SMJ Manuscripts, FHL; Joseph Townsend and Nicholas Poplin to SMJ, February 8, 1833, SMJ Papers, LV.

49. Rebecca Jane Walker to Isaac Walker, May 8, 1830, April 1, 1833, Walker Family Papers, private collection, copies in author's possession (thanks to Bronwen C. Souders who transcribed and shared these letters). On Kimberton Boarding School, see Jensen, *Loosening the Bonds*, 176–78.

50. "Hopewell Friends' Meeting, Va.," *FI*, July 18, 1896.

51. SMJ, *Conversations*, 60 (quotation).

52. Hamm, *God's Government Begun*, 65–70 (quotation 68); SMJ to Elizabeth Janney, May 12, 1844, SMJ Manuscripts, FHL; Janney, *Memoirs*, 58–66. See also Jordan, *Slavery and the Meetinghouse*, 88–90.

53. Hamm, *God's Government Begun*, 65–70, 197–98; SMJ to Elizabeth Janney, May 26, 1844, SMJ Manuscripts, FHL; Janney, *Memoirs*, 58–66. See also Jordan, *Slavery and the*

Meetinghouse, 88–90. Society of Congregational Friends, *Proceedings* (1849), 5–6; "Basis of Religious Association Adopted by the Conference held at Farmington in . . . 1848," in Elisabeth Potts Brown and Susan Mosher Stuard, eds., *Witnesses for Change*, 114.

54. SMJ, *Conversations*, 57. SMJ to Phineas Janney, September 27, 1849; SMJ to Joseph Dugdale, August 31, 1849; Elizabeth Janney to SMJ, October 29, 1844; John Comly to SMJ, June 17, 1845; and William Stabler to SMJ, May 4, 1851, all in SMJ Manuscripts, FHL. On the creation of the Society of Congregational Friends, see Densmore, "Dilemma of Quaker Anti-Slavery," 84–88; and Jordan, *Slavery and the Meetinghouse*, 92–93.

55. SMJ to Elizabeth Janney, May 5, 1845, November 4, 1851, February 26, March 1, December 6, 1852, SMJ Manuscripts, FHL; SMJ, *Memoirs*, 106–10, 128. See also Unknown to "My Dear Brother," July 4, 1852, SMJ Papers, LV. SMJ, *Life of William Penn*.

56. Hamm, *Transformation*, 28–34; Dillwyn Parrish to SMJ, November 17, 1853, April 27, 1852, December 29, 1854, SMJ Manuscripts, FHL. SMJ, *Life of George Fox*.

57. "Report of the Committee on Property . . . to the Goose Creek Monthly Meeting," (May 1852) and Dillwyn Parrish to SMJ, November 17, 1853, both in SMJ Manuscripts, FHL; SMJ to Caleb Carmalt, n.d., in SMJ *Memoirs*, 127, 128; BYM minutes, October 25–28, 1852, FHL. The BYM accepted BH and SMJ's proposal in 1864. The next year, Baltimore Friends jointly decided that Orthodox Friends should get a 20 percent share of the yearly meeting's property holdings; SMJ, *History*, 4 (pt. 2): 343–47.

58. *British Friend* 11 (April 1853), 105; ibid. 12 (February 1854), 46–47 (my thanks to Christopher Densmore for these references); William Bennett to Joseph C. Turnpenny, December 7, 1853, SMJ to William Bennett, February 4, 1854, December 1, 1856, SMJ Manuscripts, FHL. On liberalism—and its limits—among British Friends, see Isichei, *Victorian Quakers*, esp. 25–43, 61–65, 158–63.

59. "Salutation in the Love of Christ, from the Yearly Meeting of Friends in London, to All Who Bear the Name of Friends," *Friends' Review*, August 1, 1857; *FI*, August 21, 1858 ("Salutation" and SMJ and BH's response); SMJ to William Bennett, March 12, 1858, SMJ Manuscripts, FHL; SMJ, *Memoirs*, 168–69.

60. *FI*, August 28, 1858; SMJ to William Bennett, June 21, 1854, December 15, 1855, October 1, 1858, BH to SMJ, September 1, 1858, SMJ Manuscripts, FHL. SMJ published "The True Grounds of Religious Union" in *FI*, January 19, 26, 1856.

61. BH to SMJ, September 1, 1858, SMJ Manuscripts, FHL; Edward Hicks, *Little Present*, 66, 94, 65, 69, 67. The Baltimore Yearly Meetings reunited in 1968 (Forbush, *History of BYM*, 149–55); the Philadelphia Yearly Meetings reunited in 1955 (Herbert M. Hadley, "Diminishing Separation," in John M. Moore, ed., *Friends in the Delaware Valley*, 138–72); the New York Yearly Meetings reunited in 1955 (Barbour, *Quaker Crosscurrents*, 257–75); the New England Yearly Meetings reunited in 1945.

62. Jacob Janney to Mary Janney, November 24, 1832, Miscellaneous Manuscripts, FHL; Elizabeth Janney to SMJ, February 20, 1861, SMJ Manuscripts, FHL.

Chapter 6. Strengthening the Bonds of Fellowship: The Domestic and Public Lives of Quaker Women

1. Rebecca K. Williams Journal, July 12, 1857, April 18, 1863, in the Pidgeon Family Papers, FHL; "A Memorial of Fairfax Monthly Meeting Concerning our Beloved Friend, Miriam G. Gover, Deceased," *FI*, December 26, 1863; "Burial of Jesse Gover, of Waterford,

Loudon County, Va.," *FI*, June 6, 1863; "Minutes of Fairfax Monthly Meeting," *FI*, July 22, 1893; "Jesse and Miriam Gover," *FI*, November 10, 17, 24, 1900; "Fairfax Friends' Meeting," *FI*, March 23, 1901; and "A Study of Some Meetings," *FI*, September 18, 1909.

2. SMJ, *History*, 4 (pt. 2): 253; Seth Smith to Samuel Smith, April 14, 1838, Clarence H. Smith Papers, IHS. For the population in the 1780s and 1860, see Crothers, "Quaker Merchants," 50n5; and BYM minutes, November 1, 1860, FHL.

3. Levy, *Quakers and the American Family*, 205–30.

4. Fox, "To All Women's Meetings, that are Believers in Truth" (Epistle 291, 1672), in Fox, *Collection of Christian Epistles*, 2: 39; Penn, *Some Fruits of Solitude*, 33; Rebecca Larson, *Daughters of Light*, 16–23. See also Mary Maples Dunn, "Women of Light," in Berkin and Norton, eds., *Women of America*, 115–19; Mary Maples Dunn, "Latest Light on Women of Light," in Elisabeth Potts Brown and Susan Mosher Stuard, *Witnesses for Change*, 71–84; and Bacon, *Mothers of Feminism*, 7–17.

5. Frost, *Quaker Family*, 175–77; Fox, "An Encouragement to All Faithful Women's Meetings in the World . . ." (Epistle 320, 1676), in Fox, *Collection of Christian Epistles*, 2: 113; Levy, *Quakers and the American Family*, 195–204; and Mack, "In a Female Voice," in *Women Preachers*, eds. Kienzle and Walkers, 249–54.

6. Mary Maples Dunn, "Women of Light," in Berkin and Norton, *Women of America*, 119–21; Larson, *Daughters of Light*; Bacon, *Mothers of Feminism*, 24–41; Jensen, *Loosening the Bonds*, 145–66; Levy, *Quakers and the American Family*, 214–24; Journals of Rachel Neill, 1805–1808, With an Account of Friends Who Visited Hopewell Monthly Meeting, 1795–1813, March 10, 1795, November 4, 1799, in Pidgeon Family Papers, FHL.

7. Larson, *Daughters of Light*, 92, 121 (quotation), 235, 326; [Sarah Janney], "Accot. of a Family Visit to Friends of our Mo. Meeting, 1778," [Sarah Janney], "Fragment of Journey to Friends of Goose Creek Meeting, 1783," in Janney Family Papers, FHL.

8. Harriet J. Moore, *Memoir*, 69; Grose, *Hannah Janney*, 62–63; Nichols, *Legends of Loudoun*, 12–14.

9. Levy, *Quakers and the American Family*, esp. 12–14, 66–80, 205–30; Fox, "To All Women's Meetings, that are Believers in Truth" (Epistle 291, 1672), in Fox, *Collection of Christian Epistles*, 2: 40. See also, Larson, *Daughters of Light*, 30–34, 133–71; Frost, *Quaker Family*, 64–92, 150–86; and Bacon, *Mothers of Feminism*, 7–17.

10. Fox, "To All Women's Meetings, that are Believers in Truth," in Fox, *Collection of Christian Epistles*, 2: 40; Bacon, *Mothers of Feminism*, 49; BYMWF minutes, October 13–14, 1790, October 17, 1793, FHL; BYMWF minutes, May 29, 1773, HCQC. On education among Chesapeake Friends, see Dunlap, "Quaker Education."

11. BYMWF minutes, query of 1785, HCQC; BYMWF minutes, October 15, 1792, October 14, 1790, FHL.

12. BYMWF minutes, query of 1778, query of 1785, June 1, 1782, June 4, 1785, June 7–10, 1790, HCQC; BYMWF minutes, October 12, 1790, October 10, 1791, October 12, 1802, October 14, 1796, FHL.

13. FMMWF minutes, January 24, 1801–January 2, 1811, FHL. For a detailed study of women's meetings in the Philadelphia region, see Soderlund, "Women's Authority."

14. FMMWF minutes, January 24, 1801–January 2, 1811, FHL. For specific cases, see FMMWF minutes, November 28, December 26, 1801, May 23, 1802, November 23, 1805, November 22, 1806, and November 28, 1810.

15. Barbour, *Quaker Crosscurrents*, 165–67; Hewitt, "The Fragmentation of Friends," in Elisabeth Potts Brown and Susan Mosher Stuard, *Witnesses for Change*, 93–108; Bacon, *Mothers of Feminism*, 179; Bacon, "A Widening Path," 192–95; "Basis of Religious Association, Adapted by the Conference Held at Farmington . . . [October 6–7], 1848," *FI*, March 20, 1852.

16. SMJ to John Jackson, September 27, 1849, in *FI*, October 13, 1849; "Congregational Friends," *FI*, May 3, 1851; "Progress of Separation among the Adherents of Elias Hicks," *TF*, September 29, 1849.

17. Mary Maples Dunn, "Women of Light," in Berkin and Norton, *Women of America*, 121–25; Bacon, *Mothers of Feminism*, 42–54; Soderlund, "Women's Authority"; Larson, *Daughters of Light*, 30–34, 227–30; and Haviland, "Beyond Women's Sphere," 419–46.

18. Penn, in Dunlap, "Quaker Education," 2; Barbour, *Quaker Crosscurrents*, 146–48; Frost, *Quaker Family*, 93–132; and Bacon, *Mothers of Feminism*, 59–62.

19. Anthony Benezet to Samuel Fothergill, November 27, 1758, in Brookes, *Friend Anthony Benezet*, 230 (see also 52–53); PYM, *Some Observations*; Frost, *Quaker Family*, 100–102.

20. PYM, *Some Observations*; Frost, *Quaker Family*, 102–105; Dunlap, "Quaker Education," 8–9, 97–98.

21. Jensen, *Loosening the Bonds*, 167–83; Robert V. Wells, "Quaker Marriage Patterns." Frost, *Quaker Family*, 127; Kelley, *Learning to Stand*. Still, some elite northern women lamented the limitations of their education; see Skemp, *Judith Sargent Murray*, 84–94. On women's education in the South, see Lebsock, *Free Women*, 172–77; and Farnham, *Education*. Bacon, *Mothers of Feminism*, 1, 81–85, 89–90, 96–100; Mary Maples Dunn, "Women of Light," in Berkin and Norton, *Women of America*, 132.

22. Dunlap, "Quaker Education," 8–9, 98–100, 105–108, 117–18, 122–23; HF, *Hopewell Friends History*, 154–56; Janney and Janney, *Ye Meetg Hous Smal*, 67–68.

23. BH, *Memoir of Margaret Brown*, 13–14; "A Memorial of Fairfax Monthly Meeting, Concerning Our Beloved Friend, Miriam G. Gover, Deceased," *FI*, December 26, 1863. See also Harriet J. Moore, *Memoir*, 7–13; Townsend, comp., *Memoir of Elizabeth Newport*, 8; and *FI*, September 13, 1873.

24. William Stabler, *Memoir of Life of Edward Stabler*, 19–20, 97, 99–104; John J. Janney to Seth Smith, May 18, 1837, Clarence H. Smith Papers, IHS. See also Worrall, *Friendly Virginians*, 354.

25. William Stabler, *Memoir of Life of Edward Stabler*, 60–63; Dunlap, "Quaker Education," 140–41, 146, 149; AMM minutes, December 26, 1816, April 23, 1818, April 22, 1819, FHL; Jensen, *Loosening the Bonds*, 179–80 (Painter quotation); *AG*, September 21, 1819, January 5, 1820, May 6, 1824, September 6, 1826; BH, *Memoir of Margaret Brown*, 85–89; BH, *Autobiography*, 93–98, 106–107.

26. William Stabler, *Memoir of Life of Edward Stabler*, 60–63; Dunlap, "Quaker Education," 320–32; BH, *Autobiography*, 43–63, 118–22; BH, *Memoir of Margaret Brown*, 24–28.

27. BH, *Autobiography*, 52–63; Dunlap, "Quaker Education," 109–10, 118–19, 123–24, 328–32; FMM minutes, December 27, 1815, January 1, February 17, 1817, January 25, July 29, 1818, February 2, 1820, January 1821, August 14, 1822; GMM minutes, June 1, August 3, 1815, August 29, 1816; AMM minutes, April 26, 1821; HMM minutes, August 10, 1815, February 8, 1821; and Report of the Standing Committee on Education, BYM minutes,

October 31–November 3, 1853, all FHL. Friends taught three schools in Goose Creek, six in Alexandria, five in Fairfax, and four in Hopewell. Jensen, *Loosening the Bonds*, 173–79. Rebecca Jane Walker to Susannah Talbott Walker and Rebecca Hirst Talbott, April 26, 1830, Walker Family Papers, private collection, copies in author's possession; Elizabeth Griffith to Aaron and Mary Griffith, October 4, 1844, A. H. Griffith to Harriet Griffith, February 26, 1855, A. H. Griffith to [Isaac H. Griffith], February 8, 1857, and Nathaniel E. Janney to Isaac H. Griffith, May 9, 1859, in Griffith Family Papers, FHL.

28. BH, *Autobiography*, 100–109, 118–26; John C. Calhoun to Lt. Patrick Calhoun, October 21, 1842, in Meriwether, Wilson, Hemphill, Cook, and Moore, eds., *Papers of John C. Calhoun*, 16: 503. See also Bruce R. Smith, "Benjamin Hallowell," 337–38, 346–50. SMJ, *Memoirs*, 50–52; Springdale Boarding School for Girls, *Springdale Memento*, 16, 21–29; SMJ to P. Durkin and J. and W. H. Irwin, March 15, 1841, and Memoir of Julia Rebecca Headley, 1842, unpaginated, in SMJ Papers, LV.

29. SMJ to Patience Taylor, February 23, 1853, SMJ Manuscripts, FHL; Memoir of Julia Headley, 1842, SMJ Papers, LV; Springdale Boarding School for Girls, *Springdale Memento*, 11, 30–31; *AG*, August 21, 1840; and *NE*, January 17, 1850. On the demanding curriculum at women's antebellum academies, see Kelley, *Learning to Stand*, 86–91.

30. Memoir of Julia Headley, 1842, SMJ Papers, LV. On Davidson, see Irving, ed., *Biography and Poetical Remains*.

31. BH, *Autobiography*, 130, 154–55; James S. Hallowell to Edward Stabler, April 15, 1850, September 24, 1858; James S. Hallowell to Margaret Hallowell, April 29, 1857, in Hallowell-Stabler Family Papers, FHL; *AF* 11 (November 1855), 159. See also "Alexandria Female Seminary Catalogue, [1849–1850]," James S. Hallowell Collection, ALSC.

32. "Literary Institutions," *AF*, 11 (January 1856), 214; Lucy P. Dorsey to James S. Hallowell, December 31, 1860, Hallowell-Stabler Papers, FHL. See also "Reminiscences by Henry Clay Hallowell [1829–1899] . . . 1893," 49, typescript, A. Thomas Hallowell Papers, FHL.

33. Kelley, *Learning to Stand*.

34. *AG*, December 12, 1839, February 8, 1840, August 26, 1840, May 7, August 25, 1841; *AT*, April 15, 18, 1797; NCPEUS, *Proceedings of National Convention 1840*; Seale, *Alexandria Library Company*, 1–17. On the Revolution and education, see Wood, *Radicalism*, esp. 189–96; Kerber, *Women of the Republic*, esp. 185–231; and Norton, *Liberty's Daughters*, esp. 256–94.

35. Jonathan Daniel Wells, *Origins*; *AG*, April 18, 1797, February 18, 1818, January 14, February 18, 19, 1840, February 22, 1842; BH, *Autobiography*, 101–104, 123–24, 127–29. See also Bruce R. Smith, "Benjamin Hallowell," 351–54; and Seale, *Alexandria Library Company*, 1–68.

36. Jonathan Daniel Wells, *Origins*; Levy, *Quakers and the American Family*, esp. 1–5, 17–22, 193–267 (quotation 265). On Quaker domesticity, see also Levy, "Birth of the 'Modern Family,'" in Zuckerman, ed., *Friends and Neighbors*, 26–64; Levy, "'Tender Plants,'" in Katz, Murrin, and Greenberg, eds., *Colonial America*, 240–65; and Larson, *Daughters of Light*, 164–70. On the "cult of domesticity," see Welter, "Cult of True Womanhood"; Cott, *Bonds of Womanhood*; Ryan, *Cradle*; Ginzberg, *Women and the Work*; and Isenberg, *Sex and Citizenship*.

37. Ginzberg, *Women and the Work*, esp. 214–20. See also Kelley, *Learning to Stand*;

Varon, *We Mean to be Counted*; Isenberg, *Sex and Citizenship*, 191–204; and Lebsock, *Free Women*.

38. Fox-Genovese, *Within the Plantation*, 192–289, 334–71; McCurry, *Masters of Small Worlds*; Faust, *Mothers of Invention*; and Kirsten E. Wood, *Masterful Women*.

39. See Ginzberg, *Women and the Work*; and Isenberg, *Sex and Citizenship*.

40. On Quakers' racial attitudes, see McDaniel and Julye, *Fit for Freedom*. On the overlapped gender and racial hierarchies in the colonial and antebellum South, see Wyatt-Brown, *Southern Honor*; Lebsock, *Free Women*; Fox-Genovese, *Within the Plantation*; and Kirsten E. Wood, *Masterful Women*; and Kathleen Brown, *Good Wives*, esp. part 3.

41. Boysdston, *Home and Work*, esp. 1–29 (quotation 28), 155–63; Crowley, *This Sheba, Self*, 65–75 (quotation 65).

42. On the Quaker sense of the calling, see Frost, *Quaker Family*, 136, 198–99.

43. Janney and Janney, *John Janney's Virginia*, 52, 54; SMJ to Elizabeth Janney, May 30, 1851, April 21, 1857, SMJ to Cornelia Janney, May 23, 1851, SMJ Manuscripts, FHL; Gregg, *William Gregg*, 23 (Martha Ann Wilson); GMM minutes, January 17, 1851, December 14, 1854, January 17, 1856, January 15, 1857, January 14, 1858, January 12, 1860, January 17, 1861, FHL.

44. On the domestic education of younger women, see Barnard, *Dialogues on Domestic Economy*. John Moore to Moses and Hannah Coates, March 7, 1810, Walker-Conard-Cowgill Family Papers, FHL (quotation); Jensen, *Loosening the Bonds*, 168–73; Cott, *Bonds of Womanhood*, 32–35, 101–25; Farnham, *Education*, 1–5, 51 (quotation), 97–119. On Friends' discussion of coeducational schools, see Dillwyn Parrish to SMJ, December 29, 1854, July 19, 1857, SMJ Manuscripts, FHL.

45. Kelley, *Learning to Stand*, 262–72; M. A. Brooke to Rebecca Jane Walker, September 2, 1833, Rebecca Jane Walker to Isaac and Susan Walker, January 10, 1831, and Rebecca Jane Walker to Ruth Ann Jenkins, July 10, 1831, Walker Family Letters, copies in author's possession.

46. Farnham, *Education*, 4, 97–119; *AG*, March 12, 1830; Seth Smith to Jacob Smith, January 23, 1840, September 28, 1842, April 23, 1843, and Letitia Smith to Frank [Smith], January 29, 1854, in Charles H. Smith Papers, IHS; Janney and Janney, *Ye Meetg Hous Smal*, 70; Mary Ann Lupton to Mary Walker Lupton, October 28, 1860, Lupton Family Papers, VHS.

47. Routh, *Memoir of the Life . . . of Martha Routh*, in William Evans and Thomas Evans, *Friends' Library*, 12: 439; Hubbs, *Memoir*, 26–27; Cutts, ed., *Memoirs and Letters of Dolly Madison*, 121–24; James Mott to Nathaniel Barney, November 25, 1842, and Lucretia Mott to Nathaniel Barney, February 14, 1843, in Anna Davis Hallowell, ed., *James and Lucretia Mott*, 235–40.

48. Lucretia Mott to Nathaniel Barney, February 14, 1843, in Anna Davis Hallowell, *James and Lucretia Mott*, 235–40; BYMWF minutes, October 31–November 3, 1842, FHL; Townsend, *Memoir of Elizabeth Newport*, 125; *FI*, November 22, 1873, 610; Harriet J. Moore, *Memoir*, 32–33, 44, 46; BH, *Memoir of Margaret Brown*, 58, 61, 74.

49. BYM minutes, October 10–15, 1796, FHL; Minutes of the Fourth Convention of Abolition Societies [1797], Minutes of the Fifth Convention of Abolition Societies [1798], Minutes of the Seventh Convention of Abolition Societies [1801], in American Convention *Minutes*, 1: 128–30, 133–36, 164, 240–43; Janney and Janney, *John Janney's Virginia*, 56;

Stevenson, *Life in Black and White*, 276–77; "Rules for the Government of Friends First Day School, September 13, 1827," SMJ Manuscripts, FHL; Hinshaw, *Encyclopedia*, 6: 781; *FI*, August 30, 1851.

50. Harriet J. Moore, *Memoir*, 55–56; Guild, *Black Laws*, 175–76; FQM minutes, November 15, 1847, February 21, May 15, 1848, FHL; Dunlap, "Quaker Education," 495–97; Elizabeth Janney to SMJ, September 27, 1853, SMJ Manuscripts, FHL.

51. "Letter from Lydia Wierman," *PF*, November 20, 1845 (my thanks to Deborah Lee for this reference). For an account of Wierman's life, see "Memoir of Lydia S. Wierman," *FI*, September 26, 1868.

52. See Tolles, *Meeting House*, esp. 85–108; and Susan S. Forbes, "Quaker Tribalism," in Zuckerman, *Friends and Neighbors*, 145–73. Joel and M. J. Brown to Eliza Cowgill, November 24, 1838, and Mordecai R. Moore to Eliza Cowgill, January 27, 1836, in Walker-Conard-Cowgill Papers, FHL; John J. Janney to James Smith, July 12, 1847, Charles H. Smith Papers, IHS. See also E[lizabeth] Jolliffe to Eliza Cowgill, August 21, 1836, and E. J. Hirst to Robert B. Smith, June 6, 1855, Robert B. Smith Papers, IHS.

53. "Census of Our Members," BYM minutes, October 29–November 1, 1860, FHL. Overall, the four meetings of the Fairfax Quarter consisted of 255 adult men and 327 adult women. Sex ratios among minors were more balanced (185 boys versus 183 girls), reflecting the impact of the outmigration of adult men. See also Robert V. Wells, "Quaker Marriage Patterns," 426. On spiritualized Quaker marriages, see Levy, *Quakers and the American Family*, 70–75.

54. Hewitt, "Fragmentation of Friends," in Elisabeth Potts Brown and Susan Mosher Stuard, *Witnesses for Change* 93–94; see also Hewitt, "Feminist Friends."

55. Numbers generated from FMM minutes, 1800–1865; HMM minutes, 1800–1865; "Ministers and Elders Deceased, 1784–1880," BYM miscellaneous records, in FHL; and the *FI*, 1854–1910.

56. Numbers generated from AMM minutes, 1800–1865; GMM minutes, 1800–1865; "Ministers and Elders Deceased, 1784–1880," BYM miscellaneous records, in FHL; and the *FI*, 1854–1910.

57. HMMWF minutes, August 10, September 7, December 7, 1848; FMMWF minutes, January 16, 1850–December 14, 1860, FHL. For Hough, see ibid., June 13, 1855, January 16, 1856. On male control of female-dominated churches and benevolent organizations, see Cott, *Bonds of Womanhood*, esp. 126–59; Isenberg, *Sex and Citizenship*, 75–101; and Lebsock, *Free Women*, esp. 195–236.

58. Townsend, *Memoir of Elizabeth Newport*, 142; Lucretia Mott to Nathaniel Barney, February 14, 1843, in Anna Davis Hallowell, *James and Lucretia Mott*, 236; "Jesse and Miriam Gover," *FI*, November 24, 1900.

59. FMMWF minutes, July 10, 1850, October 14, 1857, November 16, 1859, FHL. On the difficulties of obtaining company for traveling ministers, see ibid., June 11, 1851. Williams Journal, December 15, 1857, December 22, 23, 28, 1859, February 15, 1860, Pidgeon Family Papers, FHL.

60. Sally J[anney] to Margaret Stabler, August 6, 1845, Hallowell-Stabler Papers, FHL; William Stabler to SMJ, September 16, 1842, February 3, 1846, SMJ Manuscripts, FHL. For women meetings assigning companions, see FMMWF minutes, November 13, 1850, November 14, 1855, FHL. See also Kirsten E. Wood, *Masterful Women*, 93–98.

61. "Rebecca Russell," *FI*, January 19, 1889.

62. Williams Journal, January 28, 1855, December 22, 1854, Pidgeon Family Papers, FHL. See Tomes, "Quaker Connection," in Zuckerman, *Friends and Neighbors*, 174–95.

63. Williams Journal, October 27, 1854, June 20, July 6–August 25, 1856, Pidgeon Family Papers, FHL.

64. Williams Journal, March 17 ("my record"), November 28, 1856, March 20, July 14, October 3, November 16 ("this mingling"), 1857, January 8, February 3, April 30, 1858, Pidgeon Family Papers, FHL.

65. Williams Journal, February 16–18, December 15, 1854, February 25, 1855, February 23, May 1, December 25–28, 1856, March 28, August 10–28, 1858, February 17–22, 1859 (quotation), Pidgeon Family Papers, FHL; Mary Lea Stabler to Elizabeth B. Lea, October 11, 1843, Stabler-Lea Family Papers, FHL.

66. Williams Journal, April 23, September 6, December 24, 1854, March 4, 1855, April 24–26, 1856, May 23, October 1, 1857, January 17, February 3, 24, June 20, October 18, 1858, January 26, February 25, March 5, 1859, Pidgeon Family Papers, FHL. "A Collection of Original Essays Written for the Friends Literary Society of Waterford," TBL (my thanks to Bronwen Souders for sharing this source).

67. Margaret Hallowell to Edward Stabler, March 10, 1858, Hallowell-Stabler Papers, FHL.

Chapter 7. A "Nest of Abolitionists": Antislavery Goals and Southern Identities

1. Dillwyn Parrish to SMJ, August 10, 1860, SMJ Manuscripts, FHL. On Daniel Dangerfield, see "Fugitive Slave Case in Philadelphia," *NYT*, April 6, 9, 1859.

2. Tallack, *Friendly Sketches*, 17–25; *Littell's Living Age*, November 22, 1851, p. 337; Horton, *Free People of Color*, 65; J. E. Snodgrass to SMJ, September 14, 1847 ("nest of abolitionists"), SMJ Manuscripts, FHL; Robert M. Steer to Albert Cook Myers, March 28, 1945, Albert Cook Myers Collection (Steer Folder), CCHS (my thanks to Debra McCauslin and Bronwen Souders for sharing this document). Steer admitted that his "rambling" account was "hazy in detail." For an examination of Quaker dress, see Lapsansky and Verplanck, *Quaker Aesthetics*.

3. Foster, *Brotherhood of Thieves*, 61–62; see also "Pennsylvania Quakerism," *TL*, July 4, 1851. Gara, *Liberty Line*, esp. 5–6, 79–81; Jordan, *Slavery and the Meetinghouse*. See also, McDaniel and Julye, *Fit for Freedom*, Part 1; Quarles, *Black Abolitionists*, 72–76; Drake, *Quakers and Slavery*, 100–200; and Aptheker, "Quakers and Negro Slavery."

4. On nineteenth century American racialism, see Fredrickson, *Black Image*, esp. 1–42, 97–164; and Harrold, *Aggressive Abolitionism*, 11–15, 35–36.

5. "Astounding Legislation," *GUE*, February 26, 1830, "Walker's Boston Pamphlet," ibid., April 1830; Thomas Earle, *Benjamin Lundy*, 247; Dillwyn Parrish to SMJ, June 1, 1838, SMJ Papers, LV; and George Truman to SMJ, March 28, 1844, in SMJ Manuscripts, FHL. On radical abolitionism, see Stewart, *Holy Warriors*; Newman, *Transformation*; and Harrold, *Aggressive Abolitionism*.

6. Drake, *Quakers and Slavery*, 133–200; Peter Brock, *Pioneers*, 242–47, 259–72; and Jordan, *Slavery and the Meetinghouse*.

7. BYM minutes, October 26–29, 1835, October 28–31, 1839, October 31–November 3, 1842, and October 30–November 2, 1843, FHL; see also, Drake, *Quakers and Slavery*, 144–50.

8. SMJ, *Memoirs*, 33–34, 37–58; SMJ to Phineas Janney, September 17, [1842], "Memoir of Phineas Janney, 1852," in SMJ Papers, LV; SMJ to BH, February 9, 1850, SMJ to Elizabeth Janney, September 1, 11, 1829, October 31, 1842, SMJ to Phineas Janney, December 25, 1844, and SMJ and Elizabeth Janney to Cornelia Janney, May 31, 1846, in SMJ Manuscripts, FHL; "A Testimony from Goose Creek Monthly Meeting, Concerning Our Beloved Friend, Samuel M. Janney," *FI*, November 27, 1880; Lucretia Mott to Nathaniel Barney, November 25, 1842, in Anna Davis Hallowell, *James and Lucretia Mott*, 238–40; Bacon, *Valiant Friend*, 107. See also Hickin "Antislavery in Virginia," 444–518; and Hickin, "Gentle Agitator."

9. "To the Senate and House of Delegates of the State of Virginia," January 19, 1843, SMJ Manuscripts, FHL; Schweninger, Shelton, and Smith, eds., *Guide*, 303. The 1843 petition responded to a legislative petition sent the previous year by 149 Loudoun County slaveholders who complained about emancipated people who did not leave the state within a year of their manumission; see ibid., 300. See also ibid., 310. Janney's essays appeared in the following newspapers: *BSV*, February 8, 15, 22, March 1, July 26, 1845; *AG*, December 11, 1844; *RW*, July 23, 25, 1844, September 12, 19, 23, October 4, 10, 24, 28, 1845; *NE*, September 28, 1848, October 18, 1849, January 31, July 11, 1850; and (Leesburg) *Washingtonian*, August 10, 1849. See also Hickin, "Antislavery in Virginia," 455–66, 483–518, 610–17; and Hickin, "Gentle Agitator." SMJ to Isaac T. Hopper, December 15, 1844, in SMJ, *Memoirs*, 88, 93.

10. SMJ to Isaac T. Hopper, December 15, 1844, in SMJ, *Memoirs*, 88, 93. Maddox, *Free School Idea*, 126–53. According to the 1840 census, Virginia's white population over twenty amounted to 329,959, while its illiterate white population over twenty was 58,787, or almost 18 percent of the total; see Historical Census Browser, UV.

11. SMJ to Elizabeth Janney, December 14, 1845, SMJ Manuscripts, FHL; SMJ, *Memoirs*, 94–95; and Maddox, *Free School Idea*, 150–51. See also *Niles National Register*, September 13, 1845, pp. 22–23; *The Huntress*, December 20, 1845, p. 2; and W. H. McGuffy to SMJ, February 22, 1847, SMJ Papers, LV.

12. SMJ, *Memoirs*, 95–96; SMJ, "Education in the Slave States," [1845], J. E. Snodgrass to SMJ, June 23, 1845, and SMJ, "Address on Popular Education," [1846], in SMJ Manuscripts, FHL.

13. Conway, *Autobiography*, 1: 225; J. E. Snodgrass to SMJ, September 14, 1847, John Janney to SMJ, July 21, 1849, Thomas C. Connolly to SMJ, August 7, 1849, John Jackson to SMJ, September 20, 1849, SMJ Manuscripts, FHL; SMJ, *Memoirs*, 95.

14. SMJ, *Memoirs*, 95.

15. SMJ to Isaac T. Hopper, December 15, 1844, and SMJ to George Truman, December 1844, in SMJ, *Memoirs*, 88, 86; SMJ to James H. Pleasants, July 7, August 26, September 13, 1845, SMJ Manuscripts, FHL; *RW*, September 12, 19, 23, October 4, 10, 24, 28, 1845; *AG*, September 12, 20, 25, October 3, 10, 27, 28, 1845; [SMJ], *Yankees*. For secondary accounts of northern settlement in the upper South, see Netherton and others, *Fairfax County*, 251–60; Abbott, "Yankee Farmers"; Harrold, *Abolitionists*, 107–26; Hickin, "Antislavery in Virginia," 604–73; and Otis K. Rice, "Eli Thayer." For contemporary accounts, see Lyell, *Second Visit*, 2: 273–75; and Howe, *Historical Collections*, 254.

16. "Hon. Mr. Rives' Address," *AF*, November 30, 1842; "Virginia Agriculture," ibid., October 16, 1844; "Mr. Rives' Speech," *SP* (December 1842), 277–78; "Virginia Lands," ibid. (November 1843), 262–63; and "Emigration to Virginia," ibid. (January 1844), 4.

17. [SMJ], *Yankees*, 2–6, 15–17. For estimates of the population of northern migrants, see S. S. Randall, "Farmers' Club in Fairfax County, Virginia," *Monthly Journal of Agriculture* (April 1847), 445–46; and Netherton and others, *Fairfax County*, 259, which states that in 1850 one in three heads of households in Fairfax were northern born or immigrants.

18. George Truman to SMJ, May 2, 1846, and Samuel Griscom to SMJ, April 21, 1846, in SMJ Manuscripts, FHL; Samuel S. Griscom, "Prospects for Settlers in Eastern Virginia," *FI*, September 5, 1846; September 19, 1846; October 10, 1846; November 28, 1846; and February 13, 1847. Griscom also published his reports in *The Farmer's Cabinet, and American Herdbook*, July 15, 1846, and September 15, 1846. Buckskin, "Virginia Agriculture," *AF*, October 16, 1844. See also S. S. R.[andall], "Emigration to Virginia—Fairfax County Lands," *Cultivator* (March 1847), 77–78, and (October 1847), 299–300; and A New-Yorker, "Letters from Virginia," *American Agriculturalist* (October 1847), 304–305, (December 1847), 368–69, (March 1848), 95–96, (April 1848), 122–23, and (May 1848), 150.

19. Gillingham Diaries, ALSC, 1849 entry (unpaginated). The AMM published the Civil War portion of the diary in 1988; see Gillingham, *Journal*, 1. Muir, *Potomac Interlude*, 38–95, 123. See also Netherton and others, *Fairfax County*, 257–59; Spann, *Carlby*, 106–15; Buckman, "Quakers Come to Woodlawn"; Wrenn, "After the Lewises"; and "The Quakers of Woodlawn," *Sunday Star*, November 19, 1905.

20. Gillingham Diaries, 1849 entry, ALSC; *AG*, December 4, 1848; John A. Washington in Netherton and others, *Fairfax County*, 284; *FI*, November 28, 1846.

21. BYM minutes, October 31–November 3, 1842, FHL.

22. Yardley Taylor, "The Pomological Convention at New-York," *HJRA* (March 1849), 425–27. For the dispute with Baldwin, see *SP* (June 1853), 167–68, (September 1855), 284–85, (February 1856), 41–42, (May 1861), 287–89; and *AF* (January 1860), 197–98, (December 1860), 163–64. On the Loudoun County Agricultural Society, see *SP* (July 1853), 205. On Taylor's involvement in the state agricultural fair, see ibid., (March 1859), 150, (September 1859), 559. For further examples of Taylor's contributions to the southern agricultural press, see *SP* (May 1858), 258, (September 1858), 569–70, (January 1859), 9–12, (March 1859), 150–54, (April 1859), 195–98, (June 1859), 342–43, 346–49, (July 1859), 430, (March 1860), 178–79, (February 1861), 95, (March 1861), 160–63; and *AF* (January 1859), 206–208, (February 1859), 245–46, (May 1859), 349–50, (December 1859), 164–65, (February 1860), 244, (March 1860), 266–71, (April 1860), 292–93, (March 1861), 278, (April 1861), 293–94.

23. BH, *Autobiography*; BH, "Renovation of Worn-Out Lands," *AF* (July 1847), 9–13; Conway, *Testimonies*, 36; Conway, *Autobiography*, 1: 106.

24. Conway, *Testimonies*, 37–38; Conway, *Autobiography*, 1: 104–106; Conway to Caroline H. Miller, October 22, 1877, in BH, *Autobiography*, 383. See also Warren Sylvester Smith, "Imperceptible Arrows of Quakerism."

25. BH, "Comparative Value [of] Manures," *Southern Agriculturalist . . .* (July 1845), 253–57; BH, "To Destroy Sassafras Bushes," *AF* (April 1849), 338; BH, "Mode of Using Guano," *AF* (January 1855), 206; "Analysis of Soils" and "Sowing Guano," *SP* (August 1851), 251–53; "Mode of Using Guano," in ibid. (October 1854), 298–99; ibid. (August 1853), 228. BH, *Address Rockville 1852*, 11, 15; BH, *Address Leesburg 1852*. See also *DNI*, August 15, 16, 1853.

26. BH, *Address Rockville 1852*, 10–11, 15; BH, *Address Leesburg 1852*, 3–4, 11–12; Gurney, *Journey in North America*, 50; *AF* (June 1859), 380–81 (BH's suggestions for the college),

(December 1859), 176 (BH's appointment), (January 1860), 208 (BH's resignation for health reasons); BH, *Autobiography*, 163–64 (last quotation). See also Winston, "Benjamin Hallowell," 45–47, 54–57, 74–77. For the southern embrace of progress in the 1850s, see Carmichael, *Last Generation*, esp. 19–61; and Jonathan Daniel Wells, *Origins*.

27. Insurance Policy No. 10993, Insurance Company of the Valley of Virginia with Aaron H. Griffith, December 19, 1859, Aaron H. Griffith to "My Dear Son," April 22, 1856, Note on the Subject of Slavery, no title, n.d. [1850s], in Griffith Family Papers, FHL. In 1855, James H. Griffith sold his brother Aaron Griffith his half share in the Brookland factory for nine thousand dollars; see receipt of James H. Griffith to Aaron H. Griffith, May 1, 1855, ibid. See also HF, *Hopewell Friends History*, 171–72. On Virginia's economic recovery in the 1850s, see Link, *Roots of Secession*, esp. 26–36.

28. Wheelock, *Robert Hartshorne Miller*, 4, 35–41, 73–93; Hirst, *Alexandria*, 4–12, 20–21, 35–36.

29. Wheelock, *Robert Hartshorne Miller*, 101–11; Hirst, *Alexandria*, 99; BH, *Autobiography*, 195–203 (quotation 197).

30. BH, *Autobiography*, 202; AG, March 10, 1874, quoted in Wheelock, *Robert Hartshorne Miller*, 112, 71; Provine, abst., *Alexandria Free Negro Registers*, 44, 58, 59, 65, 67, 76, 80, 81, 98, 112, 116, 118–19, 120, 124, 128, 136, 161, 182, 195–96, 206, 215, 218, 224, 231, 233, 273, 274, 293; William Stabler, *Memoir of Life of Edward Stabler*, 37, 111 (quotation); Jenkins, *Edward Stabler*, 14, 17–18, 24–43; McCord, *Across the Fence*, 26.

31. William Stabler, *Memoir of Life of Edward Stabler*, 269; "Memoirs of Phineas Janney, 1852," SMJ Papers, LV.

32. M. J. Brown to Eliza Cowgill, November 24, 1838, Joel Brown to Eliza Cowgill, December 31, 1839, Walker-Conard-Cowgill Family Papers, FHL; "A Farewell to an Old Home in Virginia," Seth Smith Journal, 131, Clarence H. Smith Papers, IHS; L. Wilson Shepperd to R. B. Smith, April 27, 1854, and Robert B. Smith to [J. W. Plaster], May 24, 1861, both in Robert B. Smith Papers, IHS.

33. M. R. Moore to Eliza Cowgill, June 2, July 5, 30, 1854, March 24, 1855, July 3, 1857, Walker-Conard-Cowgill Papers, FHL; Townsend, *Memoir of Elizabeth Newport*, 141–44; "A Memoir of Elizabeth Newport," FI, November 29, December 6, 1873. See also "Early Memories of Woodlawn Meeting," Woodlawn Friends Meeting House, Virginia Room, Fairfax County Public Library, Fairfax, Va. (my thanks to Dr. David M. Sa'adah for this citation). On John Janney, see Hinshaw, *Encyclopedia*, 6: 518, 520; Worrall, *Friendly Virginians*, 406–407; and Rubin, "Between Union and Chaos," 385–88.

34. GMM minutes, November 14, 1833, January 16, 1834; FMM minutes, April 12, 1837, May 12, June 16, August 11, 1841, February 16, 1842, December 12, 1855, FHL; Isaac Walker to Samuel Janney, August 24, 1841, SMJ Manuscripts, FHL.

35. FQM minutes, December 18, 1797, March 9, 1798, October 15, 1798; FMM minutes, December 28, 1805, January 1, 1806, June 13, December 12, 1855, FHL. See also AMM minutes, February 20, 1806, May 18, 1837, July 14, 1859; GMM minutes, March 29, 1821, November 11, 1824, June 16, 1830, June 14, 1832, August 14, 1856, December 17, 1857; FMM minutes, March 16, September 14, 1836, February 15, 1837, December 12, 1855, January 16, 1856; HMM minutes, November 5, December 4, 1856, all in FHL. John Newman to Nathan Lupton, February 28, 1843, Lupton Family Papers, VHS. On slave hiring in the Potomac Valley, see Stevenson, *Life in Black and White*, 175–86; Pacheco, *Pearl*, 19–21; Netherton and others, *Fairfax County*, 263–64, 274–75; Fields, *Slavery and Freedom*, 27–28, 47–49.

36. SMJ to Phineas Janney, December 25, 1844; SMJ to Patience Taylor, February 23, 1853; SMJ to Elizabeth Janney, October 29, 1849, Elizabeth Janney to SMJ, June 25, 1854, SMJ Manuscripts, FHL; Springdale Boarding School for Girls, *Springdale Memento*.

37. Mary Lea Stabler to Elizabeth E. Lea, March 5, 1843, Stabler-Lea Family Papers, FHL; SMJ to Jane Johnson, February 20, 1856 (partial text), SMJ Papers, LV; *FI*, March 6, 1897 (full text). Netherton and others, *Fairfax County*, 275; Stevenson, *Life in Black and White*, 162, 273–76, 292, 304; Estate of Henry Wells, Estate Sale, June 19, 1815, Estate of Henry Wells, Receipts, February 2, 1814, David Lupton's Administration of Henry Wells's Estate, Frederick Co., August Court, 1817, Jonah H. Lupton List of Taxable Property, 1852, all in Lupton Family Papers, VHS. Souders and Souders, *Rock in a Weary Land*, 16–17, 79; 1850 Federal Census, Loudoun County, 197A.

38. Elizabeth E. Lea to Mary Lea Stabler, November 22, 1842, Stabler-Lea Family Papers, FHL; BH, *Autobiography*, 190–92. See also SMJ to Elizabeth Janney, December 14, 1845, SMJ Manuscripts, FHL.

39. BH, *Autobiography*, 190–91. On racial prejudice among northern Quakers, see Bassett, *Society of Friends*. See also McDaniel and Julye, *Fit for Freedom*, 109–98; and Jordan, *Slavery and the Meetinghouse*, 67–79. On the mixing of northern and southern modes of production in border state households, see Cole, "Servants and Slaves: Domestic Service," and Cole, "Servants and Slaves in Louisville." On the way black domestic labor helped define the status of southern white women, see Fox-Genovese, *Within the Plantation Household*, esp. 100–45; Faust, *Mothers of Invention*, esp. 6–7, 53–79; and Kirsten E. Wood, *Masterful Women*, 40, 48–50. On domestic labor as essential to northern middle class status, see Dudden, *Serving Women*, esp. 104–54.

40. Mary Stone to Eliza Cowgill, March 10, 1847, Mary Moore to Eliza Cowgill, June 2, 1854, Walker-Conard-Cowgill Papers, FHL; D. G. Lea to Mary Lea Stabler, n.d. [December 1842], Stabler-Lea Family Papers; Lydia Lupton to Sally Lupton, April 28, 1858, Lupton (Bond) Family Papers, FHL. On free black women in the urban South, see Lebsock, *Free Women of Petersburg*, esp. 87–111; and Ira Berlin, *Slaves without Masters*, 136–37, 215. On the perceived shortage of domestics in antebellum America, see Cott, *Bonds of Womanhood*, 48–50; Boydston, *Home and Work*, 78–80; and Dudden, *Serving Women*, esp. 44–55.

41. BH, *Autobiography*, 191, 192. Elizabeth E. Lea to Mary Lea Stabler, November 28, December 7, 1842, August 26, 1843, Mary Lea Stabler to Elizabeth E. Lea, December 13, 1842, August 22, September 14, 1843, all in Stabler-Lea Family Papers, FHL. For similar responses among middle class northern women to their domestics, see Ryan, *Cradle of the Middle Class*, 206–208; and Dudden, *Serving Women*, 155–92.

42. George Truman to SMJ, March 28, 1844, SMJ Manuscripts, FHL; Joel and Mary J. Brown to Eliza Cowgill, November 17, 1844, Walker-Conard-Cowgill Papers, FHL.

43. Mary J. Pleasants to Margaret Stabler, February 23, 1842, October 23, 1843, November 13, 1845, Hallowell-Stabler Family Papers, FHL.

44. Stewart, *Holy Warriors*; Harrold, *Aggressive Abolitionism*. On Quaker antislavery moderation and support for the Whigs, see Jordan, *Slavery and the Meetinghouse*, esp. 50–54; and Drake, *Quakers and Slavery*, 114–200. On Whig political ideals and John Quincy Adams, see Howe, *Political Culture*, 11–22, 32–37, 43–68. For a local Quaker's praise for Adams, see Seth Smith to Jacob Smith, March 10, 1848, and "On John Q. Adams Living," n.d., in Seth Smith Journal, 1805–1863, 58–59, both in Clarence H. Smith Papers, IHS. On "coercive" means, see BYM minutes, October 31–November 3, 1842, FHL.

45. Jordan, *Slavery and the Meetinghouse*, 51 (Henry Clay); Runaway Slave advertisements, *GL*, 1817–1842, TBL; *AG*, March 2, 17, 1840, November 1, 1842; *TL*, June 22, August 3, October 12, 1849.

46. *VS* (Alexandria), September 20, 1855; *Virginia Free Press* (Charlestown), August 26, September 16, 1858; Ellzey, "The Cause We Lost," 6–7, VHS. Sinha, *Counter-Revolution*. On regional differences within the South, see William W. Freehling, *Road to Disunion*, vol. 1, esp. 13–38, and *South vs. the South*, esp. 17–32. On the South's honor culture, see Wyatt-Brown, *Southern Honor*. On radical abolitionism, see Harrold, *Aggressive Abolitionism*; and McKivigan and Harrold, *Antislavery Violence*.

47. On Virginia politics in the 1850s, see Link, *Roots of Secession*, esp. 121–244; Crofts, *Reluctant Confederates*, esp. 1–89; and Poland, *Frontier to Suburbia*, 95–182. On the South's support of slavery, see Cooper, *Liberty and Slavery*; and Cooper, *Politics of Slavery*.

48. Account of SMJ's indictment and trial based on SMJ, *Memoir*, 97–106; John Janney to SMJ, September 28, 1849, February 25, 1850, SMJ to Phineas Janney, March 14, June 16, 1850, SMJ Manuscripts, FHL; *NE*, August 30, October 11, 18, November 8, 1849, March 28, June 27, July 11, 1850; *TL*, October 12, 1849; and *FI*, November 10, 1849, March 30, June 29, 1850. See also Hickin, "Antislavery in Virginia," 504–508; Hickin, "Gentle Agitator," 183–86; and Eaton, *Freedom-of-Thought Struggle*, 135–37.

49. On Springdale school, see SMJ to Elizabeth Janney, October 29, 1849, SMJ to Phineas Janney, February 23, 1851, Elizabeth Janney to SMJ, May 27, 1851, September 20, 1853, May 7, 1854, and Thomas Hoopes to SMJ, February 20, 1853, all in SMJ Manuscripts, FHL; GMM minutes, August 12, 1852, FHL. On the new school, see Dillwyn Parrish to SMJ, December 29, 1854, and SMJ to William Bennett, December 15, 1855, in SMJ Manuscripts, FHL; *FI*, January 6, 1855, August 22, 1857; and *NE*, January 17, April 11, May 23, June 6, 1850.

50. SMJ to William Bennett, February 4, 1854, SMJ to Phineas Janney, September 27, 1849, July 14, 1851; SMJ to Isaac T. Hopper, September 27, 1844; SMJ to Elizabeth Janney, March 1, 1852, October 25, 1858, all in SMJ Manuscripts, FHL.

51. SMJ to Phineas Janney, December 25, 1844, SMJ Manuscripts, FHL.

52. On Chaplin, see Harrold, *Subversives*, 97–173; and Pacheco, *Pearl*, 65–71, 114, 126–36, 207, 220–22. NEYM, *Views*, 13; BH, "Some Reflections in Relation to War and Peace," and "Goods Seized for Militia Fines," in *Autobiography*, 334. SMJ, *Essays on Practical Piety*, 22–23. SMJ descendents Asa Moore and Werner Janney argue that SMJ hid runaway slaves in a hidden hole in the wall in the back stairway of Springdale. They offer, however, little corroborating evidence for a feature that could have served numerous purposes; see Janney and Janney, *Composition Book*, 20.

53. John Janney to SMJ, October 7, 10, 1852, "Receipt for Purchase of Slave and Four Children," November 9, 1852, Elizabeth Janney to SMJ, April 17, 1853, in SMJ Manuscripts, FHL; SMJ to Jane Johnson, February 20, 1856, SMJ Papers, LV; see also *FI*, March 6, 1897.

54. SMJ to Jane Johnson, February 20, 1856, in SMJ Papers, LV, and *FI*, March 6, 1897. On the deepening crisis in Virginia and the Upper South, see Link, *Roots of Secession*, esp. 97–119; William W. Freehling, *Road to Disunion*, vol. 1, esp. part 4; Harrold, *Subversives*; and Pacheco, *The Pearl*. On Alexandria's retrocession, see Crothers, "1846 Retrocession of Alexandria." For similar conditions in the Ohio Valley, see Griffler, *Front Line of Freedom*; and Hudson, *Fugitive Slaves*.

55. Yardley Taylor, *Memoir of Loudoun County*, 22; Stevenson, *Life in Black and White*, 279–81; Worrall, *Friendly Virginians*, 399–400; "To Yardley Taylor," TBL (my thanks to Deborah Lee for sharing this document); *TL*, April 11, May 16, 1856; *NE*, April 24, 1856; *North American and United States Gazette*, May 3, 1856; Benjamin F. Taylor to Moses Sheppard, July 10, 1856, Moses Sheppard Papers, FHL. On Ray, see GMM minutes, December 13, 1855, October 16, 1856, FHL.

56. *TL*, April 11, 1856 (reprint of article from Leesburg *Democratic Mirror*, March 17, 1856); Benjamin Taylor to Moses Sheppard, July 10, 1856, in Moses Sheppard Papers, FHL.

57. *TL*, April 11 (reprint of the article from the Alexandria *VS*, March 27, 1856), May 16, 1856; *FI*, August 2, 1856; Benjamin Taylor to Moses Sheppard, July 10, 1856, in Moses Sheppard Papers, FHL.

58. "To Yardley Taylor," TBL.

59. Ibid.

60. *African Repository* (September 1853), 273; *AG*, May 30, 1856; Elizabeth Janney to SMJ, September 27, 1853, SMJ Manuscripts, FHL; and *DNI*, May 6, 1857. Lydia Wierman, quoted in *PF*, November 20, 1845 (my thanks to Deborah Lee for this citation).

Chapter 8. "The Union Forever": Northern Virginia Quakers in the Civil War

1. Lippincott, *Life and Letters*, 121–22; *Shepherdstown Register*, October 22, 1859, in Duncan, *Beleaguered Winchester*, 1; *RW*, November 22, 1859, in Shanks, *Secession Movement*, 90. See also Link, *Roots of Secession*, 180–89; and Carmichael, *Last Generation*, 117–18.

2. Declaration Adopted by the Goose Creek and Fairfax Monthly Meetings, [1861], in SMJ Manuscripts, FHL. See also GMM minutes, September 10, 1861; FMM minutes, November 9, 1861; and "Address of the Meeting for Sufferings, Representing the Baltimore Yearly Meeting of Friends," September 8, 1861, BMS minutes, all in FHL.

3. AL to Eliza P. Gurney, September 4, 1864, in Basler, ed., *Collected Works of AL*, 7: 535–36.

4. On Union military policies toward southern civilians, see Ash, *When the Yankees Came*; and Grimsley, *Hard Hand of War*; and Mountcastle, *Punitive War*. On "rose water" tactics, see AL to Cuthbert Bullitt, July 28, 1862, Basler, *Collected Works of AL*, 5: 344–46.

5. SMJ to Elizabeth Janney, October 18, 1859, SMJ Manuscripts, FHL; Carson, "Mary Hollingsworth's Diary," 107. On the Shenandoah Valley Hollingsworths, see Light, "Hollingsworth Family," 12–23; and Hinshaw, *Encyclopedia*, 6: 402.

6. DeCaro, *Fire from the Midst*, 139–40; Louis Thomas Jones, *Quakers of Iowa*, 191–97; Richman, *Brown among the Quakers*, 21–31, 35–47, 57–59. See also Reynolds, *John Brown*, 245–47; and DuBois, *John Brown*, 221–25, 251–52. For contemporary references to Brown's "plainness," see Douglass, *Life and Times*, 278; Redpath, *Public Life*, 47; Anderson, *Voice from Harper's Ferry*, 9. Thomas Montague Isbell, state senator for Berkeley and Jefferson counties, in Galbreath, "Edwin Coppoc," 425. For contemporary references to Brown's invocation of the golden rule, see Hinton, *Brown and His Men*, 322, 424, 721, 725; and Redpath, *Public Life*, 278, 280, 341. For SMJ's interpretation of the golden rule, see *FI*, August 3, 1844; SMJ, *Memoirs*, 70–71, 92, 96; and SMJ, *Essays*, 14, 17.

7. *TL*, December 30, 1859; *NYT*, November 12, 1859. See also American Anti-Slavery Society, *Anti-Slavery History*, 170, 192–96.

314 · Notes to Pages 241–244

8. *TL*, December 30, 1859; American Anti-Slavery Society, *Anti-Slavery History*, 168–69; Lippincott, *Life and Letters*, 126–27; J. W. Griffith to "My Dear Letty" (Letitia Smith), January 26, 1860, Robert B. Smith Papers, IHS.

9. J. Richards to Ike Griffith, December 18, 1859, Griffith Family Papers, LV; Rebecca Buffum Spring, "A Visit to John Brown in 1859," in Salitan and Perera, eds., *Virtuous Lives*, 117–19. Spring refers to "David Howells." The HMM (Hicksite) noted that David Howell (no *s*) had joined "the separatists" (Orthodox Friends) in February 1838. The meeting disowned his sons, David and John Howell, for serving in the Union army. See Hinshaw, *Encyclopedia*, 6: 404.

10. *FI*, December 24, 1859; SMJ to William Bennett, January 22, 1860, SMJ Manuscripts, FHL.

11. *TL*, December 23, 1859 (thanks to A. J. Aiséirithe for this reference); *National Anti-Slavery Standard*, November 3, 1860 (thanks to Christopher Densmore for this reference). On antisecession sentiment in Virginia in 1860 and early 1861, see Link, *Roots of Secession*, 191–235; Crofts, *Reluctant Confederates*, esp. 66–194; and Shanks, *Secession Movement*, 103–19.

12. Link, *Roots of Secession*, 207–44; Crofts, *Reluctant Confederates*, 138–42, 261–64, 281–83, 301–15; Shanks, *Secession Movement*, 120–213. AL received sixteen votes in Alexandria, twenty-four in Fairfax County, eleven in Loudoun, and one, by Quaker Joseph Jolliffe, in Frederick; see Kundahl, *Alexandria Goes to War*, 8; Mauro, *Civil War*, 19; Poland, *Frontier to Suburbia*, 176; and Duncan, *Beleaguered Winchester*, 5. Rebecca Williams Diary, November 17, 1860, Pidgeon Family Papers, FHL (quotation). See also Lowe, "Republican Party."

13. Conley, *Fractured Land*, 35, 48–50, 68–74; John W. Deavers, claim no. 14,841, July 12, 1872, Southern Claims Commission, in Mauro, *Civil War*, 22; Chamberlin, *Where Did They Stand?*, 4, 23–29; Rebecca Williams Diary, May 23, June 17, 1861, Pidgeon Family Papers, FHL. *Winchester Virginian*, May 24, 1861, in Duncan, *Beleaguered Winchester*, 16.

14. McPherson, *Tried by War*, 37. On the distinctions between "no man's land," "the Confederate frontier," and "garrisoned towns" within the occupied South, see Ash, *When the Yankees Came*, 76–107. On Union "hard war" tactics, see Grimsley, *Hard Hand of War*. According to the 1860 agricultural census, the six counties of northern Virginia (Fairfax, Loudoun, Berkeley, Jefferson, Frederick, and Clarke), representing 4 percent of Virginia's counties and 5 percent of its total population, produced 13 percent of the state's total wheat production and 8 percent of its horses. Figures calculated from U.S. Census Office, *Agriculture of the U.S. in 1860*, 154–64. For a contrary view of Shenandoah Valley resources, see Mahon, *Shenandoah Valley*.

15. For histories of Civil War Loudoun County, see Divine, Hall, Andrews, and Osburn, *Loudoun County*; Poland, *Frontier to Suburbia*, 183–220; Mangus, "Debatable Land"; Meserve, *Civil War in Loudoun*. For histories of the war in the lower Shenandoah Valley, see Duncan, *Beleaguered Winchester*; Mahon, *Shenandoah Valley*; Berkey, "War in the Borderland"; and Edward H. Phillips, *Lower Shenandoah*. For the war in Alexandria and Fairfax County, see Netherton and others, *Fairfax County*, 302–70; Mauro, *Civil War*; Kundahl, *Alexandria Goes to War*; and Barber, *Alexandria*. On fears of Mosby in the garrisoned town of Alexandria, see Julia Wilbur Journal Briefs, May 3, June 1, 1863, ALSC.

16. Williamson, *Mosby's Ranger's*, 443.

17. Gillingham, *Journal*, 3–5 (April 21, 25, 1861); *AG*, April 20, 1861; Caleb S. Hallowell to James S. Hallowell, April 12, 1862, Hallowell-Stabler Family Papers, FHL; AMM minutes, June 7, 1864, FHL; BH, *Autobiography*, 169–70.

18. *Baltimore American*, July 15, 1861, in Divine, Souders, and Souders, eds., *Talk Is Treason*, 26; Rebecca Williams Diary, July 10, 14–16, August 11, 30, September 7, 1861, Pidgeon Family Papers, FHL; Goodhart, *Loudoun Rangers*, 24; Elizabeth Janney to SMJ, September 22, 1862, May 11, 1863, SMJ Manuscripts, FHL; SMJ, *Memoirs*, 199; *NYT*, November 1, 1862. On Rachel Ann Means, see FMMWF minutes, January 15, 1856, FHL; and Hinshaw, *Encyclopedia*, 6: 533.

19. Lydia W. Lupton Journal, June 14, 1863, FHL. The Lupton family lived west of Winchester on Apple Pie Ridge. Griffith Diary, June 16, 1861, p. 9, Harriet Hollingsworth Griffith Collection, HRL. On Early's threat to the Sandy Spring Quakers, see BH, *Autobiography*, 215–19.

20. Edward H. Phillips, *Lower Shenandoah*, 22–23; Griffith Diary, July 14, 18, 28, August 1, 1861, pp. 18, 21, 29–30, 31, Harriett Hollingsworth Griffith Collection, HRL; "Account of Sufferings," HMM (Orthodox) Minutes, March 7, 1866, FHL; Julia Chase Diary, August 20, 1863, in Mahon, ed., *Winchester Divided*, 104; Mary W. Lupton Journal, December 26, 1862, June 19, 1863, July 24, 1864, Lupton (Bond) Family Papers, FHL; Rebecca Williams Diary, March 16, 1862, Pidgeon Family Papers, FHL; HF, *Hopewell Friends History*, 130; Berkey, "War in the Borderland," 144–46.

21. Horst, *Mennonites*, 41–61; Cartland, *Southern Heroes*, 338; Hinshaw, *Encyclopedia*, 6: 460–61. For evidence of "underground railroads" for Unionists and Confederate deserters elsewhere in the South, see David Williams, *Bitterly Divided*, 135–36, 142–45. The Virginia conscription act of March 29, 1862, exempted from service conscientious objectors who paid a five-hundred-dollar substitute fee, a fine equal to 2 percent of the value of their property, and took an affirmation to the state of Virginia. The Confederate conscription law of October 11, 1862, exempted Quakers and other pacifist religious groups after members paid a five-hundred-dollar fine or furnished a substitute. Brethren and Mennonites found these acts acceptable. Friends did not because they viewed the financial penalties as morally equivalent to service and as staunch Unionists would not affirm loyalty to the Confederacy. See Wright, *Conscientious Objectors*, 91–120.

22. "Address of the Meeting for Sufferings," September 8, 1861, in BMS minutes, FHL; Berkey, "War in the Borderland," 149–50, 152; Cartland, *Southern Heroes*, 338.

23. HF, *Hopewell Friends History*, 130–31; Edward H. Phillips, *Lower Shenandoah*, 42, 53–55 (quotation 55); Mahon, *Shenandoah Valley*, 46–47; Julia Chase Diary, November 15, 1861, March 10, 11, October 30, November 7, 1862, in Mahon, *Winchester Divided*, 12, 21, 65–66; Berkey, "War in the Borderland," 157; Cartland, *Southern Heroes*, 333–34.

24. SMJ, *Memoirs*, 191–93; Chamberlin and Peshek, *Crossing the Line*, 3–4; Rebecca Williams Diary, August 12, 1861, Pidgeon Family Papers, FHL; William Williams Memoir, in Divine, Souders, and Souders, *Talk Is Treason*, 57–75. On Crenshaw, see Cartland, *Southern Heroes*, 345–62; and Bell, *Our Quaker Friends*, 266–77. In addition to the eight Friends mentioned in the text, Confederate authorities arrested Henry Beeson, L. L. Hodgson, Joseph S. Jackson, Joseph Jolliffe, Joseph P. Mahany, Nathan Parkins, Amos Wright, and Jesse Wright of the HMM; William Holmes, James Steer, Samuel Steer, James M. Walker, and G. Pusey of the FMM; and Levi B. Stiles, Hillman Troth, and Walter Walton of the AMM.

25. HMM minutes, August 10, 1865, FHL; BYM minutes, October 30–November 2, 1865, FHL; Gillingham, *Journal*, 18 (June 4, 1862); SMJ, *Memoir*, 222, 227–28; Barber, *Alexandria*, 40. AMM minutes, November 13, 1862–June 8, 1865, FHL, reveal that during the war Friends held the meeting at Woodlawn.

26. Gillingham, *Journal*, 8, 9, 11, 20 (November 27, December 15, 1861, January 26, February 2, 1862, March 17, April 5, 1863); AMM minutes, December 11, 1862, February 12, September 14, 1863, July 7, 1864, and January 5, 1865, FHL; Jay, *Autobiography*, 199–201; *FI*, November 24, 1900; Rebecca Williams Diary, August 25, 29, September 1, November 17, 1861, February 16, 17, 1862, Pidgeon Family Papers, FHL.

27. Rebecca Williams Diary, October 25, 27, November 11, December 15, 29, 1861, January 12, 1862, Pidgeon Family Papers, FHL; AMM minutes, September 14, 1863, December 11, 1863, June 8, 1865, FHL; Gillingham, *Journal*, 10 (January 12, 1862); BYM minutes, October 27–30, 1862, FHL; Lydia W. Lupton Journal, June 17, 21, 24, July 12, 1863, FHL.

28. Gillingham, *Journal*, 5, 6, 20–21 (April 25, September 1, 1861, October 10, 1863); Rebecca Williams Diary, July 10, August 24, 1861, February 15, 1862, Pidgeon Family Papers, FHL; Mary W. Lupton Journal, September 23, 30, 1862, January 18, 1864, Lupton (Bond) Family Papers, FHL.

29. Cartland, *Southern Heroes*, 333–34, 366; Julia Chase Diary, January 18, 1864, and Laura Lee Diary, January 23, 1864, in Mahon, *Winchester Divided*, 129–30, 131; Mary W. Lupton Journal, January 18, 1864, Lupton (Bond) Papers, FHL; Hare, ed., *Life and Letters of Elizabeth Comstock*, 214; "Account of Sufferings," HMM (Orthodox) minutes, March 7, 1866, FHL; Duncan, *Winchester Beleaguered*, 178–79, 245.

30. Monteiro, *War Reminiscences*, 101. On Mosby, see Ramage, *Gray Ghost*; Mangus, "Debatable Land," 228–357; Siepel, *Rebel*; Sutherland, *Savage Conflict*, 220–45; and Mackey, *Uncivil War*, esp. 6–9, 72–122, 198–99. My discussion follows Mackey's useful distinctions of *brigand*, *guerrilla*, and *partisan*, placing Mosby in the latter category. For a recent survey, see Ramage, "Recent Historiography." For an older biography, see Williamson, *Mosby's Rangers*.

31. Mackey, *Uncivil War*, 75; SMJ, *Memoirs*, 233; Chamberlin, Souders, and Souders, eds., *Waterford News: Underground Union Newspaper*, May 28, 1864; John B. Dutton to Col. Donn Piatt, August 3, 1863, in Divine, Souders, and Souders, *Talk Is Treason*, 50; Goodhart, *Loudoun Rangers*, 128–30; Gillingham, *Journal*, 20–23 (October 10, 1863, January 18, February 12, July 12, 15, 1864).

32. Monteiro, *War Reminiscences*, 100–11; SMJ, *Memoirs*, 232–35. For a different interpretation of this incident, see Mangus, "Debatable Land," 291–92; and Mangus, "Cruel and Malicious War," 50–51. For "Mr. R. T——," see Hinshaw, *Encyclopedia*, 6: 713, 714.

33. Gillingham, *Journal*, 6 (August 1, 1861); John B. Dutton to Anna Dutton, April 28, 1863, in Divine, Souders, and Souders, *Talk Is Treason*, 48–49; "Account of Sufferings," HMM (Orthodox) minutes, March 7, 1866. See also Noel G. Harrison, "Atop an Anvil."

34. Chamberlin and Peshak, *Crossing the Line*, 7–49; *NYT*, December 14, 1862; Chamberlin, Souders, and Souders, *Waterford News: Underground Union Newspaper*, June 11, 1864. On "passive" versus "active" measures, see Mackey, *Uncivil War*, 102–12.

35. Sheridan, *Personal Memoirs*, 1: 485–87; SMJ, *Memoirs*, 218–24; J. H. Taylor to [J. M.] Waite, August 18, 20, 1864, and P. H. Sheridan to C. C. Augur, August 24, 1864, in U.S. War

Department, *Official Records*, ser. 1: vol. 43: part 1: 831–32, 861–62, 898 (hereafter ser.#: vol.#: part#: p. #). See also Poland, *Frontier to Suburbia*, 216–18; and Siepel, *Rebel*, 118–19.

36. P. H. Sheridan to U. S. Grant, October 7, 1864, in U.S. War Department, *Official Records*, 1: 43: 1: 30; Sheridan to H. W. Halleck, November 26, 1864, December 3, 1864, in ibid., 1: 43: 2: 671–72, 730; "Expedition from Winchester into Fauquier and Loudoun Counties, Va.," in ibid., 1: 43: 1: 671–73; Sheridan, *Personal Memoirs*, 1: 460–61, 487–88, 2: 99–100; Carrie Taylor to Hannah Stabler, December 3, 1864, in Janney and Janney, *Ye Meetg Hous Smal*, 45–47; SMJ, *Memoirs*, 229–31; "To the Members of the Philadelphia Yearly Meeting," and "Extracts of Letters from an Authentic Source in Relation to Losses Sustained by Our Friends in Virginia, 1864," in Joint Committee to Raise Funds for the Relief of Virginia Friends, FHL. Philadelphia Friends raised close to ten thousand dollars for their Loudoun County coreligionists, and in 1872 Loudoun Unionists received from the federal government over sixty thousand dollars for their losses.

37. On cooperation across partisan lines in northern Virginia, see Berkey, "War in the Borderland," 125–26, 154–60; Edward H. Phillips, *Lower Shenandoah*, esp. 57–60; Duncan, *Beleaguered Winchester*, xvi-xvii; Mangus, "Debatable Land," 202–208, 330–31. For a contrary view, see Burkhardt, *Confederate Rage*, 207–14. On the violence into which regions of the South with significant Unionist populations often descended, see Ash, *Middle Tennessee*; Paludan, *Victims*; Sutherland, ed., *Guerrillas*; Sutherland, *Savage Conflict*; Bynum, *Unruly Women*; Inscoe and Kenzer, *Enemies of the Country*; and David Williams, *Bitterly Divided*.

38. Mollie Dutton to Frank Steer, March 1862, and Memoir of William Williams, in Divine, Souders, and Souders, *Talk Is Treason*, 36, 71, 74–75; SMJ, *Memoirs*, 195. See Berkey, "War in the Borderland," 155, 156.

39. SMJ, *Memoirs*, 192; Griffith Diary, August 12–September 3, 1864, pp. 82–100 (quotation August 18, p. 88), Harriet Hollingsworth Griffith Collection, HRL; Rebecca Williams Diary, October 25, 29–31, November 4, 5, 11, 12, 15, 1861, Pidgeon Family Papers, FHL; Mary W. Lupton Journal, September 23–October 22, 1862, July 8–27, 1863, Lupton (Bond) Family Papers, FHL; Fremantle, *Three Months*, 228, 230–31; *SCB* 1, no. 23 (October 1, 1864): 706; Laura Lee Diary, September 20, 1864, in Mahon, *Winchester Divided*, 168–69; Rutherford B. Hayes to Lucy Hayes, August 14, 1864, in Charles Richards Williams, ed., *Diary and Letters of Rutherford B. Hayes*, 2: 493.

40. *SCB* 1, no. 23 (October 1, 1864): 706; "The Commission in the Valley," ibid. 1, no. 25 (November 1, 1864): 776; Henry Root to J. Foster Jenkins, December 29, 1864, in ibid. 1, no. 30 (January 15, 1865): 952–53; Laura Lee Diary, September 30, 1864, in Mahon, *Winchester Divided*, 170. In all, Root identified twelve "loyalist" Quaker nurses who worked in Winchester's hospitals. They included three Griffith sisters, three Brown sisters, two Sidwell sisters, Rebecca Wright, Susan Jolliffe, Mary Jackson, and Mollie Hackney. See also Duncan, *Beleaguered Winchester*, 76–78, 103–105, 164–67, 223–27. On the sanitary commission, see Ginzberg, *Women and the Work*, 133–73.

41. Weld, *War Diary*, 246 (July 18, 1863); Curtis, *History of Twenty-fourth Michigan*, 196; G. Fowle to [?], July 19, 1863, in Divine, Souders, and Souders, *Talk Is Treason*, 53. For studies of women in the Civil War, see Whites and Long, eds., *Occupied Women*; Bynum, *Unruly Women*, esp. 111–50; and Fellman, *Inside War*, esp. 193–230. For studies of

Confederate women and disruption of southern gender conventions, see Faust, *Mothers of Invention*; Rable, *Civil Wars*; and Clinton and Selber, eds., *Divided House*.

42. See Levy, *Quakers and the American Family*, esp. 17–22. For southern gender assumptions, see Faust, *Mothers of Invention*; Rables, *Civil Wars*, esp. 1–30; Wyatt-Brown, *Southern Honor*, esp. part 2.

43. Faust, *Mothers of Invention*, 196–219; Rables, *Civil Wars*, 154–80; Ash, *When the Yankees Came*, 38–44, 61–62; Kirsten E. Wood, *Masterful Women*, 176–83; Bynum, *Unruly Women*; Fellman, *Inside War*, 193–230.

44. Cartland, *Southern Heroes*, 337; Myers, *Comanches*, 220; Divine, Souders, and Souders, *Talk Is Treason*, 57; Hinshaw, *Encyclopedia*, 6: 472. Asa Bond's daughter, Rachel, married Samuel C. Means, the commander of the Unionist Loudon Rangers.

45. Hare, *Life and Letters of Elizabeth Comstock*, 215–17; see also Griffith Diary, n.d., 100–101, Harriet Hollingsworth Griffith Collection, HRL. For other examples of Quaker women protected by gender, see Mary W. Lupton Journal, September 23–24, 29–30, October 3, 4, 1862, August 29, 31, September 1, 1864, Lupton (Bond) Family Papers, FHL; and Lydia W. Lupton Journal, July 19, 1863, FHL. For Mosby as "folk hero," see Ramage, *Gray Ghost*, 5–8, 73–74, 346–47; and Ashdown and Caudill, *Mosby Myth*. See also Monteiro, *War Reminiscences*, 96.

46. Sheridan, *Personal Memoirs*, 2: 2–8; HF, *Hopewell Friends History*, 135–36; "Quaker Girl of Winchester," *The Ladies' Home Journal* (December 1893), 9; Duncan, *Beleaguered Winchester*, 218, 222.

47. Sheridan, *Personal Memoirs*, 2: 28–29; Philip H. Sheridan to Rebecca Wright, January 17, 1867, in [Rebecca Wright], *Loyal Girl of Winchester*; *The Independent* (New York), February 14, 1867; HF, *Hopewell Friends History*, 136; Duncan, *Beleaguered Winchester*, 260–61. See also Cartmell, *Shenandoah Valley Pioneers*, 213; and Wayland, *Twenty-five Chapters*, 400–401.

48. Hinshaw, *Encyclopedia*, 6: 488, 567–68; Chamberlin, Souders, and Souders, *Waterford News: Underground Union Newspaper*, i–iv, August 20, 1864, January 28, April 3, 1865; Chamberlin and Peshek, *Crossing the Line*, 51–54; J. W. C. Schooley to Abraham Lincoln, June 28, 1864, and the *Waterford News*, May 28, June 11, 1864, in AL Papers, Manuscript Division, LC (thanks for Bronwen C. and John M. Souders for information about Schooley).

49. Chamberlin, Souders, and Souders, *Waterford News: Underground Union Newspaper*, May 28, June 11, August 20, 1864, April 3, 1865.

50. Chamberlin, Souders, and Souders, *Waterford News: Underground Union Newspaper*, May 28, June 11, August 20, October 15, November 26, 1864, January 28, 1865; J. W. C. Schooley to Abraham Lincoln, June 28, 1864, in AL Papers, Manuscript Division, LC.

51. Chamberlin, Souders, and Souders, *Waterford News: Underground Union Newspaper*, May 28, 1864, January 28, 1865; Kelley, *Learning to Stand*; Varon, *We Mean to Be Counted*.

52. Hinshaw, *Encyclopedia*, 6: 488; Anscomb, "Contributions of Quakers," 259–63. See also the thirty-nine numbers of "Friends Amongst the Freedmen," written by secretary Jacob M. Ellis, in *FI*, November 3, 1866–April 24, 1875. For the Woodlawn school, see ibid., December 1, 1866, March 2, 1867, February 13, 1869, January 29, 1870. For the Goose Creek school, see ibid., April 20, 1867; and Eliza F. Rawson, "Worthy Friends of the

Nineteenth Century. I. Samuel M. Janney," ibid., June 3, 1899. In 1867, Skillman married Bernard Taylor and settled in Goose Creek; she died in 1870. See Hinshaw, *Encyclopedia*, 6: 701. On northern women's role in southern reconstruction, see Faulkner, *Women's Radical Reconstruction*.

53. *FI*, March 2, May 4, August 3, November 23, 1867, February 22, November 21, 1868, February 13, 1869, March 12, 1870.

54. *FI*, December 1, 1866, May 25, August 3, 1867, January 25, 1868, February 22, September 12, 1868, April 10, 1869, March 12, April 23, 1870; FAPF, *Sixth Annual Report*, 5–6, 7.

55. FAPF, *Sixth Annual Report*, 7; *FI*, October 2, 1869, April 23, 1870, March 11, December 16, 1871, March 2, 1872; Maddox, *Free School Idea*, 170–76; Faulkner, *Women's Radical Reconstruction*, 7. Steer remained single until 1904, when at the age of sixty-six she married local Friend and widower J. Edward Walker; she died ten years later. See Hinshaw, *Encyclopedia*, 6: 567–68.

56. BYM minutes, October 31–November 3, 1870, FHL; *FI*, November 6, 1869, November 12, 1870; Forbush, *History of BYM*, 83; SMJ, "Women as Physicians," *FI*, October 12, 1867; Friends' Educational Association, *Address*. On southern white women after the war, see Faust, *Mothers of Invention*, 248–54; Rable, *Civil Wars*, 240–88; Kirsten E. Wood, *Masterful Women*, 193–98.

57. "Address from our Meeting for Sufferings," January 8, 1848, and "Address of the Meeting for Sufferings," September 9, 1861, in BMS, FHL; GMM minutes, September 10, 1861, FHL; SMJ, *Memoirs*, 189. In *Indiana Quakers Confront the Civil War*, Jacquelyn S. Nelson argues that some 20 percent of Indiana Friends eligible for service entered the Union army.

58. SMJ, *Memoirs*, 189; Gillingham, *Journal*, 15, 18, 19 (March 14, June 4, November 25, 1862); Warwick Miller, *Reminiscences*, 13–14; Eliza H. Miller, Personal Recollections, 18–20, ALSC. Warwick Miller identified "Uncle Frank" as helping his father; his sister Eliza identified "brother Frank." According to Hinshaw, *Encyclopedia*, 6: 754, 766, Robert Miller had neither a brother nor a brother-in-law by the name of Frank; he did have a son named Francis. Wilbur Journal Briefs, November 1, December 21, 1862, September 25, 1863, ALSC. On Wilbur in Alexandria, see Faulkner, *Women's Radical Reconstruction*, 15–26, 83–99. Order of H. H. Wells, June 29, 1863, in U.S. War Department, *Official Records*, 2: 6: 60–61; Edwin M. Stanton to H. H. Wells, July 3, 1863, in ibid, 2: 6: 76; H. W. Halleck to C. C. Augur, October 11, 1864, ibid, 1: 43: 2: 341; and J. P. Slough to C. C. Augur, October 16, 1864, ibid, 1: 43: 2: 388–89.

59. Rebecca Williams Journal, June 9, 13, 1861, Pidgeon Family Papers, FHL; Minutes of the Alexandria Union Association, August 28, 30, September 5, October 9, 1861, LV; Chamberlin and Peshek, *Crossing the Line*, 22–23; Virgil Lewis, *Third Biennial Report*, 265 (appendix two); VCC, *Journal*, 1–2, 7. On the creation of the Restored Virginia state government, see Lowe, *Republicans and Reconstruction*, 6–24; and Ambler, *Francis H. Pierpont*, 213–60.

60. Chamberlin and Peshek, *Crossing the Line*, 12; Myers, *Comanches*, 21; Gillingham, *Journal*, 22–23 (February 12, July 12, 1864); Minutes of the Alexandria Union Association, October 9, 1861, LV; Chamberlin, Souders, and Souders, *Waterford News: Underground Union Newspaper*, ii; Mollie Dutton to Phebe Steer, January 29, 1865, in Divine, Souders, and Souders, *Talk Is Treason*, 95.

61. John Dutton to Anna Dutton, October 25, 1864, in Divine, Souders, and Souders, *Talk Is Treason*, 88; BMS minutes, December 31, 1863, FHL; George D. Ruggles to J. W. T. Gardiner and others, December 15, 1863, in U.S. War Department, *Official Records*, 3: 3: 1173; BYM minutes, October 30–November 2, 1865, FHL. On northern Friends' political recognition by the Lincoln administration, see Wright, *Conscientious Objectors*, 39–90; Peter Brock, *Pioneers*, 273–324; and Jacquelyn S. Nelson, *Indiana Quakers*, 79–94. But see also Rufus Jones, *Record of a Quaker Conscience*, for a Vermont Friend forcibly enlisted in the Union army.

62. GMM minutes, February 15, 1861 (Henry M. Taylor), August 16, 1866 (Kirkbride Taylor), FHL; FMM minutes, February 13, August 14, 1861 (John W. Hough), March 14, 1866 (Thomas F. Miller), FHL. On Miller's membership in Mosby's partisans, see Williamson, *Mosby's Rangers*, 476. (Thanks to John and Bronwen Souders and Taylor M. Chamberlin for information on Miller and K. Taylor.) The eleven Friends who joined the Union army were: David Howell and John Howell of HMM (June 8, 1865, July 9, 1868); John M. Taylor and Hugh Janney of GMM (June 12, 1862, April 16, 1868); and Edward Bond, James F. B. Dutton, Henry C. Hough, David E. B. Hough, Isaac S. Hough, Robert W. Hough, and William Hough of FMM (July 16, 1862, May 16, 1866, January 1, 1867, July 14, 1869), all in FHL; Hinshaw, *Encyclopedia*, 6: 772, 488. Goodhart, *Loudoun Rangers*, 8, identifies eighteen Friends in Means's unit, and Mangus, "Debatable Land," 109–13, 141, argues that sixteen or thirteen Loudoun Friends served in the Union army and "several" enlisted in Confederate units. However, neither author provides convincing evidence for these claims, which are not corroborated in the minutes of the monthly meetings. The microfilmed Civil War minutes of the AMM are largely illegible and not included.

63. BYM minutes, October 30–November 2, 1865, FHL; Joseph Janney, in, Peter Brock, *Pioneers*, 293.

64. Moses Pascal, in Janney and Janney, *Composition Book*, 26–28; Conway, *Autobiography*, 1: 437–38. See also, Divine, Souders, and Souders, *Talk Is Treason*, 99.

65. BYM minutes, October 26–29, 1863, October 31–November 3, 1864, October 30–November 2, 1865, FHL. On broader understandings of war, see SMJ, *Memoir*, 208–209, 255; BH, *Autobiography*, 340; Moorhead, *American Apocalypse*; and Oakes, *Radical and Republican*, 239–43.

66. BYM minutes, October 30–November 2, 1865, October 31–November 3, 1870, FHL; *FI*, April 18, 1868, November 12, 1870; Carson, "Mary Hollingsworth's Diary," 107; Tallack, *Friendly Sketches*, 17–25; BH, *Autobiography*, 306, 328; Gillingham, *Journal*, 25 (November 1, 1865). See also Forbush, *History of BYM*, 97–98; J. William Frost, "From Plainness to Simplicity," and Mary Anne Caton, "Aesthetics of Absence," in Lapsansky and Verplanck, *Quaker Aesthetics*, 29–37, 258–61, 268–70.

67. Cartland, *Southern Heroes*, 127; William W. Freehling, *South vs. the South*.

Epilogue: Conflicting Paths of Virtue in Nineteenth-Century America

1. Nicholas D. Kristof, "How Can We Help the World's Poor," *NYT Sunday Book Review*, November 20, 2009. For a study of abolitionist tactics and goals—though critical of political abolitionists—see Kraditor, *Means and Ends*. For political abolitionists' embrace of interracial cooperation and violence, see Harrold, *Aggressive Abolitionism*.

2. SMJ, *Memoirs*, 235. BH also saw the hand of God at work in the end of slavery but took a more optimistic view of the war; see *FI*, January 10, 1880; and BH, *Autobiography*, 340.

3. Harold B. Stabler, *Some Recollections*; Harold B. Stabler, *Further Recollections*, 13. See also Luther Hopkins, *From Bull Run*, esp. 203–205, 224.

4. Kelsey, *Friends and Indians*, 118–61; Gerald Hopkins, *Mission*, 121–84; Dunlap, "Quaker Education," 371–404; Parker, *General Ely S. Parker*, 296–304.

5. *FI*, December 21, 1867; SMJ, *Memoirs*, 249–87; BH, *Autobiography*, 261–69. For secondary accounts, see Milner, *With Good Intentions*; Dunlap, "Quaker Education," 405–30; Forbush, *History of BYM*, 83–92; Worrall, *Friendly Virginians*, 460–67; Kelsey, *Friends and Indians*, 162–200. For overviews of Grant's peace policy, see Prucha, *Great Father*, 1: 499–533; and Keller, *American Protestantism*.

6. Worrall, *Friendly Virginians*, 463–66; Kelsey, *Friends and Indians*, 197; SMJ, *Memoirs*, 302–303; Milner, *With Good Intentions*, 187–99. On reconstruction in Virginia, see Foner, *Reconstruction*, 318–19, 322–28, 412–13, 421–23, 449, 452–53. Virginia reentered the Union in January 1870.

7. Ulysses S. Grant, First Annual Message to Congress, December 6, 1869, in Woolley and Peters, American Presidency Project (online); *Evening Commercial* (Baltimore), April 23, 1869, in Dunlap, "Quaker Education," 412. For abolitionist critics of the Society of Friends, see Jordan, *Slavery and the Meetinghouse*, 41–46; McDaniel and Julye, *Fit for Freedom*, esp. 86–92; and Drake, *Quakers and Slavery*, esp. 176–79. On abolitionists' embrace of violent tactics in the late 1840s and 1850s, see Harrold, *Aggressive Abolitionism*, 117–39.

8. For Quakers' central role before 1830, see Soderlund, *Quakers and Slavery*; David Brion Davis, *Problem of Slavery in Revolution*; Newman, *Transformation*. For works that emphasize the centrality of the Garrisonians, see Kraditor, *Means and Ends*; and Perry and Fellman, *Antislavery Reconsidered*. For a critique of radical abolitionists as inward directed and racist, see Friedman, *Gregarious Saints*. On black abolitionism, see Rael, *Black Identity*; Griffler, *Front Line of Freedom*; and McCarthy and Stauffer, *Prophets of Protest*. For political abolition, see Blue, *No Taint of Compromise*; and Jonathan H. Earle, *Jacksonian Antislavery*. For a work that questions the triumphalism of a "pronorthern" historiography, see Crofts, *Reluctant Confederates*, esp. 353–60.

9. See Kraditor, *Means and Ends*, 58–62, 74; Isenberg, *Sex and Citizenship*, 90–95; Stauffer, *Black Hearts of Men*, esp. 209; Abzug, *Cosmos Crumbling*; and Cumbler, *From Abolition*.

10. Isaiah Berlin, "The Pursuit of the Ideal," in *Proper Study of Mankind*, 16; SMJ, *Essays*, 7, 14.

Bibliography

Manuscript Sources

ALEXANDRIA LIBRARY SPECIAL COLLECTIONS, ALEXANDRIA, VIRGINIA

Taylor W. Blunt Diary, Quaker Vertical File.
Chalkley Gillingham Diaries, 1829–1870.
James S. Hallowell Collection, 1821–1886.
Moses Hepburn and Phillip Hamilton to Gerrit Smith, 1846.
Eliza H. Miller, Personal Recollections (1926).
Julia Wilbur Journal Briefs, 1844–1894.

THOMAS BALCH LIBRARY, LEESBURG, VIRGINIA

A Collection of Original Essays Written for the Friends Literary Society of Waterford, Loudon County, Va., 1857, '58, '59, '60.
Runaway Slave advertisements in *Genius of Liberty*, 1817–1842. http://www.balchfriends. org/Slaves/IndexedList.htm.
"To Yardley Taylor, Esq.," July 28, 1857, Broadside.

CHESTER COUNTY HISTORICAL SOCIETY

Albert Cook Myers Collection.

EARLHAM COLLEGE QUAKER COLLECTION, RICHMOND, INDIANA

Joshua Bailey Account Book, 1773–1869.
John Butler Collection.
Ladd Family Papers, 1809–1841.
Pope Family Collection.

FAIRFAX COUNTY PUBLIC LIBRARY, VIRGINIA ROOM, FAIRFAX, VIRGINIA

"Early Memories of Woodlawn Meeting," Woodlawn Friends Meeting House File.

THE FILSON HISTORICAL SOCIETY, LOUISVILLE, KENTUCKY

Autobiography of Gen'l James Taylor of Newport, Kentucky, 1792 to 1817, 1846.

HANDLEY REGIONAL LIBRARY, WINCHESTER, VIRGINIA

Harriet Hollingsworth Griffith Collection.

HAVERFORD COLLEGE QUAKER COLLECTION, HAVERFORD, PENNSYLVANIA

Allison Family Papers, 1710–1939.
Baltimore Yearly Meeting Memorials to Deceased Friends, 1786–1842.
Baltimore Yearly Meeting of Women Friends Minutes, 1760–1790.
Letters of Anthony Benezet, 1750–1936.
Cope-Evans Family Papers, 1732–1911.
Letters of Henry Drinker, 1777–1778.
Journal of Samuel Emlen, 1794.
Hartshorne Family Papers, 1797–1957.
Isaac Jackson, Short Account of a Visit Made by Isaac Jackson to Friends (Who Keep
    Slaves) on the Western Shore of Maryland, November 1776.
Janney Family Papers, 1800–1875.
Letters of American Friends, 1676–1986.
T. Chalkley Matlack Quakeriana (1934).
Barnaby Nixon (1752–1807) Manuscript Writings.
Diaries of John Parrish, 1796–1805.
Scattergood Family Papers, 1681–1909.

HISTORICAL SOCIETY OF PENNSYLVANIA, PHILADELPHIA

Ferdinand J. Dreer Autograph Collection, vol. 95: American Prose Writers, Vol. V.
Logan-Fisher-Fox Family Papers (Collection 1960), 1703–1940.
Pemberton Papers, 1641–1880.
Pennsylvania Society for Promoting the Abolition of Slavery Papers, 1748–1979.

INDIANA HISTORICAL SOCIETY, INDIANAPOLIS

Clarence H. Smith Papers, 1775–1955.
Robert B. Smith Papers, 1832–1942.

LIBRARY OF CONGRESS, MANUSCRIPT DIVISION, WASHINGTON, D.C.

Early Virginia Religious Petitions, American Memory Project, http://memory.loc.gov/am-
    mem/collections/ petitions/.
Thomas Jefferson Papers, 1606–1827, American Memory Project, http://memory.loc.gov/
    ammem/collections/ jefferson_papers/.
Abraham Lincoln Papers, American Memory Project, http://memory.loc.gov/ammem/
    alhtml/alhome.html.
George Washington Papers, 1741–1799, Ser. 4: General Correspondence, 1697–1799, Amer-
    ican Memory Project, http://www.memory.loc.gov/ammem/collections/.

LIBRARY OF VIRGINIA, RICHMOND

Minutes of the Alexandria Union Association, 1861–1866.
Nathaniel Francis Cabell Papers, 1722–1879.
John Comly to Joseph Branson, December 7, 1841.
Griffith Family Papers, 1801–1919.
William Hodgson Letterbook, 1803–1807.
Samuel M. Janney Papers, 1790–1922.

Thomas Ladd Family Papers, 1808–1936.
Joseph Riddle and Company Letterbook, 1800–1802.
Sexton Family Papers, 1774–1836.
William B. Walthall Autobiographical Notes, 1890.

MARYLAND HALL OF RECORDS, ANNAPOLIS

Robert Pleasants Letterbook, 1754–1797.
Virginia Yearly Meeting Minutes, 1702–1856.

MARYLAND HISTORICAL SOCIETY, BALTIMORE

Pouding de Singe: An Epic Promulgated by Towhead, with Illustrations by the Same

SWARTHMORE COLLEGE FRIENDS HISTORICAL LIBRARY, SWARTHMORE, PENNSYLVANIA

Alexandria Monthly Meeting Minutes, 1802–1870.
[Anonymous Friend], Account of Difficulties of Friends in Meetings in Fairfax Quarterly
    Meeting During the Civil War, n.d., Misc. MSS.
[Anonymous Friend], Journal of a Religious Visit to Maryland, 1801, Muncy Monthly
    Meeting, Misc. Papers.
Lydia Townsend (later Comly) Atkinson, Diary of a Visit to Washington, D.C., 1864, Jour-
    nals MS.
Baltimore Meeting for Sufferings Minutes, 1778–1870.
Baltimore Yearly Meeting for Ministers and Elders, 1808–1885.
Baltimore Yearly Meeting Minutes, 1790–1870.
Baltimore Yearly Meeting Miscellaneous Records, 1730–1870.
Baltimore Yearly Meeting of Women Friends Minutes, 1790–1870.
Ezekiel Cleaver Papers, 1729–1895.
Cope Family Papers, 1792–1877.
Crooked Run Monthly Meeting Minutes, 1782–1807.
Emlen Family Papers, 1796–1866.
Charles Farquhar Correspondence, 1829–1842.
Fairfax Monthly Meeting Minutes, 1745–1870.
Fairfax Monthly Meeting of Women Friends Minutes, 1801–1870.
Fairfax Quarterly Meeting Minutes, 1787–1870.
Goose Creek Monthly Meeting Minutes, 1785–1870.
Goose Creek Monthly Meeting of Women Friends Minutes, 1785–1870.
Griffith Family Papers, 1754–1890.
William Wade Griscom Family Correspondence, 1844–1896.
A. Thomas Hallowell Papers, 1851–1940.
Hallowell-Stabler Family Papers, 1811–1946.
Hopewell Monthly Meetings Minutes, 1748–1870.
Hopewell Monthly Meeting (Orthodox) Minutes, 1830–1870.
Hopewell Monthly Meeting of Women Friends Minutes, 1748–1870.
Janney Family Papers, 1763–1823.
Jacob Janney to Mary Janney, November 24, 1832, Misc. Manuscripts.
Samuel M. Janney Manuscripts, 1815–1881.

Joint Committee to Raise Funds for the Relief of Virginia Friends Who Suffered from the Devastation of the Civil War, Records, 1864–1865.

Lupton (Bond) Family Papers, 1792–1862.

Lydia Walker Lupton Journal, "Description of Civil War in Nearby Vicinity, June 14, 1863– August 1864."

Philadelphia Meeting for Sufferings, Misc. Papers and Minute Books, 1771–1790.

Pidgeon Family Papers, 1769–1979.

Moses Sheppard Papers, 1794–1927.

Thomas R[ussell] Smith Papers, 1833–1914.

Stabler-Lea Family Papers, 1835–1932.

W. and R. S. [Stabler, William and Rachel?], "A Narrative of the Principal Part of the Events which Transpired at Baltimore Yearly Meeting in the Year 1828, with the Imperfect Reports of Some of the Speeches Made by Different Individuals," typescript.

George Truman Papers, 1844–1891.

Walker-Conard-Cowgill Family Papers, 1699–1912.

Isaac Walker to Samuel Janney, August 24, 1841, Misc. MSS.

Warrington and Fairfax Quarterly Meeting, 1776–1790.

Charles Williams Diary, 1785–1787.

UNIVERSITY OF VIRGINIA, CHARLOTTESVILLE

Historical Census Browser, Geospatial and Statistical Data Center, http://fisher.lib.virginia.edu/collections/stats/ histcensus/index.html.

VIRGINIA HISTORICAL SOCIETY, RICHMOND

Carter Family Papers, 1651–1862.

George Carter (1777–1846) Letterbook, 1807–1819.

Mason Graham Ellzey, M.D., "The Cause We Lost and the Land We Love," unpublished MSS, c. 1910.

David Griffith Papers, 1788.

Werner Janney and Asa Moore Janney, eds., "Israel Janney's 'Ledger B': Being the Account Book Kept at His Store and Mill Near Goose Creek, Loudoun County, Virginia, 1784–1792," 3 vols.

Henry Knox (1750–1806) Letters, 1786–1806.

William Lee Letterbook, May 1792–May 1793.

Lupton Family Papers, 1745–1895.

Alexander MacKenzie (1765–1834) Papers, 1790–1814.

Marine Insurance Company of Alexandria, Virginia: Insurance Policies, May 18, 1807– November 8, 1810.

Massie Family Papers, 1722–1893.

Robinson Family Papers, 1740–1887.

Wilson Family Papers, 1790–1944.

IN AUTHOR'S POSSESSION

Walker Family Papers, 1817–1833, private collection (transcribed by Bronwen C. Souders).

Printed Sources

Abbott, Richard H. "Yankee Farmers in Northern Virginia." *Virginia Magazine of History and Biography* 76 (January 1968): 56–63.

Abzug, Robert H. *Cosmos Crumbling: American Reform and the Religious Imagination.* New York: Oxford University Press, 1994.

Albert, Peter Joseph. "The Protean Institution: The Geography, Economy, and Ideology of Slavery in Post-Revolutionary Virginia." PhD diss., University of Maryland, 1976.

The Alexandria Almanac, for the Year of Our Lord 1821: Being the First after Bissextile of Leap Year, and the 45th of American Independence. Alexandria: John A. Stewart, 1820.

Allen, Jeffrey Brooke. "Were Southern White Critics of Slavery Racists? Kentucky and the Upper South, 1791–1824." *Journal of Southern History* 44 (May 1978): 169–90.

Ambler, Charles H. *Francis H. Pierpont: Union Governor of Virginia and Father of West Virginia.* Chapel Hill: University of North Carolina Press, 1937.

American Anti-Slavery Society. *The Anti-Slavery History of the John-Brown Year; Being the Twenty-seventh Annual Report of the American Anti-Slavery Society.* 1861. New York: Negro Universities Press, 1969.

American Convention for Promoting the Abolition and Improving the Condition of the African Race. *Minutes, Constitution, Addresses, Memorials, Reports, Committees and Anti-Slavery Tracts, 1794–1829.* 3 vols. New York: Bergman Publishers, 1969.

American State Papers: Documents, Legislative and Executive of the Congress of the United States. Class 1, *Foreign Relations*, 6 vols. Class 5, *Military Affairs*, 7 vols. Washington, D.C.: Gales and Seaton, 1832.

Anderson, Osborn P. *A Voice from Harper's Ferry: A Narrative of Events at Harper's Ferry* (1861). In *Black Voices from Harper's Ferry: Osborn Anderson and the John Brown Raid*, edited by Jean Libby, 1–64. Palo Alto, Calif.: by the author, 1979.

Anscomb, Francis Charles. "The Contributions of Quakers to the Reconstruction of the Southern States." PhD diss., University of North Carolina, Chapel Hill, 1926.

Aptheker, Herbert. *American Negro Slave Revolts.* 1943. New York: International Publishers, 1974.

———. "The Quakers and Negro Slavery." *Journal of Negro History* 25 (July 1940): 331–62.

Archer, Adair P. "The Quaker's Attitude towards the Revolution." *William and Mary Quarterly*, 2nd ser., 1 (July 1921): 167–82.

Ash, Stephen V. *Middle Tennessee Society Transformed, 1860–1870: War and Peace in the Upper South.* Baton Rouge: Louisiana State University Press, 1988.

———. *When the Yankees Came: Conflict and Chaos in the Occupied South, 1861–1865.* Chapel Hill: University of North Carolina Press, 1995.

Ashdown, Paul, and Edward Caudill. *The Mosby Myth: A Confederate Hero in Life and Legend.* Wilmington, Del.: Scholarly Resources, 2002.

Bacon, Margaret Hope. *Mothers of Feminism: The Story of Quaker Women in America.* San Francisco: Harper and Row, 1986.

———. *The Quiet Rebels: The Story of Quakers in America.* Philadelphia: New Society, 1985.

———. *Valiant Friend: The Life of Lucretia Mott.* New York: Walker, 1980.

———. "A Widening Path: Women in the Philadelphia Yearly Meeting Move toward Equality." In John M. Moore, *Friends of the Delaware Valley*, 173–99.

Balleisen, Edward J. *Navigating Failure: Bankruptcy and Commercial Society in Antebellum America.* Chapel Hill: University of North Carolina Press, 2001.

Baltimore Yearly Meeting. *Discipline of the Yearly Meeting of Friends, Held in Baltimore . . . in the Year 1806.* Baltimore: John Hewes, 1807.

———. *Rules of Discipline of the Yearly Meeting of Friends, Held in Baltimore.* Baltimore: William Wooddy, 1844.

Bancroft, Frederic. *Slave Trading in the Old South.* 1931. Columbia: University of South Carolina Press, 1996.

Barber, James G. *Alexandria in the Civil War.* Lynchburg, Va.: H. E. Howard, 1988.

Barbour, Hugh. *Quaker Crosscurrents: Three Hundred Years of Friends in the New York Yearly Meetings.* Syracuse: Syracuse University Press, 1995.

———. *The Quakers in Puritan England.* New Haven, Conn.: Yale University Press, 1964.

Barclay, Robert. *An Apology for the True Christian Divinity: Being an Explanation and Vindication of the Principles and Doctrines of the People Called Quakers.* 1676. 8th ed. London: J. Phillips, 1780.

Barnard, Hannah. *Dialogues on Domestic and Rural Economy and the Fashionable Follies of the World . . . To Which Is Added an Appendix, on Burns, &c. with Their Treatment.* Hudson, N.Y.: [Samuel W. Clark], 1820.

Barton, Lewis N. "The Revolutionary Prisoners of War in Winchester and Frederick County." *Winchester-Frederick County Historical Society Papers,* vol. 9: *Men and Events in Winchester and Frederick County, Virginia* (1976): 30–54.

Basler, Roy Prentice, ed. *Collected Works of Abraham Lincoln.* 9 vols. New Brunswick, N.J.: Rutgers University Press, 1953–1955.

Bassett, William. *Society of Friends in the United States: Their Views of the Anti-Slavery Question, and Treatment of the People of Color.* Darlington, Pa.: John Wilson, 1840.

Bates, Elisha. *The Doctrines of Friends, or, Principles of the Christian Religion as Held by the Society of Friends, Commonly Called Quakers.* Mt. Pleasant, Ohio: By the author, 1825.

Bauman, Richard. *For the Reputation of Truth: Politics, Religion, and Conflict among the Pennsylvania Quakers, 1750–1800.* Baltimore: Johns Hopkins University Press, 1971.

———. *Let Your Words Be Few: Symbolism of Speaking and Silence among Seventeenth-Century Quakers.* New York: Cambridge University Press, 1983.

Beeth, Howard. "Between Friends: Epistolary Correspondence among Quakers in the Emergent South." *Quaker History* 76 (Fall 1987): 108–27.

———. "Historiographical Developments in Early North American Quaker Studies." *Southern Friend* 13 (1991): 1–17.

———. "Methodology, Perspective, and Utility in Early North American Quaker Studies." *Southern Friend* 13 (1991): 55–66.

———. "Outside Agitators in Southern History: The Society of Friends, 1656–1800." PhD diss., University of Houston, 1984.

Bell, James Pinkney. *Our Quaker Friends of Ye Olden Time. . . .* Lynchburg, Va.: J. P. Bell, 1905.

Benezet, Anthony. *A Caution and Warning to Great-Britain.* Philadelphia: D. Hall and W. Sellers, 1767.

Berkey, Jonathan M. "War in the Borderland: The Civilians' Civil War in Virginia's Lower Shenandoah Valley." PhD diss., Pennsylvania State University, 2003.

Berkin, Carol Ruth, and Mary Beth Norton, eds. *Women of America: A History.* Boston: Houghton Mifflin, 1979.

Berlin, Ira. *Many Thousands Gone: The First Two Centuries of Slavery in North America.* Cambridge, Mass.: Harvard University Press, 1998.

———. *Slaves without Masters: The Free Negro in the Antebellum South.* New York: Pantheon, 1974.

Berlin, Isaiah. *The Proper Study of Mankind: An Anthology of Essays.* Edited by Henry Hardy and Roger Hausheer. New York: Farrar, Straus and Giroux, 1998.

Binns, John A. *A Treatise on Practical Farming. . . .* Fredericktown, Md.: John B. Colvin, 1803.

Bliss, Willard F. "The Rise of Tenancy in Virginia." *Virginia Magazine of History and Biography* 58 (October 1950): 427–41.

———. "The Tuckahoe in New Virginia." *Virginia Magazine of History and Biography* 59 (October 1951): 387–96.

Blue, Frederick J. *No Taint of Compromise: Crusaders in Antislavery Politics.* Baton Rouge: Louisiana State University Press, 2005.

Boller, Paul F., Jr. "George Washington and the Quakers." *Bulletin of the Friends Historical Association* 49 (Autumn 1960): 67–83.

———. "Washington, the Quakers, and Slavery." *Journal of Negro History* 46 (April 1961): 83–88.

Boucher, Jonathan. *Reminiscences of an American Loyalist, 1738–1789: Being the Autobiography of the Revd. Jonathan Boucher. . . .* 1925. Port Washington, N.Y.: Kennikat Press, 1967.

Bowes, John P. *Exiles and Pioneers: Eastern Indians in the Trans-Mississippi West.* New York: Cambridge University Press, 2007.

Boydston, Jeanne. *Home and Work: Housework, Wages, and the Ideology of Labor in the Early Republic.* New York: Oxford University Press, 1990.

Braithwaite, J. Bevan, ed. *Memoirs of Anna Braithwaite. Being a Sketch of Her Early Life and Ministry, and Extracts from Her Private Memoranda, 1830–1859.* London: Headley Brothers, 1905.

Breen, Timothy. *Tobacco Culture: The Mentality of the Great Tidewater Planters on the Eve of Revolution.* Princeton, N.J.: Princeton University Press, 1985.

Brinton, Howard H. *The Religious Philosophy of Quakerism: The Beliefs of Fox, Barclay, and Penn as Based on the Gospel of John.* Wallingford, Pa.: Pendle Hill, 1973.

Brissot de Warville, J. P. *New Travels in the United States of America, Performed in 1788.* New York: T. and J. Swords, 1792.

Brock, Peter. "Colonel Washington and the Quaker Conscientious Objectors." *Quaker History* 53 (Spring 1964): 12–26.

———. *Pioneers of the Peaceable Kingdom: The Quaker Peace Testimony from the Colonial Era to the First World War.* Princeton, N.J.: Princeton University Press, 1968.

Brock, R. A., ed. *The Official Records of Robert Dinwiddie, Lieutenant-Governor of the Colony of Virginia, 1751–1758.* 2 vols. Richmond: Virginia Historical Society, 1883–84.

Brookes, George S. *Friend Anthony Benezet.* Philadelphia: University of Pennsylvania Press, 1937.

Brown, Elisabeth Potts, and Susan Mosher Stuard, eds. *Witnesses for Change: Quaker Women over Three Centuries.* New Brunswick, N.J.: Rutgers University Press, 1989.

Brown, Kathleen M. *Good Wives, Nasty Wenches, and Anxious Patriarchs: Gender, Race, and Power in Colonial Virginia*. Chapel Hill: University of North Carolina Press, 1996.

Browne, Gary Larson. *Baltimore in the Nation, 1789–1861*. Chapel Hill: University of North Carolina Press, 1980.

Bruns, Roger, ed. *Am I Not a Man and a Brother? The Antislavery Crusade of Revolutionary America, 1688–1788*. New York: Chelsea House, 1977.

Brydon, George MacLaren. *Virginia's Mother Church, and the Political Conditions under Which It Grew*. 2 vols. Philadelphia: Church Historical Society, 1952.

Buckman, Horace D. "The Quakers Come to Woodlawn." *Yearbook of the Historical Society of Fairfax County, Virginia* 9 (1964–1965): 65–67.

Burin, Eric. *Slavery and the Peculiar Solution: A History of the American Colonization Society*. Gainesville: University Press of Florida, 2005.

Burkhardt, George S. *Confederate Rage, Yankee Wrath: No Quarter in the Civil War*. Carbondale: Southern Illinois University Press, 2007.

Bynum, Victoria E. *Unruly Women: The Politics of Social and Sexual Control in the Old South*. Chapel Hill: University of North Carolina Press, 1992.

Carmichael, Peter S. *The Last Generation: Young Virginians in Peace, War, and Reunion*. Chapel Hill: University of North Carolina, 2005.

Carroll, Kenneth L. "Quakerism on the Eastern Shore of Virginia." *Virginia Magazine of History and Biography* 74 (April 1966): 170–89.

———, ed. "Robert Pleasants on Quakerism: 'Some Account of the First Settlement of Friends in Virginia. . . . '" *Virginia Magazine of History and Biography* 86 (January 1978): 3–16.

Carson, Mary Virginia. "Highlights of Mary Hollingsworth's Life." *Journal of the Winchester-Frederick County Historical Society* 10 (1997): 24–27.

———, ed. "Mary E. Hollingsworth's Diary." *Journal of the Winchester-Frederick County Historical Society* 10 (1997): 28–125.

Carter, Robert. "Merchants and Mills from the Letter Book of Robert Carter, of Nominy, Westmoreland County." *William and Mary Quarterly*, 1st ser., 11 (April 1903): 246.

Cartland, Fernando G. *Southern Heroes, or the Friends in War Time*. Cambridge, Mass.: Riverside Press, 1895.

Cartmell, T. K. *Shenandoah Valley Pioneers and Their Descendants: A History of Frederick County, Virginia, from Its Formation in 1738 to 1908*. Winchester: Eddy Press, 1909.

Cassell, Frank. "Slaves of the Chesapeake Bay Area and the War of 1812." *Journal of Negro History* 57 (April 1972): 144–55.

Caton, Mary Anne. "The Aesthetics of Absence: Quaker Women's Plain Dress in the Delaware Valley, 1790–1900." In Lapsansky and Verplanck, *Quaker Aesthetics*, 246–71.

Chamberlin, Taylor M. *Where Did They Stand? The May 1861 Vote on Secession in Loudoun County, Virginia, and Post-War Claims against the Government*. Waterford, Va.: Waterford Foundation, 2003.

Chamberlin, Taylor M., and James D. Peshek. *Crossing the Line: Civilian Trade and Travel between Loudoun County, Virginia, and Maryland during the Civil War*. Waterford, Va.: Waterford Foundation, 2002.

Chamberlin, Taylor M., Bronwen C. Souders, and John M. Souders, eds. *The Waterford*

News: An Underground Union Newspaper Published by Three Quaker Maidens in Confederate Virginia, 1864-1865. Waterford, Va.: Waterford Foundation, 1999.

Chu, Jonathan. "Recent Developments in Early North American Historiography: A Reply." *Southern Friend* 13 (1991): 40–54.

Clemens, Paul G. E. *The Atlantic Economy and Colonial Maryland's Eastern Shore: From Tobacco to Wheat*. Ithaca: Cornell University Press, 1980.

Clinton, Catherine, and Nina Selber, eds. *Divided House: Gender and the Civil War*. New York: Oxford University Press, 1992.

Cockburn, James. *A Review of the General and Particular Causes Which Have Produced the Late Disorders and Divisions in the Yearly Meeting of Friends, Held in Philadelphia. . . .* Philadelphia: Philip Price, 1829.

Cole, Stephanie. "Servants and Slaves: Domestic Service in the Border Cities, 1800–1850." PhD diss., University of Florida, 1994.

———. "Servants and Slaves in Louisville: Race, Ethnicity, and Household Labor in an Antebellum Border City." *Ohio Valley History* 11 (Spring 2011): 3–25.

Colonization Society of Loudoun, Virginia. *Address*. Annapolis, Md.: J. Green, 1819.

Comly, John. *Journal of the Life and Religious Labours of John Comly, Late of Byberry, Pennsylvania*. Philadelphia: T. Ellwood Chapman, 1853.

Conley, Brian A. *Fractured Land: Fairfax County's Role in the Vote for Secession, May 23, 1861*. Fairfax, Va.: Fairfax County Library, 2001.

Conway, Moncure D. *Autobiography, Memories and Experiences of Moncure Daniel Conway*. 2 vols. Boston: Houghton, Mifflin, 1904.

———. *Testimonies Concerning Slavery*. London: Chapman and Hall, 1864.

Cooper, William J. *Liberty and Slavery: Southern Politics to 1860*. Columbia: University of South Carolina Press, 2000.

———. *The South and the Politics of Slavery, 1828–1856*. Baton Rouge: Louisiana State University, 1978.

Costantino, Roberto. *The Quaker of the Olden Time: The Life and Times of Israel Thompson (d. 1795)*. Westminster, Md.: Willow Bend Books, 2004.

Cott, Nancy F. *The Bonds of Womanhood: 'Women's Sphere' in New England, 1780–1835*. New Haven, Conn.: Yale University Press, 1977.

Coxe, Tench. *A View of the United States of America. . . .* Philadelphia: William Hall and Wrigley Berriman, 1794.

Craven, Avery. *Soil Exhaustion as a Factor in the Agricultural History of Virginia and Maryland, 1606–1860*. Urbana: University of Illinois Press, 1926.

Cresswell, Nicholas. *The Journal of Nicholas Cresswell, 1774–1777*. New York: Dial Press, 1924.

Crofts, Daniel W. *Reluctant Confederates: Upper South Unionists in the Secession Crisis*. Chapel Hill: University of North Carolina Press, 1989.

Crosfield, George, ed. *Memoirs of the Life and Gospel Labours of Samuel Fothergill. . . .* New York: Collins, Brother, 1844.

Crothers, A. Glenn. "Banks and Economic Development in Post-Revolutionary Northern Virginia." *Business History Review* 73 (Spring 1999): 1–39.

———. "Commercial Risk and Capital Formation in Early America: Virginia Merchants and the Rise of American Marine Insurance, 1750–1815." *Business History Review* 78 (Winter 2004): 607–33.

———. "The 1846 Retrocession of Alexandria: Protecting Slavery and the Slave Trade in the District of Columbia." In *In the Shadow of Freedom: The Politics of Slavery in the National Capital,* edited by Paul Finkelman and Donald R. Kennon, 141–68. Athens: Ohio University Press, 2010.

———. "'The Projecting Spirit': Social, Economic, and Political Change in Post-Revolutionary Northern Virginia." PhD diss., University of Florida, 1997.

———. "Quaker Merchants and Slavery in Early National Alexandria, Virginia: The Order of William Hartshorne." *Journal of the Early Republic* 25 (Spring 2005): 47–77.

Crowley, J. E. *This Sheba, Self: The Conceptualization of Economic Life in Eighteenth-Century America.* Baltimore: Johns Hopkins University Press, 1974.

Cumbler, John T. *From Abolition to Rights for All: The Making of a Reform Community in the Nineteenth Century.* Philadelphia: University of Pennsylvania Press, 2008.

Curtis, Oscar Blair. *History of the Twenty-fourth Michigan of the Iron Brigade, Known as the Detroit and Wayne County Regiment.* Detroit: Winn and Hammond, 1891.

Cutts, Lucia Beverly, ed. *Memoirs and Letters of Dolly Madison, Wife of James Madison, President of the United States.* Boston: Houghton, Mifflin, 1886.

Davis, David Brion. *Inhuman Bondage: The Rise and Fall of Slavery in the New World.* New York: Oxford University Press, 2006.

———. *The Problem of Slavery in the Age of Revolution, 1770–1823.* Ithaca: Cornell University Press, 1975.

———. *The Problem of Slavery in Western Culture.* Ithaca: Cornell University Press, 1966.

[Davis, William.] *A Narrative of the Causes Which Led to the Separation of the Society of Friends in America, and the Means that Were Employed to Effect It.* Baltimore: William Wooddy, 1852.

DeCaro, Louis A., Jr. *Fire from the Midst of You: A Religious Life of John Brown.* New York: New York University Press, 2002.

Degler, Carl. *The Other South: Southern Dissenters in the Nineteenth Century.* 1974. Gainesville: University Press of Florida, 2000.

Densmore, Christopher. "Be Ye Therefore Perfect: Anti-Slavery and the Origins of the Yearly Meeting of Progressive Friends in Chester County, Pennsylvania." *Quaker History* 93 (Fall 2004): 28–46.

———. "The Dilemma of Quaker Anti-Slavery: The Case of the Farmington Quarterly Meeting, 1836–1860." *Quaker History* 82 (Fall 1993): 80–91.

Dillon, Merton L. *Benjamin Lundy and the Struggle for Negro Freedom.* Urbana: University of Illinois Press, 1966.

Divine, John E., Wilbur C. Hall, Marshall Andrews, and Penelope M. Osburn. *Loudoun County and the Civil War: A History and Guide.* Leesburg, Va.: Potomac Press, 1961.

Divine, John E., Bronwen C. Souders, and John M. Souders, eds. *To Talk Is Treason: Quakers of Waterford, Virginia, on Life, Love, Death, and War in the Southern Confederacy, from Their Diaries and Correspondence.* Waterford, Va.: Waterford Foundation, 1996.

Doherty, Robert W. *The Hicksite Separation: A Sociological Analysis of Religious Schism in Early Nineteenth Century America.* New Brunswick, N.J.: Rutgers University Press, 1967.

Douglass, Frederick. *Life and Times of Frederick Douglass: His Early Life as a Slave, His Escape from Bondage, and His Complete History to the Present Time*. Hartford, Conn.: Park Publishing, 1881.

Drake, Thomas E. *Quakers and Slavery in America*. New Haven, Conn.: Yale University Press, 1950.

DuBois, W. E. B. *John Brown*. 1909. New York: International Publishers, 1962.

Dudden, Faye E. *Serving Women: Household Service in Nineteenth-Century America*. Middletown, Conn.: Wesleyan University Press, 1983.

Duncan, Richard R. *Beleaguered Winchester: A Virginia Community at War*. Baton Rouge: Louisiana State University Press, 2007.

Dunlap, William C. "Quaker Education in Baltimore and Virginia Yearly Meetings with an Account of Certain Meetings of Delaware and the Eastern Shore Affiliated with Philadelphia." PhD diss., University of Pennsylvania, 1936.

Dunn, Mary Maples. "Latest Light on the Women of Light." In Brown and Stuard, *Witnesses for Change*, 71–85.

———. "Women of Light." In *Women of America: A History*, edited by Carol Ruth Berkin and Mary Beth Norton, 114–33. Boston: Houghton Mifflin, 1979.

Dunn, Richard S., and Mary Maples Dunn, eds. *The World of William Penn*. Philadelphia: University of Pennsylvania Press, 1986.

Dunn, Susan. *Dominion of Memories: Jefferson, Madison, and the Decline of Virginia*. New York: Basic Books, 2007.

Earle, Carville, and Ronald Hoffman. "Staple Crops and Urban Development in the Eighteenth-Century South." *Perspectives in American History* 10 (1976): 7–78.

Earle, Jonathan H. *Jacksonian Antislavery and the Politics of Free Soil, 1824–1854*. Chapel Hill: University of North Carolina Press, 2004.

Earle, Thomas, ed. *The Life, Travels, and Opinions of Benjamin Lundy*. 1847; New York: Negro Universities Press, 1969.

Eaton, Clement. *The Freedom-of-Thought Struggle in the Old South*. 1940. New York: Harper, 1964.

Eckenrode, H. J. *The Revolution in Virginia*. 1916. Hamden, Conn.: Archon Books, 1964.

Egerton, Douglas R. *Charles Fenton Mercer and the Trial of National Conservatism*. Jackson: University Press of Mississippi, 1989.

———. *Gabriel's Rebellion: The Virginia Slave Conspiracies of 1800 and 1802*. Chapel Hill: University of North Carolina Press, 1993.

———. "'Its Origin Is Not a Little Curious': A New Look at the American Colonization Society." *Journal of the Early Republic* 5 (Winter 1985): 463–80.

Einhorn, Robin L. *American Taxation, American Slavery*. Chicago: University of Chicago Press, 2006.

Essig, James D. *Bonds of Wickedness: American Evangelicals Against Slavery, 1770–1808*. Philadelphia: Temple University Press, 1982.

Evans, Charles, ed. *Journal of the Life and Religious Services of William Evans, a Minister of the Gospel in the Society of Friends*. Philadelphia: Friends Book Store, 1870.

Evans, Emory G. *A "Topping People": The Rise and Decline of Virginia's Old Political Elite, 1680–1790*. Charlottesville: University of Virginia Press, 2009.

Evans, William, and Thomas Evans, eds. *The Friends' Library: Comprising Journals, Doctrinal Treatises, and Other Writings of Members of the Religious Society of Friends.* 14 vols. Philadelphia: J. Rakestraw, 1837–1850.

Farnham, Christie Anne. *The Education of the Southern Belle: Higher Education and Student Socialization in the Antebellum South.* New York: New York University Press, 1994.

Faulkner, Carol. *Women's Radical Reconstruction: The Freedmen's Aid Movement.* Philadelphia: University of Pennsylvania Press, 2004.

Faust, Drew. *Mothers of Invention: Women of the Slaveholding South in the American Civil War.* Chapel Hill: University of North Carolina Press, 1996.

Fawcett, Thomas H. "Quaker Migration from Pennsylvania and New Jersey to Hopewell Monthly Meeting, 1732–1759." *Bulletin of Friends' Historical Association* 26 (Autumn 1937): 102–108.

Fellman, Michael. *Inside War: Guerrilla Conflict in Missouri during the Civil War.* New York: Oxford University Press, 1989.

Fields, Barbara Jeanne. *Slavery and Freedom on the Middle Ground: Maryland during the Nineteenth Century.* New Haven, Conn.: Yale University Press, 1985.

Finnie, Gordon E. "The Antislavery Movement in the Upper South before 1840." *Journal of Southern History* 35 (August 1969): 319–42.

Fischer, David Hackett, and James C. Kelly. *Bound Away: Virginia and the Westward Movement.* Charlottesville: University Press of Virginia, 2000.

Fitzpatrick, John C., ed. *The Writings of George Washington from the Original Manuscript Sources, 1745–1799.* 39 vols. Washington, D.C.: Government Printing Office, 1931–1944.

Foner, Eric. *Reconstruction: America's Unfinished Revolution, 1863–1877.* New York: Harper and Row, 1988.

——, ed. *Thomas Paine: Collected Writings.* New York: Library of America, 1995.

Forbes, Susan S. "Quaker Tribalism." In Zuckerman, *Friends and Neighbors,* 145–73.

Forbush, Bliss. *Elias Hicks: Quaker Liberal.* New York: Columbia University Press, 1956.

——. *A History of Baltimore Yearly Meeting of Friends: Three Hundred Years of Quakerism in Maryland, Virginia, the District of Columbia, and Central Pennsylvania.* Baltimore: Baltimore Yearly Meeting of Friends, 1972.

——. *Moses Sheppard: Quaker Philanthropist of Baltimore.* Philadelphia: J. B. Lippincott, 1968.

Ford, Alice. *Edward Hicks, His Life and Art.* New York: Abbeville Press, 1985.

——. *Edward Hicks: Painter of the Peaceable Kingdom.* 1952. Philadelphia: University of Pennsylvania Press, 1998.

Foster, Stephen S. *The Brotherhood of Thieves.* 1843. New York: Arno Press, 1969.

Fox, George. *A Collection of Many Select and Christian Epistles, Letters and Testimonies, Written on Sundry Occasions by That Ancient, Eminent, Faithful Friend, and Minister of Jesus Christ, George Fox.* 2 vols. Philadelphia: Marcus T. C. Gould, 1831.

Fox-Genovese, Elizabeth. *Within the Plantation Household: Black and White Women of the Old South.* Chapel Hill: University of North Carolina Press, 1988.

Frederickson, George M. *The Black Image in the White Mind: The Debate on Afro-American Character and Destiny, 1817–1914.* New York: Harper and Row, 1971.

Freehling, Alison Goodyear. *Drift toward Dissolution: The Virginia Slavery Debate of 1831–32.* Baton Rouge: Louisiana State University, 1982.

Freehling, William W. *The Road to Disunion*. Vol. 1, *Secessionists at Bay, 1776–1854*. New York: Oxford University Press, 1990.

———. *The Road to Disunion*. Vol. 2, *Secessionists Triumphant, 1854–1861*. New York: Oxford University Press, 2007.

———. *The South vs. the South: How Anti-Confederate Southerners Shaped the Course of the Civil War*. New York: Oxford University Press, 1999.

Fremantle, Arthur James Lyon. *Three Months in the Southern States: April–June 1863*. New York: John Bradburn, 1864.

Frey, Sylvia. *Water from the Rock: Black Resistance in a Revolutionary Age*. Princeton, N.J.: Princeton University Press, 1991.

Friedman, Lawrence J. *Gregarious Saints: Self and Community in American Abolitionism, 1830–1870*. New York: Cambridge University Press, 1982.

Friends' Association of Philadelphia for the Aid and Elevation of the Freedmen. *Sixth Annual Report*. Philadelphia: Thomas William Stuckey, 1870.

Friends' Educational Association. *Address of Some Members of the Society of Friends to Their Fellow Members on the Subject of Education: And on the Establishment of a Boarding School for Friends' Children and the Education of Teachers*. Philadelphia: Merrihew and Thompson, 1861.

Frost, J. William. "From Plainness to Simplicity: Changing Quaker Ideals for Material Culture." In Lapsansky and Verplanck, *Quaker Aesthetics*, 16–40.

———. "The Origins of the Quaker Crusade against Slavery: A Review of Recent Literature." *Quaker History* 67 (Spring 1978): 42–58.

———. *The Quaker Family in Colonial America: A Portrait of the Society of Friends*. New York: St. Martin's Press, 1973.

Galbreath, C. B. "Edwin Coppoc." *Ohio Archaeological and Historical Publications* 30 (1921): 396–451.

Galpin, W. F. "The Grain Trade of Alexandria, 1801–1815." *North Carolina Historical Review* 4 (October 1927): 403–27.

Gara, Larry. *The Liberty Line: The Legend of the Underground Railroad*. 1961. Lexington: University Press of Kentucky, 1996.

Garfinkle, Susan. "Quakers and High Chests: The Plainness Problem Reconsidered." In Lapsansky and Verplanck, *Quaker Aesthetics*, 50–89.

Garrison, William Lloyd. *Thoughts on African Colonization*. 1832. New York: Arno Press, 1968.

Gary, Anne T. "The Economic and Political Relations of English and American Quakers (1750–1785)." PhD diss., St. Hugh's College, Oxford University, 1935.

Genovese, Eugene. *Political Economy of Slavery: Studies in the Economy and Society of the Slave South*. 1965. Middletown, Conn.: Wesleyan University Press, 1989.

George, Christopher T. "Mirage of Freedom: African Americans in the War of 1812." *Maryland Historical Magazine* 91 (Winter 1996): 426–50.

Gewehr, Wesley. *The Great Awakening in Virginia, 1740–1790*. 1930. Gloucester, Mass.: P. Smith, 1965.

Gilbert, E. W., and Benjamin Ferris. *Letters of Paul and Amicus: Originally Published in the "Christian Repository," a Weekly Paper, Printed at Wilmington, Delaware*. Wilmington: Robert Porter, 1823.

Gillingham, Chalkley. *The Journal of Chalkley Gillingham: Friend in the Midst of Civil War*. Alexandria, Va.: Alexandria Monthly Meeting, 1988.

Gilpin, Thomas, ed. *Exiles in Virginia: With Observations on the Conduct of the Society of Friends during the Revolutionary War*. Philadelphia: [C. Sherman], 1848.

Ginzberg, Lori D. *Women and the Work of Benevolence: Morality, Politics, and Class in the Nineteenth-Century United States*. New Haven, Conn.: Yale University Press, 1990.

Good, Donald G. "Elisha Bates and the Hicksite Controversy." *Quaker History* 70 (Fall 1981): 104–17.

Goodhart, Briscoe. *History of the Independent Loudoun Rangers, U.S. Vol. Cav. (Scouts), 1862–65*. Washington, D.C.: McGill and Wallace, 1896.

Gouger, James B. "The Northern Neck of Virginia: A Tidewater Grain-Farming Region in the Antebellum South." In *Essays in the Human Geography of the Southeastern United States*, edited by David C. Weaver, 73–90. West Georgia College Studies in the Social Studies, no. 16. Carrollton: West Georgia College, 1977.

Gould, Marcus T. C., trans. *Sermons by Thomas Wetherald, and Elias Hicks, Delivered during the Yearly Meeting of Friends, in the City of New York, June, 1826. . . .* Philadelphia: M. T. C. Gould, 1826.

Gragg, Larry Dale. *Migration in Early America: The Virginia Quaker Experience*. Ann Arbor: UMI Research Press, 1980.

Graham, James. *The Life of General Daniel Morgan, of the Virginia Line of the Army of the United States. . . .* New York: Derby and Jackson, 1859.

Gray, Gertrude E., comp. *Virginia Northern Neck Land Grants, 1694–1862*. 4 vols. Baltimore: Genealogical Publishing, 1987–1993.

Gray, Lewis Cecil. *History of Agriculture in the Southern United States to 1860*. 2 vols. 1932. New York: Peter Smith, 1958.

Green, Constance McLaughlin. *Washington: Village and Capital, 1800–1878*. Princeton, N.J.: Princeton University Press, 1962.

Gregg, John William. *William Gregg: Quaker Immigrant and His Descendents*. Middleton, Wis.: n.p., 1979.

Griffler, Keith P. *Front Line of Freedom: African Americans and the Forging of the Underground Railroad in the Ohio Valley*. Lexington: University Press of Kentucky, 2004.

Grimsley, Mark. *The Hard Hand of War: Union Military Policy toward Southern Civilians, 1861–1865*. New York: Cambridge University Press, 1995.

Grose, Polly. *Hannah: The Story of Hannah Ingledew Janney, 1725–1818*. York, Eng.: William Sessions, 1997.

Gudmestad, Robert H. *A Troublesome Commerce: The Transformation of the Interstate Slave Trade*. Baton Rouge: Louisiana State University Press, 2003.

Guenther, Karen. "A Crisis of Allegiance: Berks County, Pennsylvania Quakers and the War for Independence." *Quaker History* 90 (Fall 2001): 15–34.

Guild, June Purcell, ed. *Black Laws of Virginia: A Summary of the Legislative Acts of Virginia Concerning Negroes from Earliest Times to the Present*. Richmond, Va.: Whittet and Shepperson, 1936.

Gurney, John Joseph. *A Journey in North America; Described in Familiar Letters to Amelia Opie*. Norwich, Eng.: J. Fletcher, 1841.

——. *A Letter to the Followers of Elias Hicks, in the City of Baltimore and Its Vicinity.* Baltimore: Woods and Crane, 1840.

Hallowell, Anna Davis, ed. *James and Lucretia Mott: Life and Letters.* Boston: Houghton, Mifflin, and Co., 1884.

Hallowell, Benjamin. *Address of Benjamin Hallowell, of Alexandria, at the First Annual Meeting of the Agricultural Society of Loudoun County, Va., Held at Leesburg, October 19, 1852.* Washington, D.C.: Gideon, 1853.

——. *Address of Benjamin Hallowell, (of Alexandria, Virginia,) at the Meeting of the Agricultural Society of Montgomery County, Md., Held at Rockville, Montgomery Co., September 9, 1852.* Washington, D.C.: Congressional Globe Office, 1852.

——. *Autobiography of Benjamin Hallowell.* Philadelphia: Friends' Book Association, 1884.

——. *Memoir of Margaret Brown.* Philadelphia: Merrihew and Son, 1872.

Hamm, Thomas D. *God's Government Begun: The Society for Universal Inquiry and Reform, 1842–1846.* Bloomington: Indiana University Press, 1995.

——. *The Quakers in America.* New York: Columbia University Press, 2003.

——. *The Transformation of American Quakerism: Orthodox Friends, 1800–1907.* Bloomington: Indiana University Press, 1988.

Hare, Caroline, ed. *Life and Letters of Elizabeth L. Comstock.* Philadelphia: John C. Winston, 1895.

Harrison, Fairfax. *Landmarks of Old Prince William: A Study of Origins in Northern Virginia.* 2 vols. Richmond, Va.: Old Dominion Press, 1924.

——, ed. "With Braddock's Army: Mrs. Browne's Diary in Virginia and Maryland," *Virginia Magazine of History and Biography* 32 (October 1924): 305–20.

Harrison, Noel G. "Atop an Anvil: The Civilians' War in Fairfax and Alexandria Counties, April 1861–April 1862." *Virginia Magazine of History and Biography* 106 (Spring 1998): 133–64.

Harrold, Stanley. *The Abolitionists and the South, 1831–1861.* Lexington: University Press of Kentucky, 1995.

——. *The Rise of Aggressive Abolitionism: Addresses to the Slaves.* Lexington: University Press of Kentucky, 2004.

——. *Subversives: Antislavery Community in Washington, D.C., 1828–1865.* Baton Rouge: Louisiana State University Press, 2003.

Hart, Freeman H. *The Valley of Virginia in the American Revolution.* Chapel Hill: University of North Carolina Press, 1942.

Haviland, Margaret Morris. "Beyond Women's Sphere: Young Quaker Women and the Veil of Charity in Philadelphia, 1790–1810." *William and Mary Quarterly*, 3rd ser., 51 (July 1994): 419–46.

Hening, W. W., ed. *The Statutes at Large: Being a Collection of all the Laws of Virginia, from the First Session of the Legislature, in the Year 1619.* 13 vols. Richmond, New York, and Philadelphia, 1809–1823.

Hewitt, Nancy. "Feminist Friends: Agrarian Quakers and the Emergence of Woman's Rights in America." *Feminist Studies* 12 (Spring 1986): 27–49.

——. "The Fragmentation of Friends: The Consequences for Quaker Women in Antebellum America." In Brown and Stuard, *Witnesses for Change,* 93–108.

Heyrman, Christine Leigh. *Southern Cross: The Beginnings of the Bible Belt.* New York: Alfred A. Knopf, 1997.

Hickin, Patricia E. P. "Antislavery in Virginia, 1831–1861." PhD diss., University of Virginia, 1968.

———. "Gentle Agitator: Samuel M. Janney and the Antislavery Movement in Virginia, 1842–1851." *Journal of Southern History* 37 (May 1971): 159–90.

Hicks, Edward [A Poor Illiterate Mechanic, pseud.]. *A Little Present for Friends and Friendly People in the Form of a Miscellaneous Discourse.* Philadelphia: John Richards, 1846.

———. *Memoirs of the Life and Religious Labors of Edward Hicks, Late of Newtown, Bucks County, Pennsylvania.* Philadelphia: Merrihew and Thompson, 1851.

Hicks, Elias. *Journal of the Life and Religious Labours of Elias Hicks.* New York: Isaac T. Hopper, 1832.

———. *Observations on the Slavery of the Africans and Their Descendants, and on the Use of the Produce of Their Labour.* New York: Samuel Wood, 1811.

Hill, Christopher. *The World Turned Upside Down: Radical Ideas during the English Revolution.* New York: Viking, 1972.

Hills, Timothy J. "The Origins of West End and the Little River Turnpike: Urbanization and Economic Change in Northern Virginia, 1780–1820." MA thesis, Washington State University, 1993.

Hinderaker, Eric. *Elusive Empires: Constructing Colonialism in the Ohio Valley, 1673–1800.* New York: Cambridge University Press, 1997.

Hinshaw, William Wade. *Encyclopedia of American Quaker Genealogy.* 6 vols. Ann Arbor: Edward Brothers, 1936–1950.

Hinton, Richard J. *John Brown and His Men, with Some Account of the Roads They Traveled to Reach Harper's Ferry.* New York: Funk and Wagnalls, 1894.

Hirschman, Albert O. *The Strategy of Economic Development.* New Haven, Conn.: Yale University Press, 1958.

Hirst, Harold W. *Alexandria on the Potomac: The Portrait of an Antebellum Community.* New York: University Press of America, 1991.

[Hodge, Charles]. "Davies's State of Religion among the Dissenters of Virginia," *Biblical Repertory and Princeton Review* (April 1840), 169–205.

Hofstra, Warren R. "'The Extention of His Majesties Dominions': The Virginia Backcountry and the Reconfiguration of Imperial Frontiers." *Journal of American History* 84 (March 1998): 1281–312.

———. *The Planting of New Virginia: Settlement and Landscape in the Shenandoah Valley.* Baltimore: Johns Hopkins University Press, 2004.

———. "'These Fine Prospects': Frederick County, Virginia, 1738–1840." PhD diss., University of Virginia, 1985.

Holifield, E. Brooks. *Theology in America: Christian Thought from the Age of the Puritans to the Civil War.* New Haven, Conn.: Yale University Press, 2003.

Holton, Woody. *Forced Founders: Indians, Debtors, Slaves, and the Making of the American Revolution.* Chapel Hill: University of North Carolina Press, 1999.

Hopewell Friends. *Hopewell Friends History, 1734–1934, Frederick County, Virginia: Records of Hopewell Monthly Meetings and Meetings Reporting to Hopewell.* Strasburg, Va.: Shenandoah Publishing House, 1936.

Hopkins, Gerald T. *A Mission to the Indians, from the Indian Committee of Baltimore Yearly Meeting, to Fort Wayne, in 1804 . . . With an Appendix, Compiled in 1862, by Martha E. Tyson*. Philadelphia: T. Ellwood Zell, 1862.

Hopkins, Luther W. *From Bull Run to Appomattox: A Boy's View*. 3rd ed. Baltimore: Fleet-McGinley, 1914.

Horn, James. *Adapting to a New World: English Society in the Seventeenth-Century Chesapeake*. Chapel Hill: University of North Carolina Press, 1994.

Horst, Samuel. *Mennonites in the Confederacy: A Study in Civil War Pacifism*. Scottdale, Pa.: Herald Press, 1967.

Horton, James Oliver. *Free People of Color: Inside the Arrican American Community*. Washington, D.C.: Smithsonian Institution Press, 1993.

Howe, Daniel Walker. *The Political Culture of the American Whigs*. Chicago: University of Chicago Press, 1979.

Howe, Henry. *Historical Collections of Virginia; Containing a Collection of the Most Interesting Facts, Traditions, Biographical Sketches, Anecdotes, &c., Relating to Its History and Antiquities. . . .* 1845. Baltimore: Regional Publishing, 1969.

Hubbs, Rebecca. *A Memoir of Rebecca Hubbs, a Minister of the Gospel of the Society of Friends, Late of Woodstown, N.J.* Philadelphia: Friends' Books Store, [c. 1870].

Hudson, J. Blaine. *Fugitive Slaves and the Underground Railroad in the Kentucky Borderland*. Jefferson, N.C.: McFarland, 2003.

Hunt, Gaillard, ed. *The First Forty Years of Washington Society: Portrayed by the Family Letters of Mrs. Samuel Harrison Smith (Margaret Bayard). . . .* New York: Charles Scribner's Sons, 1906.

Ingle, H. Larry. "'A Ball that has Rolled Beyond Our Reach': The Consequences of Hicksite Reform, 1830, as Seen in an Exchange of Letters." *Delaware History* 21 (Fall–Winter 1984): 127–37.

———. *First among Friends: George Fox and the Creation of Quakerism*. New York: Oxford University Press, 1994.

———. *Quakers in Conflict: The Hicksite Reformation*. Knoxville: University of Tennessee Press, 1986.

Inscoe, John C., and Robert C. Kenzer, eds. *Enemies of the Country: New Perspectives on Unionists in the Civil War South*. Athens: University of Georgia Press, 2001.

Irving, Washington, ed. *Biography and Poetical Remains of the Late Margaret Miller Davidson*. Philadelphia: Lea and Blanchard, 1841.

Isaac, Rhys. *Landon Carter's Uneasy Kingdom: Revolution and Rebellion on a Virginia Plantation*. New York: Oxford University Press, 2004.

———. *The Transformation of Virginia, 1740–1790*. Chapel Hill: University of North Carolina Press, 1982.

Isenberg, Nancy. *Sex and Citizenship in Antebellum America*. Chapel Hill: University of North Carolina Press, 1998.

Isichei, Elizabeth. *Victorian Quakers*. London: Oxford University Press, 1970.

Jackson, Maurice. *Let This Voice Be Heard: Anthony Benezet, Father of Atlantic Abolitionism*. Philadelphia: University of Pennsylvania Press, 2009.

James, Sydney V. "The Impact of the American Revolution on Quakers' Ideas about Their Sect." *William and Mary Quarterly*, 3rd ser., 19 (July 1962): 360–82.

———. *A People among Peoples: Quaker Benevolence in Eighteenth-Century America*. Cambridge, Mass.: Harvard University Press, 1963.

Janney, Asa Moore, and Werner L. Janney. *The Composition Book: Stories from the Old Days in Lincoln, Virginia*. Bethesda, Md.: Sign of the Pied Typer, 1973.

———, eds. *John Janney's Virginia: An American Farm Lad's Life in the Early Nineteenth Century*. McLean, Va.: EPM Publications, 1978.

———. *Ye Meetg Hous Smal: A Short Account of Friends in Loudoun County, Virginia, 1732–1980*. Lincoln, Va.: n.p., 1980.

Janney, Samuel M. *Conversations on Religious Subjects, Between a Father and His Two Sons*. 4th ed. 1835. Philadelphia: Friends' Book Association, 1860.

———. *Essays on Practical Piety and Divine Grace*. Philadelphia: Book Association of Friends, 1860.

———. *History of the Religious Society of Friends, from Its Rise to the Year 1828*. 4 vols. Philadelphia: T. E. Zell, 1861–1868.

———. *The Life of George Fox: With Dissertations on His Views Concerning the Doctrines, Testimonies, and Discipline of the Christian Church*. Philadelphia: Lippincott, Grambo, 1853.

———. *The Life of William Penn: With Selections from His Correspondence and Autobiography*. Philadelphia: Hogan, Perkins, 1851.

———. *Memoirs of Samuel M. Janney*. Philadelphia: Friends Book Association, 1881.

———. *The Yankees in Fairfax County, Virginia, by a Virginian*. Baltimore: Snodgrass and Wehrly, 1845.

Jay, Allen. *Autobiography of Allen Jay, Born 1831, Died 1910*. Philadelphia: John C. Winston, 1910.

Jenkins, Virginia. *Edward Stabler, 'A Kind Friend and Counsellor': A Quaker and Abolitionist in Alexandria, Virginia, 1790–1830*. Alexandria, Va.: Alexandria Archaeology Publications, 1995.

Jennings, Francis. "Brother Miquon: Good Lord!" In Dunn and Dunn, *The World of William Penn*, 195–214.

Jensen, Joan M. *Loosening the Bonds: Mid-Atlantic Farm Women, 1750–1850*. New Haven, Conn.: Yale University Press, 1986.

Johnson, Herbert A., Charles T. Cullen, and Charles Hobson, eds. *The Papers of John Marshall*. 12 vols. Chapel Hill: University of North Carolina Press, 1974–2006.

Johnston, J. H., ed. "Antislavery Petitions Presented to the Virginia Legislature by Citizens of Various Counties." *Journal of Negro History* 12 (October 1927): 670–91.

Jolliffe, William. *Historical, Genealogical, and Biographical Account of the Jolliffe Family of Virginia, 1652 to 1893*. Philadelphia: J. B. Lippincott, 1893.

Jones, Louis Thomas. *The Quakers of Iowa*. Iowa City: State Historical Society of Iowa, 1914.

Jones, Rufus M. *The Later Periods of Quakerism*. 2 vols. London: Macmillan, 1921.

———. *The Quakers in the American Colonies*. 1913. New York: Russell and Russell, 1962.

———, ed. *The Record of a Quaker Conscience: Cyrus Pringle's Diary*. New York: The MacMillan Company, 1918.

Jordan, Ryan. *Slavery and the Meetinghouse: The Quakers and the Abolitionist Dilemma, 1820–1865*. Bloomington: Indiana University Press, 2007.

Jordan, Winthrop D. *White over Black: American Attitudes toward the Negro, 1550–1812.* Chapel Hill: University of North Carolina Press, 1968.

Judge, Hugh. *Memoirs and Journal of Hugh Judge, a Member of the Society of Friends and Minister of the Gospel. . . .* Byberry, Pa.: J. and I. Comly, 1841.

Kamoie, Laura Croghan. *Irons in the Fire: The Business History of the Tayloe Family and Virginia's Gentry, 1700–1860.* Charlottesville: University of Virginia Press, 2007.

Katz, Stanley N., John M. Murrin, and Douglas Greenberg, eds. *Colonial America: Essays in Politics and Social Development.* 5th ed. Boston: McGraw-Hill, 2001.

Keller, Robert H. *American Protestantism and United States Indian Policy, 1869–82.* Lincoln: University of Nebraska Press, 1983.

Kelley, Mary. *Learning to Stand and Speak: Women, Education, and Public Life in America's Republic.* Chapel Hill: University of North Carolina Press, 2006.

Kelsey, Rayner W. "Early Disciplines of the Philadelphia Yearly Meeting." *Bulletin of the Friends Historical Association* 24 (Spring 1935): 20–30.

———. *Friends and the Indians, 1655–1917.* Philadelphia: Associated Executive Committee of Friends on Indian Affairs, 1917.

Kerber, Linda K. *Women of the Republic: Intellect and Ideology in Revolutionary America.* 1980. New York: W. W. Norton, 1986.

Kercheval, Samuel. *A History of the Valley of Virginia.* 4th ed. Strasburg, Va.: Shenandoah Publishing, 1925.

Klingaman, David C. "Colonial Virginia's Coastwise and Grain Trade." PhD diss., University of Virginia, 1967.

———. "The Significance of Grain in the Development of the Tobacco Colonies." *Journal of Economic History* 29 (June 1969): 268–78.

Knee, Stuart E. "The Quaker Petition of 1790: A Challenge to Democracy in Early America." *Slavery and Abolition* 6 (September 1985): 151–59.

Knepper, George W. "The Convention Army, 1777–1783." PhD diss., University of Michigan, 1954.

Kraditor, Aileen S. *Means and Ends in American Abolitionism: Garrison and His Critics on Strategy and Tactics, 1834–1850.* New York: Pantheon Books, 1967.

Kulikoff, Allan. *Tobacco and Slaves: The Development of Southern Cultures in the Chesapeake, 1680–1800.* Chapel Hill: University of North Carolina Press, 1986.

Kundahl, George G. *Alexandria Goes to War: Beyond Robert E. Lee.* Knoxville: University of Tennessee Press, 2004.

Lapsansky, Emma Jones. "Past Plainness to Present Simplicity: A Search for Quaker Identity." In Lapsansky and Verplanck, *Quaker Aesthetics*, 1–15.

Lapsansky, Emma Jones, and Anne A. Verplanck, eds. *Quaker Aesthetics: Reflections on a Quaker Ethic in American Design and Consumption.* Philadelphia: University of Pennsylvania Press, 2003.

Lapsanky-Warner, Emma J., and Margaret Hope Bacon, eds. *Back to Africa: Benjamin Coates and the Colonization Movement in America, 1848–1880.* University Park: Pennsylvania State University Press, 2005.

Larson, John Lauritz. *Internal Improvements: National Public Works and the Promise of Popular Government in the Early United States.* Chapel Hill: University of North Carolina Press, 2001.

Larson, Rebecca. *Daughters of Light: Preaching and Prophesying in the Colonies and Abroad, 1700–1775*. Chapel Hill: University of North Carolina Press, 1999.

Lebsock, Suzanne. *The Free Women of Petersburg: Status and Culture in a Southern Town, 1784–1860*. New York: W. W. Norton, 1984.

Lee, Arthur. *Extract from an Address in the Virginia Gazette, of March 19, 1767, by a Respectable Member of the Community*. Philadelphia: Joseph Crukshank, 1770.

Levy, Barry. "The Birth of the 'Modern Family' in Early America: Quaker and Anglican Families in the Delaware Valley, Pennsylvania, 1681–1750." In Zuckerman, *Friends and Neighbors*, 26–64.

———. *Quakers and the American Family: British Settlement in the Delaware Valley*. New York: Oxford University Press, 1988.

———. "'Tender Plants': Quaker Farmers and Children in the Delaware Valley, 1681–1735." In *Colonial America: Essays in Politics and Social Development*, edited by Stanley N. Katz, John M. Murrin, and Douglas Greenberg, 240–65. 5th ed. New York: McGraw-Hill, 2001.

Lewis, Charles. "Journal of Captain Charles Lewis of the Virginia Regiment . . . in the Expedition against the French, Oct. 10–Dec. 27, 1755." In *Proceedings of the Virginia Historical Society at the Annual Meeting Held December 21–22, 1891 . . .*, 204–18. Richmond: Virginia Historical Society, 1892.

Lewis, Virgil A. *Third Biennial Report of the Department of Archives and History of the State of West Virginia*. Charleston: Mail-New Company, 1911.

Light, Mary Jane Jolliffe. "The Hollingsworth Family." In *Journal of the Winchester-Frederick County Historical Society* 10 (1997), 12–23.

Link, William A. *Roots of Secession: Slavery and Politics in Antebellum Virginia*. Chapel Hill: University of North Carolina Press, 2003.

Lippincott, Mary S. *Life and Letters of Mary S. Lippincott, Late of Camden, New Jersey, a Minister in the Society of Friends*. Philadelphia: William H. Pile, 1893.

Littlefield, Douglas R. "The Potomac Company: A Misadventure in Financing an Early American Internal Improvement Project." *Business History Review* 58 (Winter 1984): 562–85.

Longenecker, Stephen L. *Shenandoah Religion: Outsiders and the Mainstream, 1716–1865*. Waco, Tex.: Baylor University Press, 2002.

Lowe, Richard G. "The Republican Party in Antebellum Virginia, 1856–1860." *Virginia Magazine of History and Biography* 81 (July 1973): 259–79.

———. *Republicans and Reconstruction in Virginia, 1856–70*. Charlottesville: University Press of Virginia, 1991.

Lyell, Sir Charles. *A Second Visit to the United States of North America*. 2 vols. London: John Murray, 1849.

Lynch, William O. "The Westward Flow of Southern Colonists before 1861." *Journal of Southern History* 9 (August 1943): 303–27.

Mack, Phyllis. "In a Female Voice: Preaching and Politics in Eighteenth-Century British Quakerism." In *Women Preachers and Prophets through Two Millennia of Christianity*, edited by Beverly Kienzle and Pamela J. Walkers, 248–63. Berkeley: University of California Press, 1998.

Mackey, Robert R. *The Uncivil War: Irregular Warfare in the Upper South, 1861–1865.* Norman, Okla.: University of Oklahoma Press, 2004.

Maddox, William Arthur. *The Free School Idea in Virginia Before the Civil War.* 1918. New York: Arno Press, 1969.

———. "'A Cruel and Malicious War': The Society of Friends in Civil War Loudoun County, Virginia." *Quaker History* 88 (Spring 1999): 40–62.

Mahon, Michael G. *The Shenandoah Valley, 1861–1865: The Destruction of the Granary of the Confederacy.* Mechanicsburg, Pa.: Stackpole Books, 1999.

———, ed. *Winchester Divided: The Civil War Diaries of Julia Chase and Laura Lee.* Mechanicsburg, Pa.: Stackpole Books, 2002.

Mangus, Michael Stuart. "'The Debatable Land': Loudoun and Fauquier Counties, Virginia, during the Civil War Era." PhD diss., Ohio State University, 1998.

Marietta, Jack D. "Egoism and Altruism in Quaker Abolition." *Quaker History* 82 (Spring 1993): 1–22.

———. *The Reformation of American Quakerism, 1748–1783.* Philadelphia: University of Pennsylvania Press, 1984.

Masur, Daniel. *1831: Year of Eclipse.* New York: Hill and Wang, 2001.

Mathews, Donald. *Slavery and Methodism: A Chapter in American Morality, 1780–1845.* Princeton, N.J.: Princeton University Press, 1965.

Mauro, Charles V. *The Civil War in Fairfax County: Civilians and Soldiers.* Charleston, S.C.: History Press, 2006.

Mayer, Henry. *All on Fire: William Lloyd Garrison and the Abolition of Slavery.* New York: St. Martin's Press, 1998.

Mays, David John, ed. *The Letters and Papers of Edmund Pendleton.* 2 vols. Charlottesville: University Press of Virginia, 1967.

McCarthy, Timothy Patrick, and John Stauffer, eds. *Prophets of Protest: Reconsidering the History of American Abolitionism.* New York: New Press, 2006.

McColley, Robert. *Slavery and Jeffersonian Virginia.* 1964. Urbana: University of Illinois Press, 1973.

McCord, T. B., Jr. *Across the Fence, but a World Apart: The Coleman Site, 1796–1907.* Alexandria, Va.: Alexandria Archaeology, 1985.

McCurry, Stephanie. *Masters of Small Worlds: Yeoman Households, Gender Relations, and the Political Culture of the Antebellum South Carolina Low Country.* New York: Oxford University Press, 1995.

McDaniel, Donna, and Vanessa Julye. *Fit for Freedom, Not for Friendship: Quakers, African Americans, and the Myth of Racial Justice.* Philadelphia: Quaker Press, 2009.

McDonnell, Michael A. "Class War? Class Struggles during the American Revolution in Virginia." *William and Mary Quarterly,* 3rd ser., 63 (April 2006): 305–44.

———. *The Politics of War: Race, Class, and Conflict in Revolutionary Virginia.* Chapel Hill: University of North Carolina Press, 2007.

———. "Popular Mobilization and Political Culture in Revolutionary Virginia: The Failure of the Minutemen and the Revolution from Below." *Journal of American History* 85 (December 1998): 946–81.

McGraw, Marie Tyler. "The American Colonization Society in Virginia, 1816–1832." PhD diss., George Washington University, 1980.

McIlwaine, H. R., ed. *Journal of the House of Burgesses of Virginia, 1619–1776*. 13 vols. Richmond: Virginia State Library, 1905–1915.

McIlwaine, H. R., Wilmer Lee Hall, and Benjamin J. Hillman, eds. *Executive Journals of the Council of Colonial Virginia, 1680–1775*. 6 vols. Richmond: Virginia State Library, 1925–66.

McKivigan, John R., and Stanley Harrold, eds. *Antislavery Violence: Sectional, Racial, and Cultural Conflict in Antebellum America*. Knoxville: University of Tennessee Press, 1999.

McMaster, Richard K. "Religion, Migration, and Pluralism: A Shenandoah Valley Community, 1740–1790." In *Diversity and Accommodation: Essays on the Cultural Composition of the Virginia Frontier*, edited by Michael J. Puglisi, 82–98. Knoxville: University of Tennessee Press, 1997.

McPherson, James M. *Tried by War: Abraham Lincoln as Commander in Chief*. New York: Penguin, 2008.

Meade, Everard Kidder. *Frederick Parish, Virginia, 1744–1780*. Winchester, Va.: Pifer, 1947.

Meinig, D. W. *The Shaping of America: A Geographical Perspective on 500 Years of History*. Vol. 1, *Atlantic America, 1492–1800*. New Haven, Conn.: Yale University Press, 1986.

Mekeel, Arthur J. *The Quakers and the American Revolution*. York, Eng.: Sessions Book Trust, 1996.

———. *The Relation of Quakers to the American Revolution*. Washington, D.C.: University Press of America, 1979.

Meriwether, R. L., Clyde N. Wilson, William E. Hemphill, Shirley Bright Cook, and Alexander Moore, eds., *The Papers of John C. Calhoun*. 28 vols. Columbia: University of South Carolina Press, 1959–2003.

Merrell, James H. *Into the American Woods: Negotiators on the Pennsylvania Frontier*. New York: W. W. Norton, 1999.

Meserve, Stevan F. *The Civil War in Loudoun County, Virginia: A History of Hard Times*. Charleston, S.C.: History Press, 2008.

Mifflin, Warner. *The Defense of Warner Mifflin against Aspersion Cast on Him on Account of His Endeavours to Promote Righteousness, Mercy and Peace, Among Mankind*. Philadelphia: Samuel Samson, 1796.

Miles, Lion G. "The Winchester Hessian Barracks." *Winchester-Frederick County Historical Society Journal* 3 (1988): 19–63.

Miller, T. Michael. *Artisans and Merchants of Alexandria, 1780–1820*. 2 vols. Bowie, Md.: Heritage Books, 1992.

———. "'Out of Bondage': A History of the Alexandria Colonization Society." *Alexandria History* 7 (1987): 15–29.

———. *Portrait of a Town: Alexandria, District of Columbia [Virginia], 1820–1830*. Bowie, Md.: Heritage Books, 1995.

Miller, Warwick P. *Reminiscences of Warwick P. Miller of Alexandria, Virginia, 1896*. Alexandria, Va.: Alexandria Library, 1981.

Milner, Clyde A. *With Good Intentions: Quaker Work among the Pawnees, Otos, and Omahas in the 1870s*. Lincoln: University of Nebraska Press, 1982.

Mitchell, Robert D. *Commercialism and Frontier: Perspectives on the Early Shenandoah Valley*. Charlottesville: University Press of Virginia, 1977.

Monteiro, Aristides. *War Reminiscences by the Surgeon of Mosby's Command*. Richmond, Va.: s.n., 1890.

Moore, Harriet J. *Memoir and Letters of Harriet J. Moore*. Philadelphia: Merrihew and Thompson, 1856.

Moore, John M., ed. *Friends in the Delaware Valley: Philadelphia Yearly Meeting, 1681–1981*. Haverford, Pa.: Friends Historical Association, 1981.

Moorhead, James H. *American Apocalypse: Yankee Protestants and the Civil War, 1860–1869*. New Haven, Conn.: Yale University Press, 1978.

Morgan, Edmund S. *American Slavery-American Freedom: The Ordeal of Colonial Virginia*. New York: W. W. Norton, 1975.

Morrison, Alfred J., trans. and ed. *Travels in Confederation, [1783–1784]*. 2 vols. From the German of Johann David Schoepf (1788). Reprint of 1911 translation, New York: B. Franklin, 1968.

Moss, Roger W., Jr. "Isaac Zane, Jr., a 'Quaker for the Times.'" *Virginia Magazine of History and Biography* 77 (July 1969): 291–306.

Mountcastle, Clay. *Punitive War: Confederate Guerillas and Union Reprisals*. Lawrence: University Press of Kansas, 2009.

Muir, Dorothy Troth. *Potomac Interlude: The Story of Woodlawn Mansion and the Mount Vernon Neighborhood, 1846–1943*. Washington, D.C.: Mount Vernon Print Shop, 1943.

Myers, Frank M. *The Comanches: A History of White's Battalion, Virginia Cavalry. . . . 1871*. Marietta, Ga.: Continental Book, 1956.

Nash, Gary B. "Slaves and Slaveholders in Colonial Philadelphia." *William and Mary Quarterly*, 3rd ser., 30 (April 1973): 223–56.

National Convention for the Promotion of Education in the United States. *Proceedings of a National Convention for the Promotion of Education in the United States, Held at the City Hall, in the City of Washington, May 6, 7, 8, 1840*. Washington, D.C.: P. Force, 1840.

Nelson, Jacquelyn S. *Indiana Quakers Confront the Civil War*. Indianapolis: Indiana Historical Society, 1991.

Nelson, John K. *A Blessed Company: Parishes, Parsons, and Parishioners in Anglican Virginia, 1690–1776*. Chapel Hill: University of North Carolina Press, 2001.

Nelson, Lynn A. *Pharsalia: An Environmental Biography of a Southern Plantation, 1780–1880*. Athens: University of Georgia Press, 2007.

Nelson, Thomas, Jr. *Letters of Thomas Nelson, Jr., Governor of Virginia*. Publications of the Virginia Historical Society, New Series, No. 1. Richmond: Virginia Historical Society, 1874.

Netherton, Nan, Donald Sweig, Janice Artemel, Patricia Hickin, and Patrick Reed. *Fairfax County, Virginia: A History*. Fairfax, Va.: Fairfax County Board of Supervisors, 1978.

New England Yearly Meeting. *Views of the Society of Friends in Relation to Civil Government*. Providence, R.I.: Knowles and Vose, 1840.

Newman, Richard. *The Transformation of American Abolitionism: Fighting Slavery in the Early Republic*. Chapel Hill: University of North Carolina Press, 2002.

Nichols, Joseph V. *Legends of Loudoun Valley*. Leesburg, Va.: Potomac Press, 1961.

Norris, J. E., ed. *History of the Lower Shenandoah Valley Counties of Frederick, Berkeley, Jefferson, and Clarke. . . . 1890*. Berryville: Virginia Book, 1972.

Norton, Mary Beth. *Liberty's Daughters: The Revolutionary Experience of American Women, 1750–1800*. 1980. Ithaca: Cornell University Press, 1996.

Nuermberger, Ruth Anna Ketring. *The Free Produce Movement: A Quaker Protest against Slavery*. Durham, N.C.: Duke University Press, 1942.

Oakes, James. *The Radical and Republican: Frederick Douglass, Abraham Lincoln, and the Triumph of Antislavery Politics*. New York: W. W. Norton, 2007.

Oaks, Robert F. "Philadelphians in Exile: The Problem of Loyalty during the American Revolution." *Pennsylvania Magazine of History and Biography* 96 (July 1972): 298–325.

Oates, Stephen B. *The Fires of Jubilee: Nat Turner's Fierce Rebellion*. 1975. New York: Harper Perennial, 1990.

Osborn, Charles. *Journal of That Faithful Servant of Christ, Charles Osborn, Containing an Account of His Travels and Labors in the Work of the Ministry. . . .* Cincinnati: Achilles Pugh, 1854.

Pacheco, Josephine F. *The Pearl: A Failed Slave Escape on the Potomac*. Chapel Hill: University of North Carolina Press, 2005.

Palmer, William Pitt, Sherwin McRae, Raleigh Edward Colston, and Henry W. Flournoy, eds. *Calendar of Virginia State Papers and Other Manuscripts, Preserved at the Capitol at Richmond*. 11 vols. Richmond: R. F. Walker, 1875–1893.

Paludan, Phillip Shaw. *Victims: A True Story of the Civil War*. Knoxville: University of Tennessee Press, 1981.

Parker, Arthur C. *The Life of General Ely S. Parker: The Last Grand Sachem of the Iroquois and General Grant's Military Secretary*. Buffalo, N.Y.: Buffalo Historical Society, 1919.

Penington, Isaac. *Works of the Long-Mournful and Sorely-Distressed Isaac Penington. . . .* London, Eng.: Benjamin Clark, 1681.

Penn, William. *Some Fruits of Solitude in Reflections & Maxims*. 1693. London: Fremantle, 1901.

Perry, Lewis, and Michael Fellman, eds. *Antislavery Reconsidered: New Perspectives on Abolitionists*. Baton Rouge: Louisiana State University Press, 1979.

Peterson, Arthur G. "The Alexandria Market Prior to the Civil War." *William and Mary Quarterly*, 2nd ser., 12 (April 1932): 104–114.

Philadelphia Meeting for Sufferings. *Extracts from the Writing of Primitive Friends, Concerning the Divinity of Our Lord and Saviour, Jesus Christ*. Philadelphia: Solomon W. Conrad, 1823.

[Philadelphia Yearly Meeting (Orthodox)]. *A Declaration of the Yearly Meeting of Friends, Held in Philadelphia, Respecting the Proceedings of Those Who Have Lately Separated from the Society. . . .* Philadelphia: Thomas Kitt, 1828.

Philadelphia Yearly Meeting. *Some Observations Relating to the Establishment of Schools, Agreed to by the Committee, to Be Laid for the Consideration before the Yearly Meeting*. Philadelphia: n.p., 1778.

Phillips, Catherine. *Memoirs of the Life of Catherine Phillips; To Which Are Added Some of Her Epistles*. Philadelphia: Robert Johnson, 1798.

Phillips, Edward H. *The Lower Shenandoah Valley in the Civil War: The Impact of War upon the Civilian Population and upon Civil Institutions*. Lynchburg, Va.: H. E. Howard, 1993.

Phillips, John T. *The Historian's Guide to Loudoun County, Virginia*. Vol. 1, *Colonial Laws of Virginia and County Court Orders, 1757–1766*. Leesburg, Va.: Goose Creek Productions, 1996.

Philyaw, L. Scott. *Virginia's Western Visions: Political and Cultural Expansion on an Early American Frontier*. Knoxville: University of Tennessee Press, 2004.

Pitch, Anthony S. *The Burning of Washington: The British Invasion of 1814*. Annapolis, Md.: Naval Institute Press, 1998.

Poland, Charles Preston. *From Frontier to Suburbia*. Marceline, Mo.: Walsworth, 1976.

Price, Jacob M. "The Great Quaker Business Families of Eighteenth-Century London: The Rise and Fall of a Sectarian Patriciate." In Dunn and Dunn, *The World of William Penn*, 363–99.

Provine, Dorothy S., abst. *Alexandria County, Virginia, Free Negro Registers, 1797–1861*. Bowie, Md.: Heritage Books, 1990.

Prucha, Francis Paul. *The Great Father: The United States Government and the American Indians*. 2 vols. Lincoln: University of Nebraska Press, 1984.

Pybus, Cassandra. "Jefferson's Faulty Math: The Question of Slave Defections in the American Revolution." *William and Mary Quarterly*, 3rd ser., 62 (April 2005): 243–64.

"Quakers' Petition." *William and Mary Quarterly*, 1st ser., 14 (July 1905): 23–25.

Quarles, Benjamin. *Black Abolitionists*. New York: Oxford University Press, 1969.

———. *The Negro in the American Revolution*. Chapel Hill: University of North Carolina Press, 1961.

Rable, George C. *Civil Wars: Women and the Crisis of Southern Nationalism*. Urbana: University of Illinois Press, 1989.

Rael, Patrick. *Black Identity and Black Protest in the Antebellum North*. Chapel Hill: University of North Carolina Press, 2002.

Raistrick, Arthur. *Quakers in Science and Industry: Being an Account of the Quaker Contributions to Science and Industry during the Seventeenth and Eighteenth Centuries*. New York: Philosophical Library, 1950.

Ramage, James A. *Gray Ghost: The Life of Col. John Singleton Mosby*. Lexington: University Press of Kentucky, 1999.

———. "Recent Historiography of Guerrilla Warfare in the Civil War—A Review Essay." *Register of the Kentucky Historical Society* 103 (Summer 2005), 517–41.

Reckitt, William. *Some Account of the Life and Gospel Labours, of William Reckitt; Also, Memoirs of the Life, Religious Experiences, and Gospel Labours of James Gough, Late of Dublin, Deceased*. Philadelphia: Joseph Crukshank, 1783.

Redd, George. *Late Discovery, Extremely Interesting to Planters and Farmers, Relative to Fertilizing Poor and Exhausted Lands, upon a Cheap and Easy Plan. . . .* Winchester, Va.: J. A. Lingan, 1809.

Redpath, James. *The Public Life of Captain John Brown, with an Autobiography of His Childhood and Youth*. Boston: Thayer and Eldridge, 1860.

Reynolds, David S. *John Brown, Abolitionist: The Man Who Killed Slavery, Sparked the Civil War, and Seeded Civil Rights*. New York: Vintage Books, 2006.

———. *Walt Whitman's America: A Cultural Biography*. New York: Knopf, 1995.

Rhoads, Charles. *Business Ethics in Relation to the Profession of the Religious Society of Friends: An Address*. Philadelphia: n.p., 1882.

Rice, Otis K. "Eli Thayer and the Friendly Invasion of Virginia." *Journal of Southern History* 37 (November 1971): 575–96.

Rice, Philip Morrison. "Internal Improvements in Virginia, 1775–1860." PhD diss., University of North Carolina at Chapel Hill, 1948.

Richards, Gertrude R. B., ed. "Dr. David Stuart's Report to President Washington on Agricultural Conditions in Northern Virginia." *Virginia Magazine of History and Biography* 61 (July 1953): 283–92.

Richman, Irving B. *John Brown among the Quakers and Other Sketches.* Des Moines: Historical Department of Iowa, 1897.

Ridgeway, Michael A. "A Peculiar Business: Slave Trading in Alexandria, Virginia, 1825–1861." MA thesis, Georgetown University, 1976.

Riley, Glenda. "Legislative Divorce in Virginia, 1803–1850." *Journal of the Early Republic* 11 (Spring 1991): 51–67.

Royall, Anne. *Sketches of History, Life, and Manners, in the United States, by a Traveller.* New Haven, Conn.: printed for the author, 1826.

Rubin, Anne Sarah. "Between Union and Chaos: The Political Life of John Janney." *Virginia Magazine of History and Biography* 102 (July 1994): 381–416.

Ryan, Mary P. *Cradle of the Middle Class: The Family in Oneida County, New York, 1790–1865.* New York: Cambridge University Press, 1981.

Salitan, Lucille, and Eve Lewis Perera, eds. *Virtuous Lives: Four Quaker Sisters Remember Family Life, Abolitionism, and Women's Suffrage.* New York: Continuum, 1994.

Sanderlin, Walter S. *The Great National Project: A History of the Chesapeake and Ohio Company.* Baltimore: Johns Hopkins University Press, 1946.

Sappington, Roger E. "North Carolina and the Non-Resistant Sects During the American War of Independence." *Quaker History* 60 (Spring 1971): 29–47.

Schmidt, Frederika, and Barbara Wilhelm. "Early Proslavery Petitions in Virginia." *William and Mary Quarterly*, 3rd ser., 30 (January 1973): 133–46.

Schooley, George A., ed. *The Journal of Dr. William Schooley: Pioneer Physician, Quaker Minister, Abolitionist, Philosopher, and Scholar, 1794–1860, Somerset, Belmont County, Ohio.* Baltimore: Gateway Press, 1977.

Schreiner-Yantis, Netti, and Florence Speakman Love, eds. *The 1787 Census of Virginia: An Accounting of the Name of Every White Male Tithable Over 21 Years.* 3 vols. Springfield, Va.: Genealogical Books in Print, 1987.

Schwarz, Philip J. *Migrants Against Slavery: Virginians and the Nation.* Charlottesville: University Press of Virginia, 2001.

———. *Slave Laws of Virginia.* Athens: University of Georgia Press, 1988.

Schweninger, Loren, Robert Shelton, and Charles E. Smith, eds. *A Guide to the Microfilm Edition of "Race, Slavery, and Free Blacks: Series 1, Petitions to the Southern Legislatures, 1777–1867."* Bethesda, Md.: University Publications of America, 1999.

Scully, Randolph Ferguson. *Religion and the Making of Nat Turner's Virginia: Baptist Community and Conflict, 1740–1840.* Charlottesville: University Press of Virginia, 2008.

Seale, William. *The Alexandria Library Company.* Alexandria, Va.: Alexandria Library Company, 2007.

Seebohm, Benjamin, ed. *Memoirs of William Forster.* 2 vols. London: Alfred W. Bennett, 1865.

Selby, John E. *The Revolution in Virginia, 1775–1783*. Williamsburg, Va.: Colonial Williamsburg Foundation, 1988.

Shanks, Henry T. *The Secession Movement in Virginia, 1847–1861*. Richmond: Garrett and Massie, 1934.

Shepherd, Samuel, ed. *The Statutes at Large of Virginia, from October Session 1792, to December Session 1806 [i.e. 1807] Inclusive.* . . . 3 vols. 1835. New York: AMS Press, 1970.

Sheridan, Phillip H. *The Personal Memoirs of P. H. Sheridan, General United States Army.* 2 vols. New York: Charles L. Webster, 1888.

Siepel, Kevin H. *Rebel: The Life and Times of John Singleton Mosby*. 1983. New York: DeCapo Press, 1997.

Sinha, Manisha. *The Counter-Revolution of Slavery: Politics and Ideology in Antebellum South Carolina*. Chapel Hill: University of North Carolina Press, 2000.

Skemp, Sheila L. *Judith Sargent Murray: A Brief Biography with Documents*. New York: Bedford Books, 1998.

Skivora, Joseph F. "The Surrender of Alexandria in the War of 1812 and the Power of the Press." *Northern Virginia Heritage* 10 (June 1988): 9–13, 20.

Slaughter, Thomas P. *The Beautiful Soul of John Woolman, Apostle of Abolition*. New York: Hill and Wang, 2009.

Smith, Bruce R. "Benjamin Hallowell of Alexandria: Scientist, Educator, Quaker Idealist." *Virginia Magazine of History and Biography* 85 (July 1977): 337–61.

Smith, Paul H., Ronald M. Gephart, Gerard W. Gawalt, Rosemary Fry Plakas, and Eugene R. Sheridan, eds. *Letters of Delegates to Congress, 1774–1789*. 25 vols. Washington, D.C.: Library of Congress, 1976–2000.

Smith, Warren Sylvester. "'The Imperceptible Arrows of Quakerism': Moncure Conway at Sandy Spring." *Quaker History* 52 (Spring 1963): 19–26.

Smith, William Francis, and T. Michael Miller. *A Seaport Saga: Portrait of Old Alexandria, Virginia*. Norfolk, Va.: Donning, 1989.

Society of Congregational Friends. *Proceedings of the Yearly Meeting of Congregational Friends, Held at Waterloo, N.Y., from the 4th to the 6th of Sixth Month, Inclusive, 1849.* Auburn, N.Y.: Oliphant's Press, 1849.

Soderlund, Jean R. "On Quakers and Slavery: A Reply to Jack Marietta." *Quaker History* 82 (Spring 1993): 23–27.

———. *Quakers and Slavery: A Divided Spirit*. Princeton, N.J.: Princeton University Press, 1985.

———. "Response to 'Historiographical Developments in Early North American Quaker Studies.'" *Southern Friend* 13 (1991): 34–39.

———. "Women's Authority in Pennsylvania and New Jersey Quaker Meetings, 1680–1760." *William and Mary Quarterly*, 3rd ser., 44 (October 1987): 722–49.

Souders, Bronwen C., and John M. Souders. *A Rock in a Weary Land, a Shelter in Time of Storm: The African-American Experience in Waterford, Virginia*. Waterford, Va.: Waterford Foundation, 2003.

Spangler, Jewel L. *Virginians Reborn: Anglican Monopoly, Evangelical Dissent, and the Rise of the Baptists in the Late Eighteenth Century*. Charlottesville: University of Virginia Press, 2008.

Spann, Barbara T. *Carlby*. Fairfax, Va.: Fairfax County Office of Comprehensive Planning, 1976.

Specht, Neva Jean. "Mixed Blessing: Trans-Appalachian Settlement and the Society of Friends, 1780–1813." PhD diss., University of Delaware, 1997.

Springdale Boarding School for Girls (Loudoun County, Va.). *The Springdale Memento, Consisting of Original Essays, by the Pupils, Read at the Annual Examination, 1850, and a Catalogue of Students*. Loudoun Co., Va.: n.p., 1850.

Spruill, Julia Cherry. *Women's Life and Work in the Southern Colonies*. Chapel Hill: University of North Carolina Press, 1938.

Stabler, Harold B. *Some Further Recollections*. Maryland [?]: s.n., 1963.

———. *Some Recollections, Anecdotes, and Tales of Old Times*. Maryland [?]: s.n., 1962.

Stabler, William. *A Memoir of the Life of Edward Stabler, Late of Alexandria in the District of Columbia; with a Collection of his Letters*. Philadelphia: John Richards, 1846.

Stampp, Kenneth M. "The Fate of the Southern Antislavery Movement." *Journal of Negro History* 28 (January 1943): 10–22.

Stauffer, John. *The Black Hearts of Men: Radical Abolitionists and the Transformation of Race*. Cambridge, Mass.: Harvard University Press, 2001.

Stevenson, Brenda. *Life in Black and White: Family and Community in the Slave South*. New York: Oxford University Press, 1996.

Stewart, James Brewer. "Evangelicalism and the Radical Strain in Southern Antislavery Thought during the 1820s." *Journal of Southern History* 39 (August 1973): 379–96.

———. *Holy Warriors: The Abolitionists and American Slavery*. New York: Hill and Wang, 1976.

Strickland, William. *Observations on the Agriculture of the United States of America*. London: W. Bulmer, 1801.

Sutherland, Daniel E., ed. *Guerrillas, Unionists, and Violence on the Confederate Home Front*. Fayetteville: University of Arkansas Press, 1999.

———. *A Savage Conflict: The Decisive Role of Guerrillas in the American Civil War*. Chapel Hill: University of North Carolina Press, 2009.

Swatzler, David. *A Friend among the Senecas: The Quaker Mission to Cornplanter's People*. Mechanicsburg, Pa.: Stackpole Books, 2000.

Tadman, Michael. *Speculators and Slaves: Masters, Traders, and Slaves in the Old South*. Madison: University of Wisconsin Press, 1989.

Tallack, William. *Friendly Sketches in America*. London: A. W. Bennett, 1861.

Taylor, George Rogers. *The Transportation Revolution, 1815–1860*. New York: Rinehart, 1951.

Taylor, John. *Arator*. Georgetown, Md.: J. M. and J. B. Carter, 1813.

Taylor, Yardley. *Memoir of Loudoun County, in Loudoun County, Virginia Families and History* (1853). In *Loudoun County, Virginia Families and History*, edited by Jim Presgraves, 3–29. Wytheville, Va.: Wordsprint, 1999.

Thorne, Dorothy Gilbert. "North Carolina Friends and the Revolution." *North Carolina Historical Review* 38 (July 1961): 323–40.

Tiedemann, Joseph S. "Queens County, New York, Quakers in the American Revolution: Loyalists or Neutrals?" *Historical Magazine of the Protestant Episcopal Church* 52 (September 1983): 215–27.

Titus, James. *The Old Dominion at War: Society, Politics, and Warfare in Late Colonial Virginia.* Columbia: University of South Carolina Press, 1991.

Tolles, Frederick B., ed. "A Conscientious Parson: The Reverend, William Davis and the Quakers." *Virginia Magazine of History and Biography* 59 (July 1951): 359–61.

———. *Meeting House and Counting House: The Quaker Merchants of Colonial Philadelphia, 1682–1763.* 1948. New York: Norton, 1963.

———. "Nonviolent Contact: Quakers and the Indians." *Proceedings of the American Philosophical Society* 107 (1963): 93–101.

———. *Quakers and the Atlantic Culture.* New York: Macmillan, 1960.

Tomes, Nancy. "The Quaker Connection: Visiting Patterns among Women in the Philadelphia Society of Friends, 1750–1800." In Zuckerman, *Friends and Neighbors,* 174–95.

Townsend, Ann A., comp. *Memoir of Elizabeth Newport.* Philadelphia: Friends' Book Association, 1878.

True, Rodney H. "John Binns of Loudoun." *William and Mary Quarterly,* 2nd ser., 2 (January 1922): 20–39.

U.S. Census Office. *Agriculture of the United States in 1860; Compiled from the Original Returns of the Eighth Census.* Washington, D.C.: Government Printing Office, 1864. http://www.agcensus.usda.gov/Publications/Historical_Publications/1860/1860b-01.pdf.

U.S. Congress. *House Journal.* 23rd Cong., 2nd sess., December 1, 1834.

U.S. War Department. *The War of the Rebellion: A Compilation of the Official Records of the Union and Confederate Armies.* 4 ser., 70 vols. Washington, D.C.: Government Printing Office, 1880–1901.

Varon, Elizabeth R. *We Mean to Be Counted: White Women and Politics in Antebellum Virginia.* Chapel Hill: University of North Carolina Press, 1998.

Vickers, Daniel. "Competency and Competition: Economic Culture in Early America." *William and Mary Quarterly,* 3rd ser., 47 (January 1990): 3–29.

Virginia. Constitutional Convention, Alexandria, 1864. *Journal of the Constitutional Convention Which Convened at Alexandria on the 13th Day of February, 1864.* Alexandria: D. Turner, 1864.

Virginia Convention for the Abolition of Slavery, 1828. *Minutes of the Virginia Convention for the Abolition of Slavery, Held in Winchester, Frederick County, Virginia, August 20, 21, and 22, 1828.* Winchester, Va.: Samuel H. Davis, 1828.

Virginia. General Assembly, House of Delegates. *Journal of the House of Delegates of the Commonwealth of Virginia . . . in the Year . . . 1780.* Richmond: Thomas W. White, 1827.

Virginia. State Convention, Richmond, 1829–30. *Proceedings and Debates of the Virginia State Convention of 1829–30.* Richmond: Samuel Shepherd for Ritchie & Cook, 1830.

Virginia Yearly Meeting of Friends and Benjamin Bates. *Memorial of the Religious Society of Friends to the Legislature of Virginia, on the Militia Laws, with a Letter from Benjamin Bates (Bearer of the Memorial) to a Member of the Legislature.* New Bedford, Mass.: A. Shearman, 1813.

Wahl, Albert John. "The Congregational or Progressive Friends in the Pre–Civil War Reform Movement." PhD diss., Temple University, 1951.

———. "Longwood Meeting: Public Meeting for the American Democratic Faith." *Pennsylvania History* 42 (January 1975): 43–69.

Waldstreicher, David. *In the Midst of Perpetual Fetes: The Making of American Nationalism, 1776–1820*. Chapel Hill: University of North Carolina Press, 1997.

Walvin, James. *Quakers: Money and Morals*. London, Eng.: John Murray, 1997.

Washington, George. *Letters from His Excellency George Washington to Arthur Young and Sir John Sinclair Containing an Account of his Husbandry*. Alexandria: Cottom and Stewart, 1803.

Wax, Darold D. "Quaker Merchants and the Slave Trade in Colonial Pennsylvania." *Pennsylvania Magazine of History and Biography* 86 (April 1962): 144–59.

Wayland, John W. *Twenty-five Chapters on the Shenandoah Valley, to Which Is Appended a Concise History of the Civil War in the Valley*. 1957. Harrisonburg, Va.: C. J. Carrier, 1976.

Weekley, Carolyn J. *The Kingdoms of Edward Hicks*. Williamsburg, Va.: Colonial Williamsburg Foundation, 1999.

Weeks, Stephen B. *Southern Quakers and Slavery: A Study in Institutional History*. 1896. New York: Bergman Publishers, 1968.

Weiss, John McNish. "The Corps of Colonial Marines, 1814–16: A Summary." *Immigrants and Minorities* 15 (March 1996): 80–90.

Weld, Stephen Minot. *War Diary and Letters of Stephen Minot Weld, 1861–1865*. 1912. Boston: Massachusetts Historical Society, 1979.

Wells, Jonathan Daniel. *The Origins of the Southern Middle Class, 1800–1861*. Chapel Hill: University of North Carolina Press, 2004.

Wells, Robert V. "Quaker Marriage Patterns in a Colonial Perspective." *William and Mary Quarterly*, 3rd ser., 29 (July 1972): 415–42.

Welter, Barbara Welter. "The Cult of True Womanhood, 1820–1860." *American Quarterly* 18 (Summer 1966): 151–74.

Wheelock, Perry. *Robert Hartshorne Miller, 1798–1874: A Quaker Presence in Virginia*. Alexandria, Va.: Alexandria Archaeology, 1995.

White, Steven Jay. "Friends and the Coming of the Revolution." *Southern Friend* 4 (Spring 1982): 16–27.

———. "Quaker Historiography Revisited: Another Look at Early American Quaker Studies." *Southern Friend* 13 (1991): 18–33.

Whites, LeeAnn, and Alecia P. Long, eds. *Occupied Women: Gender, Military Occupation, and the American Civil War*. Baton Rouge: Louisiana State University Press, 2009.

Whitfield, Harvey Amani. *Blacks on the Border: The Black Refugees in British North America, 1815–1860*. Burlington: University of Vermont Press, 2006.

Whitman, T. Stephen. *The Price of Freedom: Slavery and Manumission in Baltimore and Early National Maryland*. Lexington: University Press of Kentucky, 1997.

Wilbur, Henry W. *The Life and Labors of Elias Hicks*. Philadelphia: Friends General Conference Advancement Committee, 1910.

Williams, Charles Richards, ed. *Diary and Letters of Rutherford B. Hayes*. 5 vols. Columbus: Ohio State Archaeological and Historical Society, 1922.

Williams, David. *Bitterly Divided: The South's Inner Civil War*. New York: New Press, 2008.

Williamson, James J. *Mosby's Ranger's: A Record of the Operations of the Forty-Third Battalion Virginia Cavalry. . . .* 1896. Alexandria, Va.: Time-Life Books, 1982.

Windsor, David Burns. *The Quaker Enterprise: Friends in Business*. London, Eng.: Frederick Muller, 1980.

Winston, Lewis E., Jr. "Benjamin Hallowell: Educational Leader of Virginia, Maryland, and Pennsylvania, 1799–1877." EdD diss., Virginia Polytechnic Institute and State University, 1998.

Wolf, Eva Sheppard. *Race and Liberty in the New Nation: Emancipation in Virginia from the Revolution to Nat Turner's Rebellion*. Baton Rouge: Louisiana State University Press, 2006.

Wood, Gordon S. *The Radicalism of the American Revolution*. New York: Knopf, 1992.

Wood, Kirsten E. *Masterful Women: Slaveholding Widows from the American Revolution through the Civil War*. Chapel Hill: University of North Carolina Press, 2004.

Woolley, John T., and Gerhard Peters. American Presidency Project. University of California, Santa Barbara. http://www.presidency.ucsb.edu/ws/?pid=29510.

Worrall, Jay. *The Friendly Virginians: America's First Quakers*. Athens, Ga.: Iberian, 1994.

Wrenn, Tony P. "After the Lewises: Life at Woodlawn, 1846–1972." *Historic Preservation* 24 (October–December 1972): 26–31.

Wright, Edward Needles. *Conscientious Objectors in the Civil War*. Philadelphia: University of Pennsylvania Press, 1931.

[Wright, Rebecca M.]. *The Loyal Girl of Winchester, September 1864*. Philadelphia [?]: s.n., 1888.

Wyatt-Brown, Bertram. *Southern Honor: Ethics and Behavior in the Old South*. New York: Oxford University Press, 1982.

Zuckerman, Michael, ed. *Friends and Neighbors: Group Life in America's First Plural Society*. Philadelphia: Temple University Press, 1982.

Index

A. Glenn Crothers is associate professor of history at the University of Louisville, director of research at The Filson Historical Society, and coeditor of *Ohio Valley History*.

SOUTHERN DISSENT

Edited by Stanley Harrold and Randall M. Miller

www.ingramcontent.com/pod-product-compliance
Lightning Source LLC
Chambersburg PA
CBHW050330270326
41926CB00016B/3389